Other Books by

RUSSELL KIRK

ELIOT
AND
HIS AGE

ELIOT
AND
HIS AGE

❖

T. S. Eliot's Moral Imagination
in the Twentieth Century

RUSSELL KIRK

RANDOM HOUSE
New York

I S B N: 0–394–47236–5
Library of Congress Catalog Card Number: 76–159354

Manufactured in the United States of America
by The Haddon Craftsmen, Inc.,
Scranton, Pennsylvania
Designed by Andrew Roberts

2 4 6 8 9 7 5 3

First Edition

Grateful acknowledgment is extended to the following for permission
to reprint from T. S. Eliot's works:

Barnes and Noble, Inc., Faber and Faber Ltd. and Valerie Eliot:
From *The Use of Poetry* and *The Use of Criticism*,
and from articles published in *The Criterion*.

Farrar, Straus & Giroux, Inc., Faber and Faber Ltd. and
Valerie Eliot: From *On Poetry and Poets*. Copyright 1943,
1945, 1951, 1954, © 1956, 1957 by T. S. Eliot.
From *Knowledge and Experience in the Philosophy of
F. H. Bradley*. Copyright © 1964 by T. S. Eliot.
From *To Criticize the Critic*. Copyright © 1965 by Valerie Eliot.
From *The Elder Statesman*. Copyright © 1959 by Thomas
Stearns Eliot. From *The Cultivation of Christmas Trees*.
Copyright 1954, © 1956 by Thomas Stearns Eliot.

Harcourt Brace Jovanovich, Inc., Faber and Faber Ltd.
and Valerie Eliot: From *Collected Poems 1909–1962*,
*Complete Poems and Plays, Selected Essays, Murder in
the Cathedral, The Idea of a Christian Society, Notes
Towards the Definition of Culture, The Cocktail Party,
The Confidential Clerk*. Copyright 1932, 1935, 1936
by Harcourt Brace Jovanovich, Inc. Copyright 1939,
1949, 1950, 1954, © 1960, 1964 by T. S. Eliot.

Haskell House Publishers Ltd., Faber and Faber Ltd.
and Valerie Eliot: From For Lancelot Andrewes.
Copyright © 1960 by Valerie Eliot.

To Monica, Cecilia, and Felicia,
three little charmers
enchanted by *Old Possum's Book of Practical Cats*

I'll strip the ragged follies of the time
Naked, as at their birth—

—BEN JONSON

But if that which is only submission to necessity
should be made the object of choice, the law is
broken; nature is disobeyed; and the rebellious are
outlawed, cast forth, and exiled, from this world of
reason, and order, and peace, and virtue, and fruitful
penitence, into the antagonist world of madness,
discord, vice, confusion, and unavailing sorrow.

—EDMUND BURKE

We mean all sorts of things, I know, by Beauty. But
the essential advantage for a poet is not to have a
beautiful world with which to deal: it is to be able
to see beneath both beauty and ugliness; to see the
boredom, and the horror, and the glory.

—T. S. ELIOT

CONTENTS

(*ix*)

CONTENTS

(x)

CONTENTS

CHAPTER VII

Christians and Ideologues in Heartbreak House

page 227

CHAPTER VIII

The Communication of the Dead

page 273

CHAPTER IX

Culture and Cocktail Parties

page 315

(xi)

CONTENTS

ELIOT
AND
HIS AGE

I

Eliot and the Follies
of the Time

❖

Nowadays, a few years after the death of T. S. Eliot, we
vacillate in a literary interregnum. From 1960 to 1970, say,
most survivors from what I call the Age of Eliot entered one
after another into eternity; and though here and there some
stalwart Gerontion still writes, or some hopeful new talent
starts up, for the most part we encounter literary ephemera,
or else the prickly pears and Dead Sea fruit of literary
decadence.

Yet no civilization rests forever content with literary
boredom and literary violence. Once again, a conscience may
speak to a conscience in the pages of books, and the parched
rising generation—like bushmen at the back of beyond—
may grope their way toward the springs of moral imagination.
There endure, however much defaced and neglected, what
Eliot called "the permanent things."

A fresh examination of the work of T. S. Eliot may assist

in that reinvigoration. This book is an endeavor at once to criticize an important body of literature, and to relate that literature to the events and circumstances and prospects of civilization in this century.

As yet, we have no biography of Eliot, nor any large collection of his letters.[1] "How I should hate you!" Samuel Butler (disliked by Eliot) wrote of his presumptive future biographer. The kindly Tom Eliot felt no such acrimony toward those who, in the fullness of time, would write about him as a man. Always reticent about his private tribulations, nevertheless, and careful to distinguish between his private emotions and the sentiments expressed in his poems, Eliot desired no Boswell.

Although this book is not that biography, a prefatory note on Eliot the man may be found appropriate here. He had many acquaintances, some friends, few intimates. Others knew him better than I did, but I do not believe that I failed to apprehend his character. People who are acquainted with Eliot only through his writings may fancy that he was a man chilly and almost impersonal. The truth was otherwise.

We first met in 1953, in an obscure little private hotel, unattractive wicker furniture in its parlor, where Eliot was staying in Edinburgh before the first performance of *The Confidential Clerk*. I called upon him because he had persuaded Faber & Faber, of which firm he had been a director for many years, to publish the London edition of a fat book of mine, and because I had been asked to criticize *The Confidential Clerk* in the pages of *The Month*.

Kindliness, simplicity, and directness were among Eliot's characteristics, I discovered; and this impression was confirmed by our later meetings, in London, over the years—at the Garrick Club or in his little office upstairs at Faber & Faber, in Bloomsbury. Disciplined like his literary style, Eliot's mind was humane with a consistency rare today. It was easy to talk with him, because he was both keenly intelligent (though never abstract in discourse) and gracefully unassuming.

A thoroughly different sort of person—Somerset Maugham—argued two decades ago that it has become impossible for us moderns to venerate anybody. True, there remain few men of our time whom anyone is tempted to venerate. Yet though Eliot never expected reverence for himself, and would have smiled affably at the notion, he deserved to be revered, in those later years of his, if anybody so deserved. Nowadays I hesitate to attribute "compassion"—what with the mawkish corruption of that word—to a sensible man. Yet compassion, in its root sense, could be read in Eliot's face: not the condescending sentimentality of the humanitarian, but a consciousness of the community of souls.* Now and again there came into my head, as I sat with Eliot, those lines from his "Preludes" which he had written in his Harvard days:

> I am moved by fancies that are curled
> Around these images, and cling:
> The notion of some infinitely gentle
> Infinitely suffering thing.

Those lines had struck Wyndham Lewis, too, in 1915. Lewis then, and I later, did not take Eliot himself to be pathetic: he had passed through suffering, by the time I

* Carl Sandburg, no lover of Eliot's poetry or principles, was similarly impressed at the one brief (and accidental) encounter of the two poets. They met in Robert Giroux's office: ". . . Sandburg had already drawn up a chair and was moodily gazing across my desk into Eliot's eyes. 'Just look at him!' Sandburg said to me, pointing at Eliot. 'Look at that man's face—the suffering, and the pain.' By this time Eliot was wearing a great big grin. Sandburg continued, 'You can't hold *him* responsible for the poets and critics who ride on his coat-tails!' With that, he walked out of the office and I realized that one of the great literary encounters of our time had occurred, and as far as I know Eliot had not uttered a single word." See Giroux, "A Personal Memoir," in Allen Tate (ed.), *T. S. Eliot: The Man and His Work* (1967), pp. 339–340.

knew him, to resignation and hope; but the vanity of human wishes clung about him always, not unpleasantly. His appetites were reduced, his manners perfect—and his patience boundless. He might have sat for Sir Thomas Browne, or for his own friend Father Martin D'Arcy, as an exemplar of Christian morals.

All about him, in those late years when I knew Eliot, he perceived inner and outer disorder, but was not dismayed. One winter I told him that he ought to come with me to Cyprus. (He could not have walked with me, then, as he had walked beside the Loire and in Brittany with Wyndham Lewis, just after the First World War; but if I had sat by him in the roofless Queen's Lodging of the castle of St. Hilarion, say, where the cliff-face drops away more than two thousand feet, I might have known one of Eliot's moments when time and the timeless intersect.) What with his arthritis, he may have been tempted; but he had duties to perform. True, he said, his doctor had advised him that he ought to spend the cold months in some "dry, quiet place —Egypt, perhaps." At that hour, Egypt was made hideous by revolution and massacre; Eliot suggested that the doctor was rather an old-fangled practitioner, not given to chewing the newspapers.

His physician's unworldiness notwithstanding, I replied, really he and I ought to embrace that prescription: at Cairo or Alexandria, or in the City of the Dead at Luxor, we might end gloriously as two Roman candles ignited by Saracens, not with a whimper but a bang. Eliot smiled, perhaps regretfully, aware that nothing melodramatic ever had occurred to him, nor would—except in the realm of mind and spirit.

Standing still while men were arming, Eliot lived secure, full of years and honors, amidst the crash of empires. He might have said, with Don Quixote, "I know who I am," a rare discovery—teaching resignation to any man who makes it—that Eliot had achieved painfully. Not attracted by power or wealth, Eliot was content to be poet and critic. He had no passionate desire for the fame that settled upon him, and was not easily wounded by hostility among reviewers and ideologues.

Yet for the present condition of culture, and for the future of man, Eliot knew a concern that (at least by 1953, when we met) he had ceased to feel for himself. For five decades, from *Prufrock and Other Observations* to the essays that were published after his death, Eliot labored to renew the wardrobe of a moral imagination, that generation might link with generation—and that, beyond the boredom and the horror, men might perceive the glory.

Through poem and play and essay, Eliot hoped to work upon his age—through what he wrote, not through what he experienced privately; and in that spirit this book has been undertaken. With what might have been arrogance in a man less amiable by nature, Thomas Stearns Eliot aspired to represent in his day the power of moral imagination possessed by his Mantuan and Florentine exemplars. He was an ethical poet, bent upon redeeming the time. What Unamuno called "the tragic sense of life" was Eliot's to the full—although, as old Robert Burton had written in *The Anatomy of Melancholy*, melancholy men are the wittiest. In his austere and subtly humorous way, Eliot perceived his own age more poignantly than did anyone else in the republic of letters.

T. S. Eliot was the principal champion of the moral imagination in the twentieth century. Now what is the moral imagination? The phrase is Edmund Burke's. By it, Burke meant that power of ethical perception which strides beyond the barriers of private experience and events of the moment—"especially," as the dictionary has it, "the higher form of this power exercised in poetry and art." The moral imagination aspires to the apprehending of right order in the soul and right order in the commonwealth. It was the gift and the obsession of Plato and Virgil and Dante.

In Burke's rhetoric, the civilized being is distinguished from the savage by his possession of the moral imagination— by our "superadded ideas, furnished from the wardrobe of a moral imagination, which the heart owns, and the understanding ratifies, as necessary to cover the defects of our naked shivering nature, and to raise it to dignity in our estimation." Drawn from centuries of human experience, these ideas of the moral imagination are expressed afresh from age to age.[2] So it is that the men of humane letters in our century whose work seems most likely to endure have not been neoterists, but rather bearers of an old standard, tossed by our modern winds of doctrine: the names of Eliot, Frost, Faulkner, Waugh, and Yeats may suffice to suggest the variety of this moral imagination in the modern age.

Burke's moral imagination is contrasted by Eliot's teacher, Irving Babbitt (who probably introduced to Eliot this aspect of Burke), with Rousseau's idyllic imagination. In the twentieth century, the idyllic imagination may be giving way to the diabolic imagination. Eliot would contend against both the disciples of Rousseau and the disciples of Lawrence—against the worshipers of strange gods.

Eliot and some of his contemporaries agreed, tacitly or explicitly (again in Burke's phrases), "that *we* have made no discoveries, and we think that no discoveries are to be made, in morality. . ." Their achievement was to reinvigorate in the twentieth century those perennial moral insights which are the sources of human normality, and which make possible order and justice and freedom.

Good books and essays already have been written about Eliot's style, his sources, his power as literary innovator, his critical talents. Yet many critics have touched somewhat uneasily or glancingly upon Eliot's moral and political principles. His Christian orthodoxy has been tolerated by some, sneered at by others; his social ideas frequently have been ignored or disparaged. To strip the ragged follies of the time, nevertheless, was Eliot's undertaking all his long literary career. Deliberately he wrote within a great tradition and in conformity to orthodox teaching. Like Samuel Johnson, Eliot would have chosen to be judged upon his merits as moralist and statist, not as stylist merely. As philosophical poet, as dramatist, as literary critic, and as social essayist, Eliot labored for the recovery of order: the order of the soul, and the order of the commonwealth.

It is the power of moral imagination that will give long life to Eliot's work. And some fifty-five years after "The Love Song of J. Alfred Prufrock" was published, tardy discursive judgment needs to be rendered. So I propose to examine Eliot's chief endeavors, and to touch now and again upon the work of his allies or of his adversaries. If we apprehend Eliot—who is not easy to plumb—we apprehend the intellectual and moral struggles of our time.

My own object in this present book is to discuss the significance of Eliot's convictions for this age, and to set in his social perspective the most eminent writer of the past half-century. I do not serve under the flag of those gentlemen whom F. O. Matthiessen (after Eliot) calls "the sociological critics": participating in a high continuity, Eliot was not simply a product or a representative of social influences within his lifetime. Yet I agree with Irving Babbitt that all important literature is ethical in character, and that the man of letters moves his society for good or ill. This book, then, has to do with Eliot the champion of the moral imagination and with Eliot the critic of the civil social order.

In humane letters, ours has been the Age of Eliot, as once there was an Age of Dryden, and an Age of Johnson. As an historical and a literary epoch, our time commences with the First World War: the preceding years of this century were the tag-ends of nineteenth-century opinions, and until 1914 the social institutions of the nineteenth century stood little impaired. After the deluge of what optimists called the "Great War," a new current flowed in literature, as in the social order. The past half-century has been Eliot's age, in that Thomas Stearns Eliot, a shy colossus, bestrode the period as Virgil or Dante or Dryden or Johnson had dominated very different times. Relish him or not, we encounter Eliot everywhere in twentieth-century intellectuality and social speculation and literary controversy.

Since Eliot's death, we have slipped further still into the antagonist world of armed doctrine and consuming appetite. This book may help to explain the strong relevance of Eliot's thought and imagery to our present passionate discontents.

I have put into the ten following chapters of prose what James McAuley expresses in three stanzas:[3]

> A distant shepherd on the plain
> Changed his tune, and the city fell;
> But, syllable by syllable,
> Amphion raised the walls again.
>
> The ratios of the vibrant string,
> The trembling column of breathed air,
> Ordain a measure to despair
> And bind ambition in a ring.
>
> Justly framed, the metre gives
> This meaning, meaning's counterpart:
> "Set love in order in the heart—
> For in these modes the polis lives."

It is conceivable that in some distant future time, when the history of the twentieth century seems barbarous and bewildering as the chronicles of Scotland's medieval age, the piercing visions of Eliot may be regarded as the clearest light which endured in that general darkness.

II

The Burial of Matthew and Waldo

❖

❡Sir Edmund Gosse and the Hippopotamus

In June, 1917, there was published by The Egoist Press, in Bloomsbury, a slim book of verse: *Prufrock and Other Observations*. This was the first volume brought out by The Egoist Ltd., which later would publish books by James Joyce, Wyndham Lewis, and other new writers; it was also the first book of the creator of Prufrock. Five hundred copies were printed, and it took four years to sell out the edition; the author's royalties would amount to ten guineas, and the publisher's profits to eighteen shillings and eightpence.

The poet, though an American, was a London bank clerk, then twenty-nine years old. In one short innovating poem, "Cousin Nancy," he broke good-naturedly with the attenuated genteel tradition of his Bostonian kinsfolk:

> Upon the glazen shelves kept watch
> Matthew and Waldo, guardians of the faith,
> The army of unalterable law.

(11)

Riding, smoking, and dancing, Cousin Nancy would not be governed by Matthew Arnold and Ralph Waldo Emerson; neither would the new antagonist world, baptized by fire a few months before *Prufrock* appeared. In the battle of the Somme, from July through October, 1916, almost half a million British soldiers had been killed or wounded or captured; myriads more would die on that front—the obsession of Field Marshal Haig—in 1917 and 1918. By June, 1917, the Great War seemed a stalemate that could not be broken until all conscript armies lay dead. Rudyard Kipling had published, in the fatal spring of 1917, his frightful description of the boy-soldiers' corpses in no-man's land, "blanched or gay-painted by fumes," given to corruption:

For this we shall take expiation.

But who shall return us our children?

Those children had died beside the Somme; their bones would not speak in the bent world after the War. The old civilized order of Europe and America was laid waste by this devastation. Arnold and Emerson, those pillars of nineteenth-century sweetness and light (such as it had been), lay cindered by fires beside the corpses in the craters.

J. Alfred Prufrock, strolling mean streets in Boston at tea-time, oppressed by small timidities and a vast ennui, unable to love or to escape from the stuffy closet of self, never saw the Somme; but he knew his own Hell. Prufrock, too, would be an aspect of the new antagonist world. After 1917, many a man like a pair of ragged claws would scuttle about the world; and the Prufrocks would be such a man's prey. No longer would Matthew and Waldo slice tea-time's cake of custom. Not out of the War, but out of a bank's cellar beneath a London street, emerged the poetic vision that was to take the measure of the century.

As if bent on giving the lie to Darwin's notion of the survival of the fittest, the War was thinning the talents of the time. Military principles of selection, especially for regimental officers, sent "to be senselessly tossed and retossed in stale mutilation" the younger professional men, scientists, teachers, engineers, administrators, artists, public leaders— and poets. In the world after the War, places that might have been occupied by men like George Wyndham and T. E. Hulme and Rupert Brooke—by young men of high promise who, instead, suffered from "the heart-shaking jests of Decay where it lolled on the wires"—would be filled by another breed. Their successors, too often, were the new sort of politicians (those "hard-faced men who looked as if they had done very well out of the war," in Stanley Baldwin's honest description); or the ideologues of totalist politics; or a variety of Hollow Men.

Matthew and Waldo, too, were blanched or gay-painted by the fumes of the Somme. The antagonist world was at hand; but so was the Age of Eliot, with its resignation, its penitence, its defense of the permanent things, and its stubborn hope.

As yet little known, the young writers whom Wyndham Lewis called "the men of 1914"—Eliot, James Joyce, Ezra Pound, T. E. Hulme, and Lewis himself—had begun to make their mark in London just about the time the War erupted. In Ezra Pound's rooms at the foot of Notting Hill (later to become the Rotting Hill of Lewis' sardonic sketches after the Second World War), that detached observer Wyndham Lewis first met, in 1914, the young T. S. Eliot of those years, "a figure entering the portals—seated in the parlour—of Heartbreak House." Was this youthful unknown, placidly smiling, one of Ezra's "preposterous people"? In his magazine *Blast*, Lewis would publish in July, 1915, Eliot's "Preludes" and "Rhapsody on a Windy Night."

Lewis, so readily displeased with people, took to Eliot: "He growled softly at me, as we shook hands. American. A graceful neck I noted, with what elsewhere I have described as a 'Gioconda smile.' Though not feminine—besides being physically large his personality visibly moved within the male pale—there *were* dimples in the warm dark skin; undoubtedly he used his eyes a little like a Leonardo. He was a very attractive fellow then; a sort of looks unusual this side of the Atlantic. I liked him, though I may say not at all connecting him with texts Ezra had shown me about some fictional character dreadfully troubled with old age, in which the lines (for it had been verse) 'I am growing old, I am growing old, I shall wear the bottoms of my trousers rolled'—a feature, apparently, of the humiliations reserved for the superannuated—I was unable to make head or tail of."[1]

Ezra Pound was engaged in stiffening, rather than molding, T. S. Eliot for the world of London letters; Eliot would lend Pound and Miss Harriet Weaver a hand in editing *The Egoist*, a periodical promising, troubled, and doomed to early dissolution. In June, 1917, Eliot was appointed assistant editor of that paper, with a salary of nine pounds a quarter, much of that sum (without Eliot's knowledge) contributed by Pound. Perhaps the paper's title was not altogether happy. Eliot already was aware, from observing people in parlors and pubs, and from reading Kipling, that a principal affliction of twentieth-century man is this: he has too much ego in his cosmos.

His association with *The Egoist* led to Miss Weaver's publishing *Prufrock*, and so to a certain limited celebrity. That winter, Osbert Sitwell—an officer returned from horrors to literary drawing rooms—met the shy emerging Eliot at a fashionable public reading by several poets. This was a charity benefit for the Red Cross, held on December 12, 1917, at a house in South Kensington; Sir Edmund Gosse chaired the affair. The evening before this reading, a dinner party was held for the chairman, the benefit's organizers, and the "performing poets"—among them Robert Graves, Robert Nichols, Irene Rutherford McLeod, Sherard Vines, Aldous Huxley, Edith Sitwell, Sacheverell Sitwell, Osbert Sitwell, Viola Tree, Siegfried Sassoon (who, however, did not turn up), and Eliot.

Sir Edmund Gosse was then England's arbiter of literary taste; the Age of Eliot would dethrone him. Gosse was so fiercely detested by the rising generation of literary men, the men of 1914, that they have damned him to immortal fame. Although his deserts may have been small, distinctions had been heaped upon him. "At a good word from him—and at this time, from him alone—the sales of a young author's books, even of a poet's, mounted higher," Sir Osbert Sitwell writes, "while the insolence he would naturally otherwise have had to encounter would diminish or altogether disappear."[2]

Gosse was given to administering rebukes, however, to presumptuous young writers. Evelyn Waugh (whose father, a distant kinsman of Gosse, had been helped by Sir Edmund in earlier years) looked upon this martinet-critic as an abominable charlatan: "To me he epitomized all that I found ignoble in the profession of letters": a charlatan as a scholar, the author of next to nothing, a sycophant with men of power and fashion. "I saw Gosse as a Mr. Tulkinghorn, the soft-footed, inconspicuous, ill-natured habitué of the great world, and I longed for a demented lady's-maid to make an end of him."[3]

At that Gosse-dominated dinner, the Sitwells first saw Eliot: "A most striking being, having peculiarly luminous, light yellow, more than tawny, eyes: the eyes, they might have been, of one of the greater cats, but tiger, puma, leopard, lynx, rather than those of a lion which, for some reason, display usually a more domesticated and placid expression. His face, too, possessed the width of bony structure of a tigrine face, albeit the nose was prominent, similar, I used to think, to that of a figure on an Aztec carving or bas-relief."[4]

The next day, the poets read from a platform in Lady Colefax's drawing room in Onslow Square. Having been detained overlong at his bank, Eliot arrived late—and was rebuked before everybody by that pomposity Sir Edmund. "He showed no annoyance at being reproved," Sitwell recollects, "for one manifestation of [Eliot's] good manners was that he never allowed his companions to suspect the fatigue he must have been suffering: nor did he ever repine openly at the extraordinary fate which constrained such a poet to such a task, but endured it, if puzzled at times, with a jaunty patience—though doubtless with all a tiger's fiery core of impatience at the heart."

The suzerainty of Gosse was collapsing, and in this fashion the Age of Eliot was ushered in, grumpily, by Gosse himself –all unwitting. Gosse's interest in literature for literature's sake —or perhaps for fashion's sake—would be swept away by Eliot's interest in literature for the sake of the moral imagination.

Aldous Huxley was one of the performing poets on this occasion. Sir Edmund Gosse—so Aldous wrote to his brother Julian—was "the bloodiest little old man I have ever seen"; various "young bards" (Gosse's phrase) succeeded other young bards on the platform, "troops of Shufflebottoms, alias Sitwells bringing up the rear: last and best, Eliot. But oh— what a performance: Eliot and I were the only people who had any dignity: Bob Nichols raved and screamed and hooted and moaned his filthy war poems like a Lyceum villain who hasn't learnt how to act: Viola Tree declaimed in a voice so syrupy and fruity and rich, that one felt quite cloyed and sick by two lines; the Shufflebottoms were respectable but terribly nervous: the McLeod became quite intoxicated by her own verses; Gosse was like a reciter at a penny reading."[5]

Eliot read "The Hippopotamus"; whether or not he had intended to outrage Gosse, he succeeded:

> He shall be washed as white as snow,
> By all the martyr'd virgins kist,
> While the True Church remains below
> Wrapt in the old miasmal mist.

Probably few present suspected that this ironical young poet, within a few years, would be almost venerated by the *Church Times.* Arnold Bennett, present at that afternoon's readings, was mightily impressed by Eliot; he wrote in his diary, "If I had been the house, this would have brought the house down." Thereafter, whenever the two of them met, he would ask Eliot if he were going to write another "Hippopotamus." Despite his bank-weariness, Eliot, usually adept at making himself inconspicuous, was charismatic that afternoon.

"Though he was reserved, and had armored himself behind the fine manners, and the fastidiously courteous manner, that are so particularly his own," Osbert Sitwell continues; "though, too, the range and tragic depths of his great poetry were to be read in the very lines of his face; and though, in addition, he must have been exhausted by the long hours of uncongenial work, his air, to the contrary, was always lively, gay, even jaunty." Elegant of dress, easy of movement, this young poet not long out of Harvard and known, until the publication of *Prufrock,* chiefly for his contributions to *The Egoist,* would play David to Gosse's Goliath.

The comic, but not irreverent, lines of "The Hippopotamus" were Gosse's bane. Nearly fourteen years later, when Eliot had come to dominate London letters after a fashion very different from Gosse's, the author of "The Hippopotamus" reviewed in his quarterly *The Criterion* Evan Charteris' biography of Gosse.

"The place that Sir Edmund Gosse filled in the literary and social life of London," Eliot would write in 1931, "is one that no one can ever fill again, because it is, so to speak, an office that has been abolished. . . . I will not say that Sir Edmund's activity was not a very useful activity, in a social-literary world which is rapidly receding into memory. He was, indeed, an amenity; but not quite any sort of amenity for which I can see any great need in our time." Charteris' comparison of Gosse with Sainte-Beuve was not happy, Eliot continued. "Sir Edmund could not have written a masterpiece like *Port-Royal,* because he was not interested enough; he could not even have written a book comparable to *Chateau-briand.* I think that people whose interests are so strictly limited, people who are not gifted with any restless curiosity and not tormented by the demon of thought, somehow miss the keener emotions which literature can give. And, in our time, both temporary and eternal problems press themselves upon the intelligent mind with an insistence which they did not seem to have in the reign of King Edward VII."[6]

Keener emotions and urgent concern with temporal and eternal problems were to be conspicuous marks of literature in the Age of Eliot. Although the Sitwells and Arnold Bennett and Aldous Huxley and others glimpsed genius in this newcomer, relatively few people detected in Eliot, at first, his soberness and his power of intellect. Literary gentlemen like Arthur Waugh—writer, publisher, and father to Evelyn Waugh—still enjoyed their "capital evenings" at Sir Edmund Gosse's house in Hanover Terrace, even if they were a little afraid of that potentate. The Gosse set took Eliot for a poet of negation and bad manners; Arthur Waugh compared the author of *Prufrock* to a drunken helot, capable only of chastening the rising generation by his ignominious example.

Eliot rejected the nineteenth century's liberalism and its vogue of Culture, undone by the War; Eliot would observe that the nineteenth century—which he abhorred—must end sometime, even if in the middle of the twentieth century. In time it would become clear (to the chagrin of some early neoterist votaries of Eliot) that this American was affirming a belief old and tough, if sardonic. Eliot would turn, presently, to the Anglican divines, to the seventeenth century (the century of genius), and to still older sources of thought and feeling.*

To those tired of Gosse, the poems of *Prufrock* were a tardy relief. Eliot did not attempt to write what Huxley called "filthy war poems": that variety of literature he left to those who had fought, among them Sitwell and Sassoon and Graves and Edmund Blunden and the young poets who had died among the poppies of Flanders. Eliot's health had not been vigorous enough for the American Navy to accept him. Ford Madox Hueffer's "Antwerp" was "the only good poem I have met with on the subject of the war," Eliot wrote in an *Egoist* review of November 10, that year. But he was no pacifist, he had told Bertrand Russell in October, 1914. He wrote of what he knew—the inner disorder, not the outer.

Reading *Prufrock* in 1917, E. M. Forster was heartened to encounter verse "innocent of public-spiritedness"; Eliot, he wrote, carried on the human heritage by singing of "private disgust and diffidence, and of people who seemed genuine because they were unattractive or weak." Eliot, Forster continued, had uttered a feeble protest against obsession with

---

* What Eliot found foolish in the adulation of Emerson and Arnold is suggested in a sentence from a book by a forgotten American literary journalist: William Winter, *Gray Days and Gold* (1892). Having declared that "the welfare of the future lies in the worship of beauty," Winter proceeds to this praise of Arnold, sufficiently representative of the time:

"The man who heeds Matthew Arnold's teaching will put no trust in creeds and superstitions, will place no reliance upon the cobweb structure of theology, will take no guidance from the animal and unthinking multitude; but he will 'keep the whiteness of his soul'; he will be simple, unselfish, and sweet; he will live for the spirit and not the flesh; and in that spirit, pure, tender, fearless, strong to bear and patient to suffer, he will find composure to meet the inevitable disasters of life and the awful mystery of death."

patriotism and the like—a protest "the more congenial for being feeble."

Two decades after *Prufrock*—by which time, sentiments revolutionary, rather than pacifist, would be in vogue among poets—Louis MacNeice, in his *Modern Poetry,* would sneer at Forster's judgment expressed in *Abinger Harvest* (1926). Eliot, MacNeice would write, had "sat back and watched other people's emotions with ennui and an ironical self-pity. . . . Ten years later less feeble protests were to be made by poets and the human heritage carried on rather differently. . . . . The contemplation of a world of fragments becomes boring and Eliot's successors are more interested in tidying it up."

To MacNeice, there would reply in 1940 a writer with some experience of war, revolution, poverty, and the literary dogmas of the Left: George Orwell, who took up Eliot's defense on this point. MacNeice wished his readers to believe that he and his friends somehow had protested more effectively than had Eliot, by publishing *Prufrock* at the moment when the Allied armies were assaulting the Hindenburg Line. Orwell would remark:

"Just where these 'protests' are to be found I do not know. But in the contrast between Mr. Forster's comment and Mr. MacNeice's lies all the difference between a man who knows what the 1914–18 war was like and a man who barely remembers it. The truth is that in 1917 there was nothing that a thinking and sensitive person could do, except to remain human, if possible. And a gesture of helplessness, even of frivolity, might be the best way of doing that. If I had been a soldier fighting in the Great War, I would sooner have got hold of 'Prufrock' than *The First Hundred Thousand* or Horatio Bottomley's *Letters to the Boys in the Trenches.* I should have felt, like Mr. Forster, that by simply standing aloof and keeping touch with pre-war emotions, Eliot was carrying on the human heritage. What a relief it would have been at such a time, to read about the hesitations of a middle-aged highbrow with a bald spot!"[7]

Neither Forster nor MacNeice understood *Prufrock* well: the poems in that book were not concerned directly with order in the commonwealth, but they did reflect a strong concern for the order of the soul. Yet certainly Eliot's poems refreshed that part of the public which retained a taste for humane letters. Joined to the novelty of Eliot's verse-forms and his grimy new images with a touch of Laforgue, the ironies, levities, evocations, and allusions of *Prufrock and Other Observations* succeeded in rousing the attention of the younger literary public, weary both of patriotic sloganeering and of Georgian bucolic poses. As the War put an end to the complacent political notions of the nineteenth century, so Eliot demolished nineteenth-century smugness about the human condition.

About this time, George Santayana, another fugitive from Harvard Yard, described the end of an era: "The days of liberalism are numbered. . . . It is in the subsoil of uniformity, of tradition, of dire necessity that human welfare is rooted, together with wisdom and unaffected art, and the flowers of culture that do not draw their sap from that soil are only paper flowers."[8] That, in substance, would become Eliot's discourse on modern society.

Anarchy, certainly, Eliot was to resist with all his strength. Eliot's culture would more nearly resemble that of the old Schoolmen. We moderns are dwarfs mounted upon the shoulders of giants, Bernard of Chartres had said in the twelfth century: "If we see more and further than they, it is not because of our own clear eyes or tall bodies, but because we are raised on high by their gigantic stature." In certain medieval churches, the figures of the Evangelists sit or stand upon the shoulders of the Prophets. So it was to be with

Eliot's understanding of cultural and social tradition. His protests—even his protest against Sir Edmund Gosse—were an affirmation of the permanent things.

The Youngest Eliot of St. Louis

Thomas Stearns Eliot never cast off affection for family or place or the culture he inherited, but modern life was to efface, as it has for millions of other people, the setting he knew in his childhood. The house at 2635 Locust Street, in St. Louis, where he was born in 1888, has vanished without trace: on the site stands a new flat-roofed industrial building. In recent years, that whole neighborhood has been devastated beyond recognition. On Locust, and in the nearby streets, almost no population remains, everything having become shoddy commercial development, or having sunk into ghastly dereliction.

Indeed, the river-city that Eliot knew is three-quarters obliterated. A few hundred yards to the north of what was Laclede's Landing, on the Mississippi, there survive some buildings he would have recognized—and those saved from demolition only at the eleventh hour. Most of the old French town was swept away deliberately in the 1940's, and for a quarter of a century the cathedral stood solitary in the rubble-strewn urban desert called the Jefferson Memorial. Blight has spread outward for miles, from the city's heart. We are destroying our ancient edifices, Eliot would write in 1948 "to make ready the ground upon which the barbarian nomads of the future will encamp in their mechanized caravans."

Yet the St. Louis into which Eliot was born—the seventh child of middle-aged parents—then enjoyed swift growth and high prosperity. His was one of the families that gave

St. Louis a culture and a tone of its own. If a gentleman may be defined as a person who never refers to himself as a gentleman, so in America an aristocracy has led without ever calling itself an aristocracy.

The descendants of Andrew Eliot, cordwainer (who emigrated from Somerset to Massachusetts Bay Colony in 1667), soon were eminent in the peculiar austere New England aristocracy of ministers and merchants. On both his father's side and his mother's, Eliot's ancestors were woven into this class—although sometimes suffering vicissitudes. The sixth president of the United States, for one, was a collateral connection. "My great-grandfather's cousin John," T. S. Eliot wrote to me in 1956 (referring to John Quincy Adams), "was extremely useful to my family. My great-grandfather was a shipowner whose fortunes were ruined by that little maritime war between Britain and the United States in 1812, and my cousin John saved the situation by finding him a job in the Civil Service in Washington, where my grandfather was born."*

From Harvard Divinity School, the Reverend William Greenleaf Eliot, doctor of divinity, had gone straight out to St. Louis in 1834 and had established the Unitarian Church of the Messiah. He founded Washington University, becoming in 1872 its first chancellor; he read and wrote much; was great in charities; labored against slavery and for prohibition

---

* A few months before this correspondence (Eliot's letter to me being dated 13th January, 1956), I had published, with an introduction, a paperbound edition of Gentz's *American and French Revolutions Compared*, which had been translated and published by John Quincy Adams while Adams was American minister to Prussia. Eliot had not known of this essay until I sent him a copy of my edition. In the letter quoted above, T. S. Eliot is a trifle inaccurate: William Greenleaf Eliot, his grandfather, was born in New Bedford in 1811, although he spent much of his childhood in Washington. Much as he had no very strong interest in the culture of New England, the poet similarly did not share intensely his father's and his uncle's relish for the genealogy of the Eliots and the Greenleafs.

of drink; helped to keep Missouri in the Union, when the Civil War began. This grandfather of T. S. Eliot was all New England conscience.

"I never knew my grandfather," the poet said in St. Louis in 1953; "he died a year before my birth. But I was brought up to be very much aware of him: so much so, that as a child I thought of him as still head of the family—a ruler for whom *in absentia* my grandmother stood as vicegerent. The standard of conduct was that which my grandfather had set; our moral judgments, our decisions between duty and self-indulgence, were taken as if, like Moses, he had brought down the tables of the Law, any deviation from which would be sinful. Not the least of these laws, which included injunctions still more than prohibitions, was the law of Public Service: it is no doubt owing to the impress of this law upon my infant mind that, like other members of my family, I have felt, ever since I passed beyond my early irresponsible years, an uncomfortable and very inconvenient obligation to serve upon committees."[9]

Henry Ware Eliot, second son of William Greenleaf Eliot and father of the poet, prospered as president of a brick-making company. ("Too much pudding choked the dog," Henry Ware said of his father's plan to make a clergyman of him.) Henry Ware's wife, Charlotte Champe Stearns, came of a Massachusetts family still older than the Eliots; she wrote a dramatic poem, *Savonarola*, and a life of her father-in-law; she was active in the reform of prisons for women and of courts for juveniles. Pious in both classical and Christian senses of that abused word, the parents of the Eliot children thought much—justifiably—of their ancestors, and more of their religious and civic duties.[10] Though T. S. Eliot was to transcend this kindly family culture, at once conservative and reforming, he never would repudiate it.

His was a good boyhood. Long later, he would write of "the long dark river, the ailanthus trees, the flaming cardinal birds, the high limestone bluffs where we searched for fossil shellfish . . ." The Mississippi fascinated him, and in the preface he would write for an edition of *Huckleberry Finn,* that river would be called the clue to the meaning of the book. "I feel that there is something in having passed one's childhood beside the big river," he would write in 1930, "which is incommunicable to those who have not. Of course my people were Northerners and New Englanders, and of course I have spent many years out of America altogether; but Missouri and the Mississippi have made a deeper impression on me than any other part of the world."[11]

He was fortunate to have been born in St. Louis, he would say in 1953, rather than in New York, Boston, or London. The Church of the Messiah, the old city, and Washington University became for him symbols of Religion, the Community, and Education: "I think it is a very good beginning for any child, to be brought up to reverence such institutions, and to be taught that personal and selfish aims should be subordinated to the general good which they represent." At Smith Academy, "a good school" since vanished, he was taught "as is now increasingly rare everywhere, what I consider the essentials: Latin and Greek, together with Greek and Roman history, English and American history, elementary mathematics, French and German. Also English! I am happy to remember that in those days English composition was still called *Rhetoric*."[12]

Religion and Education, in those days, were healthy enough in St. Louis; but what occurred in the old courthouse and the city hall, down toward the river, was not always so salubrious. The political corruption of that city was the subject of Lincoln Steffens' first chapter in *The Shame of the Cities* (1904). There had arisen in St. Louis, too, an avaricious plutocracy for which the Eliots and their kind knew contempt; "Bleistein with a Cigar" and other gross figures in Eliot's early poems had their St. Louis models. For honest industry and commerce, T. S. Eliot—like his ancestors of New England and St. Louis—had a liking all his life; for that matter, he would make himself into an efficient man of business. But the financial predator was a different being. Some of Eliot's recurrent scorn, in his poems, for the shady barbarous financier may be in part the reflection of the scandals that plagued St. Louis while he was a boy at Smith Academy. The young Eliot knew affluence, in St. Louis and in Massachusetts; but lifelong he despised Sir Epicure Mammon.

Harvard, Babbitt, and Paris

Boston and London, rather than St. Louis, would provide the background for his early verse. Eliot departed for Harvard College in 1906; from that year forward, St. Louis had only a subtle claim upon him. The Somerset village of East Coker, from which Andrew Eliot had gone out to America, in time would be dearer to Eliot than mutable St. Louis—dear enough for him to have his ashes interred there, at the last. For permanence and continuity, Eliot was to long all his life; and East Coker today might be recognizable by a returned Andrew Eliot, while the St. Louis of T. S. Eliot's youth is little more than a ghost.

As he had grown up in St. Louis at a fortunate time, so he came to Harvard in happy years. It was the Harvard where a distant kinsman, Charles William Eliot, was president; the Harvard of Irving Babbitt (who detested President Eliot), of Barrett Wendell, George Santayana (who held Wendell in contempt), Josiah Royce, Charles T. Copeland, and other famous professors whose books have endured. F. O. Matthiessen suggests that of Harvard's professors, Babbitt and Santayana most influenced Eliot; certainly Eliot and Santayana had in common a mordant criticism of political

liberalism; but Santayana's materialism did not settle upon
the young Eliot.* From Babbitt, too, Eliot would dissent
in part; but Eliot would be grateful always to Irving Babbitt,
who, assailed on all sides by his intellectual adversaries,
nevertheless built more strongly than he knew.

During Eliot's years at Harvard, Babbitt published his
first three books: *Literature and the American College, The
New Laocoön,* and *The Masters of Modern French Criticism.*
These, and indeed all of Babbitt's later writings, were to find
renewed expression or clear sympathy—if sometimes disagreement, too—in Eliot's poetry and prose. In the fullness of
time, Eliot would pass beyond Babbitt's ethical humanism,
as already he had passed beyond his family's Unitarianism;
but his debt to Babbitt remained Babbitt's closest tie to the
writers of his own century. That fact requires a digression.

"I do not believe that any pupil who was ever deeply
impressed by Babbitt, can ever speak of him with that mild
tenderness one feels towards something one has outgrown or
grown out of," Eliot would write in 1941. "If one has once
had that relationship with Babbitt, he remains permanently
an active influence; his ideas are permanently with one, as a
measurement and test of one's own. I cannot imagine anyone
coming to react *against* Babbitt. Even in the convictions one
may feel, the views one may hold, that seem to contradict
most important convictions of Babbitt's own, one is aware
that he himself was very largely the cause of them. The
magnitude of the debt that some of us owe to him should be
more obvious to posterity than to our contemporaries."[13]

In 1908—the year before Eliot enrolled in his class in

* In 1954, when Eliot was arranging for Faber & Faber to publish
the London edition of my book *The Conservative Mind,* he objected
mildly to my American publisher concerning my subtitle, *From Burke
to Santayana.* George Santayana, Eliot suggested, had insufficient substance for such a station. At the time, I let that subtitle stand; but
some years later, in the American revised editions, I altered it (without consulting Eliot) to *From Burke to Eliot.*

"Literary Criticism in France with Special Reference to the Nineteenth Century"—Babbitt published *Literature and the American College,* the fruit of fifteen years of study and reflection. This was the prolegomenon to the intellectual movement that came to be called American Humanism, or the New Humanism, which for nearly a generation filled the serious journals of the United States with friendly or hostile criticism—and which, in England, would be a major concern of Eliot's review *The Criterion.* This Humanism (not to be confounded with John Dewey's "Religious Humanist" association, which was neither religious nor humanistic) remains a living force today, though professed only by a remnant. Babbitt thought it inexpedient to push beyond ethics into theology or dogma; besides, he could not persuade himself of the operation of divine grace. Babbitt's disciple Eliot would become a Christian, in time; but Eliot remained to the end a humanist also.

"What Is Humanism?" This is the first chapter of *Literature and the American College,* and all the rest of Babbitt's books enlarge upon this subject. To put matters briefly, humanism is the belief that man is a distinct order of being, governed by laws peculiar to his nature; there is law for man, and there is law for thing. Man stands higher than the beasts that perish because he recognizes and obeys this law of his nature. The disciplinary arts of *humanitas* teach man to put checks upon his will and his appetite. Those checks are supplied by reason—not the private rationality of the Enlightenment, but by the higher reason that grows out of a respect for the wisdom of one's ancestors and out of the endeavor to apprehend the character of good and evil. The sentimentalist, who would subject man to the mastery of impulse and passion; the pragmatic materialist, who would treat man as an edified ape; the leveling enthusiast, who would reduce human personality to a collective mediocrity

—these are the enemies of true human nature, and against them Babbitt directed this book and all his later books.

Against the humanist, Babbitt set the humanitarian. The humanist struggles to develop, by an act of will, the higher nature within man; the humanitarian, on the contrary, believes in "outer working and inner *laissez faire*," material gain and emancipation from moral checks. What the humanist desires is a working in the soul of man; but what the humanitarian seeks is the gratification of appetites. Francis Bacon represented for Babbitt the utilitarian aspect of humanitarianism, the lust for power over man and over physical nature; Rousseau stood for the sentimental side of humanitarianism, the treacherous impulse to break what Burke had called "the contract of eternal society" and to substitute for moral obligation the worship of a reckless egoism.

Much read in Indian philosophy, Babbitt drew from the Buddha the truth that the greatest of vices is "the lazy yielding to the impulses of temperament (*pamâda*), the greatest virtue (*appamâda*) is the opposite awakening from the sloth and lethargy of the senses, the constant exercise of the active will." Babbitt's respect for Indic wisdom helped to persuade Eliot to embark upon graduate work in Indic studies at Harvard—studies Eliot would abandon later, nevertheless, fearing that he might fall into an amorphous syncretism at the expense of full participation in classical and Christian culture. "A good half of the effort of understanding what the Indian philosophers were after—and their subtleties make most of the great European philosophers look like schoolboys—lay in trying to erase from my mind all the categories and kinds of distinction common to European philosophy from the time of the Greeks," Eliot would say in 1933, regarding his Indic studies at Harvard under Lanman and Woods. He did not wish to forget how to think and feel as an American or a European. "And I cannot but feel that in some respects Irving Babbitt, with the noblest intentions, has merely made matters worse instead of better."[14]

This demurrer notwithstanding, the mark of Babbitt is strong upon Eliot's poetry and prose—even the mark of Babbitt's admiration for Buddhist insights. In *The Waste Land*, the Buddha's Fire Sermon would become relevant to twentieth-century culture. In the apprehension of cultural continuity, especially, Eliot's work continues Babbitt's undertaking; in the reaction against romanticism; in theories of education; in political principle; in grasp of the ethical end of letters; in emphasis upon the essential and the succinct; in the rousing of the moral imagination.

So Babbitt became imprinted upon Eliot's mind; but in general, Eliot became no representative Harvard Man. The Genteel Tradition did not attract him, and of old New England's writers, only Hawthorne impressed him much. With some New England authors whose convictions he might have shared, Eliot was acquainted only superficially, or perhaps not at all.*

We see Eliot during his Harvard years chiefly through the eyes of Conrad Aiken, his fellow-student and closest early friend: through Aiken's short sketch "King Bolo and Others," and through Aiken's inimitable autobiography, *Ushant.* (Eliot is the "Tsetse" of Aiken's cast of characters in *Ushant.*) Aiken was the first to spy out in "the fabulously beautiful and sibylline Tsetse" those literary gifts which would go unpublished until 1915. They were fellow editors of the *Harvard Advocate,* and shared many interests, though

---

* Eliot had not heard of Orestes Brownson, for one, until he read my book *The Conservative Mind*; and a paperbacked edition of selected essays by Brownson, which I brought out with an introduction in 1955, provided Eliot's first direct introduction to the American champion of orthodoxy and tradition. "I am not altogether pleased by Brownson's style," Eliot wrote to me early in 1956, "which strikes me as wordy and diffuse. But it is remarkable that a Yankee a century ago should have held such views as his, and depressing that he has been so ignored that most of us had never heard of him."

dissimilar in character. (Aiken spent much of his life in an almost obsessive pursuit of women, while Eliot was shy with everyone in the beginning, and lifelong was severe in the encounters of the sexes.) In London, a few years later, Aiken's "Uncle Dracula" kept "wagging an accusatory finger at the embarrassed Tsetse, and repeating over and over, 'I think you are a very wicked man' (the last thing, of course, that could possibly have been said of him)." Aiken describes Eliot as "a singularly attractive, tall, and rather dapper young man, with a somewhat Lamian smile," writing farcical verse about King Bolo (which he continued to do for many years, showing it only to a select circle). Eliot wrote, too, the Class Ode, when he graduated from Harvard College.

It is useful to know something of Harvard and Boston and Eliot in those days, if one wishes to understand *Prufrock and Other Observations*. The lack of such acquaintance leads one critic, Graham Martin, perceptive in more theoretical questions, to the absurd aside that "The lover in the 'Portrait' [of a Lady, in *Prufrock*] reports visits to his mistress . . ." But Eliot's Beacon Hill Lady is, in fact, an elderly "dear deplorable friend, Miss X, the *précieuse ridicule* to end all preciosity, serving tea so exquisitely among her bric-a-brac . . ." So says Aiken, who knew the Lady's original, "pinned like a butterfly to a page" of *Prufrock*. Her snares were not those of Circe, and her like survives in Boston today. Doubtless Graham Martin has been misled by the epigraph to "Portrait of a Lady," which (from *The Jew of Malta*) mentions fornication. One needs to bear in mind always Eliot's subtle sense of fun.

Although Harvard and Boston in those years had charms now desiccated, they could not attach Eliot. In 1908 and 1909, he had read Arthur Symons' *Symbolist Movement in Literature* and the three volumes of Jules Laforgue's poems; admiration for the French Symbolists (combining, perhaps,

with the influence of Babbitt's lectures on French literature)
transported him out of Harvard Yard. He obtained a master's
degree in English literature in 1910, and went off to Paris
for most of a year. *

Nearly a quarter of a century later, Eliot would write with
some nostalgia of his Parisian year. At that time, he remarked,
England had been an intellectual desert where one could see
a few tall and handsome cactuses: the "art for art's sake"
sterility of such as Sir Edmund Gosse; while America had
been an intellectual desert "without the least prospect of
even desert vegetables." But Paris had been in bloom:

"The predominance of Paris was incontestable. Poetry,
it is true, was somewhat in eclipse; but there was a most
exciting variety of ideas. Anatole France and Remy de Gour-
mont still exhibited their learning, and provided types of
skepticism for younger men to be attracted by and to repudiate; Barrès was at the height of his influence, and of
his rather transient reputation. Péguy, more or less Berg-
sonian *and* Catholic *and* Socialist, had just become important,
and the young were further distracted by Gide and Claudel.
Vildrac, Romains, Duhamel, experimented with verse which
seemed hopeful, though it was always, I think, disappointing;

---

* During his years as a student, Eliot wrote, at intervals, the poems
that would be collected in *Prufrock and Other Observations*. The chro-
nology of his formal studies is as follows: he entered Harvard College
in 1906 and took his bachelor's degree in 1909; was a graduate student
at Harvard from the autumn of 1909 to the autumn of 1910, obtaining
a master's degree; read French literature and philosophy at the Sorbonne from October, 1910, to July, 1911; spent some time at Munich
in the summer of 1911; returned to Harvard Graduate School in the
autumn of 1911, and spent three years in Indic studies and philosophy;
was made an assistant in philosophy at Harvard for the academic year
of 1913–14; proceeded to Marburg, on a traveling fellowship, in the
summer of 1914; removed to England at the outbreak of the War;
studied Greek philosophy at Merton College, Oxford, for some months
in 1914 and 1915; married in June, 1915. Although he completed his
dissertation on Francis Herbert Bradley in 1916, he never applied for
a Harvard doctorate or sought a university post.

something was expected of Henri Franck, the early deceased author of *La Danse devant l'arche*. At the Sorbonne, Faguet was an authority to be attacked violently; the sociologists, Durkheim, Lévy-Bruhl, held new doctrines; Janet was the great psychologist; at the Collège de France, Loisy enjoyed his somewhat scandalous distinction; and over all swung the spider-like figure of Bergson. . . . I am willing to admit that my own retrospect is touched by a sentimental sunset, the memory of a friend coming across the Luxembourg Gardens in the late afternoon, waving a branch of lilac, a friend who was later (so far as I could find out) to be mixed with the mud of Gallipoli."[15]

After some months, Aiken joined Eliot there, "for the first visit to the *pâtisserie* and then *sirop de fraises* and soda at the sidewalk café." While at the Sorbonne, Eliot had learned to compose critical reviews directly on the typewriter; and he had found that "it tends to compel one to use periodic sentences rather than loose," he had informed Aiken. They read poems in a garret; they talked at "the marble-topped table . . . the chestnut blossoms fell from the lamplit spring trees into the book or the *bière blonde,* or onto the heads of poets . . ." So writes Aiken, who nevertheless withdrew (abandoning, too, a pretty little American coquette) to London—the seat of his only pair of trousers being nearly worn through.

During that Parisian year, Eliot read—along with much else—the writings of Charles Maurras and of Julien Benda, a man of the Right and a man of the Left, whose ideas would work upon him for decades, though not half so strongly as Babbitt's. He read, too, Henri Massis; he heard Bergson lecture—but did not become a disciple; he knew Alain-Fournier and Jacques Rivière; he studied Paul Claudel. He would return to Harvard "in exotic Left Bank clothing, and with his hair parted behind"; he had entertained some thought of settling in France permanently.

Yet the claim of Paris upon Eliot was less strong than upon many other Americans who made their way to the Left Bank, or to the Right, in those years. Though he had been "early inoculated by the subtle creative venoms of Laforgue and Vildrac" (Aiken's phrase), even the influence of Laforgue, as Aiken remarks, has been too strongly emphasized by some commentators on Eliot's poetry. Eliot was no imitator of Laforgue; it was more a matter of somewhat similar minds regarding somewhat similar subjects. Already Eliot was writing verse that, though not to be published for another four or five years, was something quite new; in Aiken's eyes, Eliot "adumbrated a form which might be exactly the solution they were looking for—something freer, certainly, than the strictly stanzaic, or the monotonies of classic blank verse; with varying length of line, and, to some degree, a substitution of cadence for metrical beat or measure; but using both these and rhyme, too, when it wished, or when it suited."

The young Eliot ought not to be taken for a sobersided devotee of Gallic high culture: Aiken tells us of Eliot's fun with what now would be called "pop art" and "pop culture," during "the first 'great' era of the comic strip," of Krazy Kat, Mutt and Jeff, Rube Goldberg, and Nell Brinkley; of their passion for discovering and inventing slang; these were not quite the usual diversions of a representative Harvard graduate student. Yet returning to Harvard in the autumn of 1911, Eliot entered upon Indic studies and pure philosophy. He was appointed an assistant in philosophy—his promise being detected by Alfred North Whitehead and Bertrand Russell more clearly than it had been by Irving Babbitt—and the Harvard professors expected him to join them permanently, once he had obtained his doctorate.

He was one of the dozen graduate students of Russell, that aristocratic eccentric then delivering the Lowell lectures while visiting professor of philosophy at Harvard; with the others, Eliot took tea with Russell once a week, saying little. He made Russell into "Mr. Apollinax" of *Prufrock and Other Observations*:

When Mr. Apollinax visited the United States
His laughter tinkled among the teacups.
I thought of Fragilion, that shy figure among the birch-trees,
And of Priapus in the shrubbery
Gaping at the lady in the swing.

Those similes were apt. This acquaintance would lead, a year later, to an intimacy with Bertrand Russell which had curious consequences.

Graduate study at Harvard was a brief interlude: Eliot did not mean to abide with Professor Channing-Cheetah and dowager Mrs. Phlaccus. Eliot had gone back to Cambridge "already Europeanized," Aiken writes; "He made the point, for a while, a conspicuously un-American point, of carrying a cane—was it a malacca?—a little self-conscious about it, and complaining that its 'nice conduct' was no such easy matter." In his room Eliot hung a Crucifixion by Gauguin; and he took lessons in boxing from a Boston Irishman, perhaps the original of Eliot's tough Sweeney. (Long later, when asked what sort of person his creator supposed apeneck Sweeney to be, Eliot would reply that he had in mind a moderately successful pugilist who had retired to keep a public house.) "He was early explicit, too, about the necessity, if one was shy, of disciplining oneself," Aiken recollects, "lest one miss certain varieties of experience which one did not naturally 'take' to. The dances, and the parties, were a part of this discipline, as . . . was his taking of boxing-lessons."[16]

At Harvard, the varieties of experience were limited; Santayana, finding this so, had just departed forever. Europe offered diversity. A student of Idealism, in those years, necessarily spent some time at German universities; and so Eliot proceeded to handsome old Marburg in the spring of 1914. He would not see America again for many a year.

Expatriation

T. S. Eliot scarcely had begun to settle down in Marburg—indeed, he had not yet received the suitcase that Aiken had forwarded to him—before the events that began at Sarajevo sent Americans scurrying out of the Continent: the beginning of that disruption of civilization which was to weigh upon Eliot all the rest of his life. Retreating to England, he read philosophy at Merton College for a year, loving Oxford's buildings but not much taken with Oxford's professors. The accident of departure from Marburg, Aiken says, "would prove to have been decisive, and in England he would remain, exploring and consolidating the new cultural terrain, and beginning the laborious work of marking out what was to be his own domain in it."

In October, 1914, by chance he met Bertrand Russell, back from Harvard, in New Oxford Street. The lonely young American and the iconoclastic mathematical philosopher fell into friendship; certainly Eliot then needed someone's help. At Oxford he completed his doctoral dissertation on F. H. Bradley, the English Idealist philosopher. He never returned to Harvard to take his doctoral degree: poetry had lured him away from metaphysical disciplines and professorial possibilities, and England had won him away from the United States. As late as May, 1916, Eliot's mother would write to Bertrand Russell to express her hope that Russell would encourage Tom to choose "Philosophy as a life work. . . . I had hoped he would seek a University appointment next year. If he does not I shall feel regret. I have absolute faith in his Philosophy but not in the vers libres."[17] That could not come to pass.

For Tom Eliot had been married to Vivienne Haigh-Wood in June, 1915, and at first the two of them lived with her parents in Hampstead; more of that union presently. Presumably they had not the money to shift to France or America, had they wished to; besides, Bertrand Russell suggests that Vivienne was afraid to meet the Eliots of St. Louis. More than anything else, an accident of marriage converted him into an expatriate.

To support the two of them, for more than a year Eliot served as a school usher, chiefly at Highgate Junior School, "then a rough place," says John Betjeman, a boy at that school, who put into the hands of The American Master a manuscript modestly entitled *The Best Poems of Betjeman*. Eliot taught French, Latin, lower mathematics, drawing, swimming, geography, history, and baseball.* The situation was unpromising, and he found instead a clerkship at Lloyd's Bank, in the City. From that time forward he resided in London, returning to the United States only at rare intervals, the first of these seventeen years after he had left Harvard Graduate School.

Another reason for Eliot's settling in London, and later becoming a British subject, is suggested in the concluding sentences of his review of Paul Elmer More's *Aristocracy and Justice* (1916), reprinted in *The Sacred Wood* under the title "A Note on the American Critic": "But it is not the fault of Mr. More or Mr. Babbitt that the culture of ideas has only been able to survive in America in the unfavourable atmosphere of the university." He did not change his mind: he would write, in 1931, "The American intellectual of today has almost no chance of continuous development upon his own soil. . . . He must be an expatriate." It was better to be an expatriate in London than in New York—this latter the worst form of expatriation from American life, Eliot declared.

---

* "I know from experience," Eliot would tell a Chicago audience in 1950, "that working in a bank from 9:15 to 5:30, and once in four weeks the whole of Saturday, with two weeks' holiday a year, was a rest cure compared to teaching in a school." See *To Criticize the Critic* (1965), p. 101.

He took a whimsical pride in becoming a man of business. To Lytton Strachey he would write, in 1919: "You are very—ingenuous—if you can conceive me conversing with rural deans in the cathedral close." (He dealt with documentary bills, acceptances, and foreign exchange.) "I do not go to cathedral towns but to centres of industry. My thoughts are absorbed in questions more important than ever enter the heads of deans—as *why* it is cheaper to buy steel bars from America than from Middlesbrough, and the probable effect —the exchange difficulties with Poland—and the appreciation of the rupee."[18]

He was not altogether pleased with English life; but he had little choice. "Where to live? The letters are full of the question," Conrad Aiken recollects from his correspondence with the newly married Eliot. "England was clearly impossible. 'A people which is satisfied with such disgusting food is *not* civilized.' London is at first detested. But Oxford, and Merton, with its 'Alexandrian verse, nuts and wine,' the professors with pregnant wives and sprawling children, and hideous pictures on their walls, make him long even for London, perhaps to work in the British Museum. 'Come, let us desert our wives, and fly to a land where there are no Medici prints, nothing but concubinage and conversation. Oxford is very pretty, but I don't like to be dead.'"

So Eliot wrote to Aiken in 1915. Earlier, during a visit to London, Aiken had endeavored in vain to find a publisher for the manuscripts of "The Love Song of J. Alfred Prufrock" and "La Figlia che Piange" that he had carried with him there on Eliot's behalf. Those poems had satisfied him, Eliot told Aiken in 1915, whether they were good or not; he was uncertain whether he could or would write more like them. "Why should one worry about that? I feel that such matters take care of themselves, and have no dependence upon our plan." He threw his incertitudes into Byron's verse; he had nothing planned, he said, "Except perhaps to be a moment merry . . ."

Merriment, nevertheless, was not precisely what Eliot would find, most days, during those next few years. As much by accident as from choice, he stuck to London. He was not totally alienated from America: rather, gradually he became immersed in England, and that, the seventeenth-century England of Little Gidding and East Coker as much as the twentieth-century London where he earned his living and his reputation.

By 1915, at the age of twenty-seven, T. S. Eliot had made only one grave mistake in his life, but that very grave: his marriage. Vivienne (sometimes Vivien) Haigh Haigh-Wood, who became the first Mrs. Eliot, was a pretty chatterbox, and had danced in ballet; Eliot learned to fox-trot with her. "Poor Tom Eliot married the landlady's daughter," Roy Campbell said to me once, in his unsparing, good-natured way. Vivienne was a thin-skinned young woman, whimsical and impatient of restraint, a product of her times: a flapper. "She wanted to enjoy life," Stephen Spender says, "found Eliot inhibiting and inhibited, yet worshipped him." Someone called her "the river girl." She possessed a petulant intelligence, and some literary gift, recognized by Eliot; during 1924 and 1925, she would write several vignettes and reviews for her husband's quarterly. It is not difficult to understand why a shy and solitary young American in London, philosophically adrift and parted from his early moorings in Missouri and Massachusetts, should have been drawn to this hyacinth-girl of the idyllic imagination.

But Vivienne Haigh-Wood suffered from poor health, from obscure neuroses, and, in the judgment of several, from vulgarity. Bertrand Russell dined with this newly married pair in July, 1915:

"I expected her to be terrible, from his mysteriousness;

but she was not so bad. She is light, a little vulgar, adventurous, full of life—an artist I think he said, but I should have thought her an actress. He is exquisite and listless; she says she married him to stimulate him, but finds she can't do it. Obviously he married in order to be stimulated. I think she will soon be tired of him."

Still, Russell liked them both—so much so that he invited them to occupy one of the bedrooms in his London flat; and being wretchedly poor, they accepted. Also Russell gave, or lent, Eliot some debentures in a munitions-making firm—Russell being a pacifist, and Eliot not. This strange conjunction of personalities could not endure. "It is quite funny how I have come to love him, as if he were my son," Russell was writing about Eliot in November. "He is becoming much more of a man. He has a profound and quite unselfish devotion to his wife, and she is really very fond of him, but has impulses of cruelty to him from time to time. It is a Dostojevsky type of cruelty, not a straightforward everyday kind. I am every day getting things more right between them, but I can't let them alone at present, and of course I myself get very much interested. She is a person who lives on a knife-edge, and will end as a criminal or a saint—I don't know which yet. She has a perfect capacity for both."

Russell was no ideal marriage counselor. About this time, Bertrand Russell—who had been chaste until his marriage, but had steered another course thereafter—was carrying on simultaneously affairs with Lady Ottoline Morrell, with the famous Colette (Constance Malleson), and with an American girl whom he had more or less promised to marry if a divorce might be obtained. By September, 1916, Russell was writing to Lady Ottoline, to whom he was candid about all his other amours, "I shall soon have come to the end of the readjustment with Mrs. E. [Mrs. T. S. Eliot]. I think it will be all right, on a better basis. As soon as it is settled, I will come to Garsington."[19]

Russell's relationship with the Eliots terminated about that time; T. S. Eliot made some endeavor by correspondence to renew the friendship, a decade later, when Vivienne's decline was far advanced, but he would have made an odd sort of son to Bertrand Russell. The Eliots took a house at Marlow (which place-name Vivienne adopted as her pseudonym), where Aldous Huxley called upon them in June, 1918, finding both in excellent form: "I rather like her; she is such a genuine person, vulgar, but with no attempt to conceal her vulgarity, with no snobbery of the kind that makes people say they like things, such as Bach or Cézanne, when they dont."[20] That "excellent form" would not endure.

Rebellion against the Abstruse

"Cousin Nancy" was published in *Poetry*, through Ezra Pound's good offices, in October, 1915. Eliot's burial of Matthew and Waldo, in that poem, was the act of a young man who had discovered through Babbitt, Bradley, and his other literary and philosophical studies (as, indeed, through his brief experience of three cultures) the hollowness of those nineteenth-century guardians.

Anyone who reads Eliot's dissertation, *Knowledge and Experience in the Philosophy of F. H. Bradley* (not published until 1964), will find Eliot's one excursion into pure philosophy worthy of Josiah Royce's description of it, "the work of an expert." Believing Arnold and Emerson had become, to employ a word coined by Ambrose Bierce, "incompossible" with believing Bradley. The Harvard Graduate School and Francis Herbert Bradley had made something of a metaphysician of Eliot—if, like Bradley, a metaphysical skeptic; and in metaphysics, Matthew and Waldo seemed nerveless.*

* The heritors of the American Transcendentalist school, with its ideals of "unity, cosmopolitanism, brotherhood, and progress through

Bradley's writings, unlike Babbitt's, did not endure in Eliot as a strong conscious influence for much more than a decade; and in his preface to the dissertation, Eliot disclaimed, somewhat after Bradley's manner, any lasting importance for his early study: "Forty-six years after my academic philosophizing came to an end, I find myself unable to think in the terminology of this essay. Indeed, I do not pretend to understand it."[21]

As Eliot remarked more than once, he shared with Bradley a distrust of abstruse ideas. Bradley did much for him, Hugh Kenner argues: "A view of the past, a view of himself and other persons, a view of the nature of what we call statement and communication: these delivered Eliot from what might well have been, after a brilliant beginning, a cul-de-sac and silence."[22]

Bradley confirmed what perhaps Eliot's understanding of his own family already had suggested to him, that the past is not a thing frozen, but lives in us; one might as well aspire to separate the desired from desire. From Bradley, Eliot acquired, too, defenses against the prevalent latter-day utilitarianism of his age, and arguments that distinguish the person, and the claims of art and science, from the claims of social life.

"It is only on the supposition that physical existence is the ultimate end of society that art and science can be held to be essentially means to social ends," Lewis Freed com-

---

peaceful means," were enraged at "Cousin Nancy"; they promptly detected heresy. Waldo Browne—editor of *The Dial* and namesake of Waldo Emerson—and his colleagues and faithful readers denounced this blasphemy against Arnold and Emerson; they even accused Eliot of plagiarism, in the hope of squelching him. (Eliot had borrowed "the army of unalterable law" from Meredith's sonnet "Lucifer in Starlight"; this was an early instance of that deliberate technique of evocation by inserting other men's flowers which Eliot was to employ in most of his poems.) See *The Dial*, November 25, 1915; and Nicholas Joost, *Years of Transition, The Dial, 1912–1920* (1967), pp. 61–71.

ments on Bradley's help to Eliot. "And such a supposition, Bradley holds, is in direct conflict with the facts of moral consciousness. The end of society, on a secular level, is the realization of the moral ideal, the content of which is both social and cultural. And although Bradley does not impugn the importance of social life, he holds that art and science constitute the higher part of that ideal. It is our moral duty to perfect our nature by the cultivation of art and science, not merely as a means to social ends, but as ends in themselves."[23]

Also Bradley confirmed what Eliot had learned from Babbitt and Santayana and others: that utilitarianism and pragmatism cannot sustain the norms of civilization, the permanent things. As Freed puts it, "Bradley offers more modern weapons than scholasticism, and more penetrating ones than Arnold, for controverting the 'Utilitarian mind.'" Thus Bradley did his part in armoring Eliot against ideology —against the endeavor to apply abstruse ideas to personal and public concerns, and especially against trying to reduce everything in life to the alleged "greatest good of the greatest number." As J. M. Keynes was to write, Marxism is the final *reductio ad absurdum* of Benthamism: so, in coming to understand the fallacies of the English Utilitarians, Eliot began to form a criticism of Marxist doctrine much more penetrating than the materialistic arguments against Communism which most publicists of "democracy" and "free enterprise" would employ after 1918.

Moreover, Eliot acquired from Bradley something he much needed personally: a glimpse of the Self, as distinguished from what we are accustomed to calling "personality." Bradley reasoned that all personality is an artificial creation: it is not eccentric individualism, a cult of personality, that we ought to seek, but rather realization of the self in a cultural order. From his early years, Eliot seems to have felt what everyone (including apeneck Sweeney) feels in some degree: an isolation from others, a difficulty in relating his soul to the people he encounters. This tendency toward solipsism—toward the isolation of the self, toward doubting the reality of anything but one's own sensations and observations—was a danger among Idealists, Bradley pointed out. Eliot, indeed, found that even Bradley did not erect barriers sufficient to wall off altogether the pit of solipsism.

For human presumption tempts the man of intellect— especially if he is a shy man of intellect, as Eliot was—to assume that only the self can be known, or perhaps that only the self exists. Men tend to mistake their private immediate experience for certain knowledge; thus they stumble into a prison of spirit, shut off from the painfully acquired wisdom of the species.

Bradley led Eliot toward understanding that the world is real, but that the self perceives the world only in a glass, darkly. A general intention among men to reconcile their different—and fragmentary—points of view through common references cannot suffice to avert solipsism; neither can the possession of a common language. For us to catch some glimpse of what we really are, and to act with some apprehension of the human condition, we have to pass beyond abstruse ideas. In effect, Eliot began to perceive that we must nurture the moral imagination, which draws upon theology and history and poetic images. As Richard Wollheim writes of Eliot's dissertation on Bradley, "He thought that the requirement stretched beyond this [a common language to bind together points of view] and necessitated a community of souls upon which the individual was dependent for his existence."[24]

Harvard was surprised that young Eliot, so brilliant a student of philosophy, did not return to the university and metaphysics. But his close analysis of Bradley had led Eliot beyond metaphysics. Idealism could not satisfy him, and the mild disdain with which, nearly half a century later, he regarded his dissertation may have come to him not long after he finished his work on Bradley. Eliot was to be a philosophical poet—even a metaphysical poet—but no closet metaphysician.

He was thereafter opposed to abstract systems created out of private rationality—whether systems metaphysical or systems political. He had burrowed within dusty metaphysics; he understood the powers and the limits of that discipline; and he found himself seeking still. Reason, as opposed to passion and sentiment, he would defend in his essays: the reason of classicism, set against the impulses of romanticism. The more imagination a man possesses, the more he must wonder about the mysterious essence that is himself; the more he must be aware of his uniqueness; the more he must torment himself by suspecting that his face reflected in a mirror, or his conscious behavior with other people, cannot be really *himself*. And if an imaginative man does not know himself, or know the source from which that self has come, how can he venture to intrude upon those appearances which are called "other people"?

Eliot could not find in metaphysics satisfactory answers to these questions. To Burke's reproaches against the heart of the thoroughbred metaphysician, and to Johnson's thunder against presumptuous intellectuality, ruinous in personal concerns as in public life, Eliot soon would subscribe, implicitly at least. Already, in his own poems, he was groping his way toward other means than metaphysics for warding off solipsism: toward faith and moral imagination.

Like Burke, Eliot came to dread not the intellect itself —certainly not to dread right reason—but rather to dread defecated rationality, arrogantly severed from larger sources of wisdom. He dreaded this presumption in the person, and he dreaded it in the commonwealth. William Hazlitt said that Burke overwhelmed opposing polemicists because Burke was a metaphysician, not a mere logician—and this despite

Burke's abhorrence of the *philosophes*. So it was with Eliot: he came to dominate the literature of a rationalistic age because of his own powerful rational faculties, which informed him that individual rationality and private judgment have their limits. Those who took Eliot to be ignorant of metaphysics or natural science—or, for that matter, of economics—sometimes would find themselves humiliated by a swift rejoinder, Eliot citing Whitehead or alluding to some experiment in chemistry.

Formal philosophy, after all, is merely the ordering and examination of knowledge; philosophy is not the *source* of knowledge.* Eliot felt compelled to try to penetrate beyond analysis of sensations and words to the sources for understanding of Self and World and Time. This is not to abandon right reason, but to look beyond abstruse ideas. If "all a rhetorician's rules teach him but to name his tools," all a metaphysician's apparatus is but a critical armory. Eliot submitted, if you will, to a force: to a tormenting but ineluctable conviction that the Enlightenment's neat constructions called "ideas" cannot of themselves satisfy the higher reason.

Eliot had a high respect for ideas; but he knew that there exist other means to enlargement of the reason than abasement before isolated ideas—which ideas ordinarily are simply some one else's analysis and refinement of his own experience and his own vision. Metaphysics has its uses; but so has the moral imagination. With Virgil and Saint Augustine and Dante, Eliot drew upon the moral imagination, as well as upon private rationality. Resort to the moral imagina-

---

* In the conversation of mankind, says Michael Oakeshott, there is "no fixed number to the voices which engaged in this conversation, but the most familiar are those of practical activity, of 'science,' and of 'poetry.' Philosophy, the impulse to study the quality and style of each voice, and to reflect upon the relationship of one voice to another, must be counted a parasitic activity; it springs from the conversation, because this is what the philosopher reflects upon, but it makes no specific contribution to it." (Michael Oakeshott, *The Voice of Poetry in the Conversation of Mankind* [1959], p. 12.)

tion as a path to wisdom liberates the thinker from the narrow limits of personal experience and individual rational faculties.

What we call "the moral imagination" has connections with Newman's "illative sense." Its evidences may be fragmentary and irregular, but they are numerous; and, entering the mind over a long period of time, they may bring conviction. The moral imagination, embracing tradition, looks to theology and history and humane letters, especially, for evidences of human nature and of the permanent things. Through the moral imagination, one may escape from the pit of solipsism: the moral order is perceived to be something larger than the circumstances of one's time or one's private experience; one becomes aware of membership in a community of souls; one learns that consciousness and rationality did not commence with one's self or with one's contemporaries.

It was toward this moral imagination—even if he did not use the phrase—that Eliot was turning even while at Harvard. Having studied Bradley, one could not rest content with such as Arnold and Emerson, whom the young Eliot found all too soft in their ideas, surely. The rising generation revolted. Cousin Nancy rebelled in ignorance, but Eliot rebelled metaphysically. Rebellion against the shaken theism and moralism of the nineteenth century set Eliot searching for older certitudes.

Emerson, with other free spirits of the nineteenth century, was dear to Eliot's mother; perhaps for that reason, and possibly because he was not much learned in New England's men of letters, Eliot was to confine his early dissent from Emerson to four lines of "Sweeney Erect":

> The lengthened shadow of a man
> Is history, said Emerson
> Who had not seen the silhouette
> Of Sweeney straddled in the sun.

(47)

"I never could give much reality to evil and pain," Emerson had said on his fifty-eighth birthday. Eliot, however, just out of Harvard, already saw the reality of evil and pain: on a grand scale, the slaughter of the Somme was sufficient demonstration. Sweeney, shadowing the twentieth century, undid Emerson.

Matthew Arnold, a more formidable adversary whose regenerative ambition considerably resembled Eliot's own, was to be drubbed by Eliot several times, most notably in his essays "Arnold and Pater" (1930) and "Matthew Arnold" (1933). Arnold "failed to ascend to first principles"; he fondly endeavored to make poetry do duty for religion. "The total effect of Arnold's philosophy is to set up Culture in the place of Religion, and to leave Religion to be laid waste by the anarchy of feeling. And Culture is a term which each man not only may interpret as he pleases, but must indeed interpret as he can."[25]

It was not in Boston only that Eliot found Arnold paving Hell with good intentions: in England, even more, Arnold's despairing elegiac tone made difficult the recovery of hope and principle which Eliot sought. Ian Gregor puts the relationship well:

"To distinguish himself from Arnold became for Eliot a way of characterizing that revolution of taste which he was concerned to bring about, a revolution which, while it set 'the poets and the poems in a new order,' also enabled him to create a climate of opinion favorable to his own poetic practice. When we see Arnold in this perspective we begin to understand something about why he haunted Eliot at every stage of his career, 'a familiar compound ghost' arousing him to admiration and dislike."[26]

When he wrote "Cousin Nancy," Eliot may not have been quite sure why he disliked Arnold, except that Bostonians ranked Arnold with the law and all the prophets, and so stultified their imagination. By 1932, when Eliot had been a Christian for some years, what Arnold had done to Bostonians would be clearer to Eliot: "Like many people the vanishing of whose religious faith has left behind only habits, he placed an exaggerated emphasis upon morals. Such people often confuse morals with their own good habits, the result of a sensible upbringing, prudence, and the absence of any very powerful temptation; but I do not speak of Arnold or any particular person, for only God knows."[27]

Dover Beach had been cold and barren enough; but by 1917, Eliot and his contemporaries found themselves on a strand still more desolate. Eliot had taken up residence in Heartbreak House, a ruinous edifice: the England, and the civilized world, that the War was pulling down. The mood of the time was George Bernard Shaw's:

"Heartbreak House was far too lazy and shallow to extricate itself from this palace of evil enchantment. It rhapsodized about love; but it believed in cruelty. It was afraid of the cruel people; and it saw that cruelty was at least effective. Cruelty did things that made money, whereas Love did nothing but prove the soundness of Larochefoucauld's saying that very few people would fall in love if they had never read about it. Heartbreak House, in short, did not know how to live, at which point all that was left to it was the boast that at least it knew how to die: a melancholy accomplishment which the outbreak of war presently gave it practically unlimited opportunities of displaying. Thus were the firstborn of Heartbreak House smitten; and the young, the innocent, the hopeful expiated the folly and worthlessness of their elders."[28]

A mild-mannered bank clerk, writing verses and reviews in a London flat, was commencing a labor of intellectual restoration quite different from Shaw's vagrant expectations.

Through the moral imagination, order in the soul and order in the commonwealth might be regained; and Eliot, though no lover of neat systems of a sociological character, had begun to rouse in his generation that dormant imaginative faculty.

III

Hell and
Heartbreak House

❖

Henry James's Successor

Upon the crumbling terraces of Heartbreak House, as German bombs fell in 1917, there strutted the energetic figure of the prime minister, David Lloyd George: the Waste Land stretched before him. No stronger contrast could occur than that between the temporary political master of England and the clerk-poet who was to dominate English letters for decades. "He was akin to the eighteenth-century view of a Welshman," Lloyd George's best biographer sums up that flamboyant and canny politician: "'Full of pride, petulance, and pedigree, hot as a leek and amorous as a goat.'"[1]

The reticent, humorous, elegant American scholar transplanted to London had no touch of Taffy. In 1917 and for years thereafter, Eliot was searching in the Buddha or in Saint Augustine for what Arnold and Emerson could not give him. London might not seem the best of all conceivable places to conduct such an inquiry, but Samuel Johnson and

William Blake and many other poets had sought there before him.

Genius ought to be centric, G. K. Chesterton was to write, not eccentric; and Eliot was centric almost to inflorescence. To Lloyd George, popular journalists pinned such adjectives as "colorful"; had they known of Eliot, they might have called him shadowy. Yet there is graven upon Eliot's stone in Westminster Abbey a burning rose. Interiorly, in 1917, Eliot was burning, burning, burning, while centrifugal force scattered the slates of Heartbreak House.

Lloyd George grew rich amidst general disasters; Eliot then was wretchedly poor. Even at the height of his reputation, Eliot could not have subsisted by poetry alone. During 1916, 1917, and 1918, he contrived to supplement his little salary from Lloyd's by writing reviews, rewarded by meager honoraria, for serious journals, and by teaching extension courses for Oxford University and the University of London; also he lectured to adults for the London County Council —his subjects being Victorian, Elizabethan, and modern French and English literature.

Eliot the writer felt the spur of necessity; also he knew the goad of sorrow. If Vivienne meant to stimulate him through their marriage, she succeeded—but not after the fashion she had intended. She gave to her husband chiefly what Thackeray's wife had given to that great Victorian —an occasion for the discipline of compassion. Soon Eliot's friends would inquire awkwardly after his wife's health.

"I was a close witness of the tragic progress of his first marriage," Sir Herbert Read reminisces. "Vivienne was a frail creature and had not been married long before she began to suffer from serious internal ailments. These exasperated an already nervous temperament and she slowly but surely developed the hysterical psychosis to which she finally succumbed. Eliot's sufferings in these years were acute . . .

Posterity will probably judge Vivienne harshly, but I remember her in moments when she was sweet and vivacious;
later her hysteria became embarrassing . . ."[2]

Read would tell Eliot that he ought to divorce his wife;
Read himself had done just that, and Eliot's friend Conrad
Aiken was forever dropping one mate and finding another.
But for Eliot, as for C. S. Lewis, there was something of the
eternal in even the shabbiest union of the sexes, and mar-
riage was morally indissoluble.

So the decades of Eliot's creative and critical achievement
were darkened by a knowledge of the vanity of human
wishes; and Eliot's work cannot be well understood unless
one is aware of this weight upon him for most of his life.
A fastidiousness, perhaps an austerity, toward the "dance of
life" was to run through Eliot's poetry and criticism; when,
for instance, he had occasion to quote Jonson's Sir Epicure
Mammon, he deleted the words "naked between my suc-
cubae." Freud was as alien to him as was Marx; and he felt
almost an aversion against D. H. Lawrence. "Perhaps the
force of his attack against Lawrence," Stephen Spender
observes, "is not that of the puritan against the sensualist,
but of this truth—that there can be no synthesis—against
the false idea of Lawrence that the modern world can be
saved by the sexual relation of the human pair."[3] Eliot came
to know that early.

But this is to anticipate the sorrow. In those days, Eliot
sometimes was sallow and sickly, yet cheerful of face and
even dapper. His features, his talk (when he could be drawn
out), and his clothes made him a young man of mark. "At
a Sunday evening performance," Clive Bell recalls, "I used
to admire Mr. Eliot's faultless dress, white waistcoat and all:
whether at an evening party, or in the country (you will
remember the 'four piece suit') or in the city, always the
poet made himself inconspicuous by the appropriateness of

his costume."[4] And there is Frank Morley's description of Eliot as a City man (for a time, a little earlier, he had worn a monocle, and neighbors had called him Captain Eliot):

"His strong-set acquiline features and his well set-up figure were observed to advantage in the traditional costume of bowler hat, black coat and striped trousers which marked him as one of the class who give us our crack volunteer regiments, and who turn out more athletes and sportsmen than any body of men in these islands. Was that a deliberate disguise? It might fool you to know which of his disguises was which. He carried a malacca-handled umbrella which was always neatly rolled, and with which, when he wished for a taxicab, he waved in the air. Such a display, however, was unusual; for the most part his behavior was subject to an iron control."[5]

Eliot had come to know nearly everyone, with the exception of G. K. Chesterton, in the realm of London letters. Bertrand Russell had introduced him round; Eliot's poems and reviews in *Poetry, Blast, The New Statesman, The International Journal of Ethics, The Monist, The Little Review, The Egoist,* and other periodicals had attracted the attention of people worth interesting. Leonard and Virginia Woolf, John Middleton Murry, the Sitwells, Herbert Read, and the hostesses of the drawing rooms took him up. Lady Ottoline Morrell would have him out to Garsington Manor often. For with the publication of *Prufrock*, a new literary domination had commenced.

To his brother Julian, Aldous Huxley wrote concerning Eliot, at the end of 1916, "You ought to read his things. They are all the more remarkable when one knows the man, ordinarily just an Europeanized American, overwhelmingly cultured, talking about French literature in the most uninspired fashion imaginable." A few months later, Huxley wrote to a friend that Eliot was "a very nice creature." He called on Eliot at Lloyd's Bank, where the author of *Prufrock* "was the most bank-clerky of all bank clerks. He was not on the ground floor nor even on the floor under that, but in a sub-sub-basement sitting at a desk which was in a row of desks with other bank clerks."[6]

It was a time of famous men of letters. Yeats stood high; Robert Graves, Siegfried Sassoon, Edmund Blunden, and others were writing from the trenches; H. L. Mencken published his *Book of Prefaces* that year; Pound was a rising power; George Saintsbury's *History of the French Novel* appeared; Joseph Conrad and Rudyard Kipling loomed large still; there were grand or ascending literary names on either side of the Atlantic; yet it was to be Eliot's age.

For by 1917, a literary revolution was in process, which Eliot would describe thirty-seven years later, in 1954: "In the first decade of the century, the situation was unusual. I cannot think of a single living poet, in either England or America, then at the height of his powers, whose work was capable of pointing the way to a young poet conscious of the desire for a new idiom. It was the tail-end of the Victorian era. Our sympathies, I think, went out to those who are known as the English poets of the nineties, who were all, with one exception, dead. The exception was W. B. Yeats, who was younger, more robust, and of more temperate habits than the poets of the Rhymers' Club. And Yeats himself had not found his personal speech . . . What the poets of the nineties had bequeathed to us, besides the new tone of a few poems by Ernest Dowson, John Davidson, and Arthur Symons, was the assurance that there was something to be learned from the French poets of the Symbolist Movement —and most of them were dead, too."[7]

It was Eliot himself who filled this vacuum of the poetic imagination. He would become what Henry James* had been, but also something more; and he was aware of the

* Henry James had died on February 28, 1916, after many years' residence in London.

difficulties of a "Europeanized American." In 1928, after he had become a British subject, he would write to Herbert Read a letter touching on this matter:

"Some day I want to write an essay about the point of view of an American who wasn't an American, because he was born in the South and went to school in New England as a small boy with a nigger drawl, but who wasn't a southerner in the South because his people were northerners in a border state and looked down on all southerners and Virginians, and who so was never anything anywhere and who therefore felt himself to be more a Frenchman than an American and more an Englishman than a Frenchman and yet felt that the U.S.A. up to a hundred years ago was a family extension. It is almost too difficult even for H. J. [Henry James] who for that matter wasn't an American at all, in that sense."[8]

Having chosen Heartbreak House, Eliot would remain there during a second and greater war, when other literary men found it prudent to cross the Atlantic westward. "If we take the widest and wisest view of a Cause," he would write a decade later, "there is no such thing as a Lost Cause because there is no such thing as a Gained Cause. We fight for lost causes because we know that our defeat and dismay may be the preface to our successors' victory, though that victory itself will be temporary; we fight rather to keep something alive than in the expectation that anything will triumph."[9] As a poet with a cause, he would win victories in literary London and in America, too; yet much fortitude, Stoic and Christian, would be required of Eliot as he contended against the dominant forces of the twentieth century. Lloyd George, at the head of the Conservative party in 1917, was the symbol of much that Eliot detested; but the real champion of conservative causes would be Eliot.

Prufrock and Tradition

With the publication of *Prufrock* in 1917, Eliot captured
something more important even than the admiration of established men of letters: he won the rising generation.
Whether most of the rising generation understood him well
may be another matter; only some years later did the tendency of his thought become manifest. From first to last,
Eliot's poems had mystery in them, and were susceptible of
many interpretations; the poet himself always permitted his
critics and commentators to find what significance they
might like or dislike in his verses, acknowledging that a
writer, and a poet especially, may express truths dim enough
to himself, yet illuminating to another mind; he did not
elucidate.

"For my generation," declares Kathleen Raine (who was
nine years old when *Prufrock* appeared), "T. S. Eliot's early
poetry, more than the work of any other poet, has enabled us
to know our world imaginatively."[10] Yet to know the world
with what sort of imagination? The mass of criticism of
Prufrock, from 1917 down to this writing, includes a wide
range of views; sometimes that criticism reflects the Freudian imagination or the Marxist imagination. To explain what
Eliot was saying, rather than to praise the manner in which
he said it, is a principal purpose of this book. One needs to
commence this task with "The Love Song of J. Alfred
Prufrock," so obscure, so evocative, so surprising a poem.

At heart, "The Love Song" is the first of Eliot's several
poems about Hell. In this instance, it is the Hell of the
solipsist, unable to credit the reality of those who appear
about him: a genteel solipsist unable, even when he has had
some glimpse of the essence of things, to tell his phantom
neighbors the Truth. "The Love Song of J. Alfred Prufrock"

(57)

is not merely a description of a vacillating gentleman at a tea party, too timid to declare his affections; nor is it a condemnation of bourgeois society; nor yet an effusion of world-weariness. Really, Prufrock is a flaccid Everyman—though a modern man surfeited with comforts and embarrassed when he is confronted by revelation—who refuses to bear witness to the truth. J. Alfred Prufrock is not identical with Thomas Stearns Eliot, except so far as the characters created by every poet must contain something of their author; but the poem does reflect the mind of a young man in search of firm ground.

Prufrock is granted a peep at the timeless; but being infirm of will, he creeps back into the prison of Time, and hereafter must chafe at the prospect of growing old. The mermaids of the moral imagination will not sing to him. Our every decision, lifelong, is irrevocable for good or evil, Eliot was to say often in his later years. But Prufrock can hold to no decision for so much as a minute—certainly not to a decision that might make him absurd in the eyes of those who live by the formulations of tea parties; he lacks the strength "to force the moment to its crisis." He is a Hollow Man.

The poem's epigraph is from *The Inferno*. Like Lazarus, Prufrock has seen Death, the "eternal footman"; but trivialities and dread of being misunderstood beset him; and he descends, like Dante's Guido, to the hell of a bestower of evil counsels. The best gloss upon this poem is John Halverson's.

Prufrock has lived the existence of empty form, Halverson writes. "Yet he also at least contemplates the possibility of freeing himself. It would have to be an heroic leap, that self-liberation, requiring nothing less than a complete revolution in his life; yet it might bring with it the possibility of meaningful existence, of communication and love."[11]

He lacks the courage for that leap. For love to endure, there must exist a community of souls. But Prufrock has rejected his part in the moral conversation of mankind; his song is a monologue without auditors; he ends in an infernal isolation.

What no reviewer of *Prufrock* predicted in 1917, with that slim book of verse there commenced a renewal of the moral imagination in literature. Many were bewildered by Eliot's early poems; some were attracted only by the novelties of style; others took the poems for "social commentary" merely; to some sober critics, Eliot had expressed successfully a generation's disillusionment with everything. Had its moral significance been clear to most readers, *Prufrock* might have been rejected as hopelessly old-fangled in inspiration. Yet gradually the literary public of 1917 and succeeding years became aware that Eliot had something of the seer in him; that perhaps one literary era had been buried and another was being born. Some people even sensed that the earthly hell of the War was paralleled, in this innovating "Prufrock," by the enduring hell of fallen human nature.

Kathleen Raine writes that "Mr. Eliot gave hell back to us. . . . The shallow progressive philosophies both religious and secular of our parents' generation sought to eliminate evil from the world. Mr. Eliot's visions of hell restored a necessary dimension to our universe."[12] To describe Hell is not to despair of salvation; nor to convert one's self into a Prufrock; nor to be a humorless fanatic; certainly not to condemn one's self to literary sterility.

"Prufrock" drew its images and phrases from the bewildering variety of sources that has rejoiced the regiment of Eliot scholars—from Dante and Saint Augustine, obviously, but also from Benson's life of Edward FitzGerald, to which book the imagery of "Gerontion," too, would owe much.[13] Prufrock may be damned, but he is comical after his fashion. Though Dante wrote no *Old Possum's Book of Practical Cats*, in Eliot there was a touch of Democritus; one often was unsure precisely when he jested, yet certain that he jested frequently. J. Alfred Prufrock's resignation to the role of Polonius was not to be emulated by Eliot. It would become one of Eliot's qualities that cheerfulness might break unexpectedly, like rain, into the Waste Land.

The course set by Eliot ought to have been descried by anyone who read his first major critical essay, "Tradition and the Individual Talent," which was published in *The Egoist* in 1919 and reprinted in Eliot's first collection of essays, *The Sacred Wood*, the next year. This declaration of principles rang with the aggressiveness of youth; it has been attacked by both friends and enemies of Eliot right down to the present, but Eliot never disavowed it. If this essay served well enough as armor for Eliot's shy and reserved nature, still it represented his literary and social principles from beginning to end. Eliot's own talent was not to be revolutionary, but conservative; he did not become a lost leader of the Party of Progress, because even in *Prufrock* he was defending what he came to call "the permanent things" against the follies of the time.[14] It is no paradox, he said in substance, to be at once an innovator and a reactionary.

In "Tradition and the Individual Talent," Eliot argued that the true poet, restraining private emotions, almost extinguishing visible personality, immerses himself in a profound continuity of literature: he may add to the body of great literature (indeed, he ought to innovate, if he has the power, that he may renew the vitality of tradition), but only if he has absorbed great literature. Tradition has life; we contribute to it and are nurtured by it.

"Yet if the only form of tradition, of handing down, consisted in following the ways of the immediate generation before us in a blind or timid adherence to its successes," Eliot wrote, " 'tradition' should positively be discouraged. We have seen many such simple currents soon lost in the sand; and novelty is better than repetition. Tradition is a matter of much wider significance. It cannot be inherited, and if you want it, you must obtain it by great labor. It involves, in the first place, the historical sense, which we may call nearly indispensable to anyone who would continue to be a poet beyond his twenty-fifth year; and the historical sense involves a perception, not only of the pastness of the past, but of its presence . . . This historical sense, which is a sense of the timeless as well as of the temporal and of the timeless and of the temporal together, is what makes a writer traditional. And it is at the same time what makes a writer most acutely conscious of his place in time, of his contemporaneity."

The intersection of time and the temporal: this understanding was to run through the whole of Eliot's work. This idea is bound up with what Burke called "the contract of eternal society" and with Burke's "great mysterious incorporation of the human race." We are not creatures of the hour only—the poet, least of all. "And he is not likely to know what is to be done," Eliot says of the poet, "unless he lives in what is not merely the present, but the present moment of the past, unless he is conscious, not of what is dead, but of what is already living." No enduring literature can be written by men deficient in this understanding; no society can long subsist without it.[15]

In defying both Gosse and *The Dial*, Eliot was not breaking tradition, but restoring it. (No man can make a tradition, Nathaniel Hawthorne had written; it takes a hundred years to make one.) Eliot's verses seemed eccentric to readers who thought of tradition as yesterday's styles merely; but Eliot meant to be centric. "One error, in fact, of eccentricity in poetry is to seek for new human emotions to express; and in this search for novelty in the wrong place it discovers the perverse." Not a dead past, or an unknowable future, was Eliot's destination: life is for action here and now, but that life can have meaning only if we know what has been

said and done before our hour; only if we subordinate ourselves to civilization's continuity and essence; only, indeed
(though this last was not to become clear in Eliot's writing
for some time), if we accept certain ancient sources of
authority that describe the intersection of time and the
timeless. "Someone said: 'The dead writers are remote from
us because we *know* so much more than they did.' Precisely,
and they are that which we know."

This is true of literature, Eliot saw; and true also of the
commonwealth. He never passed through a phase of political
radicalism, and the continuity essential to great poetry had
for him its parallel in the continuity of the civil social order.
Literature and society know no wall of separation.

True, the poet ought not to convert himself into the
politician, Eliot stated in the introduction to *The Sacred
Wood* (1920); Matthew Arnold had done just that, to his
harm. "Arnold is not to be blamed; he wasted his strength, as
men of superior ability sometimes do, because he saw something to be done and no one else to do it. The temptation, to
any man who is interested in ideas and primarily in literature,
to put literature into the corner until he cleans up the whole
country first, is almost irresistible." H. G. Wells and G. K.
Chesterton had done just that; doubtless it was their proper
role, Eliot suggested; but it should not have been Arnold's
role.

Yet though the poet should steer clear of ideology and
passionate involvement in practical political movements—
though, indeed, the poet is no giver of laws or captain of
hosts—still the poet lives in a civil social order. That public
order is intertwined with the order of the soul; therefore the
poet cannot ignore it. With considerable courage, three
years after he wrote the essays of *The Sacred Wood*, Eliot
was to attempt, through the editing of a literary review, a
work of social regeneration, inseparable from literary regeneration. And in some slim tracts, later, he would defend

prescription in politics as stoutly as he had reaffirmed tradition in literature. So it had been with Johnson and Coleridge, exemplars for Eliot; so it had been with Plato in his duststorm.

"And certainly poetry is not the inculcation of morals," Eliot was to write in his preface to the 1928 edition of *The Sacred Wood*, "or the direction of politics; and no more is it religion or an equivalent of religion, except by some monstrous abuse of words." Just so. Yet T. S. Eliot was a moralist, a political thinker, and a Christian (later), as well as a poet.

Gerontion and Servitude to Time

During 1917, the old order of society in Europe had been falling apart with vertiginous speed. The Czar had abdicated in March; by November, the Bolsheviks had overthrown Kerensky. Everything collapsed into chaos by the autumn of 1918 (when Eliot published, in *The Little Review*, four new poems, the chief of them "Sweeney Among the Nightingales"); the Armistice was signed in November, settling upon Germany a peace in some ways worse than war. At Versailles, in June, 1919, the map of Europe was drawn anew—in a fashion that would bring on a war yet more catastrophic.

T. S. Eliot, dealing in foreign exchange at his bank and helping to edit *The Egoist,* brought out his *Poems,* published by the Woolfs: from those quatrains, it might have been difficult to guess at his later eminence. Eliot then enjoyed a grand reputation in a tiny circle: fewer than two hundred and fifty copies of his *Poems* were printed, and when *Ara Vos Prec* (collecting all his earlier verses) was published—in as limited a printing—in 1920, only three copies were sent out for review.

Ara Vos Prec (published in America as *Poems*) contained "Gerontion," written in 1919; and "Gerontion" made it clear that Eliot's was no mere clever ephemeral talent. In 1919 and 1920, the collected poems of Hardy and Kipling were published; and books of verse by Richard Aldington, Laurence Binyon, Walter de la Mare, D. H. Lawrence, John Masefield, Siegfried Sassoon, Edith Sitwell, Amy Lowell, Ezra Pound, John Crowe Ransom, Edmund Blunden, Robert Bridges, Aldous Huxley, Wilfred Owen, Conrad Aiken, Vachel Lindsay, Edna St. Vincent Millay, Edwin Arlington Robinson, Carl Sandburg, Sara Teasdale, and Glenway Westcott. It was as prosperous a time for poetry as it was unprosperous for the social order.[16]

Wise after his fashion, little old Gerontion has become, since 1919, an evangelist—quite against his will and intention. His palsied finger points toward the path that Eliot, half unwitting, already had begun to follow. Certainly "Gerontion" is no "equivalent of religion" after the manner of Arnold; but as a description of life devoid of faith, drearily parched, it is cautionary—even though Eliot himself, at that time, had traveled only half the distance toward the mutilated shrine at Canterbury.

This poem—its Jacobean strength of expression mingling with touches of the year of Versailles—is a station on Eliot's path, and yet also it reflects the condition of the bent world of 1919, and the condition of graceless man in every age. To me, the blank verse of "Gerontion" is Eliot's most moving poetry, but he never tried this virile mode later. A desolate splendor of utterance issues from the dying Gerontion, who has lived for the senses alone. "His problem," Marion Montgomery writes of Gerontion, "is that he can discover no vital presence in the sinful shell of his body, the part of his existence which may be named Sweeney Supine."[17] Gerontion believes in the existence of God and disbelieves in the possibility of his own salvation from the body of this death.

Musing and half dreaming, Gerontion awaits his end in a rented house—a Heartbreak House. The wisdom of the world, which he possesses, is of no avail now. Having rejected Christ long ago, soon Gerontion must encounter the retributive Christ, the tiger. Christ having been denied, neither fear nor courage can relieve the blight of spirit. Gerontion's acquaintances, now not even ghosts, sought in necromancy or in aestheticism or in sensuality some escape from this drought. They have fallen into the gulf before him, and now Gerontion will be annihilated:

I that was near your heart was removed therefrom

To lose beauty in terror, terror in inquisition.

I have lost my passion: why should I need to keep it

Since what is kept must be adulterated?

I have lost my sight, smell, hearing, taste and touch:

How should I use them for your closer contact?

Gerontion is what the Spaniards call a desperado: he has despaired of the operation of divine grace. There remains for him not even thorough damnation, but the vestibule of Hell only; he has been too petty and unadventurous a sinner to become a companion of Farinata, in *The Inferno*. With a hopeless egoistic bravado he awaits the Tiger's final leap: his life has been unheroic, but his destruction, "in fractured atoms," may be melodramatic enough. The jade History lures men into "cunning passages, contrived corridors and issues," like a gypsy witch, deceiving through ambition, guiding by vanity—and then one is lost, deprived of light, vainly athirst.*
Empty ritual, formal acceptance without living faith, bring no salvation. In the end, the lost fall into the Gulf.

Eliot is saying this: the modern and perennial appetite

* As Elizabeth Drew puts it, Gerontion's " 'History' is human experience lived without the framework of a Logos; lived by the 'knowledge' supplied by empirical science. It is man relying on his own desires and 'whispers,' believing that he can control his own fate; directed only by arbitrary expediency . . ." See Drew, *T. S. Eliot: the Design of His Poetry* (1949), p. 54.

to "multiply variety in a wilderness of mirrors" (with Sir Epicure Mammon, again) leads to destruction. The practical statesmen of the Hall of Mirrors at Versailles, talking of history, strolling into contrived corridors, forget the weevil and the spider—the symbols of death and corruption; while Sweeney, the average sensual man in Eliot's imagery, rejects grace every hour—and so must be whirled "beyond the circuit of the shuddering Bear."

Some who read Eliot in 1919 and 1920 relished "Gerontion" as a cleverly labyrinthine expression of their own pose of despair and disillusion, the enervate state of half-belief, half-disbelief: the lamentations of impotent defiance. (It still was possible, in England or America, to delight in so Byronic an attitude.) But Eliot wrote in earnestness. Unless faith is regained—*if* it may be regained—unless we become something better than "the sapient sutlers of the Lord"— why, we end desperate as Gerontion or simian as Sweeney. We end barren. Eliot's state of mind then was like that of Joseph Wood Krutch in *The Modern Temper*—although Eliot would write years later that he had more in common with even a Communist than with such a secularistic liberal as Krutch. If faith is lost, then all is lost; but those who have eaten of the tree of knowledge cannot forget that they have learned the emptiness of the universe. Knowledge, not ignorance, is Gerontion's undoing.

In "Gerontion," Eliot's perplexity is not far distant from Matthew Arnold's; and his implicit argument—that belief is a necessity for the person and for the commonwealth, so help Thou my unbelief—resembles those of Arthur Balfour and W. H. Mallock, two or three decades earlier. The difference is this: Eliot was creating a language and a style which, he hoped, might wake the imagination of the rising generation. Could the modern rationality, having tasted in pride the fruit of the wrath-bearing tree of Eden, grope back through those cunning passages toward the fear and the love of the Lord? "After such knowledge, what forgiveness?" In 1919, Eliot doubted the existence of any such Ariadne's thread.

Yet only a few years later, those doubts would have diminished. At tea in Tavistock Square, Stephen Spender recalls, "Virginia Woolf needled Eliot about his religion. Did he go to church? Yes. Did he hand round the plate for the collection? Yes. Oh, really! Then what did he experience when he prayed? Eliot leaned forward, bowing his head in that attitude which was itself one of prayer ('Why should the aged eagle stretch his wings?'), and described the attempt to concentrate, to forget self, to attain union with God."[18]

Gerontion had lodged in the decrepit Heartbreak House of the Armistice and the Treaty, its gardens now "rock, moss, stonecrop, iron, merds"; and there would he be devoured. But Eliot was making his way to other mansions. To have lost one's certitude in an order spiritual and an order temporal, during the years of school and college and university, had been a commonplace experience ever since the beginning of the eighteenth century. To lament this loss and to search for curious substitutes had been a widespread game among men of intellect during the latter half of the nineteenth century. But for a young man of poetic genius, in the years after the Great War, to find his way beyond the common preoccupation with doubt toward a fresh apprehension of the transcendent, and toward a reinvigorated understanding of the principles of social order—this was something more rare.

Any other such seeker might have been found vexatious or ridiculous by Bloomsbury; but that circle could not dismiss Eliot with a sneer or a chuckle. He knew his poets, his metaphysicians, even his theologians. Endowed with humor, he was anything but one of David Hume's "gloomy, hairbrained" enthusiasts who "may have a place in the calendar; but will scarcely ever be admitted, when alive, into the intimacy of society." Indubitably Eliot was an innovator in verse, moreover; if Bloomsbury had excluded any talented man of originality, Bloomsbury would have been false to its own convention of unconventionality.

So it came to pass that Bloomsbury—where dwelt a good many Gerontions—puffed and patronized Eliot, although his beliefs soon would shake its complacency (including its complacent doctrines of originality and creativity) and would sap its intellectual hegemony. Leonard and Virginia Woolf had published Eliot's *Poems* in 1919, and would publish the first English edition of *The Waste Land* in 1923, and his *Homage to John Dryden* in 1924; to Virginia Woolf, by 1922, Eliot was the "Great Tom." Yet, in *The Waste Land* and in his review *The Criterion,* that year of 1922, Eliot would lay his petards beneath the philosophical convictions of the Woolfs and their set.

It was not that the creator of Gerontion disliked the Bloomsbury set more than other intellectual circles of those years; Bloomsbury at least was humane and inquisitive. America, surely, had nothing half so imaginative. Virginia Woolf was better company than Eliot could have found in Harriet Monroe, queen of *Poetry*—who had been nearly as much outraged by Eliot's early poems as had been Waldo Browne and the old *Dial* set. Pound had sent Harriet Monroe a copy of "The Love Song of J. Alfred Prufrock" in October, 1914; but what she approved was Vachel Lindsay's "Fireman's Ball." Pound had written to her that "Prufrock" was "the most interesting contribution I've had from an American"; Eliot actually had "trained himself *and* modernized himself *on his own.*" As Noel Stock comments, Miss Monroe "was disappointed when she found that Eliot had betrayed his heritage into the hands of the very cosmopolitanism which American civilization was destined to overcome."[19]

Nor did Eliot take to the expatriates—or holiday expatriates—of the Left Bank. Conventional on principle, Eliot became suspected of deliberate sartorial mockery of friends who affected bohemianism. At Paris, in May, 1924, Eliot frequented "the Dôme and other bars in top hat, cutaway, and striped trousers." William Carlos Williams grumbles that Eliot's incongruously correct attire "was intended as a gesture of contempt" for American arts-and-letters types proud of their new-found Parisian emancipation.[20] Probably it was so. His poetry, innovating in form as Williams and his friends had aspired to innovation, took a direction of thought and substance as repugnant to the Williams set as was Eliot's morning coat.

Eliot had struck out for himself, regardless of these and other literary coteries. During 1921 and 1922, he was sending to the new *Dial* his much-admired "London Letters." Soon after *The Dial's* assault upon "Cousin Nancy," that periodical had shifted from St. Louis to New York, had passed into the direction of very different editors, had embraced innovation, literary and political, and had welcomed Eliot, whose politics were not then discernible. This connection gave Eliot opportunity to assail both the complacent Georgian poets in England and the egalitarian disciples of Walt Whitman, particularly Carl Sandburg, in America. Both schools, in their opposed fashions, gave the public what the public was believed to relish; both were false to reality—both the "green and pleasant land" sentimentality and the American cult of the colossal. A few months later, Eliot would flog both schools with his new whip of scorpions in *The Waste Land*.

The way of this solitary innovator was hard enough, the admiration of Bloomsbury notwithstanding. Difficulties with Vivienne increased, and may be reflected, veiled, in certain lines of *The Waste Land*. And he was poor still. In his first year at Lloyd's, his annual salary was a hundred and twenty pounds, less than he had been paid as a school usher; it had risen by increments, but it did not suffice. His brilliant review-essays were turned out in swift succession, to add a pittance to a pittance. Only a blockhead writes except for money, according to Samuel Johnson: like Johnson at a similar age and stage in London, Eliot wrote under strong pressure to maintain himself at all. One does not grow affluent by writing for such eminent literary reviews as *The Dial* and, a little later, *La Nouvelle Revue Française*. The clerkship at Lloyd's might be time-consuming; yet without it, Eliot might have been reduced to the poverty of George Gissing in a shabby-genteel New Grub Street.

Nor was the way of this innovator easy philosophically and pyschologically. Beyond the troubles of marriage and occupation, Eliot the Seeker seems to have been experiencing a crisis of the Self about 1921. He perceived that decadent rationalism and liberalism could not sustain a man concerned with ultimate questions. Yet though in "Gerontion," and even in "Prufrock," he had delineated the Great Refusal, still he could not submit himself to religious doctrine. He thought as much of becoming a Buddhist as of professing Christian belief.

Moreover, just who *was* Tom Eliot? What is the Self? What is Time? The pitfall of solipsism that he had discovered in Idealism still yawned before him: an appalling prospect of solitude. F. H. Bradley had argued that what we call the Self is the product merely of a limited private experience; indeed, the "known" world is such an arbitrary construction. Gerontion found Self and World such. But Eliot looked for some surety, some real knowledge of Self and World—for revelation, conceivably, if the discursive reason might not afford such certitude.

Especially he seems to have hungered for an understanding of Time. Is what we call "time" also a mere private construction, shifting and amorphous as the self, signifying no more than a private growing old—and death around the corner for Prufrock, imminent for Gerontion? So Bradley had written, and so Eliot still feared. Or can it be that Time is objective; that Time has an Author; that the acts of the person signify in Time? If Time should be a genuine continuity, and not simply a human convention, then the Self would have meaning. Such problems fretted even apeneck Sweeney; they obsessed Eliot.

Probably it is true, as Graham Martin suggests, that in 1921 Eliot still was convinced philosophically by Bradley's concepts of Self and World and Time; and that nevertheless, in his early poems, he was expressing his eagerness for certitude, permanence, meaning, and realization of the self. What Eliot then took to be metaphysically honest, he found to be psychologically unendurable. This pathetic tension was at its harshest as he turned over in his moral imagination the reflections and fragments that make up *The Waste Land.*

Since Eliot's death, several critics have suggested that Eliot's sorrow in *The Waste Land* was the result chiefly of frustration in his marriage—which, one may conjecture from that poem and other writings, was no harmony of body and spirit. Doubtless some trouble of this sort contributed to his vision of barrenness, and even gave that vision a particular focus. But his concern for the public order, too, went deep in him, from beginning to end; he would write in 1939 that his greatest depression of spirits, lifelong, followed upon the shameful yielding to Hitler at Munich. And with such a mind as Eliot's, philosophical conundrums may produce a disquiet as strong as any erotic harassment. About this time, Eliot was tormented also by the "God is Dead" problem since so vulgarized, and Marion Montgomery describes this well:

"The science of the mind that Eliot studied proved insufficient," Montgomery writes. "Phenomenology is after all a development of subjectivity as if it were self-sufficient. What it leads to is a separation of subjective being from any Other. The possibility of any dialogue, that word used so desperately in our time, is doomed. For phenomenology, as that branch of learning had developed by the time of Prufrock, was a heresy to the orthodox family relationship of minds very like the Albigensian in its effective isolation of the individual. So considered, one sees how such a heresy is destructive to the sanity of the artist no less than to other men, for a part of the definition of the artist is that he communicates vision, whether simple simile or complex metaphysical system. The pure application of phenomenology means not only that the poet cannot write for others but that he cannot even write for himself."[21]

An intellectual tension, then, lies back of *The Waste Land,* as back of "Gerontion." More than personal poems or social poems, these are philosophical poems. Breaking out of the confines of phenomenology, Eliot is searching for sources of knowledge and love that may enable the human pair to commune fully, and that may enable the human agglomeration to become a human community. Gerontion knows no Other; Eliot is more fortunate, suspecting that the Other is knowable, though not yet known.

In 1921, Eliot was hard ridden by necessity. The spur of necessity brought out Eliot's talents, rather than debasing them; but he paid a heavy price in his health. Haunting philosophical preoccupations—which, a century earlier, might have been called "religious melancholy"; an uncongenial workaday occupation; too intense a literary endeavor; an ailing wife and an imperfect marriage: these, settling upon his constitution, for a few months overcame him.*

While recuperating at Margate and in Switzerland, he produced that strange great poem *The Waste Land,* which

---

* This collapse was physical chiefly—certainly not intellectual, for during it Eliot produced his most famous poem. In *The Cocktail Party,* years later, Eliot would have his psychiatrist, Dr. Harcourt-Reilly, object to patients' using the term "nervous breakdown"— because that phrase might mean anything or nothing.

was to turn the literary world upside down. After he had written "Gerontion" and *The Waste Land,* Eliot would understand Self and World the better. But for a few more years he still would lack the grammar of assent.

The Inner Waste Land and the Outer

For a man like Eliot, imbued with the idea of the contract of eternal society, the prospect of Europe in the autumn of 1921 was dismal enough. The Hapsburg system had been torn apart, and the impoverished succession-states, riven by faction and ideology and ethnic rivalries, clearly could achieve no enduring order. Ruined Germany, the Weimar Republic feeble from the first, was hard pressed to withstand Communist insurrection. The face and the spirit of France were ravaged. In Italy, Communist and Fascist bands, terrible simplifiers, struggled for power; Mussolini would triumph a year later. The Bear, now Red, glowered upon the West. Ireland was lost to the United Kingdom, as Sinn Fein and the Black and Tans competed in terror. Lloyd George's inflation was followed by an abrupt deflation; two million men were unemployed in Britain. "The glory of Europe is extinguished forever," Burke had declared in 1789; if the indictment had been hyperbole then, it seemed accurate enough in 1921.

This decay of order and justice and freedom within the old European community was paralleled by the decadence of the old moral order, the Church falling into disrepute and the governing motive of many eminent men being merely "put money in thy purse." For the charlatan and the cheat, large opportunities were opened everywhere; while the old motives to integrity were fearfully shaken. Out of the War's brutality had emerged gross appetites and violent ambitions, and everywhere egoism swaggered. A mind disciplined by a classical education thought of the Roman decadence. One heard endless prating about democracy, but the actual tendency of the time seemed to be toward the servitude to desire in private life, and the servitude to ideology in public affairs. It was a loveless prospect, and the community of souls was stricken.

Were *The Waste Land* only the poetic lament of a man whose marriage had not fulfilled his hopes, and who had worked himself to the bone, it would remain interesting— but it could not have spoken as a conscience to a multitude of other consciences. A widespread decay of love is no accident: causes may be discerned, and remedies—however difficult—may be suggested. In short, Eliot has described in *The Waste Land* not merely his ephemeral state of mind; much more important, he has penetrated to causes of a common disorder in the soul of the twentieth century.

Disdaining the Romantic lyric poet's exaltation of the ego, Eliot subordinated private emotion to the expression of general truths. A few brief passages from "Tradition and the Individual Talent"—published only two years earlier—may suggest his determination to rise above personal comment on the universe:

"The progress of an artist," Eliot had reasoned, "is a continual self-sacrifice, a continual extinction of personality. . . . the more perfect the artist, the more completely separate in him will be the man who suffers and the mind which creates; the more perfectly will the mind digest and transmute the passions which are its material. . . . Impressions and experiences which are important for the man may take no place in the poetry, and those which become important in the poetry may play quite a negligible part in the man, the personality. . . . It is not in his personal emotions, the emotions provoked by particular events in his life, that the poet is in any way remarkable or interesting. . . . Poetry is not a turning loose of emotion, but an escape from emotion; it is not the expression of personality, but an escape from personality."

So *The Waste Land* ought not to be read as a sublimation of Eliot's emotions in 1921—which, whether or not complex, certainly were not unusual. It is Eliot's thought and expression that matter. He was troubled in 1921, privately; but he knew that most men have been troubled, and that many have endured troubles with resignation and fortitude. Not his private misgiving, but his concern with the condition of modern man, is what gives *The Waste Land* an enduring force. Before him sprawled a prospect of private and public disorder. Although he suffered under this general distemper, it is anything but a private perplexity that Eliot sets before us.

Confronted with this scene, Eliot is not "disillusioned" (for when had he been the dupe of illusion?) or despairing, though gloomy enough. The first necessity, he implies, is to ask the right questions. How have we come to this pass? The "protagonist" (as the critics generally call him) really is the Seeker; and he is searching for the springs of love.

The Waste Land might have been more coherent and less puzzling had Ezra Pound let it alone—although then it would have stirred up less of a sensation. Eliot, in part recovered from his collapse, brought to Pound at Paris, near the end of 1921, a poem twice as long as *The Waste Land* we know; moreover, Eliot proposed to publish it with "Gerontion" as a prologue. There were lyrics that Pound excised; they appeared later as portions of "The Hollow Men" and as "Dream Songs" in Eliot's *Minor Poems*. Eliot had strained his hand while rowing, and so gave Pound a draft typewritten, for the most part; Pound crossed out his large deletions and wrote in his amendments.

"Pound was, in fact, a dominating director," Eliot would write in 1946. "He has always had a passion to teach. In some ways, I can think of no one whom he resembled more than Irving Babbitt—a comparison neither man would have relished." Babbitt's influence upon himself was evident, Eliot went on; and he suggested that Pound, like Babbitt, was one of those "men so devoted to ideas, that they cannot engage in profitable discussion with those whose ideas differ from their own." But Eliot accepted Pound's authority, and the manuscript (or typescript, rather) of *The Waste Land* shrank. "I should like to think that the manuscript, with the suppressed passages, has disappeared irrecoverably; yet, on the other hand, I should wish the blue pencilling on it to be preserved as irrefutable evidence of Pound's critical genius."*

So the seeming discontinuity and the abrupt—often jarring—succession of images and evocations and incorporated quotations that we encounter in *The Waste Land* result in considerable part from Pound's advice; these aspects seem to have disconcerted, at first, even Eliot himself. It had not been his intention, while writing at Margate and Lausanne, to employ these kaleidoscopic or cinematographic devices to such an extent; he had in mind a more smoothly flowing monologue. Had he not yielded to Pound's energy, we might have had a long poem less magical, yet better fulfilling Eliot's intention: the Great Refusal of Gerontion, fol-

---

* See Eliot, "Ezra Pound" (1946), in Peter Russell (ed.), *Ezra Pound, a Collection of Essays . . . on his Sixty-Fifth Birthday* (1950), pp. 27–28. Actually, Eliot had given the manuscript of *The Waste Land*, in October, 1922, to John Quinn, of New York, to express his thanks for Quinn's many services to him; also he had sold to Quinn, for a hundred and forty dollars, a mass of other early manuscripts of his. This manuscript of *The Waste Land* remained in Quinn's possession and (after 1924) in that of Quinn's sister, until the New York Public Library bought these materials in 1958; this acquisition was kept secret until 1968.

"Criticisms accepted so far as understood, with thanks," Eliot wrote to Pound from London, in January, 1922. Their correspondence at this time contains considerable information as to Pound's changes in the manuscript. See D. D. Paige (ed.), *The Letters of Ezra Pound, 1907–1941* (1950), pp. 167–172.

lowed by the delineation of sterility in the Waste Land, and incorporating the picture of the Hollow Men's vacuity—altogether, with transitional and elucidatory passages, a more coherent denunciation of modern disorder, more fully representative of Eliot's own intellect and method. In the long run, this might have been better teaching. Beyond any doubt, nevertheless, the enthusiasm and the scandal that resulted from publication of the Pound-revised poem would have been less if Eliot had withstood Pound.

When first I read *The Waste Land*, in my student days, I was annoyed by the seeming pedantry—ineffectual pedantry, at that—of Eliot's Notes, which explain little enough and have misled many readers and critics. The Notes to *The Waste Land* were in part an endeavor to compensate for Pound's merciless deletions, and some of them carry a hint of Eliot's whimsy and self-mockery; he was no lover of a heavy ostentatious apparatus of scholarship. But chiefly the Notes were improvised to satisfy the printer: there were sixty-four pages, altogether, to be filled in the little book, and the poem itself was too short for that compass, so padding must be provided. Eliot did not fall into that folly ever again.

The Notes may be ignored; so may some of the criticism of *The Waste Land*. Certain critics have offered theories about the poem so openly in conflict with Eliot's own literary principles and with his later writings that one wonders whether those commentators ever read the poem itself with a desire to understand; they have read the Notes and have read earlier critics—whom they imitate or denounce. But the poem may be read appreciatively without the possession of a doctoral degree in literature; and it is no allegory, but rather after its fashion a narrative poem, as the *Aeneid* and *The Divine Comedy* are narrative and philosophical.

In October, 1922, this poem was published in *The Criterion*, Eliot's own new review, without notes; it appeared in

The Dial, across the Atlantic, in November—again without notes, because *The Dial's* editors declined to print them. The first edition of the book was published in New York (a thousand copies, with the Notes) by Boni and Liveright, that December; the first English edition (less than five hundred copies) was brought out by the Woolfs in September, 1923. The Age of Eliot had arrived with a clap of thunder.

For with *The Waste Land,* Eliot completed the success he had commenced with *Prufrock:* he won over, horse, foot, and dragoons, the rising generation of aspiring literary talents.* With a certain disrelish, E. M. Forster was to acknowledge Eliot's ascendancy over the young:

"For Mr. Eliot's work, particularly *The Waste Land,* has made a profound impression on them, and given them precisely the food they needed. And by 'the young' I mean those men and women between the ages of eighteen and thirty whose opinions one most respects, and whose reactions one most admires. He is the most important author of their day, his influence is enormous, they are inside his idiom as the young of 1900 were inside George Meredith's, they are far better qualified than their elders to expound him, and in certain directions they do expound him."[22]

True, *The Waste Land* suggested better than had Eliot's earlier poems the way the "Invisible Poet" was steering—and so waked the justified suspicions of those young neoterists who had taken up with ideology, the inversion of religious dogma. Malcolm Cowley has described the mixed feelings of the young progressivists and levelers who were enchanted

---

* Eliot even captured, as Roy Campbell rejoices, "those who were then the most fervent admirers of J. E. Flecker, Brooke, and Lascelles Abercrombie," that "green and pleasant land" set, who abruptly turned from depreciation of Eliot to adulation, becoming his "most ardent admirers and imitators. . . . From then on the influence of Eliot literally swallowed up many of these minor poets as a blue whale swallows mites of krill." See Roy Campbell, *Light on a Dark Horse* (1952), p. 203.

by the novelty of *The Waste Land,* but uneasy with its moral and social implications. "Strangeness, abstractness, simplifications, respect for literature as an art with traditions—it had all the qualities demanded in our slogans." They would defend the poem against the old entrenched schools of criticism, and against popular misunderstanding; but at heart they did not like it:

"When *The Waste Land* first appeared, it made visible a social division among writers that was not a division between capitalist and proletarians. . . . But slowly it became evident that writers and their theories were moving toward two extremes (though few would reach one or the other). The first extreme was that of authority and divinely inspired tradition as represented by the Catholic Church; the second was Communism. In Paris, in the year 1922, we were forced by Eliot to make a preliminary choice. Though we did not see our own path, we instinctively rejected his."[23]

From the publication of *The Waste Land,* indeed, men of the Left would begin to fulminate against Eliot—as presently they would complain of Robert Frost; for those two poets became defenders of the moral imagination, with its roots in religious insights and in the continuity of civilization. This the intelligent ideologue could not abide, committed as he was to mechanism and futurism.

Nearly half a century after the arrival of *The Waste Land,* it still remains desirable to inquire—for the common reader, and for a good many uncommon readers—just what Eliot was saying in that startling poem. Although merely to list the commendable critical essays about *The Waste Land* would require the equivalent of a chapter of this book, mystery and mystification continue to shroud Eliot's intentions. Some critics descend so deep into a line-by-line analysis (often in the flickering light of the befuddling Notes) that they are themselves lost, like their readers, in contrived corridors. A close examination of Eliot's sources and allusions is all to the good; but that has been accomplished already by several competent hands.[24]

My own summary analysis, which follows, is an endeavor to penetrate to the heart of this poem, necessarily refraining from comment upon Eliot's technique, and avoiding most excursions into his evocation of prophets, saints, poets, potentates, and anthropologists. Now that we may read at our leisure the whole body of Eliot's work, it is possible to see *The Waste Land* in the perspective of Eliot's later poetry and prose, and so to emancipate ourselves from the understandable limitations of those critics who wrote only a few years after the poem burst upon them. This verb "burst" I employ deliberately, upon the authority of William Carlos Williams, whose school of poetry was undone by Eliot: "Then out of the blue *The Dial* brought out *The Waste Land* and all our hilarity ended. It wiped out our world as if an atom bomb had been dropped upon it and our brave sallies into the unknown were turned to dust."[25]

At the heart of this poem of exploration lies the legend of the Grail, and more especially the symbol of the Chapel Perilous. (Eliot, not expecting *The Waste Land* to achieve so surprising a popularity, assumed that those who might read him would know tolerably well the Chapel Perilous and many other allusions and symbols in his lines. But already the decline of the old humane schooling, in classroom and home, had diminished in his audience the thrill of recognition; already the American college, as Babbitt had said, was turning out more pedants and more dilettantes, but fewer young people of truly liberal learning.)

How may a man be born again and a blasted land made to bloom anew? Why, screw your courage to the sticking-place: dare to ask terrifying questions, and you may be answered.

In some versions of the Grail legend, questing knights

who entered the Chapel Perilous—ringed about with tombs
—beheld the cup, the lance, the sword, the stone. If they
found the hardihood to inquire, they would be answered:
they would be told the meaning of these things; told at once,
perhaps, or perhaps later. And of that questioning great good
would come: the Fisher King's wound would be healed,
and the desolate land would be watered again. "So in a civilization reduced to 'a heap of broken images' all that is requisite is sufficient curiosity," Hugh Kenner comments keenly;
"the man who asks what one or another of these fragments
means . . . may be the agent of regeneration. The past exists
in fragments precisely because nobody cares what it meant;
it will unite itself and come alive in the mind of anyone who
succeeds in caring, . . . in a world where 'we know too much,
and are convinced of too little.' "[26]

Knowing that past and present really are one, Eliot draws
upon the myths and the symbols of several cultures to find
the questions that we moderns ought to ask. Myth is not
falsehood; instead, it is the symbolic representation of reality.
From ancient theological and poetical and historical sources,
burningly relevant to our present private and public condition, we summon up the moral imagination. We must essay
the adventure of the Chapel Perilous if we would not die of
thirst; we must confront the Black Hand and the dead
Wizard-Knight, there in the ruinous Chapel; if we face down
the horror, and dare to ask the questions, we may be heard
and healed.*

The most superficial adverse criticism of The Waste Land,
advanced chiefly by doctrinaire progressivists and humani-
tarians or by grimmer ideologues, is this: "Eliot," they say,
"is snobbishly contrasting the alleged glory and dignity of

---

* "The horror! The horror!", from Conrad's Heart of Darkness, was
the epigraph Eliot first chose for The Waste Land; Pound persuaded
him to supplant it with Petronius' account of the bored sibyl.

the Past with what he takes for the degradation of the democratic and industrialized Present. This is historically false,
and ought to be repudiated by all Advanced Thinkers."

But that is not at all Eliot's intention. The Present, Eliot
knew, is only a thin film upon the deep well of the Past; the
Present was ceasing to exist even as he wrote at Margate
or at Lausanne; the Present evaporates swiftly into the cloud
of the Future; and that Future, too, soon will be the Past.
The ideological cult of Modernism is philosophically ridiculous, for the modernity of 1971, say, is very different from the
modernity of 1921. One cannot order his soul, or participate
in a public order, merely by applauding the will-o'-the-wisp
Present. Our present private condition and knowledge depend upon what we were yesterday, a year ago, a decade
gone; if we reject the lessons of our personal past, we cannot
subsist for another hour. Just so it is with the commonwealth,
sustained by a community of souls: if the community rejects
its past—if it ignores both the insights and the errors of
earlier generations—then soon it comes to repeat the worst
blunders of past times. Whether or not Time is a human convention merely (on which point, Eliot had not made up his
mind as he wrote *The Waste Land*), the Past is not dead,
but lives in us; and the Future is not a foreordained Elysium,
but the product of our own decisions in this vanishing moment that we enjoy or endure.

The Waste Land, then, is no glorification of the Past.
What the reader should find in this poem, rather, is Eliot's
understanding that, by definition, human nature is a constant;
the same vices and the same virtues are at work in every age;
and our present discontents, personal and public, can be apprehended only if we are able to contrast our present circumstances with the challenges and the responses of other times.
Aside from this, Eliot's glimpses and hints of a grander style
and a purer vision in other centuries are chiefly the established device of the satirist, who awakes men to their parlous

(82)

condition of abnormity by contrasting living dogs with dead lions.

Lost, we must ask for directions; and those directions do not come from living men only.* For authoritative guidance, Eliot turned especially, in this poem, to Saint Augustine, the Buddha, and the Upanishads. "The unexamined life is not worth living," as Socrates told his disciples. *The Waste Land* is the endeavor of a philosophical poet to examine the life we live, relating the timeless to the temporal. A Seeker explores the modern Waste Land, putting questions into our heads; and though the answers we obtain may not please us, he has roused us from our death-in-life. For just that is the Waste Land: the realm of beings who think themselves quick, but who exist only in a condition sub-human and sub-natural, prisoners in Plato's cave.

In *The Waste Land,* tremendous questions echo round the Chapel Perilous. In the progress of a terrifying quest, some wisdom is regained, though no assurance of salvation. We end by knowing our peril, which is better than fatuity: before a man may be healed, he must recognize his sickness.

Regeneration is a cruel process: so commences "The Burial of the Dead," the first of the four parts of *The Waste Land*: the half-life underground seems preferable to many. No sooner is this said than there breaks in the querulous voice of a woman, Marie—encountered in an Alpine hotel, perhaps overheard in chance conversation: she is a displaced or stateless person from the wreck of the Austro-Hungarian

---

* John Ruskin's name rarely is coupled with Eliot's; yet it was Ruskin who, in the literature of the previous century, gave the best expression of cultural continuity, defended in the twentieth century by Eliot. Take this passage from *Sesame and Lilies:*

"We play with the words of the dead that would teach us, and strike them far from us with our bitter, restless will; little thinking that those leaves which the wind scatters had been piled. not only upon a gravestone, but upon the seal of an enchanted vault—nay, the gate of a great city of sleeping kings, who would awake for us, and walk with us, if we knew but how to call them by their names."

structure, with memories of staying at the archduke's, her cousin's; the mountains conceal her, and she takes that for freedom; her roots withered, she drinks coffee in the Hofgarten, and drifts. Such is the condition of Europe in 1921, for Heartbreak House is roofless in the Continent, too.*

As she falls silent, a voice is heard, prophetic or ghostly, inviting the son of man to take shelter under a red rock, where he will be shown fear in a handful of dust. (In Hadrian's villa, the subterranean mock Hell could be entered from any building of that sprawling expanse; just so, it is easy to pass from a café by the Starnbergersee, in one moment, to the Waste Land, where "the dead tree gives no shelter, the cricket no relief.")

The next moment, memory and desire have wafted in the hyacinth girl, the image of lost love; four lines from *Tristan und Isolde* summon her up from the dead, in this month of lilac and hyacinth and illusory spring. The episode in the hyacinth garden had been like the trance of those who sought the Grail but were unworthy. The hyacinth is withered now, and the girl vanished, amid stony rubbish. Aye, that episode's done for: will the future bring consolation?

So we come to Madame Sosostris, with her Tarot cards, decadent sibyl misreading her own pack. Fear death by water, she says—to people perishing of thirst. Her counsels would deny us rebirth through grace in death, the fertilizing power of water; she does not find the Hanged Man—Christ, or the Dying God—in the fortune she tells. But perhaps, unwittingly, this witch has conjured up a ghost: Stetson, who

---

* "Marie" and her murmurs are drawn from the autobiography of Countess Marie Larisch, *My Past* (1916), closely connected with the Archduke Rudolph and Maria Vetsera, who died mysteriously at Mayerling: the suggestion of private and public disorder is obvious. See George L. K. Morris, "Marie, Marie, Hold on Tight," in *Partisan Review*, XXI (March-April, 1954); reprinted in Hugh Kenner (ed.), *T. S. Eliot: A Collection of Critical Essays* (1962), pp. 86–88.

died a coward at Mylae—which might have been the Dardanelles, these wars having much of a likeness.

Thus "The Burial of the Dead" concludes with the Searcher's reproach to dead Stetson, not far from London Bridge:

"That corpse you planted last year in your garden,
"Has it begun to sprout? Will it bloom this year?
"Or has the sudden frost disturbed its bed?
"O keep the Dog far thence, that's friend to men,
"Or with his nails he'll dig it up again!"

This is a play upon Webster's lines in *The White Devil*:

But keep the wolf far thence, that's foe to man,
For with his nails he'll dig them up again.

An aside concerning the Dog is excusable here, for these particular lines of *The Waste Land* illustrate admirably the wide variety of interpretations of Eliot possible and even plausible. (Some critics abstain altogether from comment upon this particular passage.) Consider three glossators of good reputation, far apart.

First, George Williamson, in his *Reader's Guide to T. S. Eliot* (pp. 134–135): "If Dog involves Sirius—as in 'Sweeney among the Nightingales'—he becomes a sign of the rising of the waters and is friendly to growth. But Dog may also involve Anubis, guardian of the dead, who helped to embalm the broken Osiris. By his ambiguity the Dog presents an ironical aspect, and this irony centers in the intent of the planting . . ."

Second, D. E. S. Maxwell, in his *Poetry of T. S. Eliot* (p. 39): "The Dog may be spiritual awareness or conscience, which Stetson makes no attempt to arouse, in the fear that it might force him to recognize his spiritual failings, to attempt to redeem himself—this none of the people of the waste land wishes to do, for it requires effort and positive action."

Third, Cleanth Brooks, in his *Modern Poetry and the Tradition* (pp. 145–146): "I am inclined to take the Dog . . . as Humanitarianism and the related theories which, in their concern for man, extirpate the supernatural—dig up the corpse of the buried god and thus prevent the rebirth of life." He adds a footnote: "The reference is perhaps more general still: it may include Naturalism, and Science in the popular conception as the new magic which will enable man to conquer his environment completely."

Would it have been well to be disinterred by the Dog, or not well? Eliot never explained, and such controversies may continue so long as English poetry is criticized. This catacomb, layer upon layer, of evocation and suggestion in *The Waste Land* makes this poem subtle and strange and ambiguous as the Revelations of Saint John. Many lines are puzzling as the characters written by the sibyl on the leaves she scattered. Yet the general meaning of *The Waste Land* is as clear as its particular lines are dark.

So the Seeker clambers over the heap of broken images, leaving "The Burial of the Dead," to enter upon "A Game of Chess," the second part of the poem—and he stumbles into a boudoir. At first this room is mistaken for Cleopatra's; but really this is no chamber of grand passion and queenly power; it is only the retreat of a modern woman, rich, bored, and neurotic. On a wall, the picture of the metamorphosis of Philomel is a symbol of the reduction of woman to a commodity—often a sterile or stale commodity—in modern times. (The levelers would bring us down, Burke had said, to the doctrine that "a woman is but a woman; a woman is but an animal, and an animal not of the highest order.") Modern woman is ravished, but nowadays she is transformed into no sweet nightingale.

In this boudoir the woman is haunted, starting at noises on the stair, seeking in empty talk the quieting of a subtle dread; no diversion satisfies her—surely not "O O O O that

Shakespeherian Rag." "Think," she tells the Seeker; and indeed he does:

> I think we are in rats' alley
> Where the dead men lost their bones.

So it is with the woman of fashion—and not otherwise with the woman of the ladies' lounge of the London public house, talking of adultery and abortion. The game of chess that modern woman plays is her undoing; sexual power is atrophied to the parched attempt at gratification of an appetite which cannot be satisfied by flesh only; love becomes an empty word. And the bartender calls out repeatedly, "HURRY UP PLEASE IT'S TIME": like the woman of the boudoir, the woman of the pub idles away the hours and days and years until death knocks.

Leaving the pub, the Seeker drifts down the Thames: we hear the Fire Sermon, the third part of this poem. The polluted river does not cleanse; dull lusts, sexual or acquisitive, hang about it now; the Seeker finds no gaiety and no glory. He becomes hermaphrodite Tiresias, impotently witnessing copulation without ardor and loss of chastity without either pleasure or remorse:

> When lovely woman stoops to folly and
> Paces about her room again, alone,
> She smoothes her hair with automatic hand,
> And puts a record on the gramophone.

Against this degradation, the Seeker appeals to the true City of love and gaiety, with music upon the waters. One hears, as a distant echo, the voices of children singing of the Grail. But the Fisher King himself, perhaps the wounded Fisher of Men, casts his lines in a dull canal behind the gashouse, even the romantic memory of his crumbling castle departed. Here the dead do not rise to the surface, their bones being cast into a dry garret and "rattled by the rat's foot only, year to year." From Highbury down to Margate Sands, this river—once life-bestowing—has turned sinister.

The varieties of concupiscence have driven out love. Those who amuse themselves beside the river or drift down it (to their undoing) fancy that they are safe enough:

But at my back in a cold blast I hear
The rattle of the bones, and chuckle spread from ear to ear.

Infatuation with transitory impulses, the Buddha had said in his Fire Sermon, oppresses man; abjure desire. And as Augustine sought redemption from the unholy loves of Carthage, so the Seeker prays that the Lord may pluck him as a brand from the burning.

Out to sea the Thames carries us—and to the ten enigmatic lines of the fourth part of this poem, "Death by Water." Passing beyond profit and loss, Phlebas the drowned Phoenician entered the whirlpool. In time, we all are swallowed by the whirlpool; yet what we have taken for "life" may be worse than death; and perhaps through dying we come to the life eternal. Madame Sosostris had predicted death by water. Yet is this "dying" really annihilation? May it not be rebirth, as by baptism? However that may be, a surrender to the element of water is better than endless torment in the fire of lust.

It is not in the ocean depths that the Seeker ends his quest. In the concluding part of this poem, "What the Thunder Said," he ascends into the mountains—once the source of life-giving water—Gethsemane and the slaying of God in his mind. The "red sullen faces" that sneer upon him from "doors of mudcracked houses" are God-forsaken; the thunder is dry and sterile. Someone walks beside him: the Fisher King, perhaps, who once guarded the Grail; and a mysterious third being, hooded. Is this the Christ, or the Tempter of the Wilderness, or some Hollow Man? In this delusory desert, the traveler can be certain of nothing.

This upland desolation, ravaged by hooded hordes, is the waterless expanse of Sinai for lost peoples—of this century and of many centuries—who wander aimlessly, uprooted by terrible events; it is the eastern Europe of 1921, and also the "Hell or Connaught" of all the vanquished. "Cracks and reforms and bursts in the violet air" of twilight work the ruin of cities: Athens and Alexandria and Vienna and London become as the Cities of the Plain; the terrible simplifiers contend against one another in the Last Days.

Here the landscape is by Bosch or Breughel, and woman's sexuality, sunk into witchcraft, engenders a brood of monsters, "bats with baby faces." The world is turned upside down: voices call from dry cisterns and wells. Threading his way upward through this horror, the Seeker arrives at the Chapel Perilous, dry bones and tumbled graves.

Empty and forgotten the Chapel stands, "the wind's home." Yet the Seeker has arrived at the place where, even now, questions are answered in the moonlight for those who dare to ask in earnest. At a cock's crow from the rooftree, the diabolical powers round about are dispersed for the moment. A damp gust brings rain, and the thunder speaks.

That thunder is the voice of revealed wisdom: it is the Indo-European "DA," a root from which have sprung up many trunks; it is, if you will, the "I am that am" from the Burning Bush. And the thunder of DA utters three sounds that are the answers—sibylline indeed—to the Seeker's questions. They are "datta," "dayadhvam," and "damyata," from the Brihadaranyake-Uphanishad. And they signify "give," "sympathize," and "control."

So saith the Lord: give, sympathize, control. But though the Seeker had found courage to carry him to the Chapel Perilous and to ask the dread question, has he resolution and faith sufficient to induce him to obey the thunder? Some rain has fallen; but the sacred river wants a flood; mind and flesh are feeble. For lack of human daring, the Waste Land may remain ghastly dry.

Give? That means surrender—yielding to something outside one's self. If sexual union is to be fertile, there must occur surrender of self in some degree, momentary self-effacement in another. Lust, too true, may produce progeny; but those are the bats with baby faces. Larger even than procreation, giving or surrender means the subordination of the self(as of the arrogant private rationality) to an Authority long derided and neglected. Can modern man humble himself enough to surrender unconditionally to the thunder from on high?

Sympathize? That means love and loyalty, and the diminishing of private claims. We all lie in the prison-house of self-pity; and to recognize the reality of other selves—more, to act upon that reality—must require unusual strength: the virtue of *caritas*. The overweening modern ego has grown fat on the doctrine of self-admiration; the community of souls has been falling apart for some centuries now.

Control? That, as Babbitt had said, is to place restraints upon will and appetite. True control is exerted not through force and a master, but by self-discipline and persuasion of others. But can the strutting will restrain itself by its own act? Can modern appetites, so long unchecked—so long gorged on blood and foulness, as during the War—be confined once more to their proper place? We have indulged the *libido*; now can we return to the other kind of freedom, *voluntas*—to Cicero's ordered and willed freedom? Our desires are insatiable, and the thunder is distant.

So the thunder has answered the questions that were put in the Chapel Perilous. It was painful to seek for those answers; it will be agony to obey. Still the Seeker hesitates, though now the arid plain is behind him. He casts his lines upon the waters. London Bridge is falling down: the outer order of civilization disintegrates. But may not ruins be shored up? And should not a man commence the work of renewal, spiritual and material, by setting his lands in order: by recovering order within his own soul? The world may deride as folly such aspirations; but this is a mad world, my masters. Play Quixote. Give, sympathize, control; and the peace that passes all understanding be upon you.

"This seemed a new voice, revealing ancient things in a new way," Rose Macaulay recollects concerning the mark made at once by *The Waste Land* among other seekers; "the dark corridors where dreams lurk, where primeval history hides, were furnished with what seemed at times (but was not) a haphazard, inconsequent juxtaposition of images, and with fragments of social dialogue at tea parties, in streets, in pubs, fragments thrown up out of what mysterious context of experience? They drifted by, slipping again into the mist; their echoes disturbed. . . . The known landscape sprang to life: the stony waste, the decayed hole among the mountains, the empty chapel the wind's home. All this we know by nature, it is our heritage. But it is not left as we leave it; into it break thunder and voices and talk, turning the scene upside down; one has to think, to understand and follow . . . "27

Eliot had asked the great questions; and in the Waste Land, here and there, blades of grass had begun to sprout.

IV

A Criterion in a Time of Hollow Men

❖

Raising a Standard

Like other poets before him, Eliot woke to find himself famous; but still he labored in the cellars of Lloyd's Bank— tidying the estate of the lately deceased Houston Stewart Chamberlain, among other chores, and dealing with all claims and obligations of Lloyd's that arose out of the Versailles Treaty. *The Waste Land* had been a high success: yet a success, at first, chiefly among those who themselves wrote or aspired to write. It was nothing like the popular triumphs of Scott and Byron, more than a century before, or even like the popularity of John Betjeman, four decades later.

"Success" meant that the American first edition (for which its publisher paid Eliot a tardy advance of a hundred and fifty dollars) sold out promptly, and that another thousand copies were printed. It meant that the Dial Award (two thousand dollars, actually by pre-arrangement in lieu of payment by that magazine for publishing the poem) went to Eliot. It would mean, in time, that Eliot's name would be known to millions who had read next to nothing that he wrote. Yet this early success left him literally beneath a London pavement, people's heels tapping incessantly on the green glass cubes of the walk just above his head as he sat at his Lloyd's table.

Success as a poet made Eliot more noticed in the Bank itself. In Switzerland, young I. A. Richards encountered an officer of Lloyd's, Mr. W., who inquired of him whether Mr. Eliot was a good poet; and on Richards having assured him that Eliot was such, Mr. W. declared himself pleased:

"You know, I myself am really very glad indeed to hear you say that. Many of my colleagues wouldn't agree at all. They think a Banker has no business whatever to be a poet. . . . But I believe that anything a man does, whatever his *hobby* may be, it's all the better if he is really keen on it and does it well. . . . In fact, if he goes on as he has been doing, I don't see why—in time, of course, in time—he mightn't even become a Branch Manager."[1]

Actually, Eliot might have risen still higher than that in the City, had he persisted—as he might have risen at Harvard, or at Oxbridge; it was his talent for executing business, indeed, that soon would find him a place with a new publishing house. Like Harvard, the Bank had expected him to persist. Probably he preferred his work at Lloyd's to a university lectureship; he told Richards, in those days, that "No, he wasn't at all sure that an academic life would be what he would choose."

But either he must leave the bank and find some other means of supporting himself and his wife, or else cease to write: he had collapsed before from overwork, and now that he was editing a review in addition to his other undertakings, he was on the verge of a second collapse. In June, 1920, Ezra Pound had written to John Quinn, a New York patron of arts and letters, asking for a subvention for Eliot: "His wife hasn't a cent and is an invalid always cracking up, & needing doctors, & incapable of earning anything—though she has tried—poor little brute." By the beginning of 1923, Lloyd's was paying Eliot a salary of six hundred pounds annually; it was not so much lack of money that oppressed him as it was the endeavor to be simultaneously a banker and a man of letters. What might be done for him?

The Woolfs hoped that a salaried editorship might be secured for Great Tom. At this time, the leading lights of Liberalism were reorganizing their chief serious periodical, *The Nation and Athenaeum*. Would not Eliot make a good literary editor—or perhaps assistant literary editor, under Leonard Woolf? Virginia Woolf appealed to Lytton Strachey for support, writing to him in February that Eliot was becoming, "in his highly American way, which is tedious and long-winded to a degree," desperate; he might have to leave the Bank in any event. Maynard Keynes also strongly supported Eliot's candidacy for this post. But most of the *Nation*'s directors either had not heard of Eliot or entertained certain reservations, perhaps suspecting his politics—not without cause. At length they did offer him a place, but at a salary less by two hundred pounds than that he received from Lloyd's, and guaranteeing only six months' tenure; he could not take that. Early in March, he wrote to John Quinn that he had not leisure enough to visit a dentist or a barber. "I am worn out. I cannot go on."

During 1922, two attempts had been made to raise a regular subsidy for the author of *The Waste Land*. In March, Ezra Pound, Richard Aldington, and May Sinclair, associated in *Bel Esprit* (a little association got up by Pound), had commenced endeavors to obtain three hundred pounds annually, for at least five years, the money to be paid to Eliot that he might "devote his whole time to literature." To William Carlos Williams, Pound wrote: "The point is that Eliot is at the last gasp. Has had one breakdown. We have got to do something at once." A *Bel Esprit* circular, concocted without Eliot's knowledge, appealed for substantial help. "The facts are that his bank work has diminished his output of poetry, and that his prose has grown tired. Last winter he broke down and was sent off for three months' rest."

John Quinn contributed three hundred dollars in cash, and twenty-one other donors were found; *Bel Esprit* appears to have obtained money or pledges that might have sufficed to provide a hundred and twenty pounds annually for Eliot. Pound also had urged donors to send money directly to Eliot, if they liked, and the appeal leaked into newspapers: anonymous gifts, including four postage stamps, reached Eliot, and his family in America grew indignant on learning of the scheme. Eliot then refused to accept *Bel Esprit*'s benefaction. Having accomplished nothing for Eliot or any other writer or artist, Pound's creation, *Bel Esprit*, ceased to exist in 1923, though the group's example had persuaded some Frenchmen to subsidize Paul Valéry. Quinn later sent Eliot four hundred dollars, promised annual gifts, and tried to obtain another annual two hundred dollars from Otto Kahn; but Quinn already was near his end.

What Pound could not do from Paris, Bloomsbury might essay. During the summer of 1922, the Woolf circle took up the good cause, trying to found the Eliot Fellowship Fund; Aldington was treasurer, and Lady Ottoline Morrell, Leonard Woolf, and Harry Norton formed the fund's committee for England. Calling Eliot "one of the most original and distinguished writers of our day," the committee had declared that "It is impossible that he should continue to produce good poetry unless he has more leisure than he can now hope to obtain, but his literary work is of far too high and original a quality to afford by itself a means of livelihood."

Lytton Strachey, though he gave a hundred pounds to

this fund, thought the appeal somewhat absurd—especially after Eliot formally objected that it must be his own decision as to whether he should leave the Bank; Strachey parodied the Eliot appeal in a letter to the Woolfs, asking for his own fund, "The Lytton Strachey Donation." This project, too, fell through.*

In the end, very little was done for the exhausted Eliot during 1922 and 1923. While all these futile negotiations were in progress, Eliot was embarking upon the heavy and unremunerated labor of founding his own literary review, *The Criterion.* That quarterly—for one brief period a monthly —was to endure for nearly seventeen years, the most important journal of criticism and reflection on either side of the Atlantic. The first number appeared in October, 1922.

This bold act of commencing *The Criterion* signified that Eliot, unlike Gerontion, did not despair of grace; and that he hoped to restore and reinvigorate Heartbreak House. *The Criterion* was meant to be a work of renewal, stirring up the hopes and enlivening the imagination of educated people who might recognize some worth in Tradition. Then, too, it was intended to assist in the recovery of the common cultural patrimony of Europe by attracting to its pages writers from many countries, the men who would recognize their common cause. And it would scourge the ragged follies of the time. Even though this review's subscribers (as things would turn out) at no time numbered more than eight hundred, Eliot was addressing himself to what Matthew Arnold (after Isaiah) had called The Remnant. Of missions to the masses, the twentieth century knew too many; Eliot's mission was to

---

* The somewhat complicated story of these attempts to raise money on Eliot's behalf may be traced through various recent collections of letters: see B. L. Reid, *The Man from New York: John Quinn and His Friends* (1968), pp. 436–437, 489, 534–535, 582–583; D. D. Paige (ed.), *The Letters of Ezra Pound, 1907–1941* (1950), pp. 172–176; Noel Stock, *The Life of Ezra Pound* (1970), pp. 244–245; Michael Holroyd, *Lytton Strachey* (1968), Vol. II, p. 393.

the educated classes. The drift toward Marxism, or toward some other totalist ideology, was apparent already among literary people: Eliot would offer them an alternative—in philosophy and religion, in humane letters, in politics.

Three numbers of *The Criterion* appeared without editorial apology; but in the number for July, 1923, the editor would insert a leaflet explaining his review's purpose: "The *Criterion* aims at the examination of first principles in criticism, at the valuation of new, and the revaluation of old works of literature according to principles, and the illustration of these principles in creative writing. It aims at the affirmation and development of tradition. It aims at the determination of the value of literature to other humane pursuits. It aims at the assertion of order and discipline in literary taste."

Also it aimed at political resurrection, though this was not proclaimed. From the first, *The Criterion* published essays touching upon political theory and institutions—this despite Eliot's smiling rebuke to Chesterton and Wells for some recent offenses of that character.

As *The Criterion* progressed, Eliot's coldness toward Matthew Arnold diminished: for Arnold had endeavored in similar fashion to do the work that Eliot had chosen—to restore culture and put down anarchy through an appeal to men of intellect. In *The Criterion*'s final number at the beginning of 1939, Eliot would acknowledge the bent of his quarterly—a bent long before discerned by all its subscribers: "For myself, a right political philosophy came more and more to imply a right theology—and economics to depend upon right ethics; leading to emphases which somewhat stretched the original framework of a literary review." (This sentence nearly paraphrases a passage in Irving Babbitt's *Democracy and Leadership*—even though that book had been somewhat condescendingly reviewed by Herbert Read in *The Criterion* for October, 1924.) The order of the soul could not be parted from the order of the commonwealth.

No sooner had Eliot written his draft of *The Waste Land* than he flung himself into what Walter Bagehot had called "The Age of Discussion": through discussion among thinking people, the Waste Land might be watered. Eliot had found a patroness, Lady Rothermere, for his review by the end of 1921, and by the following autumn the first number made its strong impact—upon the sort of readers who might perceive reality among *The Waste Land's* symbols of disorder. Eliot accepted no salary as editor; Richard Aldington (said by Herbert Read to have entertained some jealousy of their friend Eliot) became assistant editor.

Since the beginning of the Age of Discussion, in the latter half of the eighteenth century, the tone of civilized life and the fabric of social order had been maintained in considerable part by the serious journals of opinion and criticism. These magazines, carrying on discussion of first principles and current controversies among educated and reflective people, had exerted a profound influence upon those who more directly shaped public opinion—clergymen, professors, newspaper editors, lawyers, public men, and a great many of the men and women whose names no one ever hears, but who individually command the respect of friends and neighbors, and thus turn the mind of the public in one direction or another. In 1921, the number and influence of such sober periodicals already were decreasing; and this retreat would become a rout, after the Second World War (on the close approach of which disaster, *The Criterion* folded its tent).

If serious reviews should go by the board, Eliot knew, the public might be left with nothing better than what, after much experience, Arthur Machen called "that damnable vile business," daily journalism of the (then) halfpenny variety; for the better newspapers generally took their tone from the reflective quarterlies, monthlies, and weeklies. Henry Adams had said that though his *North American Review* enjoyed a direct circulation of merely a few hundred copies, its indirect influence was incalculable, the editors of daily papers reading it and diffusing its ideas by plagiarism.

To Eliot, much about the Age of Discussion was unattractive—and had been unattractive, ever since its infancy in the Reformation. That age had been an age of presumption, egoism, and frantic voices; it had challenged prescriptive wisdom, had denied every authority, had scoffed at tradition, and might bring mankind to the brink of destruction.

It is not always agreeable to live in a time when everything under the sun is brought perennially into question—when every principle in life is haggled over incessantly, as if the world were one sophistical debating society. Yet once men have got into an Age of Discussion, they are unlikely to return into an Age of Faith; the danger is that they may slide into an era of secular propaganda, of unthinking conformity to fad and foible, and of mass manipulation.

Serious journalism, in the sense of regularly published reflective periodicals, is not very old: it commenced not long before the approach of the French Revolution, when people in power began to find it prudent to consult or to persuade public opinion on the principal questions of the day, rather than simply to ascertain the opinions of the court, the upper clergy, the territorial magnates, and the great bankers and merchants. In Britain, as the Age of Discussion approached its zenith, *The Edinburgh Review* and *The Quarterly* had led the way; similar journals of opinion and criticism had sprung up in France, Italy, Spain, the German states, and the new United States. Such periodicals attained the height of their influence in the latter half of the nineteenth century (a period, incidentally, much distrusted by Eliot), when they were found on the tables of every substantial householder. As a class of publications, already they were in decay when Eliot entered the field: during his own few years in London,

The Egoist, Arts and Letters, and other reviews had come forth from the womb only to die in infancy.

In many countries after 1914, and especially in Britain, the diminished income of the upper and middle classes who had made up the bulk of the subscription lists had affected those journals. New diversions, with radio and films beginning to fill leisure hours, and the automobile functioning as a mechanical Jacobin, had begun to take their toll of leisurely readers. Despite much talk about the enlightenment of the working classes, late-Victorian and Edwardian endeavors of that sort already were collapsing before Eliot settled in London; George Gissing, in his novels, had remarked this failure. Nor had the increase of public literacy done anything to sustain the serious journals: it had become clear enough that there exists no sure relationship between compulsory schooling and voluntary reading; indeed, an inverse ratio might be postulated.

During the years of Eliot's editorship of *The Criterion,* Britain—despite centuries of fairly popular government and a long history of free schools, which were made compulsory in consequence of the Reform of 1867 and the coming of economic competition from abroad—was subjected to perhaps the most vile popular press in the world. *The Fortnightly* and *The Contemporary Review* and *Blackwood's* and *The Quarterly* and periodicals more serious survived—but survived only, dwindling in circulation; such popular magazines as the British edition of *Harper's* (which, edited by Andrew Lang at the beginning of the century, had circulated a hundred thousand copies monthly) were to vanish altogether. And when the first number of *The Criterion* came out, few of today's university-sponsored quarterlies had come into existence on either side of the Atlantic.

With the serious reviews that did exist in Britain or America in 1921, Eliot was unsatisfied, although he contributed to them; not altogether pleased with the new *Dial*, for instance, as he had been less than pleased with the old *Dial*.[2] What reviews asked the tremendous questions? What editors shared his convictions? Was there something more to literature than diversion, or the "art for art's sake" pose of Gosse, or the "green and pleasant land" silliness, or the American cult of the colossal, from Whitman to Sandburg? Was there something more to society than economic efficiency, and something more to politics than what H. L. Mencken called boob-bumping? What periodical was giving expression to the moral imagination and to the claims of tradition? If a serious journal might begin to raise such questions afresh, the Age of Discussion might not sink into an Age of Hollowness. *The Criterion* was one of T. S. Eliot's several strong attempts to redeem the time. He would do what he might to restore standards of judgment.*

Why did not Eliot state more fully, at the beginning, his purpose for *The Criterion*? One reason for this reticence, probably, was the new quarterly's financial sponsorship. Its benefactress, for its first three years, was Lilian, Lady Rothermere—who meant well, but who understood and shared little of Eliot's concerns.

Viscountess Rothermere was the consort of a most eminent baron of the halfpenny press—of Harold Harmsworth, created (1913) Lord Rothermere, who had made a tremendous financial success of the journalistic enterprises founded by his brother, Alfred Harmsworth, created Lord Northcliffe. They had commenced by building up, in the judgment of R. C. K. Ensor, "a most lucrative business in periodicals supplying chatty unintellectual pabulum for uneducated

---

* In a letter to John Quinn, in 1920, Eliot had scoffed at the new *Dial*, although one of its editors, Schofield Thayer, had been at school and at Harvard with Eliot. *The Dial*, Eliot wrote, was an exact copy of the dull *Atlantic Monthly*. "There is far too much in it, and it is all second-rate and exceedingly solemn." London had nothing better. See Reid, *The Man from New York, op. cit.*, p. 434.

minds."[3] They had secured a Glasgow Irishman from the slums, Kennedy Jones, to create a daily paper with the biggest circulation (already achieved by 1896) in Britain. Their papers, as Lord Salisbury had said, were "written by office-boys for office-boys."

This denigration from Hatfield House was mild: for these papers were precisely what Arthur Machen meant by "that damnable vile business." Northcliffe is described as boyish by his biographer, Hamilton Fyfe—"boyish his irresponsibility, his disinclination to take himself or his publications seriously; his conviction that whatever benefits them is justifiable, and that it is not his business to consider the effects of their contents on the public mind."[4] The newspapers of the Harmsworths were meant to bring money and power to the Harmsworths, and that they did. Quarter-educated men at best, Northcliffe and Rothermere were figures of the Waste Land.

Of the politics of these barons of the press, nothing more charitable may be said than that they shared what Bagehot had called "the ignorant democratic conservatism of the masses." They stuffed their newspapers with fraudulent and distorted "news" for the sake of sensation and circulation. Readers enjoy a good hate, said Alfred Harmsworth; the brothers and their editors conjured up images to be detested; they did well out of hothouse anger, successively, against the French, the Boers, the Boxers, the Germans. In the gratified expectation of more money, the Harmsworths had done their full share to extend the boundaries of the Waste Land.

A brother-in-law's and a husband's tastes are not necessarily those of a lady patroness of a new critical quarterly; yet from the first Eliot must have been acutely uncomfortable with such a connection. What he hoped to undo, the Harmsworth interest was increasing. With such backing, it was best not to mention at all, in early numbers of The Criterion, certain ends of that quarterly.

Happily for Eliot, the sponsorship did not continue long. Though she did not interfere overmuch with her editor, Lady Rothermere had desired a different sort of publication. In 1925 she summoned Eliot to Switzerland, and he learned that her subsidy (through Cobden Sanderson, who had published the magazine during its first three years) was to be discontinued. A few months earlier, Eliot had written to Herbert Read concerning his ambitions for the review and concerning Lady Rothermere's different expectations. She had desired "a more chic and brilliant Arts and Letters, which might have a fashionable vogue among a wealthy few"; Eliot had no complaint, for she had been "quite as appreciative as one could expect a person of her antecedents and connections to be."

Some thought, he told Read, that as editor he had been making money from *The Criterion*—though actually he had taken no salary; others, including his American relatives, had thought that he must be bringing out the review "for other discreditable reasons." He had been silent as to his motives and policy in editing the quarterly, he went on, because he did not wish to be accused of a hunger for leadership. "If one maintains a cause, one is either a fanatic or a hypocrite: and if one has any definite dogmas, then one is imposing those dogmas upon those who cooperate."

Although he desired to bring together writers of similar views, this homogeneity was indefinable: "I do not expect everybody to subscribe to all the articles of my own faith, or to read Arnold, Newman, Bradley, or Maurras with my eyes." Dogma and a creed were desirable at that time, he added, but none of us is wholly consistent; he did not trouble himself about the charge that his own verse and his own prose did not well consist. "Why then should I bother myself about particular differences of formulation between myself and those whom I should like to find working with me?"[5]

This new review would become the principal rival of the well-established, but dull, *London Mercury*; indeed, the *Mercury* would cease publication before *The Criterion* did. From the first, the "Criterion group" included many men whose views did not coincide with Eliot's—John Middleton Murry the most frequent contributor among those. Eliot succeeded in attracting most of the writers he had hoped for —although the irascible Wyndham Lewis deserted *The Criterion*, perhaps from pressure of work, perhaps from some obscure grudge.

Eliot certainly did not intend to advance the principles— or non-principles—of Northcliffe and Rothermere. What did he mean to stand for? Even though he did not declare his "dogmas" in the first number of his review, it is easy enough to describe those doctrines by a glance at Eliot's background.

Orthodoxy Is My Doxy

If a man believes earnestly in Tradition, as Eliot did, it becomes lost endeavor to look for the source of his convictions mainly in the writings of his contemporaries, or even in formal political theories. Eliot's politics took form early in his life, and were not altered substantially, though his expression of those principles improved with the passing of the decades.

The real roots of Eliot the social thinker were entwined with the history of his family and of the republic into which he had been born; with English social experience and political prescription; with the Christian concept of social order, particularly in its Anglican aspect; and with the political imagination of certain great men of letters whom he admired —notably Virgil, Dante, Dryden, Johnson, and Coleridge. Against the various political messiahs of his time, he reacted strongly, in part because they were hostile to Christian teaching and the Church. And he set his face against various political literati and social theorists of his day, from H. G. Wells to Karl Mannheim.

Of political writers during his era, two especially are mentioned in his essays and editorial commentaries: Charles Maurras and T. E. Hulme. The latter was reinforcement only, for Eliot knew nothing of Hulme until Herbert Read brought out (in 1924) the dead man's *Speculations*—by which year Eliot had made up his mind already concerning the first principles of society. Maurras, read much by Eliot as early as 1910, endured with him a long while: Eliot admired in the founder of *Action Française* his advocacy of cultural continuity, his defense of the genius of Christianity (even though Eliot himself was not yet a professed Christian), his zeal for order: all these expressed in a noble prose. Yet on most points, Babbitt's *Democracy and Leadership* is closer to Eliot than any of Maurras' writings.

As for those political philosophers whose names stand grand in the college manuals of politics, Eliot was to mention them seldom—and then perhaps slightingly. (Of Thomas Hobbes, he was contemptuous in truly cavalier fashion.) J. M. Cameron, the shrewdest essayist on Eliot's politics, wonders why "Mr. Eliot fails to see that his real affinities are not with Maurras (so radical in his positivism) but with those who are the prophets and apologists of the liberal societies of England and the United States: with Jefferson and Burke, with Acton and Maitland."[6] The reasons are not far to seek, however. As for Jefferson, T. S. Eliot grew up an heir of the Federalists, like his distant kinsman Henry Adams, and the name of Jefferson was anathema, with cause; more than once, Eliot remarked that *his* America had ended with the public's rejection of John Quincy Adams as president of the United States. As for Burke (who, nevertheless, influenced Eliot through Babbitt in his early years, and directly during his last two decades)—why, Burke was a Whig; and Samuel

Johnson had told everyone that the first Whig was the Devil.

The political exemplar of Eliot's youth had been a gentleman as real to the St. Louis boy as if he still had sat at the
head of the dining table on Locust Street: the grandfather
he never actually saw, the Reverend William Greenleaf Eliot,
"the nineteenth-century descendant of Chaucer's parson."[7]
That grandfather had been a Christian hero—and a pillar of
the visible community, a reforming conservative, as well
as a buttress of the community of souls. In St. Louis he had
reformed the schools; founded the university; become the
apostle of gradual emancipation of the slaves, the champion
of national union, the leader in a dozen other turbulent
causes of reform—but always in the light of the permanent
things. William Greenleaf Eliot had cherished, in the words
of Tom Eliot's mother, "all that was sacred and memorable in
the past, as a priceless legacy, a repository of truth, even
though commingled with error." His grandfather's notion
of perfectibility, and some other beliefs (among them the
grandfather's zeal for prohibiting strong drink), T. S. Eliot
would discard; yet a grandfather like that must weigh more
lifelong, for an adherent of Tradition, than all the political
metaphysicians in the books.

Some commentators on Eliot tend to forget how American he remained in some aspects, despite his having become
a British subject; and the conservative side of the American
political experience, as represented by Federalism and even
by St. Louis Republicanism, colored Eliot's thought more
strongly than did anything from the European continent of
his own years. He remained familiar with American practical politics to his last years, and I conversed with him on
such topics (corruption in the United States Senate, for
instance) several times in the 'fifties; he quickly apprehended political allusions by which almost any Englishman
would have been bewildered. Despite his veneration of King
Charles the Martyr, there ran through Eliot's political as-

sumptions much of his learned and fearless kinsman President John Adams—a fertile virgin teritory, this, for any doctoral candidate.* "No one wholly English in culture could have brought himself in the nineteen-twenties to confess to 'Royalism' as a political creed," J. M. Cameron comments; "and though the Anglo-Catholicism with which Mr. Eliot linked his Royalism is by definition English, as worn by him it has a less insular cut than is common. This slight eccentricity to English styles of thinking has sometimes, though not always, been of immense advantage to Mr. Eliot in his political writings. In the heady days of the Popular Front he managed to keep his balance when many writers lost theirs, and this without yielding to the complacency which marked the conservatism of Mr. Chamberlain and Lord Halifax."[8]

Just so: Eliot remained sufficiently American in political background to judge of British political affairs with something like detachment. There was no English writer on politics of his own time who influenced Eliot so much as had Irving Babbitt and Paul Elmer More. Consider this passage, for instance, that Eliot took to heart:

"Reaction may be, and in the true sense is, something utterly different from this futile dreaming; it is essentially to answer action with action, to oppose to the welter of circumstance the force of discrimination and selection, to direct the aimless tide of change by reference to the co-existing law of the immutable fact, to carry the experiences of the past into the diverse impulses of the present, and so to move forward in an orderly progression. If any young man, feeling now within himself the power of accomplishment, hesitates to be called a reactionary, in the better sense of this term,

---

* The strong influence of John Adams upon Ezra Pound is more obvious, even though Pound's paraphrasing of Adams probably passes unnoticed by many readers of the *Cantos*—as does, for that matter, Pound's unmarked quoting of phrases and sentences from Adams. Adams and Confucius become Pound's own cherished Guardians of the Law.

because of the charge of effeminacy, let him take courage."

Charles Maurras? Not at all: this is drawn from Paul Elmer More's volume *On Being Human,* the final collection of *The New Shelburne Essays,* published early in 1936, a few months after More's death. In Eliot's editorial Commentary for July, 1936, will be found these sentences:

"The only reactionaries today are those who object to the dictatorship of finance and the dictatorship of a bureaucracy under whatever political name it is assembled; and those who would have some law and some ideal not purely of this world. But the movement, towards the Right so-called, . . . is far more profound than any mere machinations of consciously designing interests can make it. . . . "

Paul Elmer More's "young man, feeling now within himself the power of accomplishment," had been a Harvard undergraduate when, in 1906, More became literary editor of *The Nation.* It was More's call to imaginative reaction, echoing down the years, that reinforced Eliot's courage in scourging the follies of the time. Through Eliot, as through More, there spoke something out of the old New England; and with Eliot, that voice returned, affirming, to the country from which it had withdrawn, negating, three centuries earlier.*

So his American background remained powerful in the politics of Eliot. No one would deny that his embracing of English life and institutions contributed mightily to the conservative inclination of his social convictions. As much by accident as from choice, the young Eliot had taken lodging in Heartbreak House; and he had found his apartment agreeable enough, despite the holes in the roof and the rats in the cellar. He came to love London, from the Wren spires to the Underground; and the English villages and countryside. Heartbreak House though Britain might be, and much

---

* But More was no admirer of Eliot's verse: *The Waste Land* was abhorrent to him, as he told Eliot to his face.

though Eliot might despise most of Britain's public men in his time, still there was shade in this corner of the Waste Land, as under the red rock. Freedom and order and justice survived more hopefully in Britain, during those years, than anywhere else in the world: the crown in parliament, the constitution, and the common law still protected a national community. To this prescriptive pattern of politics, Eliot gave his allegiance.

Distrust of political abstractions had served the English well for a long while. Theirs had been called the politics of empiricism; but more accurately, the British social structure and the British political institutions were the product of custom and convention, prescription and prejudice, a beneficent continuity centuries old. Here much that was good in the civil social order might be preserved, and perhaps reinvigorated. In Britain, Eliot found a Tradition worth defending: a Tradition imperilled, but not doomed utterly. Eliot took up a cause conservative, having faith in that Tradition, though not (at least until his later years) a Conservative with a capital. The politicians of that party which professed attachment to continuity and convention were a feeble lot, Eliot perceived. As a body, the Conservative leaders of Eliot's years have been sufficiently described by W. L. Burn:

"Having abandoned the old aristocratic concept of government they did nothing to create a new aristocracy; they relied confidently on their skill in riding the wild horses of democracy; they were gamblers who would pocket their winnings and pay their losses cheerfully without seeking to alter the rules of the game. What did they do to maintain the family as the basic unit of society? There may be answers to this question, but they are not, in recollection, very obvious. . . . A certain tolerance and a certain efficiency, of which Baldwin and Chamberlain were the respective representatives; and in addition, the opportunity to pad oneself against the more unpleasant impacts of society. The process of proletarianisation was allowed to continue, but a man who was sufficiently wealthy could withdraw himself from contact with it. The chief difference today is that the process of proletarianisation has been accelerated while most of the exemptions have been cancelled."[9]

To that, Eliot would have said Amen. To redeem the time in England from the Conservatives, as well as from the Socialists and the Liberals and various glum ideological factions, was from the first a principal purpose of Eliot's *Criterion*. A standard must be raised, in politics as in literature. Eliot did not hesitate to proclaim himself a reactionary in twentieth-century Britain: he had no desire to conserve decadence and ugliness; something might be accomplished if thinking Englishmen could be reminded of what had been said and done in that realm during the sixteenth and seventeenth centuries, and earlier. Nothing was more natural for Eliot than that he should become, in these circumstances, a Tory. (Toryism, John Henry Newman had said, is loyalty to persons.) "I always was a natural Tory," James Russell Lowell had written to Thomas Hughes in 1875, "and in England should be a staunch one. I would not give up a thing that had roots to it, though it might suck up its food from graveyards."[10] What Lowell might have become, Eliot did become—but trusting that England still had more life in it than did the graveyard round the Chapel Perilous. Coleridge's "constitution of church and state, according to the idea of each" would be Eliot's thereafter.

Eliot's fundamental assumptions about social order, then, were drawn in considerable part from his American inheritance and his English situation, illuminated by his historical consciousness. What of influence by political theorists? In England, there had been only five practical leaders who also were men of thought and rhetoric, Eliot suggests in his essay on Charles Whibley (1931): Clarendon, Halifax, Bolingbroke, Burke, and Disraeli; and of those, he entertained doubts about Bolingbroke. But the most certain influence upon Eliot came from three poets and critics, incidentally men of political thought, who loom large in Eliot's writings: John Dryden, Samuel Johnson, and Samuel Taylor Coleridge. Of these, probably Johnson, in politics, meant most to Eliot.[11]

Far from being an absolutist, Johnson stood for the rule of law in a polity, the *libido dominandi* restrained by custom and statute. He was not particular as to the frame of government, provided that it was a government founded upon prescription: if men's morality is tolerably strong, Johnson reasoned, almost any political system will work well enough; while if morality is decayed, constitutions are ropes of sand. These assumptions, together with the loyalty of the Tories to the throne and their strong attachment to the Church of England, were what Johnson and Coleridge and others passed on to Eliot.

So it was natural enough that Eliot, whose understanding of political man closely resembled Johnson's, stood up for something very like the high old Toryism—in a time at least as uncongenial for Tories as Johnson's age had been. Eliot's politics, like Johnson's, were far more historical than theoretical in their roots. With Johnson, Eliot retained strong sympathies for the Old Cause—even though, as he would write later, "We cannot follow an antique drum." He believed in the need for aristocracy, hereditary and intellectual: the alternative to an aristocratic element in a polity was the rule of an oligarchy. He saw the Whigs as fathers of the Liberals of his own day; like Yeats, he abhorred the thoroughgoing Whig, the shallow rationalist and sophister, with—

> A levelling, rancorous, rational sort of mind
> That never looked out of the eye of a saint
> Or out of drunkard's eye.

The Criterion would take its stand against leveling radicalism and against plutocracy. It would oppose political cults of personality. It would endeavor to find a middle ground between the degradation of the democratic dogma and the new totalism of Communists, Nazis, and Fascists. It would try to save men of intellect from dishonest servitude to ideology and faction: from what Benda was to call "the treason of the intellectuals" (more accurately translated, by borrowing a word from Coleridge, as "the treason of the clerisy").

"The Whigs will live and die in the heresy that the world is governed by little tracts and pamphlets," Walter Scott once wrote to a friend. Eliot did not fall into that Whiggish error: he knew that his journal could work only upon a few minds, and upon those slowly. But in Britain, when the early numbers of *The Criterion* appeared, the old framework of class and politics still stood, if here or there eaten through by rust. Through persistence and appeal to the literate, the Fabians had moved the nation in one direction; by similar endeavors, conceivably Eliot and a handful of friends could contrive to shift the nation in another direction.

The Criterion's first issue appeared at an hour of crisis for true-blue Tories. On October 17, 1922, at the Carleton Club, Lloyd George's Coalition government was brought down by Stanley Baldwin, then President of the Board of Trade. Lloyd George was a dynamic force, Baldwin told the Conservatives at that meeting, but "a dynamic force is a very terrible thing." Withdrawing from the Coalition, the Conservatives resolved to fight the next general election as an independent party with their own leader. At least Heartbreak House was freed of Lloyd George's management.

In the general election of 1922, the Conservatives won 344 seats out of the 615 in the House of Commons, and Bonar Law became prime minister as a Conservative, rather than as a Coalitionist (which had been his standing for a short time after Lloyd George's resignation). Law scarcely fulfilled Eliot's model of a statesman, though a man more honest than Lloyd George had been. Might it be possible, in the confusion of parties then, for something like the moral imagination of Dryden and Johnson and Coleridge to work upon the practical politics of Britain? Such hope was indulged by Eliot when he launched *The Criterion*; and though never rewarded, that hope persisted in Eliot so long as his magazine endured.

A Strong Cry from a City Cellar

Despite Eliot's talk of dogma, *The Criterion* welcomed a wide variety of literary schools and a diversity of social and religious persuasions. The first number contained, in addition to *The Waste Land*, George Saintsbury (an older staunch Tory, if a skeptical one) on Dullness; T. Sturge Moore on Tristram and Isolt; a ghostly tale by May Sinclair; the plan of Dostoevsky's novel *The Life of a Great Sinner*; Hermann Hesse on recent German poetry; Valery Larbaud on Joyce's *Ulysses*. Later numbers during the first year of publication included contributions by Ernst Robert Curtius, Ezra Pound, Roger Fry, Luigi Pirandello, Julien Benda, Virginia Woolf, Herbert Read, W. B. Yeats, Owen Barfield, E. M. Forster, Paul Valéry, and other people of stature. The only directly political piece, in 1922–23, was an appreciation of Bolingbroke, in two parts, by Charles Whibley.

Eliot himself contributed to the second number one of his more enduring short essays, "In Memoriam: Marie Lloyd." This praise of "the greatest music hall artist in England" touched upon the decay of class, now extending to the lower class: "The middle classes, in England as elsewhere, under democracy, are morally dependent upon the aristocracy, and the aristocracy are morally in fear of the middle class, which is gradually absorbing and destroying them." With the coming of a classless society, boredom reigns. The Melanesians, W. H. R. Rivers had written, are dwindling toward extinction because "civilization" has deprived them of their native culture: literally they are bored to death. "When every theatre has been replaced by 100 cinemas," Eliot concluded, "when every musical instrument has been replaced by 100 gramophones, when every horse has been replaced by 100 cheaper motor-cars, when electrical ingenuity has made it possible for every child to hear its bedtime stories through a wireless receiver attached to its ears, when applied science has done everything possible with the materials on this earth to make life as interesting as possible, it will not be surprising if the population of the entire civilised world rapidly follows the fate of the Melanesians." The boredom of a total egalitarianism would run through Eliot's writings thereafter, as it had been an occasional theme with George Saintsbury before him.

From the third number forward, reviews of French, German, and American periodicals were published. Although the cultural unity of Europe was a principal interest of the editor of *The Criterion,* the early contributions from famous European writers who looked upon Europe as one historic community may have been somewhat disappointing to Eliot; articles *about* these leaders of European thought were more satisfactory. More Continental writers were persuaded to contribute to the second volume of the quarterly—among them Hofmannsthal, Lévy-Bruhl, Proust, and Cavafy—and the roster of distinguished authors grew: Ford Madox Ford, Wyndham Lewis, Hugh Walpole, J. Middleton Murry, Sacheverell Sitwell, W. B. Yeats, Osbert Sitwell, Harold Monro, David Garnett. F. W. Bain wrote on Disraeli, and Charles Whibley on Chesterfield. Book reviews commenced with the number for July, 1924.

In its second year, Eliot contributed to his magazine two essays, two reviews, and two editorial Commentaries. In "The Function of Criticism" (October, 1923), he belabored Romanticism and Whiggery, on behalf of Classicism and

Catholicism; he defended Tradition and Outside Authority against Middleton Murry's Inner Voice:

"If, then, a man's interest is political, he must, I presume, profess an allegiance to principles, or to a form of government, or to a monarch; and if he is interested in religion, and has one, to a Church; and if he happens to be interested in literature, he must acknowledge, it seems to me, just that sort of allegiance . . . There is, nevertheless, an alternative, which Mr. Murry has expressed. 'The English writer, the English divine, the English statesman, inherit no rules from their forebears; they inherit only this: a sense that in the last resort they must depend upon the inner voice.' This statement does, I admit, appear to cover certain cases; it throws a flood of light upon Mr. Lloyd George. But why *in the last resort*? Do they, then, avoid the dictates of an inner voice up to the last extremity? My belief is that those who possess this inner voice are ready enough to hearken to it, and will hear no other. The inner voice, in fact, sounds remarkably like an old principle which has been formulated by an elder critic in the now familiar phrase of 'doing as one likes.' The possessors of an inner voice ride ten to a compartment to a football match at Swansea, listening to the inner voice, which breathes the eternal message of vanity, fear, and lust."

Nothing could better express the ethical character of *The Criterion* than the preceding passage. Another of Eliot's principal ethical essays appeared in February, 1924: the preface to "Four Elizabethan Dramatists." If critics who argued that Eliot idealized the past (because of his description, in *The Waste Land,* of Elizabeth and Leicester on the Thames, and similar lines) had read this essay with any attention, they might have been hard put to it to explain away these sentences:

"Even the philosophical basis, the general attitude toward life of the Elizabethans, is one of anarchism, of dissolution, of decay. It is in fact exactly parallel and indeed one and the same thing with their artistic greediness, their desire for every sort of effect together, their unwillingness to accept any limitation and abide by it. The Elizabethans are in fact a part of the movement of progress or deterioration which has culminated in Sir Arthur Pinero and the present regiment of Europe."

An age that prates of progress, Eliot suggested repeatedly, probably is on its way to Avernus. In his Commentary (the first of many *Criterion* Commentaries) of April, 1924, Eliot discussed T. E. Hulme's posthumous *Speculations*, edited by Herbert Read. Hulme is "classical, reactionary, and revolutionary; he is the antipodes of the eclectic, tolerant, and democratic mind of the end of the last century," in Britain a solitary figure. "A new classical age will be reached when the dogma, or *ideology,* of the critic is so modified by contact with creative writing, and when the creative writers are so permeated by the new dogma, that a state of equilibrium is reached.

"For what is meant by a classical moment in literature is surely a moment of *stasis,* when the creative impulse finds a form which satisfies the best intellect of the time, a moment when a type is produced."

Aspiring to formulate that new dogma which would introduce a classical era, Eliot laid about himself manfully in this first Commentary, cudgeling Bertrand Russell for his opinions on men of culture (which had been published in *The Dial*), and cudgeling Dean Ralph Inge for his "violence, prejudice, ignorance, and confusion," unworthy of the Dean of St. Paul's talents, when Inge wrote for newspaper readers. In his Commentary of July, 1924, Eliot assailed various literary critics for obliterating just distinctions, confounding "attitudes" toward life or religion or society with literature. The most dangerous of these tendencies, he wrote, "is the tendency to confuse literature with religion—a tendency which can only have the effect of degrading literature and annihilating religion." In the same Commentary, he cast a suspicious eye upon The Society for Cultural Relations between the Peoples of the British Commonwealth and the Union of Socialist Soviet Republics—possibly an agency for official Soviet propaganda, he suggested. The ideologue—that is, the zealot who subverts religion to make way for the new Savage God's fierce commandments—was Protean in his talents; but in *The Criterion* Eliot kept watch upon the ideologue.

In the third volume of *The Criterion*—the last under Lady Rothermere's patronage—still more well-known men of letters made their appearance, among them D. H. Lawrence, whom Eliot recognized as important though distasteful. Conrad Aiken, Clive Bell, Edith Sitwell, F. G. Selby, Gilbert Seldes, A. E. Coppard, Benedetto Croce, James Joyce, and Edwin Muir were published. F. W. Bain's essay "1789" was a blast against Jacobinism. There was considerable attention in these four numbers to music, the theater, and the ballet.

In January, 1925, appeared "Three Poems by Thomas Eliot"—to be discussed later, for they were fragments of "The Hollow Men." In the same number, Eliot published his "dialogue" or short story "On the Eve"; much of its first draft had been the work of Vivienne Eliot, and it was a literary form in which Eliot did not persevere. Its theme is the phenomenon of the rich and well-connected anarchist— an interesting subject that had been taken up some years earlier by Robert Louis Stevenson, Joseph Conrad, and G. K. Chesterton. In this dialogue, the remarks of one of the aristocratic diners, Alexander, generally reflect Eliot's own misgivings and suspicions—except for Alexander's acceptance of dictatorship as a palliative.

Alexander, quoting Disraeli, expresses his loathing for those rich Liberals who play at pulling down the laws, the empire, and the religion of England. "They are 'capitalists'

because they live upon a civilisation to which they contribute nothing—and they are 'anarchists' because they
are ready to destroy the civilisation which bore and nourished
them. There is a certain irony, of course, about the fate of
these Gadarene swine. They have always stood for "progress'
—and the progress which they have set in motion is on the
point of obliterating them for ever . . .

"They have stood for the extension of democracy—and
now that democracy is extended to the utmost, democracy
is on the point of deposing them in favour of a new oligarchy
stronger and more terrible than their own . . .

"They cling, at the last, to the paltry satisfaction of 'holding the balance of power' between the two parties both of
which they affect to despise. They have been squandering
everything that the humble people have worked to create—
soldiers and generals and diplomats and administrators are
humble people, in my opinion," said Alexander acidly. "The
Whigs have no principles," he continued, summing up judici-
ally. "Look at their policies toward Russia, and Ireland, and
India . . .

"But they will never see what has happened. It is at their
dinner-tables that one hears the most antiquated political
theories, and the most unintelligent expressions of the most
snobbish and insincere literary taste. . . ."

Here Eliot, through Alexander, was excoriating the Liberals who had entered into the "Lib-Lab" government of
Ramsay MacDonald, which took office as a coalition after
the general election of 1923 (even though Labour had obtained only 30.7 per cent of the votes, and the Liberals 29.9
per cent, the Conservatives remaining the largest party).
Sidney and Beatrice Webb were the intellectual architects of
this domination; and Eliot knew that the Webbs looked to
the Soviets for light.[12] But Britain was not really on the eve
of revolution. By the autumn of 1924, as D. C. Somervell
observes, "The Liberals were heartily sick of maintaining in

office by their votes a government which, in order to convince the world that it was not a protégé of Liberalism, did nothing but revile and abuse its benefactors."[13]

In the general election, which occurred between the writing of "On the Eve" and that story's publication, the MacDonald government fell; and never again would the Liberals win a general election. Yet the phenomenon of the rich radical would rise again—though Eliot would not again discuss the danger with such vehemence.

In his Commentary of January, 1925, Eliot made some amends to Matthew Arnold—who now appeared as the champion (despite many weaknesses) of genuine culture against Marxist degradation of culture. Were Arnold still alive, said Eliot, "he would find Populace and Barbarians more philistinised, and Philistia more barbaric and proletarianised, than in his own time." Trotsky's *Problems of Life* had been published in English translation. In that book, Eliot had hoped to find the description of a new revolutionary culture that doubtless would have been repellent to him, but fascinating. Instead, what he found in Trotsky's pages was boredom. The Soviet culture could not justify the horror of the Revolution:

"It is not justified by the dreary picture of Montessori schools, crèches, abstinence from swearing and alcohol, a population warmly clad (or soon to be warmly clad), and with its mind filled (or in process of being filled) with nineteenth-century superstitions about Nature and her forces. Yet such phenomena as these are what Mr. Trotsky proudly presents as the outcome of his revolution; these form his 'culture.' Here is the Eastern prophet of the new age speaking in the smuggest tones of a New Bourgeoisie:

" 'The cinema amuses, educates, strikes the imagination by images, and liberates you from the need of crossing the Church door.'

"It remains only to observe that there is no mention in

Mr. Trotsky's Encheiridion of Culture of such an institution as the ballet; and that his portrait shows a slight resemblance to the face of Mr. Sidney Webb."

That the Trotskys and the Webbs should not dominate the culture of the future, Eliot in his poverty was working fifteen hours a day. He chose a passage from Arnold—that on Oxford, in *Culture and Anarchy*—to describe the endeavor of *The Criterion*:

"We have not won our political battles, we have not carried our main points, we have not stopped our adversaries' advance, we have not marched victoriously with the modern world; but we have told silently upon the mind of the country, we have prepared currents of feeling which sap our adversaries' position when it seems gained, we have kept up our communications with the future."

Those communications with the future, nevertheless, Lady Rothermere was about to suspend. For three years, Eliot—an amiable autocrat as editor—had brought out a wonderfully interesting quarterly, in it the promise of moving the minds and hearts of the rising generation, as already *The Waste Land* functioned as catalyst. He had made his quarterly better than Paris' *Nouvelle Revue Française* and New York's *Dial*. Yet *The Criterion* was about to slide into oblivion, when Eliot's circumstances were altered.

Publishing and Placemen

One change was misery: the deterioration of Vivienne Eliot. Under the pseudonyms of Fanny Marlow, Feiron Morris, Felix Morrison, and F. M., Eliot's wife had written a half-dozen flirtatious vignettes and some book reviews for *The Criterion;* she would write no more. She had contributed a poem, too: "Necesse est Perstare?" Now she was ceasing to endure.

In Vivienne Eliot's verses, people insist upon talking at lunch about "the eternal Aldous Huxley—Elizabeth Bibesco —Clive Bell—unceasing clamour of inanities." Her husband, "like some very old monkey," grows weary of this chatter; she grows wearier:

Is it necessary—

Is this necessary—

Tell me, is it *necessary* that we go through this?

Hyacinths bloom in two of her *Criterion* vignettes; in the winter of 1924 her hyacinths "are bursting clumsily out of their pots, as they always do, coming into misshapen bloom before their time. And this is the essential spring—spring in winter, spring in London, grey and misty spring, grey twilights, piano organs, flower women at street crossings. . . .

"Now one begins to beat against the bars of the cage: the typewriter and the telephone, and the sight of one's face in the glass. One's soul stirs stiffly out of the dead endurance of the winter—but toward what spring? . . . What happy meetings, what luminous conversations in twilight rooms filled with the scent of hyacinths, await me now? The uncompromising voice of truth inside me answers, None at all. For I am not the same person who once played—as it seems to me—a leading part in those spring fantasies. . . .

"Why do I always feel when I see Bernard Shaw that I must go up to him and take his hand and tell him all about the winter's isolation, the typewriter and the telephone, the sight of one's face in the glass and how one started life by being a beautiful Princess admired and worshipped by all men and living in a house of rosy glass through which one watched the envious world go by and how one is cast out of the glass house and wants to get back, inside, safe and beautiful and secure?"*

* F. M., "Necesse est Perstare?", *The Criterion*, Vol. III, No. 4 (April, 1925), p. 364; F. M., "Letters of the Moment—I", *The Criterion*, Vol. IV, No. 6 (February, 1924), pp. 220–222. Perhaps Vivienne

Yes, those hyacinths: one thinks immediately of the "hyacinth girl" in her husband's "Burial of the Dead," the first part of *The Waste Land,* written two and a half years earlier. Which came first—*The Waste Land,* or Vivienne's recurrent misshapen and premature hyacinths?

> You gave me hyacinths first a year ago;
> They called me the hyacinth girl.

However one takes the hyacinth symbol, the marriage that may have been an idyll in 1915 steadily descended into torment: people rarely return to houses of rosy glass. Not long after *The Waste Land* had been published, that Hyacinth Girl whom Eliot had won—to his later sorrow—had begun to recede into a Waste Land of her own. In the spring of 1923—so Eliot had written to Bertrand Russell—Vivienne had barely weathered a frightful illness. By May, 1925, he was writing to Russell that Vivienne's health was a thousand times worse than it had been a decade earlier, when Russell had known her. It might be better—were it possible—for her to live alone, Eliot thought: "living with me has done her so much damage . . ." After ten years of marriage, he still found Vivienne baffling and deceptive, "like a child of six with an immensely clever and precocious mind"; she could write extremely well, Eliot declared. He felt desperate.*

Now that Vivienne was too ill for money to do much for

Eliot's vignettes were a concession to the taste of Lady Rothermere; once the review obtained new sponsors, Mrs. Eliot's contributions ceased.

* Eliot's letters to Russell during this period will be found in the fourth chapter of the second volume of Russell's *Autobiography, The Middle Years, 1914–1944.* "I can never escape from the spell of her persuasive (even coercive) gift of argument," Eliot confessed to Russell. Perhaps, as Eliot suggested, Russell understood Vivienne Eliot better than did her husband. But where women were concerned, Russell's genuine kindness frequently came into conflict with his irrepressible lustfulness. As Freda Utley writes in her *Odyssey of a Liberal* (1970), she could not forget "an all too vivid vision of his hungry lips and avid eyes blotting out the image of philosopher and friend which mattered most."

her (if ever it could have), Eliot's material circumstances abruptly improved. During 1925, Geoffrey Faber—a poet turned entrepreneur, whose second volume of verse Eliot had reviewed in 1918—decided to shift from brewing into general publishing. The existing firm of The Scientific Press, managed by C. W. Stewart, became the partnership of Faber & Gwyer, and the proprietors looked about for a staff. Bruce Richmond of the *Times Literary Supplement,* and Hugh Walpole, and Charles Whibley, are said to have suggested Eliot's name for a post. An offer was made and accepted: Eliot's leanest days were over, and with this publishing firm (later Faber & Faber) he was to remain until his retirement. Thereafter Faber & Faber would publish Eliot's own books, and he would help, as author and as director, to make the firm famous.

As a man of business, rather than as a man of letters, Eliot was engaged. "It isn't even as if his colleagues at Faber & Gwyer were acknowledged or ardent admirers of Eliot's literary judgement," Frank Morley writes. "In 1925 I doubt if any of them saw any particular reason to defer to him in literary matters. What then were his assets? He was a gentleman; he was literate; he was patient; he got on well with difficult people; he had charm; and, he had been in the City. . . . At the start of a publishing house solvency is the greatest aim, and there was possibly something solid and comforting, something magical, in having a banker in the crew."[14]

As a man of business, Eliot was to perform efficiently, after his fashion at Lloyd's Bank. Morley describes him a few years later, when (in 1929) Faber & Gwyer had become Faber & Faber:

"He no longer wore the black coat. His face, rather pale from overwork, was now to be seen above an ordinary dark lounge suit but he had not given up the caution of the banker. He had a theory you were not likely to lose money on the books you didn't publish. It was difficult to bully him; he had the courage to say No. But he could also say Yes. He was extremely perceptive in detecting the right character in manuscripts which might have been thought beyond his range. He made mistakes, of course, but his mistakes as a rule were not costly, and some of his far shots paid well. . . . One of the nicknames for Eliot was Possum (the reference here is to Uncle Remus), and another was Elephant (because he didn't forget). . . . He wasn't apt to fight for anybody that any other publisher would publish; but he could fight for people at whom no other publisher would look."[15]

Eliot already was with Faber & Gwyer when Lady Rothermere's subsidy to *The Criterion* ceased. It appears that the directors of Faber & Gwyer may have expected him to propose that the firm should assume publication of his quarterly; the annual deficit of the magazine was not large. But to the "Criterion group" that was accustomed to meet frequently at The Grove public house in South Kensington, Eliot gave no hope that he ever would make any such suggestion. Although *The Criterion* and "the Criterion crowd" mattered much to him, he would not propose to his employers a project that must bring loss in the short run, whatever eventual prestige it might confer upon Faber & Gwyer: he was too much the man of business for that.

Frank Morley, a new friend of Eliot's, conferred with C. W. Stewart, who suggested that he and Richard de la Mare (now production manager for Faber & Gwyer) could manage affairs if some outside benefactor should pay the deficit; with that prospect, probably Faber & Gwyer would invite Eliot to let them publish his review. Morley advised Eliot not to dissolve *The Criterion,* even though one number (Autumn, 1925) already had been canceled: funds might yet be found. " 'All right,' said Tom. 'I'm tough. Who pays the bills?' "[16]

Morley went next to Bruce Richmond, who chuckled—

and ten minutes later presented Morley with a list of a dozen names, probable sponsors of a *Criterion* fund. That money was found speedily; Charles Whibley and Frederick Scott Oliver, staunch Tories, were among the donors. Both Faber and Gwyer soon invited Eliot to put their firm's imprint upon *The Criterion,* having this subsidy to defray loss; and after publication of a few more numbers, Faber made the review (by this time the *New Criterion*) a subsidiary of the publisher. There was no need until 1928 for a fresh subsidy fund.

The poet had been emancipated from the Bank, and the review had been snatched back from Limbo. But Eliot, grand though his reputation was in certain circles, still could not be called a popular author. His slim *Homage to John Dryden,* published in 1924, had come out in an edition of approximately two thousand copies—and there was no New York edition. Late in November, 1925, Faber & Gwyer published his *Poems, 1909–1925,* in an edition of 1,460 copies. This volume included *Prufrock,* the *Poems* of 1920, *The Waste Land,* and "The Hollow Men"; the collection was dedicated to his father, who had died in 1919, and whom the younger Eliot had not seen since he had left America for Marburg and Oxford and London.

"The Hollow Men" describes the spiritual vacuity of the modern age—and the vacuity not merely of ordinary people who have ceased to attend church services. In "The Idea of a Literary Review," Eliot's preface to the resurrected *Criterion* of January, 1926, Eliot declared that he could perceive a tendency toward "a higher and clearer conception of Reason, and a more severe and serene control of the emotions by Reason": a new classicism, thrice welcome. This tendency might be found in books by Sorel, Maurras, Benda, Hulme, Maritain, and Babbitt.

"And against this group of books I will set another group

of books . . . which represent to my mind that part of the present which is already dead:

"*Christina Alberta's Father*, by H. G. Wells; *St. Joan*, by Bernard Shaw; and *What I Believe*, by Bertrand Russell. (I am sorry to include the name of Mr. Russell, whose intellect would have reached the first rank even in the thirteenth century, but when he trespasses outside of mathematical philosophy his excursions are often descents.) Between these writers there are many and great differences, as between the others. And they all have their moments: at one point in his novel Mr. Wells lapses from vulgarity into high seriousness; at two points, if not more, in his long series of plays Mr. Shaw reveals himself as the artist whose development was checked at puberty. But they all hold curious amateur religions based apparently upon amateur or second-hand biology, and on *The Way of All Flesh*. They all exhibit intelligence at the mercy of emotion. . . . But we must find our own faith, and having found it, fight for it against all comers."

Not simply, then, at the hollowness of nameless folk is "The Hollow Men" directed: it is aimed, too, at such as Wells and Shaw and Russell, at the intellectual enemies of the permanent things, those who wander amusingly into contrived corridors of the spirit—and beguile others, less gifted, after them. Also, as Hollow Men, Eliot has in mind the politicians of his time—though in Britain the Conservatives then held office. Political measures devoid of moral imagination are hollow indeed. In foreign affairs, as the politicians held out fond promises of the perpetual peace to be achieved through the League of Nations, they stumbled toward a greater war; in affairs domestic, the politicians were proceeding to settle for the boredom of the welfare state, rather than to undertake the hard and austere labor of thinking through a program for restoring true community. (In this last stricture, Eliot took common ground with Chesterton.)

During the years 1925 and 1926 there may have been drawn an historical line of demarcation, after which Eliot's imaginative Toryism had scant prospect of success. The politicians who drew that line were not all Socialists: some were the men of Stanley Baldwin's second Conservative government.

"Our party differences of the old sort were almost extinct," Keith Feiling writes of this period. "One dividing line vanished with the Irish treaty; another, older still, of Church against Dissent, faded away with a decline of religious faith. A third, of free trade against protection, was in abeyance. . . . Nor, again, was the democracy, which Peel had so dreaded and which Salisbury found so perilous in foreign affairs, any longer in question. . . . In essence, the controversy was no more about democracy, or even about Socialism: rather, over the degree to which Socialism could be wisely applied or economic democracy asserted. So with Conservative Cabinets, as with Labour, the power of the State continually advanced."[17]

For in 1925 and 1926, acts of Parliament established pensions for all widows and for all the aged—not for the destitute or in emergency, but for everyone, forever. Similar provisions for unemployment and sickness would follow. That these acts promised far more than they could provide in reality, and were wretchedly financed, escaped notice for a time. "The State was no longer to be the occasional intervener in times of stress and strain and the reliever of dire poverty, but the habitual and actually compulsory channel to which, in many of the normal eventualities of life, all people without distinction of means, class, and occupation would look for financial assistance."[18] After the Second World War, the Beveridge Plan would be merely an enlargement of the policies of Stanley Baldwin and Neville Chamberlain. It was ominous that the great General Strike followed right on the heels of these welfare-state measures: the working classes were not conspicuously grateful, and the Baldwin government would fall in 1929.

To make the whole people pensioners of the state, Eliot believed, was to resolve none of the discontents of modern society, but rather in time to exacerbate them: it was humanitarian concession, but not imaginative and charitable reform. In foreign policy, similarly, the Baldwin years were a time of illusion in all three British parties. Lord Curzon (one leader whom Eliot might have approved in office), only a few years earlier nearly chosen prime minister, was denied any place in the Baldwin cabinet of 1925. In Curzon's stead, Austen Chamberlain was made secretary of state for foreign affairs: he proceeded to the silliness of Locarno, presently, and after him Neville Chamberlain would proceed to the shame of Munich. Although no economist and no diplomat, Eliot detected the hollowness of the statesmen of the 'twenties. Those gentlemen, too, plod round the prickly pear at five o'clock in the morning.

Death's Dream Kingdom

With "The Hollow Men" (mostly left over from the first draft of *The Waste Land*, and published fragmentarily in *The Chap Book*, *The Dial*, and *The Criterion*, before its final form appeared in *Poems, 1909–1925*), Eliot terminates that period of his life during which he peered into the Abyss. Thereafter he becomes a poet of belief. Some of his critics took "The Hollow Men" for a despairing epilogue to a hopeless quest; but it was neither that, nor yet an affirmation of triumph of spirit.

These Hollow Men—with their evoking of Kurtz in Conrad's *Heart of Darkness*, of Guy Fawkes' effigy, of figures in Dante, and of Shakespeare's murdered Caesar—are the souls that will be spewed out of His mouth. They choose to linger in their despicable death-in-life, rather than to pass through the jaws of death into "death's other kingdom," which might be Paradise. It is not that they have sinned violently: their vice is flaccidity of will. Life is for action, but they have not acted in spirit. Phlebas the Phoenician sailor, dying by water that he might experience rebirth, was more happy than they.

These Hollow Men dare not meet those Eyes—Christ's, or the reproachful eyes of Dante's Beatrice—that would demand repentance and the ordeal of regeneration; fearful, they hide in "death's dream kingdom," preferring illusion to transcendent reality. In one sense, they are the humanitarian and secularistic liberals who put their faith in the trauma of immanent perfection; in another sense, they are the large majority of mankind in this century, preferring the feeble comforts they know to the quest of the Chapel Perilous. John Henry Newman described them: "They who realize that awful day when they shall see him face to face whose eyes are as a flame of fire, will as little bargain to pray pleasantly now as they will think of doing so then."

No, it is safer to scuffle about in the dream kingdom, where no Eyes invade the darkness. By their timorousness, these Hollow Men have lost personality. They huddle together in a cheerless collectivity that is not community. They are guisers, scarecrows, venerating graven images, sightless.

Upon them falls the Shadow, frustrating their feeble aspirations: their ideas slide away unrealized, their gestures accomplish nothing, their imagination is sterile, their emotions wake no responses, their desires end in barrenness, their powers remain latent only, and their being itself is nerveless. Their attempts at supplication are tardy and vain: it is too late for them to profess faith with humility. They cannot even disintegrate, with Gerontion, in fractured atoms; they will put no match to gunpowder under Parliament House; their world ends "Not with a bang but a whimper."

In a Boston drawing room, Prufrock dared not speak of truth revealed, and so found himself in a Hell of the isolated self; in death's dream kingdom, in the desolation of cactus and prickly pear, such Hollow Men are confined forever. This poem is the last of Eliot's delineations of Hell. From "The Hollow Men" forward, he would be a Seeker still—but a seeker after "the perpetual star, multifoliate rose" of timeless love, now knowing that rose to be real. A man who has emptied himself of vanity and fleshly desire may struggle through suffering to that rose; but a Hollow Man, a stuffed man, stirred only by the wind of the dead land, circles endlessly round the prickly pear.

In "The Hollow Men," Eliot gives us the image of "such a Hell as modern minds can believe in, and find worse, not better, than Limbo," Harold F. Brooks writes. "The Hell of the Jesuit sermons in Joyce would provide disbelief; the 'lost violent souls,' Dante's Farinata, Byron's Cain, Baudelaire's Don Juan, like Satan himself, attract romantic admiration. The Hollow Men resemble the old guy, not Fawkes the hero-villain; and what they are finally damned to is total paralysis, corresponding, for the mind and soul, to the doom forecast by scientists, in accordance with the principle of entropy, for our 'valley of dying stars.' "[19] It is the Hell of energy exhausted altogether, of universal erosion to sea level; and it may be paved with good intentions.

This is the Hell of those intellectuals who put their trust in "that part of the present which is already dead"; it is the Hell of the trimmer in politics; it is the Hell of the average sensual man who prefers ephemeral diversion to duty and sacrificing love. It is the Hell into which many men have fallen in all ages; also it is the Hell most consonant with twentieth-century infidelity. Though it is not the Hell of the diabolic imagination, surely it is the Hell to which the idyllic imagination lures us. It is a Hell where no one reigns: even the Grand Anarch cannot be espied.

V

Catholic, Royalist, Classicist

❖

Pilgrim's Progress Toward Ember Day

From the end of 1925 to the spring of 1930, Eliot published no collection of verse or major poem. These were the years of transition from visions of damnation to visions of purgation and affirmation. Eliot's time was spent principally in the editing of *The Criterion* and in the writing of a great many essays and reviews. (He contributed to periodicals, between publication of *Poems, 1909–1925* and publication of *Ash-Wednesday*, some one hundred and forty prose pieces.) This was the time when Eliot's theological and political convictions achieved fullness; though he would refine and enlarge his first principles after 1930, no substantial change in his position occurred after that year.

Between 1925 and 1930, Eliot passed from misgiving to belief; from horror to peace; from the politics of youthful aspiration to an understanding of politics as the art of the possible. It is convenient to look first at Eliot's verse during these years—the short "Ariel Poems" and the parts of the unfinished drama which later was published as *Sweeney Agonistes*—reserving for the conclusion of this chapter *Ash-Wednesday*.

The poem "Fragment of a Prologue" was published in *The Criterion* for October, 1926; the poem "Fragment of an Agon" was published in the same review for January, 1927. These were intended to be parts of a play with the title *Wanna Go Home, Baby?* But that intended tragedy of the jazz age never took on more flesh; these two fragments were published together as *Sweeney Agonistes: Fragments of an Aristophanic Melodrama* at the end of 1932, and a stage version (with a brief final scene, somewhat incongruous, added) of a one-act play resulted.[1] Pursuit by the Furies, suggested in *Sweeney Agonistes,* was to become the theme of *The Family Reunion,* in 1939. The two Fragments are important chiefly because they bring to a close Eliot's visions of horror that began with "The Love Song of J. Alfred Prufrock"; after them, Eliot discerns the way to purgation and redemption.

The Fragments, with their two young women of dubious virtue, their Tarot pack, their empty-headed male visitors, and their haunted Sweeney, probably never could have been enlarged into a successful drama. "The theme of Mr. Eliot's early verse finds supreme expression in *The Waste Land,* to which *Sweeney Agonistes* appears a rather sterile appendix," Helen Gardner declares. "Confined within the limits of scenic presentation, with this limited circle of people, the 'boredom,' which in *The Waste Land* seems universal, is capable of dismissal as an accident of a certain class and period; and the 'horror' is either trivial, and rather obviously symbolic, as in the telephone bell and the knocking, or grotesque as in Sweeney's anecdote from the *News of the World*."[2]

This criticism being sound, there remains small point in adding here another exegesis to the numerous commentaries on *Sweeney* already published. Eliot abandoned *Wanna Go Home, Baby?* not merely because dramatic progression was impossible in the frame he had chosen, but also, surely, because his own mind was moving from the perception of horror to the perception of man regenerate.

What I find surprising in some criticisms of *Sweeney* is the assertion that Sweeney is a puppet merely; that intellectual Eliot speaks, unconvincingly, through apeneck Sweeney; that the average sensual man could not understand the boredom and the horror of existence limited to "birth, and copulation, and death." Our asylums, after all, are packed nowadays with average sensual men whom the Furies have tracked down. Sweeney has committed an unpardonable act of horror, and he cannot turn back to what he was before that act. Though "I've gotta use words when I talk to you," and though Sweeney cannot command words sufficient to express his terror and loathing, still he knows the hopeless frightfulness of his condition. Under the bamboo tree, in a jazz version of Rousseau's idyllic imagination, Sweeney may look for sanctuary; but he cannot find it; he understands now that for one like himself, "life is death," whether in this flat or on that cannibal isle.

Nevill Coghill went to see Rupert Doone's production of *Sweeney Agonistes* (before an audience of thirty, including the poet himself). A good deal later, he had opportunity to question Eliot about that production. "I had no idea the play meant what he made of it . . . that everyone is a Crippen," Coghill said of Doone's interpretation. "I was astonished."

"So was I," Eliot told him; he had meant something very different from Doone's implication that every man labors under a compulsion to murder a girl and dissolve her in an acid bath. Yet any play, Eliot laconically revealed to Coghill, may have more meanings than one. Nevertheless, Coghill's interpretation of the meaning of *Sweeney Agonistes* (which he takes to be similar to the meaning of Eliot's "Marina") is consonant with the whole drift of Eliot's moral imagination at that time:

"The governing idea (for me) is that of rebirth into supernatural life through a cycle of which a descent into the dark night of the soul is a recurring preliminary. This appears as a process for the common man as much as for the professed mystic, whether he recognizes it or not, and Sweeney is the common man, the average, decent lout.

"Such a man is put to torture by his soul, of whose existence he is at first but dimly aware, as a maturing man becomes aware of the upthrust of a wisdom-tooth. It hurts, and it drives him, naturally, to violence."[3]

Unredeemed by grace, and weak of intellect and will, Sweeney discovers his soul only to know Hell. But T. S. Eliot, with his Ariel Poems, was moving away from the Abyss. Seven months after "Fragment of an Agon," Faber & Gwyer published Eliot's "Journey of the Magi," a kind of greeting card (five thousand copies), especially commissioned by the firm. It would be followed in the Ariel series by Eliot's "A Song for Simeon" (1928), "Animula" (1929), and "Marina" (1930). These verses arch as a bridge between the dim hope of "The Hollow Men" and the compassionate Lady of *Ash-Wednesday*.

"The Journey of the Magi," suggested by Lancelot Andrewes' sermon at Whitehall in 1622, is the plain narration of an old Magus who belongs to the Old Dispensation—and who, though he has beheld the Child, would "be glad of another death," for to him this Birth was "hard and bitter agony." The old order, though still standing visible, is undone; the new order cannot be comprehended as yet.

"A Song for Simeon," in the spirit of the second chapter of the Gospel according to Saint Luke, has its "Roman hyacinths blooming in bowls" as symbols of the New Dispensation, which Simeon can prophesy but cannot live to enjoy; the ultimate vision is denied him. The city shall be sacked, and the people take to "the goat's path, and the fox's home." But all this Simeon accepts calmly, consoled, "having seen thy salvation."

"Animula" contrasts the soul that issues from the hand of God with the soiled soul that issues from the hand of Time. Feeble and unperceiving, this poor Soul subsists upon illusions in childhood and upon other illusions in mature years: "Irresolute and selfish, misshapen, lame . . ." The world deceives and corrupts; yet after the viaticum, the soul may be cleansed and may endure.

"Marina" (published a little later than *Ash-Wednesday,* but nevertheless the last span of the bridge from "The Hollow Men") is spoken by King Pericles, whose lost daughter has been restored by the sea; it is an expression of the victory of the life eternal over death. And yet this poem remains ambiguous: Pericles may be dreaming and self-deluding, his wish nurturing his vision. Tenderness suffuses this poem, as it does "Animula"; but tenderness is not faith, and "Marina" cannot be well understood until one has read *Ash-Wednesday.*

Good poems of religious aspiration though these four are, they could not have helped greatly in redeeming the time had there come no *Ash-Wednesday* and no *Four Quartets.* They are fingerposts along Eliot's painful route from the awareness of death-in-life to the awareness of that real life which is found in the conjunction of time with the timeless. How was it, many admirers of Eliot the Innovator demanded, that in a mere eight years the gloomy delineator of the Waste Land could mount the stair toward the multifoliate rose? How could the poetic modernist find it possible to take refuge in an antique orthodoxy?

Eliot's journey toward Christian faith was no peculiar phenomenon in his time, of course: that pilgrimage had been made, or was being made, by men of letters so diverse as G. K. Chesterton, C. S. Lewis, Roy Campbell, Charles Williams, Edwin Muir, Paul Elmer More, and Evelyn Waugh. Yet no two such seekers followed precisely the same path. In Eliot's instance, there is nothing surprising about his recovery of belief (for a recovery it was, rather than a providential fall on the road to Damascus). It would have been strange if a man so much in love with English tradition, and so deeply read in Dryden, Johnson, and Coleridge, had not felt himself drawn toward the living and visible Church of England—and within that Church, toward that party which was heir to the Oxford Movement.

"Belief will follow action," John Henry Newman had said. Long before his confirmation, Eliot had been living a Christian life and reading a powerful body of Christian literature—with especial attention to Newman. If the imperial intellects of Johnson and Newman, say, had made submission to dogma, why should not T. S. Eliot accept the authority of the Church? Eliot had grown familiar with the philosophies, the ideologies, and the neoterist cults of his time; and he had found them whited sepulchres, manifestations of decadence of spirit. But the Church still was a rock, great and ancient. "The reason first why we do admire those things which are greatest," the judicious Hooker had written, "and second those things which are ancientest, is because the one are the least distant from the infinite substance, the other from the infinite continuance, of God." When writing "The Hollow Men," Eliot still murmured, "I believe, O Lord; help thou my unbelief." The Ariel Poems are the beginning of that action which belief follows. And there existed several reasons why belief did follow more swiftly than Eliot may have hoped.

First, Eliot never had been anti-Christian or an atheist; it was only that he had slipped away from the Unitarianism

of St. Louis and New England.* Since his schooldays, his
condition had been one of distressed doubt, but not one of
belligerent negation. Twentieth-century American Protestantism, with its tendency to decline into the ethos of
sociability, had satisfied him neither intellectually nor emotionally. Yet the Christian patrimony he had inherited from
generations of upright New Englanders lay at the heart of
his tradition; it could not be ignored; what he needed was
a grammar of assent. In the Church of England, with its
grand liturgy, its ancient intellectual power, its splendid
churches of every period, its virtual identity with English
culture, he came to discover what he had found wanting in
the Church of the Messiah and in the latter-day sectarianism
of Beacon Hill.

Second, Eliot's encounter with Humanism, through Irving
Babbitt and others, had led him to ask ultimate questions.
Economics leads upward into politics, Babbitt had said, and
politics into ethics. But what sanctions exist for ethics? Like
Paul Elmer More, Eliot found it necessary to pass beyond
ethics into theology. Eliot's essays and asides on Humanism,
a subject perennially discussed by British and American and
Continental contributors to his review, are evidence of how
strong his sympathies were with the twentieth-century
Humanists—and how much he learned from them—and how
they left him unsatisfied and thirsting for stronger assurance.
In a letter to Bonamy Dobrée, early in 1929, he went to the
heart of the matter:

"I don't object in the least to the position of Babbitt for
Babbitts. It is a perfectly possible position for an individual.
I only say: this is not a doctrine which can help the world in

---

* The best aspect of Unitarianism, Eliot wrote in a review of several
books for *The Criterion* (May, 1927), is not its allegedly comfortable
nineteenth-century liberalism, but rather "a kind of emotional reserve
and intellectual integrity."

general. ⌊The individual can certainly love order without loving God. The people cannot. And when I say people, don't think I mean any slum or suburb or Belgravian square; I mean any number that can be addressed in print. I should say of humanism as many say of mysticism: it is unutterable and incommunicable. It is for each humanist alone. It is not only silly, but damnable, to say that Christianity is necessary for the people, until one feels that it is necessary for oneself. I'm not attacking humanism: I should be more hostile toward a catholicism without humanism; I only mean that humanism is an ingredient, indeed a necessary one, in any proper catholicism; and I want to point out the danger⌋ of Babbitt's leading some of his followers into a kind of catholicism which I should dislike as much as he does."[4]

Humanism, then, stung Eliot as if it had been a gadfly, rousing curiosity and inquiry; his reaction, after his leaving Harvard, was a gradual transcending of the humanist argument, a fulfillment rather than a rejection of Babbitt's teachings. Like Thomas More and Erasmus, Eliot became both humanist and Christian.

⌊Third, Eliot's study of F. H. Bradley and Idealism had propelled him into his quest for a reality that is more than the time-continuum of past, present, and future. Is everything ephemeral? Does not a permanent reality exist? Idealism sought to penetrate beyond the world of appearances; but Idealism could offer only a misty apprehension of the Absolute through some immediate experience uniting reason, will, and sensation. The Idealist himself is no master of such a transcendent experience: one must turn to the mystics for that. And if one turns to the mystics, must one not turn also to the source of mystical communion—to the being of God? Eliot's Indic studies inclined him to this same conclusion. Moreover, few of us are mystics; to such a man of genius as Pascal, mystical vision came but once, and then was inexpressible in words, except for "Fire, fire, fire!" Are we not dependent for knowledge of the true self (as distinguished from the hungry and deluded ego) and for knowledge of others and of this world, upon revelation and the Logos— upon divine penetration into human consciousness? His metaphysical studies had thrust Eliot forward toward religious insights.

Though always a partisan of right reason, Eliot understood that the discursive reason is not the sole way of approaching truth. Repeatedly he took the side of reason against impulse and ideology; he distrusted the notion of an intuition unguided by authority and not subject to discursive analysis—as he disliked the fallacy of an untutored conscience. Yet the insights of faith—the "leap in being" of the man of vision, the sudden direct experience of reality— are essential to Eliot's later poetry. During 1927, *The Criterion* published a long running debate or symposium concerning intelligence and intuition, the participants being Middleton Murry, Father Martin D'Arcy, Charles Mauron, Ramon Fernandez, and Eliot himself.

"Mr. Murry suggests that I must mean one of two things; either I must deny 'intuition' altogether, or I affirm 'intuition' to be a form of 'intelligence,'" Eliot wrote ("Mr. Middleton Murry's Synthesis," *The Criterion*, October, 1927). "I certainly do not mean the former; I do not at all wish to expunge the word 'intuition' from the dictionary. What I mean is much more like the latter; I am willing to admit, in a rough and ready way, that 'intelligence is the genus, intuition and discourse the species'. . . . I mean that intuition must have its place in a world of discourse; there may be room for intuitions both at the top and at the bottom, or at the beginning and the end; but that intuition must always be tested, and capable of test, in a whole of experience in which intellect plays a large part." The insights of *Ash-Wednesday*

—and still more, of *Four Quartets*—would be intuitions at the top of a world of discourse.*

Fourth, Eliot moved toward Christian faith because he had seen to what the modern world was descending in the decay of that faith. If the land is an arid waste when the waters of faith have dried up, then those waters must have been the source of life in the person and in the commonwealth. He accepted a legitimate presumption that Christian belief might be judged by its fruits—or by what fruits it once had yielded: he had seen how the ignoring or the denial of Christian teaching had been followed by private and public disorder.

From "Prufrock" to "The Hollow Men," he had described the evil half-life of fallen man in this age. With *Ash-Wednesday*, he would begin to describe the possibility of regeneration. As Hoxie Neale Fairchild says of Eliot, "Slowly and gradually he discovers that frustrated romantic hankerings are impotent to cope with his awareness of the reality of evil, and that the problem of evil makes no sense unless it is interpreted in Christian terms. For a time he recognizes this truth without being willing to act upon it. Then he becomes a Christian and begins to write Christian poetry."[5]

So, once Eliot had begun to act, he was impelled soon to write *Ash-Wednesday*. His most signal action was to be

---

* This point may be made more clear by reference to a conversation between St.-John Perse (whose *Anabasis* Eliot translated and published in 1930) and Albert Einstein. The scientist had invited the poet to Princeton to ask him a question:

" 'How does a poet work? How does the idea of a poem come to him? How does this idea grow?' St.-John Perse described the vast part played by intuition and by the subconscious. Einstein seemed delighted: 'But it's the same thing for the man of science,' he said. 'The mechanics of discovery are neither logical nor intellectual. It is a sudden illumination, almost a rapture. Later, to be sure, intelligence analyzes and experiments confirm (or invalidate) the intuition. But initially there is a great forward leap of the imagination.' " See André Maurois, *Illusions* (1968), p. 35.

confirmed in the Church of England in 1927—the year in which he became, too, a British subject. In his prose writings for several years after 1925, one finds a sufficient, if fragmentary, explanation of how reason and sentiment worked upon him, after he had anatomized the Hollow Men, to bring him to certitudes. For the remaining four decades of his life, he would be sustained by those Permanent Things.

In his essay "Second Thoughts on Humanism" (1929), Eliot would put the substance of all this very clearly. He quoted T. E. Hulme on the realism of Christian dogmas, which matter far more than "the sentiment of Fra Angelico." Then, in words close to John Henry Newman's, Eliot stated that he came to profess Christianity because he had come to conclude that its dogmas are true:

"Most people suppose that some people, because they enjoy the luxury of Christian sentiments and the excitement of Christian ritual, swallow or pretend to swallow incredible dogma. For some the process is exactly opposite. Rational assent may arrive late, intellectual conviction may come slowly, but they come inevitably without violence to honesty and nature. To put the sentiments in order is a later and an immensely difficult task: intellectual freedom is earlier and easier than complete spiritual freedom."

A Capacity for Salvation

For Lancelot Andrewes was published (fifteen hundred copies) in November, 1928. The eight essays "on style and order" in that volume had appeared in periodicals previously; nevertheless, many readers on either side of the ocean were startled by Eliot's prefatory proclamation that, in effect, orthodoxy was his doxy, as she had been Dr. Johnson's. Eliot declared himself a classicist in literature, a royalist in politics, and an Anglo-Catholic in religion. "I am quite aware that the first term is completely vague, and easily lends itself to clap-trap; I am aware that the second term is at present without definition, and easily lends itself to what is almost worse than clap-trap, I mean temperate conservatism; the third term does not rest with me to define."

What a far cry from Bloomsbury! Yet Eliot had undergone no sea-change, except in the symbolic sense that he had emerged from the dark night of the soul to the confidence of faith. The convictions of 1928 followed naturally enough from the inclinations of 1915.

An Anglo-Catholic? That might scandalize Bloomsbury, but Christianity always had been a scandal. It might be asked, nevertheless, why (being much influenced by Newman) Eliot had not proceeded all the way to Rome. Yet doubtless Eliot's desire to participate, in England, in a living tradition had secured him for Canterbury. The Church of England's liturgy was interwoven with the body of great literature he knew so well; the Church of England's splendid architectural monuments were all about him; the Church of England's consecration of the English state still endured— however precariously; the preachers and scholars of the Church of England, from the reign of Elizabeth onward, had filled his mind in recent years. In London, the Catholicism of Rome seemed an exotic thing, more Irish than Latin. Eliot would profess the Catholic faith in its Anglican establishment.*

A royalist? That word sounded odd even to most Englishmen. Nearly everyone in Britain was a royalist, in the sense

---

* Almost all writers who turned Christian in those years, George Orwell observes, went "to the Church with a world-wide organization . . . Perhaps it is even worth noticing that the only latter-day convert of really first-rate gifts, Eliot, has embraced not Romanism but Anglo-Catholicism, the ecclesiastical equivalent of Trotskyism." See Orwell, *Inside the Whale* (1940), in Orwell and Angus (eds.), *The Collected Essays, Journalism, and Letters of George Orwell*, Vol. I, p. 515.

that the British democracy had not the faintest intention of storming Windsor: even in the Labour party, a republican was regarded as rather an unpleasant eccentric. But Eliot was re-expressing Newman's observation that Toryism is loyalty to persons. He meant that his allegiance (sworn some months earlier) was to the Crown—and not, say, to the Conservative party of 1928, then about to lose a general election. Eliot meant that he supported the prescriptive political institutions of the nation which he had chosen for his own; that he rejected revolution and ideology; that, at worst, he preferred King Log to King Stork, or a legitimate sovereign to a dictator like Mussolini.

A renewed respect for kings endowed with Burke's "unbought grace of life," it should be added, was in the air, late in the 1920's; not a few intelligent people (including some highly unconventional thinkers) had begun to reflect that constitutional monarchs might possess sufficient sense of honor and attachment to just authority to restrain squalid oligarchs and predatory interests and ideological mobs. Bernard Shaw then seemed nearly as much a royalist as was Eliot. Consider Shaw's preface to *The Apple Cart*, first performed in August, 1929. Shaw's King Magnus is the hero —and the tragic hero—of that play, despite Shaw's tardy endeavor to plead impartiality.

Some people still cling to the error that in the contest between royal authority and democracy, the underdog is democracy, Shaw wrote; such people are long out of date. "But to me it is the king who is doomed to be tragically in that position in the future into which the play is projected; in fact, he is visibly at least half in it already; and the theory of constitutional monarchy assumes that he is wholly in it, and has been so since the end of the seventeenth century.

"Besides, the conflict is not really between royalty and democracy. It is between both and plutocracy, which, hav-

ing destroyed the royal power by frank force under democratic pretexts, has bought and swallowed democracy." For
one moment, the sentiments of Shaw and Eliot coincided.

Eliot meant that he saw monarchy, wherever it survived
or might be restored in his time, as a bulwark against disorder: the feebleness of the succession-states of Europe,
during the previous decade, had attested to that. Eliot no
more entertained some notion of royalism in America or
in any other long-established republic than had his kinsman
John Adams; rather, he was saying that wherever kings have
long reigned, as in England, to overturn the throne is to
subvert order and justice and freedom. Eliot looked upon
Charles Maurras' royalism—despite certain extravagances
of language in Maurras—as a barrier against dictatorship:
a strong king and an able prime minister would be preferable far to a dictator masquerading as minister, dominating
a shadow-king.

A classicist? Many of Eliot's admirers, and many of his
adversaries, have denied that he was anything of the sort;
other critics have supported his declaration. But generally
it is best to accept a man at his own sincere assessment.
Here Eliot meant that he lived and breathed within Tradition: the classicist is assimilative, for the ability to assimilate
is the ability to absorb culture. (So Dryden had said of Ben
Jonson, so Samuel Johnson—as Rasselas—had written of
poetry, and so Pope had acted.) Here he meant, too, that
he stood for right reason, as opposed to obsession with alleged originality, personality, and creativity; for the permanent things, as opposed to the lust for novelty; for normality,
as opposed to abnormity.

"If we are to be qualified as 'neo-classicists,'" Eliot had
written in his *Criterion* Commentary for June, 1927, "we
hope that 'neo-classicism' may be allowed to comprise the
idea that man is responsible, *morally* responsible, for his
present and his immediate future." Classicism, he stated

repeatedly, meant judicious balance, derived from conscious participation in a great tradition; it meant appreciation of the living past. In the same Commentary, he had declared that *The Criterion* would continue to "use the word 'classicism,' unsatisfactory as it is—to most people it connotes little more than alexandrine couplets, the painting of David, and the architecture of the Madeleine or possibly the British Museum. . . . Those persons who find even a little stay and comfort in the word 'classicism' are always at a disadvantage. If they confine themselves to criticism, they are reproached for their lack of creative power; if they do 'create,' and if (as is sure to happen) what they create bears little resemblance in form to the work of Racine, or Dr. Johnson and Landor, then it is immediately said that their precept and practice are utterly in divorce: for if you cannot deny that their creative work has merit you can always deny that it has any of the characteristics of 'classicism.' "

In this preceding long sentence, Eliot refutes successfully, I think, various critics who argue, in effect, that Eliot cannot be a classicist because *The Waste Land* is unlike *The Rape of the Lock*. But these literary categories "romantic" and "classical" were diminishing in accuracy during Eliot's early successes as critic, and today have fallen into confusion worse confounded. (Indeed, how much in common did a "romantic" like Scott ever have with a "romantic" like Shelley?) However one may wish to define "classicist," it is clear enough that Eliot's literary convictions were coherent, and that he endeavored to stand in the succession of Virgil and Dante. (His little book on Dante would appear in 1929, and Dante's classical splendor was in his mind when he wrote the preface to *For Lancelot Andrewes*.) In essence, Eliot's classicism was the literary expression of the moral imagination, contending against the idyllic and the diabolical imagination.

So much for Eliot's pronunciamento. Of the essays in *For*

Lancelot Andrewes, two especially (both later reprinted in his *Selected Essays*) bear upon his Anglo-Catholicism and his politics of prescription. The reading of Pascal and Newman had helped Eliot on his way to settled principle; so had reflection upon Baudelaire; and two Anglican bishops of the century of genius, Andrewes and Bramhall, had been invisible sponsors at his confirmation. He had read Richard Hooker and Jeremy Taylor well; what not many others had done then, he had read much also in Lancelot Andrewes, Bishop of Winchester, and in John Bramhall, Bishop of Derry.

A church must be judged by its intellectual fruits, its influence upon sensibility, and its architectural monuments, Eliot wrote in his essay on Andrewes. "The English Church," he admitted, "has no literary monument equal to that of Dante, no intellectual monument equal to that of St. Thomas, no devotional monument equal to that of St. John of the Cross, no building so beautiful as the Cathedral of Modena or the basilica of St. Zeno in Verona." Yet the Church of England is worthy of intellectual assent, if one studies Hooker and Andrewes.

It may not be smooth going: "To persons whose minds are habituated to feed on the vague jargon of our time, when we have a vocabulary for everything and exact ideas about nothing—when a word half-understood, torn from its place in some alien or half-formed science, as of psychology, conceals from both writer and reader the meaninglessness of a statement, when all dogma is in doubt except the dogmas of sciences of which we read in the newspapers, when the language of theology itself, under the influence of an undisciplined mysticism of popular philosophy, tends to become a language of tergiversation—Andrewes may seem pedantic and verbal. It is only when we have saturated ourselves in his prose, followed the movement of his thought, that we find his examination of words terminating in the ecstasy of assent." Andrewes is stronger than John Donne, because Andrewes is deeper rooted in tradition.

Eliot contrasts Bishop Bramhall with Hobbes, "one of those extraordinary little upstarts whom the chaotic motions of the Renaissance tossed into an eminence which they hardly deserved and have never lost." Thomas Hobbes was an early popularizer of scientism, applied to faith and politics; he left the human will quite out of consideration, substituting for it a shallow theory of sense perception; and Hobbes' theory of government was not philosophical at all. Hobbes' psychology led to political tyranny—though through the temperament, rather than in any rational fashion. Bramhall, in his vindication of church and state against Hobbes, was the champion of moral order and public order—including ordered freedom; for Bramhall saw that the king had a religious obligation toward his people, as well as a civil obligation. Hobbes, indeed, is an early ideologue:

"It is extraordinary that a philosophy so essentially revolutionary as that of Hobbes, and so similar to that of contemporary Russia, should ever have been supposed to give any support to Toryism. But its ambiguity is largely responsible for its success. Hobbes was a revolutionary in thought and a timid conservative in action; and his theory of government is congenial to that type of person who is conservative from prudence but revolutionary in his dreams. . . . Hobbes's violence is of a type that often appeals to gentle people. His specious effect of unity between a very simple theory of sense perception and an equally simple theory of government is of a kind that will always be popular because it appears to be intellectual but is really emotional, and therefore very soothing to lazy minds."

When a Bramhall is forgotten and a Hobbes is puffed up by the intellectuals, public and private order are in decadence: that is the lesson of these essays on Andrewes and Bramhall. Although it would be heresy and folly to erect a religious establishment out of alleged political necessity, church and state cannot be separated; a state professedly atheistic will erect, after all, its own secularistic caricature of a church, with its heretical hierarchy, and will decree its own inverted dogmas. Church and state both must wither if the attempt is made to erect between them a wall of separation, Eliot believed. He wrote his essays on Andrewes and Bramhall, and took communion in the Church of England, at a time when disestablishment seemed probable, and when several beautiful City churches were threatened with demolition. In 1926, he and Bonamy Dobrée had led a hymn-chanting procession through the streets, in protest against schemes to pull down "redundant" City churches; and they had succeeded in preventing that atrocity. But Eliot was not much cheered by this small victory. In August of that year, he wrote to Dobrée that no reunion with Rome might be expected:

"What I meant was that after Disestablishment the Church of England will lose its whole reason for existence; and that its more serious members will gradually go over to Rome. Some will fall into nonconformity; the majority will content itself with civil marriages and individual Gods (my God for my dog, my pipe, my golf-tools and my allotment garden, your God for yours) but Rome will very slowly become stronger."[6] Eliot assumed that he was casting his lot with the vanquished.

And why adhere to a failing cause? Because the Church is the guardian of the truth. "I should say that it was at any rate essential for Religion that we should have the conception of an immutable object or Reality the knowledge of which shall be the final object of that will; and there can be no permanent reality if there is no permanent truth," he wrote to Dobrée. "I am of course quite ready to admit that human apprehension of truth varies, changes and perhaps develops, but that is a property of human imperfection rather than of truth. You cannot conceive of truth at all, the word has no meaning, except by conceiving of it as something permanent."[7] Repository and expounder of the Permanent Things, the Church makes possible the inner and the outer order. An England without the Church would be an England deprived of truth.

Among the truths that the Church guards, the knowledge of Sin and Redemption looms large. In his introduction to Baudelaire's *Intimate Journals* (1930), Eliot declared that even evil is preferable to the "cheery automatism of the modern world. . . . So far as we are human, what we do must be either evil or good; so far as we do evil or good, we are human; and it is better, in a paradoxical way, to do evil than to do nothing: at least, we exist. It is true to say that the glory of man is his capacity for salvation; it is also true to say that his glory is his capacity for damnation. The worst that can be said of most of our malefactors, from statesmen to thieves, is that they are not men enough to be damned."

The Hollow Man is more wretched than Dante's Farinata. "In the middle nineteenth century, the age which (at its best) Goethe had prefigured, an age of bustle, programmes, platforms, scientific progress, humanitarianism and revolutions which improved nothing, an age of progressive degradation, Baudelaire perceived that what really matters is Sin and Redemption . . . ; and the possibility of damnation is so immense a relief in a world of electoral reform, plebiscites, sex reform and dress reform, that damnation itself is an immediate form of salvation—of salvation from the ennui of modern life, because it at least gives some significance to living."

The Church, then, stands for freedom of the will—for the freedom to choose salvation or damnation—as it stands for voluntary community. If the Church falls, so falls tolerable social order. But few men support a church out of mere social expediency, and no man should. The mission of the Church is the ordering of souls, not the ordering of the state—though from a community of souls there should arise a social community. Faith is not the product of the fallacious concept of the Church as a moral police.

How, then, is a man persuaded to accept Christian doctrine and the Christian Church? In his introduction to Pascal's *Pensées* (1931) Eliot dealt with this question in phrases very like Cardinal Newman's:

"The Christian thinker—and I mean the man who is trying consciously and conscientiously to explain to himself the sequence which culminates in faith, rather than the public apologist—proceeds by rejection and elimination. He finds the world to be so and so; he finds its character inexplicable by any non-religious theory: among religions he finds Christianity, and Catholic Christianity, to account most satisfactorily for the world and especially for the moral world within; and thus, by what Newman calls 'powerful and concurrent' reasons, he finds himself inexorably committed to the dogma of the Incarnation. To the unbeliever, this method seems disingenuous and perverse: for the unbeliever is, as a rule, not so greatly troubled to explain the world to himself, nor so greatly distressed by its disorder; nor is he generally concerned (in modern terms) to 'preserve values.' "

Eliot made no fuller formal statement touching upon his conversion—or rather, his reunion with Christianity. Such apologies had been written by others of similar mind, and presumably any detailed profession of faith by Eliot would have resembled closely Chesterton's *Orthodoxy*. In his *Thoughts after Lambeth* (1931) Eliot relegates to a parenthetical remark the protests of those marchers in the secularistic dawn who looked upon him as a lost leader: "I dislike the word 'generation,' which has been a talisman for the last ten years; when I wrote a poem called *The Waste Land* some of the more approving critics said that I had expressed the 'disillusionment of a generation,' which is nonsense. I may have expressed for them their own illusion of being disillusioned, but that did not form part of my intention."

The illusion of being disillusioned, and the actual servitude of the "new freedom" in morals, are principal subjects of Eliot's observations upon the Church of England's Lambeth Conference in 1930. (Indeed, that ineffectual and unimaginative Conference would be utterly forgotten today, were it not for Eliot's *Thoughts*.) Morals flow from faith, Eliot wrote; a faith built upon moralism is unendurable and, happily, transitory. In the course of this argument, Eliot drubbed his old patron Bertrand Russell:

"I cannot regret that such views as Mr. Russell's, or what we may call the enervate *gospel of happiness,* are openly expounded and defended.* They help to make clear, what the nineteenth century had been largely occupied in obscuring, that there is no such thing as just Morality; but that for any man who thinks clearly, as his Faith is so will his Morals be. . . . Emancipation had some interest for venturous spirits when I was young, and must have been quite exciting to the previous generation; but the Youth to which the bishops' words apply is grey-haired now. . . .

* In *The Georgiad* (1933) Roy Campbell put into verse Eliot's stricture upon Russell:
"Hither flock all the crowd whom love has wrecked
Of intellectuals without intellect
And sexless folk whose sexes intersect:
All who in Russell's burly frame admire
The 'lineaments of gratified desire,'
And of despair have baulked the yawning precipice
By swotting up his melancholy recipes
For 'happiness'—of which he is the cook
And knows the weight, the flavour, and the look,
Just how much self-control you have to splice it with:
And the right kind of knife you ought to slice it with:
How to 'rechauffe' the stock-pot of desire
Although the devil pisses on the fire . . ."

(153)

Christian morals gain immeasurably in richness and freedom by being seen as the consequence of Christian faith, and not as the imposition of tyrannical and irrational habit. What chiefly remains of the new freedom is its meagre impoverished emotional life; in the end it is the Christian who can have the more varied, refined and intense enjoyment of life; which time will demonstrate."

It has been objected by certain critics that Eliot's regaining of faith did not make him joyous. (One wonders whether these writers' notion of a professed Christian is a pillar of sanctimony with an imbecilic grin.) True, the imitation of Christ sometimes suffuses believers with joy; but that is not the usual experience, for faith does not transform circumstance. What faith offers, ordinarily, is peace, resignation, and hope, not overflowing euphoria. Eliot's regaining of belief did not restore his wife in mind and body, or alter the bent world which he surveyed in those years. Faith does not abolish sorrow: it makes sorrow endurable.

Yet those who fancy that the later Eliot was a doleful pomposity never knew him. Can it be that they take sobersidedly his comical self-mockery in the lines (published in *The Criterion*, January, 1933) "For Cuscuscaraway and Mirza Murad Ali Beg"?

> How unpleasant to meet Mr. Eliot!
> With his features of clerical cut,
> And his brow so grim
> And his mouth so prim
> And his conversation, so nicely
> Restricted to What Precisely
> And If and Perhaps and But.

He would become a churchwarden; but still he was Old Possum, student of feline extravagances; still the devotee of the recordings of the Two Black Crows, Moran and Mack; still possessed of a sense of the ridiculous, frequent in his letters; still good company, generous of praise, ready of sympathy. The brow was not really grim: he would even enter into a correspondence with Mr. Groucho Marx.*

The recovery of belief gave Eliot the theological virtues. But the denial of faith brought on, for many rationalistic intellectuals, the Age of Anxiety; and brought to the mass of mankind, the Age of Ideology. The recovery of belief gave to Eliot what had glimmered faintly in the Waste Land: the hope that the time might be redeemed. That aspiration rises from the concluding sentences of *Thoughts after Lambeth*:

"The Universal Church is today, it seems to me, more definitely set against the World than at any time since pagan Rome. I do not mean that our times are particularly corrupt; all times are corrupt. I mean that Christianity, in spite of certain local appearances, is not, and cannot be within measurable time, 'official.' The World is trying the experiment of attempting to form a civilized but non-Christian mentality. The experiment will fail; but we must be very patient in awaiting its collapse; meanwhile redeeming the time: so that the Faith may be preserved alive through the dark ages before us; to renew and rebuild civilization, and save the World from suicide."

Abide with Me

Religion and ethics occupied much space in *The Criterion* from 1925 through 1930, and among those who wrote on such subjects were William Butler Yeats, Ramon Fernandez, Jacques Maritain, Martin D'Arcy, Julien Benda, G. K. Chesterton, Mario Praz, Paul Elmer More, and Allen Tate.

* Six letters from Eliot, and five to him from Marx, are included in *The Groucho Letters: Letters from and to Groucho Marx* (1967).

But except for some book reviews and for his part in the prolonged discussion of intuition and intelligence, the editor himself wrote little that touched upon such matters. In his own review, Eliot was a political critic during this period.

In Britain and throughout most of the world, this was the time of the uneasy lull between the Versailles settlement and that series of disasters (the financial collapse of 1929–30, the Spanish Civil War, the Italian conquest of Abyssinia, the German reoccupation of the Rhineland) which brought on worse disorder than ever. It was a period of ascendancy for the Conservative party, with Stanley Baldwin at Number Ten Downing Street from November, 1924, to May, 1929. It was a period of complacency for many.

This was a time when the world knew a respite from violence: a time when political imagination ought to have been employed, and when the principles of order might have been examined. But Eliot saw the Conservative party unimaginative and timorous, the Labour party dully ideological and materialistic, the Liberal party enfeebled and unprincipled. He saw nothing better in other great states; indeed, the prospect was that democracy (for which Eliot felt no passionate affection) would give way to something worse—a force and political dogmatism of a fanatical character. The sands were running out. From 1925 through 1930, Eliot did what he could to stimulate discussion among educated people concerning the first principles of social order.

During *The Criterion*'s early years, one could have read between its lines Eliot's strong hope that Catholicism, royalism, and classicism might reinvigorate society. During these middle years of his review, however, he endeavored chiefly to maintain a tolerable balance—to resist the extremes of Communism and Fascism. With something like a sigh, he settled for the imperfect possible; he even found himself a defender of democracy against totalists—or, at least, a friend of a democracy of elevation, though still resisting a drab leveling democratism.

So far as universal suffrage could establish a democratic society, Britain now approached the limits of reform. In 1918, the Representation of the People Act had extended the franchise to virtually all adult males and to nearly all women more than thirty years old; though this measure had no discernible effect upon the strength of particular parties and did not seem to have roused women to activity in public affairs, still there persisted pressures toward the old radical idea of "one man, one vote"—or rather, one adult, one vote—"and only one vote."

The Act of 1928 would bring in the "flapper vote"—that is, it would enfranchise women between the ages of twenty-one and thirty. Also it would abolish the last remnants of plural voting, except for the university seats (which would survive until the Attlee government after the Second World War). Eliot looked upon the final triumph of the Benthamite concept of democratic representative government and wondered whether that triumph really would be final. Would not mass democracy, badly led, smug, and sacrificing everything to creature-comforts, fall before some hard new domination? These circumstances, and this question, form the background for Eliot's political arguments between the defeat of the first MacDonald government and the coming of the Great Depression.

With considerable impartiality, *The Criterion* opened its pages to discussion of questions of political principle. During these years, Charles Maurras contributed an essay in two parts, much discussed by other contributors in several numbers; Shaw's *Intelligent Woman's Guide to Socialism and Capitalism* was the subject of four parallel reviews, from as many points of view; J. S. Barnes defended Fascism; A. L. Rowse, then a "sympathetic critic" of Communism, wrote several essays and reviews; Christopher Dawson predicted the end of the liberal era; Julien Benda appeared in this quarterly; later, Eliot would go so far as to publish C. M. Grieve's "Second Hymn to Lenin."

Despite this interest in political thought, *The Criterion* remained primarily a review of literature and philosophy. In June, 1928—when *The Criterion* reverted to its quarterly form, after a single year's attempt to attain comparative popularity as a monthly review—Eliot stated in his Commentary that journal's general attitude toward political discussion:

"In the theory of politics, in the largest sense, *The Criterion* is interested, so far as politics can be dissociated from party politics, from the passions or fantasies of the moment, and from problems of local and temporary importance. Which party is in power at home, or what squabble may be taking place in the Balkans, is of no interest, nor is jockeying for positions in treaties and peace-pacts. But the general relations of civilized countries among each other should be examined; and the philosophies expressed or implicit in various tendencies, such as communism or fascism, are worthy of dispassionate examination." Similarly, he added, *The Criterion* would discuss religious ideas, but would stop where emotional conviction begins.

"What unites, we believe, the various writers, both in England and in foreign countries, who constitute what has been vaguely called 'the *Criterion* group' is not a common adhesion to a set of dogmatic principles, even of literary criticism, but a common interest in what we believe to be the most important matters of our time, which allows the widest variation in attitude and tendency. . . . Individually, the various contributors (including the editor) inevitably have their own passions and prejudices; as a whole, *The Criterion* is quite disinterested."

Two especial political interests of the editor recur in Eliot's Commentaries during these years: American copyright law, and censorship in Britain. On the latter subject, he opposed censorship of books by the Home Office; were there to be any censorship at all, he argued, it ought to be the responsibility of the Church of England, not of a political functionary. (He would have controlled films severely, however, because of their power to debase or delude an undiscriminating mass audience.)

Of more immediate interest are Eliot's several *Criterion* contributions to the understanding of democracy, Fascism, and Communism; were these articles more widely known, a good deal of confusion about Eliot's politics might be dissipated. From the first, he was a consistent and intelligent opponent of both Fascist and Communist ideologies; and somewhat to his own surprise, perhaps, on occasions he found himself defending the constitutional democracies of Britain and the United States. He never entertained any foolish hopes of Mussolini or Lenin, Hitler or Stalin.

Power, he knew, was shifting: yet shifting, he feared, not into the hands of a peaceful multitude, but into the clutch of oligarchs and demagogues. He observed the degradation of the democratic dogma in many quarters—even in the new Prayer Book of the Church of England, in which the words "incomprehensible" and "everlasting" had been supplanted by "infinite" and "eternal":

"The Preface reads like a rather embarrassed apology for change: everything is changing, so the Prayer Book must change. 'Far and wide the country has yielded place to the town, and the growth of knowledge has given to millions instead of thousands new means of earning their daily bread.' That may be so; but what connexion have these economic phenomena with the revision of a Prayer Book; and if they are connected, are they connected *rationally*? 'With the rise of numbers has come also a shifting of power from the few to the many.' A shifting of power, certainly; but is it from the few to the many? or from demagogue to demagogue? And what, again, has Universal Suffrage (now approaching its consummation) to do with revision of a Prayer Book? The editors continue: 'in religion as in all else truth is not prized less highly because it is no longer fenced on any side.' But when fences are down the cattle will roam, including two vagrant beasts named *infinite* and *eternal*, words which will wander so far, the fence of meaning being down, that they will cease to belong anywhere."[8]

In the Baldwin years, little concern for the infinite and the eternal was to be observed among leaders of the Conservative party, Eliot believed. In July, 1927, reviewing Anthony M. Ludovici's *Defense of Conservatism*, Eliot pointed to a ruinous weakness: "He isolates politics from economics, and he isolates it from religion. He would build a conception of the Tory without taking account of those vast and international economic transformations, a vague awareness and anxiety about which is what drives most of us to think about politics at all." And Ludovici would have had England discard the Church of England in favor of the Church of Rome—a blunder for those who support monarchy. "The problem of Toryism should be rather to make the Church of Laud survive in an age of universal suffrage, in an age in which a Parliament elected by persons of every variety of religious belief or disbelief (and containing now and then a Parsee) has a certain control over the destinies of that Church."[9]

Might Toryism be redeemed from the Tories of the hour? Three events of the previous decade had turned the attention of men of letters toward politics, Eliot wrote in November of that year: the Russian Revolution, the transformation of Italy, and the Vatican's condemnation of the *Action Fran-çaise*. "All of these events compel us to consider the problem of Liberty and Authority, both in politics and in the organization of speculative thought. Politics has become too serious a matter to be left to politicians. We are compelled, to the extent of our abilities, to be amateur economists, in an age in which politics and economics can no longer be kept wholly apart. Everything is in question—even the fundamental dogma of modern society that debentures are safer than common stocks. . . . We have to adapt our minds to a new age—new certainly to this extent, that the nineteenth century gave us a very inadequate preparation for it." He was looking for fresh views. Wyndham Lewis had just published *Time and Western Man;* Eliot welcomed that book, describing Lewis as "the most remarkable example in England of the actual mutation of the artist into a philosopher of a type hitherto unknown."[10]

During 1928, Eliot wrote against Fascists and Socialists and Communists. Italian Fascism was inconsonant with the British constitution, he suggested in a comment on *The Lion,* the organ of the British Fascist party.[11] But the ideas of Charles Maurras were another matter; and he took up Maurras' defense against Leo Ward. Maurras' royalism and traditionalism, Eliot said, were bulwarks against totalist ideology: "If anything, in another generation or so, is to save us from a sentimental Anglo-Fascism, it will be some system of ideas which will have gained much from the study of Maurras." Nor was Maurras anti-Christian: "I have been a reader of the work of Maurras for eighteen years; upon me he has had exactly the opposite effect." Eliot appended to his essay a considerable bibliography on Maurras and *Action Française.*[12]

In the same issue of his review, Eliot published the second part of Maurras' "Prologue to an Essay on Criticism." Leo Ward replied to Eliot in the June number of *The Criterion;* in the same issue, the editor replied to the reply; and Ward was given a final rejoinder. Ward had argued that Maurras produced what John Adams had called "political

Christians," men who accepted religious doctrine because it might lead to their political advantage. Eliot's rebuttal was characteristic of his coolness in political dispute:

"Mr. Ward asks: 'is it not only for those who identify Conservatism with Christianity that an adhesion to the former has been preparatory to a conversion to the latter?' With all reserves as to the meaning of the word 'conservatism,' I say that I never supposed anything else. I never supposed that M. Maurras could influence towards Christianity anyone who was not influenced towards his political theory. But those who are not affected by his political theory will not be influenced by Maurras at all, so that their Christianity is not in question. I say only that if anyone is attracted by Maurras' political theory, and if that person has as well any tendency towards *interior* Christianity, that tendency will be quickened by finding that a political and a religious view can be harmonious."[13]

Three months later, Eliot gave a knock to the democratism of Emil Ludwig, who had declared that Britain need not fear Germany, because Germany now was a socialist country: only the Hohenzollern monarchy had been bellicose. Eliot saw otherwise: "A nation is neither more nor less aggressive because it has a king, or an emperor, or a president, or a committee as its nominal head. The fact that 'the people' does not want war is no security against war; and a 'people' is not a whit more reliable than an individual sovereign. The causes of modern war—and 'war' means here war between peoples on the same level of civilization—lie deep in economic and financial matters. . . . All peoples above the barbaric level desire peace—in general; but they should not be allowed to persuade themselves that the desire for peace is enough to ensure it; though intelligent vigilance and independent criticism will help to preserve it."[14]

If democrats and socialists were quite capable of waging war, so innocent psychologists were quite capable of repressing human freedom and variety. Eliot took up Sigmund Freud's book *The Future of an Illusion*, and found in it an ominous slant:

"So far as culture means merely social organization, then Dr. Freud's next remarks, on the necessity of defending culture against the individual, are quite just. But this leads him to the view that culture and civilization are always 'imposed' on the many by the few—which is only intelligible if we continue to restrict culture to the maintenance of law and order, and not altogether true at that.

"But we are hopelessly bewildered on the next page . . . where we read [in Freud] that 'one thought at first that the essence of culture lay in the conquest of nature for the means of supporting life, and in eliminating the dangers that threaten culture by the suitable distribution of those among mankind . . .' If one really thought that the essence of culture lay in eliminating the dangers that threaten culture, then there must be something very wrong with one's reasoning powers. I can feel only stupefaction on reading such a course of argument. And throughout this first chapter, one has the impression that the truly cultured and civilized man is the highly efficient Policeman. Dr. Freud observes with a sigh that 'probably a certain percentage of mankind . . . will always remain asocial.' The word 'asocial' has perhaps some deep psychological meaning beyond my comprehension; but it seems to me that some contributions have been made to what I call civilization by men who have been solitaries or rebels."[15]

These scarcely were sentiments consonant with the image of Eliot the remorseless pillar of things established that hostile critics have erected. Nor was Eliot really a political partisan at all. As the British general election of 1929 approached, Eliot foresaw no improvement over the Baldwin government: "All that can be predicted this year is the usual waste of time, money and energy, a very small vote in consequence of the increased number of voters, and the return, known to Dryden, of 'old consciences with new faces.' " The rhetoric of English politicians reflected their meagre talents:

"Perhaps British statesmen once had more leisure, time to re-read their sentences, and even look up their words in a dictionary. Mr. Lloyd George was always a busy little man." Ramsay MacDonald was no better; Winston Churchill, worse. "Beyond a certain point, degrees of inferiority are indifferent; and in this sense there can be nothing appreciably worse than the style of Mr. Churchill's recent reminiscences in *The Times* newspaper. . . . In our ideal Platonic Republic, of course, the country would be governed by those who can best write and speak its language—those, in other words, who can best think in that language."

At this juncture, Eliot remarked that Bernard Shaw, H. G. Wells, and Wyndham Lewis, in their several ways, all were inclining toward Fascism. (Wells, indeed, said Eliot, masked his inclinations toward a total society behind mockery of Benito Mussolini.)* This was not then so damning a charge as it later became. And the aging Fabians were shifting toward some sort of autocracy. Eliot took alarm; he understood the intellectual's attraction toward concentration of political power, but the consequences (once writers' ideas should penetrate, vulgarized, to "thousands of unthinking people") might be most unpleasant. "The extreme of democracy—which we have almost reached—promises greater and greater interference with private liberty; but despotism might be equally despotic. . . . A rational government would

---

* At this time, although Wells ridiculed Mussolini's posturing, various of Wells' own writings seemed to imply that Wells would not oppose the central direction which was the essence of Fascism, so long as the dictator or the oligarchs were under the influence of intellectuals. A year later, however, Wells burlesqued his own notion of an autocratic government guided by a visionary professor, in his novel *The Autocracy of Mr. Parham* (1930).

be one which acted for itself in matters concerning which 'the people' does not know its own mind; which did as little governing as possible, and which left as large a measure of individual and local liberty as possible."

Eliot (whom some radical critics have tried to label "crypto-fascist," a term extracted from the Marxist publicist's jargon about the time of the Second World War) was, actually, one of the first editors to oppose a drift toward Fascism among men of intellect. The men of letters were growing discontented with the inefficiency and the dullness of democracy. "If, as we believe, the indifference to politics as actually conducted is growing, then we must prepare a state of mind towards something other than the facile alternative of communist or fascist dictatorship."[16] For men of letters do possess power, either latent or immediate; the ordinary man was coming to regard as incompetent both major parties in Britain; and should the clerisy's inclination coincide with that of the crowd, the constitution might give way.

In 1918 and 1919, there had existed danger that Communists might attempt a coup in England; the government had been seriously alarmed then. But a decade later, the danger came from the Fascists; and, unlike many other writers at that time, Eliot perceived the evil in that movement. What might be done to shore up ordered freedom and to restore vigor to the political commonwealth? The general election of June, 1929, brought MacDonald and Labour to power for a second time—though the Conservatives won a plurality of the popular vote. A month later, Eliot offered his "Second Thoughts on the Brainless Election." The members of the new cabinet—or rather, the old Lib-Lab ministers restored—had not one new idea among them. What might be done, in an hour when Fascists and Communists grew in influence among the intellectuals and among the mass of citizens?

"There is of course a great opportunity—for the Conservative Party; an opportunity which we are quite certain it will fail to seize. It is the opportunity of thinking in leisure, and of appreciating the efforts of private persons who have committed some thinking already. The Labour Party is a capitalist party in the sense that it is living on the reputation of thinking done by the Fabians of a generation ago (we do not know whether any Fabian veterans are still thinking or not)..... The Conservative Party has a great opportunity, in the fact that within the memory of no living man under sixty, has it acknowledged any contact with intelligence. . . . It has, what no other political party at present enjoys, a complete mental vacuum: a vacancy that might be filled with anything, even with something valuable."[17]

If the defeated Conservatives would not rouse themselves to confront the peril of totalist politics, a man of letters must do what he could. At the end of 1928, Eliot had published in *The Criterion* his essay on "The Literature of Fascism." This was followed by J. S. Barnes' "Fascism," in the April, 1929 number; and by A. L. Rowse's "The Literature of Communism: Its Origin and Theory," also in the April number. Eliot replied to these ideological writers: "Mr. Barnes and Mr. Rowse" (*The Criterion*, July, 1929).

Describing himself as a "political ignoramus," Eliot proceeded to expose both these ideologies as insufficient for the difficulties of the time. Now that everyone enjoyed the vote in Britain, he wrote, the real power became more concentrated in the hands of "a small number of politicians, or perhaps in the Civil Service, or perhaps in the City, or perhaps in a number of cities." Upon the mass of people, increasingly aware that "popular government" had shrunk to a shadow, ideological slogans must operate powerfully.

The fundamental menace of Fascism and Communism, Eliot continued, is that these ideologies attempt to supplant religious faith. "The more a political creed usurps the place of religious creed, the more risk of its becoming merely a façade. The popular result of ignoring religion seems to be merely that the populace transfer their religious emotions to political theories. Few people are sufficiently civilized to afford atheism. When a political theory becomes a creed, one begins to suspect its impotence."

Fascism, founded in Italy upon expediency rather than upon any body of sound ideas, might destroy democracy throughout Europe, what with the general dissatisfaction with democratic governments. And that prospect dismayed Eliot: "I cannot share enthusiastically in this vigorous repudiation of 'democracy.' When the whole world repudiates one silly idea, there is every chance that it will take up another idea just as silly or sillier. It is one thing to say, what is sadly certain, that democratic government has been watered down to almost nothing. . . . But it is another thing to ridicule the *idea* of democracy. A real democracy is always a restricted democracy, and can only flourish with some limitation by hereditary rights and responsibilities. . . . The modern question as popularly put is: 'democracy is dead; what is to replace it?' whereas it should be: 'the frame of democracy has been destroyed; how can we, out of the materials at hand, build a new structure in which democracy can live?'

"Order and authority are good: I believe in them as wholeheartedly as I think one should believe in any single idea; and much of the demand for them in our time has been soundly based. But behind the increasing popular demand for these things, the parroting of the words, I seem to detect a certain spiritual anaemia, a tendency to collapse, the recurring human desire to escape the burden of life and thought. . . . And in this state of mind and spirit human beings are inclined to welcome any regime which relieves us from the burden of pretended democracy. Possibly also, hidden in many breasts, is a craving for a regime which will

relieve us of thought and at the same time give us excitement and military salutes."

Much in the thought of Maurras and his friends had attracted him, Eliot concluded, but Fascism was empty—and grim. "A new school of political thought is needed, which might learn from political thought abroad, but not from political practice. Both Russian communism and Italian fascism seem to me to have died as political ideas, in becoming political facts."[18]

In his reply to Barnes and Rowse, Eliot suggested that Fascism and Communism "are merely variations of the same doctrine: and even that they are merely variations of the present state of things." Political philosophers, alas, never recognize the irrational element in their own philosophies. "Mr. Barnes seems to me to confound the rational and irrational elements in fascism; and Mr. Rowse seems to me to try to isolate the rational and ignore the irrational element in communism." Fascism is Napoleonic, rather than royalist. "In the *success* of a man like Mussolini (a man of 'the people') a whole nation may feel a kind of self-flattery; and the Russian people deified itself in Lenin. Both Italy and Russia seem to me to be suffering from Napoleonism."

Of the two, Eliot concluded, he would prefer Fascism, as the less overwhelming; but he wanted neither. "Fascism is (begging Mr. Barnes' pardon) nationalistic, and communism internationalistic: yet it is conceivable that in particular circumstances fascism might make for peace, and communism for war. The objections of fascists and communists to each other are mostly quite irrational. . . . But my chief purpose in venturing to criticize two authors immeasurably more learned and competent than myself, is to affirm my previous contention that neither fascism nor communism is new or revolutionary as *idea*."[19]

Fascism and Communism, that is, could offer only old consciences with new faces: neither could make that leap by which a decadent civilization might be renewed. Men of letters would be attracted to one or the other of these shallow ideologies, Eliot feared, and balance would be lost. His reply to Barnes and Rowse was published only three months before The Crash of October 29, 1929. When the New York stock exchange fell into chaos, the way was opened for terrible simplifiers to rally an immense following. Many literary men, so often sentimental and superficial in their practical politics, fell into Benda's "treason of the intellectuals."

Some of the Criterion group would admire the rhetoric that resounded from the balcony of the Palazzo Venezia—or, later, would mistake the *superbia* of a Munich beer-cellar orator for political inspiration; others would carry their offerings to the shrine of the god that failed, in Moscow, as if the mummified Lenin could work secular miracles. But Eliot and those closest to him in their convictions would persist in the endeavor to restore a personal and a public order that they had inherited from Jerusalem and Athens and Rome, and that in England was upheld by Westminster and Windsor and Canterbury.

"We can hardly believe that there are not, scattered over the continents of Europe and America, a few men of thought and observation, who are concerned with the Theory of Politics," Eliot wrote in January, 1930. "And we are very badly in need of that; and half a dozen Aristotles working together would be only enough to supply the need. All that we have is confusion of voices in popular discussion, exaggerating the importance of various details." The forming of public opinion must not be left to popular newspapers. "To amuse people is to have power over them; and power is power, even if its possessors have not the slightest notion what they are doing with it."[20]

Could men of thought avert another great war and another series of revolutions? Could they reconcile the claims of order with the claims of justice and freedom? "I think we are in agreement that 'Order' and 'Authority' are more dangerous catchwords now, than 'Liberty' and 'Reform' were fifty or seventy-five years ago," he wrote to Dobrée, in November, 1930. "Order and Authority may point more directly to the yellow press and the crook capitalists than Liberty and Reform pointed to Socialism. I am terrified of the modern contempt of 'democracy' . . . I am as scary of Order as of Disorder."

Later, as Hitler loomed large in Germany, Dobrée met Eliot by chance in Piccadilly. "I suppose one must have order," Dobrée said. "Yes," Eliot replied, "but there are different kinds of order."[21]

Eliot meant that constitutional order is legitimate and —whatever the imperfections of democratic states—bound to certain principles of justice and freedom; while the order of dictator or oligarchy, which in the totalist states recognizes little or no source of higher authority, overthrows the healthful tension between the claims of authority and the claims of freedom: such a state may commit atrocities in the name of order. He may have thought of Talleyrand's remark, after the fall of Napoleon, that "You can do everything with bayonets—except sit upon them." Eliot was as strongly attached to the prescriptive British constitution, in all its complexity, as most Americans profess to be attached to the formal document of their federal constitution. If a scheme of political reform could not be reconciled with the essence of the British constitution, for Eliot that was sufficient reason to reject the proposal.

If the order of the soul is decayed, Freud's civilized Policeman cannot suffice to maintain the outer order of the state; the power of the Stormtrooper succeeds; and even that power, in the long run, must fall to ruin. In 1930, Stephen Spender met Eliot for the first time. At their luncheon, Spender asked Eliot what future he foresaw for their civilization. "Internecine fighting . . ." Eliot said. "People killing one another in the streets."[22]

Regaining the Higher Dream

Nothing could be more remote from the realm of politics than is *Ash-Wednesday*. As Helen Gardner writes, the poem arises from a personal experience "so painful that it cannot be wholly translated into symbols."[23] Yet that poem accomplished more to redeem the time—to attract support for a tolerable civil social order, as well as to restore a consciousness of spiritual order—than did everything Eliot wrote for his *Criterion*.

Ash-Wednesday turned toward Christianity many of the rising generation, when others were gravitating toward Communism, Rose Macaulay suggests.[24] Faith of some sort, all aspiring talents seek; and if those vigorous people in any society ignore or reject religious understanding, they will take to the pseudo-religion of ideology—which inverts the religious symbols of transcendence, promising here and now, upon earth and tomorrow, the perfection of our nature that religion promises through salvation of the soul. Or, if a people ignorant of religion escape the clutch of fanatic ideology, then they will turn, at best, to the self-worship and gross indulgence of Sir Epicure Mammon. *The Waste Land* and "The Hollow Men" had made it possible to disbelieve in the nineteenth-century liberalism of Matthew and Waldo—and yet to remain intellectually respectable; *Ash-Wednesday* made it possible to believe in Christian insights—and yet, again, to remain within the pale of modern intellectuality.

As he published the first three sections of *Ash-Wednesday* in various periodicals during 1927, 1928, and 1929, Eliot had given much thought to political questions. Yet *Ash-*

Wednesday shows no connection whatever with those concerns, nor could he have expected that his purgatorial visions would reduce at all the appeal of ideology—except, perhaps, for indulging a hope that his exhortation (in the fourth section) to "redeem the time" might reach some eyes. Throughout *Ash-Wednesday*, Eliot is addressing not the community, but the conscience.

Experiences of guilt, concupiscence, error, and ennui are universal; so are feelings of remorse, and renewed temptation after repentance; so is the search for enduring love, however mistaken or perverted the course of that quest; and the longing to be purged and redeemed, that one may find abiding peace, presumably exists in every full human being, at least below the surface of consciousness. Once more, we should remind ourselves that Eliot believed the poet's own emotions to be irrelevant or trivial: what matters in a poem, so far as emotion is concerned, is the poet's touching upon universal emotions. Thus the romantic egoism of Shelley may make a study of Shelley's private life relevant to his poems; but the classical objectivity of Eliot reduces his personal experience to incidental interest—if, indeed, it was anyone's business but his own. A man so insistent upon privacy as Eliot was, and so sensitive to the feelings of others, could not have published *Ash-Wednesday* at all, had he expected his readers to recognize the immediate private affliction that his poem transforms into general truths.

Here, then, one need only suggest that *Ash-Wednesday* mirrors no guilt that Sweeney, say, would recognize as reprehensible. Though the moral imagination may emancipate its possessor from the tyranny of time and ego, that imagination often brings with it an acute awareness of personal failings—including the sins of omission—that the average sensual man is spared. Eliot's scarcely was a life of license. (Some hasty critics have taken his early "La Figlia che Piange" for a reminiscence of a faithless affair of the heart;

actually, that poem has for its inspiration Eliot's failing to find, during his visit to an Italian museum, a certain statue of a weeping girl. And we have mentioned elderly Miss X, the Boston Lady of the "Portrait," who later sent to Eliot, in England, her Christmas card with "ringing greetings from friend to friend"—no inamorata.) One man's agony of remorse is another man's dismissal of a peccadillo.

We now know what most readers of *Ash-Wednesday* did not know when it was published (only six hundred copies) in April, 1930. They may have noticed the dedication to his wife; they (except for a few friends) were unaware of Vivienne Eliot's downward spiral. Anyone who wishes may find in Grover Smith's analysis of this poem, for instance, strong implications that the dedication (whether or not his wife so recognized it) is to one in a sense already lost; it has become necessary to weigh the counsel of Saint John of the Cross that one must divest himself of the love of created beings. Purgatory's garden of the single rose, the garden where all loves end, is consolation for the lost hyacinth-garden of *The Waste Land;* in that garden of Mount Purgatory is a Lady, but if there remains in her some essence of the Hyacinth Girl, all dross has been purged away. "That garden is paradise regained," Grover Smith comments; "the Hyacinth garden of *The Waste Land* is paradise lost. . . ." The Lady of that garden with the two yew trees, in *Ash-Wednesday,* "is a symbol of the desire beyond desire and of the fusion of human and celestial. She, better than the vague ghost of 'lilac and brown hair,' is the true counterpart of the hyacinth girl, holding, with ephemeral intensity, the central focus of all impulse toward clarity and beauty."[25]

Vivienne Eliot still was with her husband while he wrote *Ash-Wednesday,* and they did not part finally until 1933. So he does not divest himself altogether of the love of created beings: the *via negativa* of Saint John of the Cross (though the protagonist of *Ash-Wednesday* renounces "the blessèd face . . . and the voice," because he cannot do otherwise) as yet is possibility only. Several years later, Eliot wrote to Bonamy Dobrée (who was horrified by the *via negativa*) that John of the Cross meant this "divesting" for people "seriously engaged in the Way of Contemplation. It is only to be read in relation to that Way: i.e. merely to kill one's human affections will get one nowhere, it would be only to become rather more a completely living corpse than most people are. But the doctrine is fundamentally true, I believe. Or to put your belief in your own way, that only through the love of created beings can we approach the love of God, that I believe to be UNTRUE."[26]

Whatever Vivienne's descent toward madness may have contributed to the remorse and renunciation of *Ash-Wednesday*, that poem would be no less moving if one surmised nothing at all of Eliot's private suffering.* It is unnecessary to know anything about the actual Beatrice Portinari for understanding the Beatrice of the *Paradiso*. The student, indeed, will do well to turn to Eliot's brief illuminating study of Dante (published in 1929, and reprinted in the *Selected Essays*, two years later) before he reads the abundant criticism of *Ash-Wednesday*. The "Divine Pageant" of the *Para-*

---

* If the sacrament of marriage consecrates a timeless spiritual union, there can be no total renunciation of the love of one especial created being, at least. This point may be made clearer by some words from Eliot's friend Father Martin D'Arcy. When Father D'Arcy, my wife, and I dined together in Los Angeles in 1965, my wife inquired of him whether, if in Heaven there be no marriage or giving in marriage, husband and wife are to expect beyond death the fullness of union they have known in this time-captive world. Father D'Arcy replied that in the heavenly state all the good things of one's existence in time will be present, in every way, whenever one desires them; while the evil will be unknowable. That being so, what was good in the episode of the Hyacinth Garden, say, is good beyond time; and the Lady who is the protagonist's guide at the beginning of *Ash-Wednesday*, the earthly Lady, will be reconciled with the man who must renounce knowledge of her in this world.

diso, Eliot wrote, "belongs to the world of what I call the
high dream, and the modern world seems capable only of
the *low* dream. I arrived at accepting it, myself, only with
some difficulty." *Ash-Wednesday* is an endeavor to give back
the high dream to the twentieth century, and the proximate
causes of his high dream do not signify much if set beside
the intellectual sources of his vision: Dante, John of the
Cross, Cavalcanti, and even Jakob Grimm. The *experience*
of private anguish moved him immensely, of course; but the
expression of that experience is our concern.

As for the larger meanings of *Ash-Wednesday*, there is
general agreement among the closer critics, although of
course they differ (as upon every poem of Eliot's) about
particular sources and significances. The three white leopards
of the poem's second section are variously interpreted in
symbol: as the sins of avarice, gluttony, and lust, and also as
the three aspects of love (by Father Genesius Jones); as
Communion and also as cannibal ritual (by Leonard Unger);
as the world, the flesh, and the devil, and as agents of purgation (by Grover Smith); as, possibly, God's agents of destruction (see Jeremiah v, 6, and Hosea xii, 7) (by B. C.
Southam); and as without allegorical significance (by Helen
Gardner).[27] In 1929, when asked about the leopards, Eliot
himself recited the line in question, but said no more. Yet
this existing body of criticism of *Ash-Wednesday* is ample
and, for the most part, lucid enough. Here, then, I do no
more than describe the poem summarily—and thereafter
comment upon its influence.

These six lyrical poems, Allen Tate wrote a year after
publication of *Ash-Wednesday*, "are a brief moment of religious experience in an age that believes religion to be a
kind of defeatism and puts all its hope for man in finding the
right secular order. . . . It is possibly the only kind of imagery
that is valid for religious verse today."[28] No more convincing
imagery has been devised since then.

(*175*)

With a touch of irony, referring to himself as an "agèd eagle" and aware that poets' reputations are precarious, Eliot begins the first section or movement of *Ash-Wednesday* with a line from Cavalcanti: "Because I do not hope to turn again." What has been done in time and place cannot be undone; it is possible only to "construct something upon which to rejoice." Repining is torment and boredom; we are left with repentance, resignation, and prayer: with the possibility, so faintly whispered in "The Hollow Men," of Purgatory.

Those three white leopards, in the second section of the poem, have devoured the sinner, except for some rejected remnants; his white bones sing to the Lady of Silences, saying that it is well to be quit of the flesh, to have done with the torment of love unsatisfied and the greater torment of love satisfied. The Rose of forgetfulness is the contemplating Lady. "And I who am here dissembled/Proffer my deeds to oblivion . . ."

These poems are not a unity, but so many aspects of purgation. In the third section or movement, the protagonist ascends stairs—turning, after all, in penitence: he ascends, looking back upon avarice and gluttony and lust, having passed by the devil of the stairs; he rises toward the three aspects of love—Charis, Agape, and Eros.[29] At the first turning of the third stair he looks through the "slotted window bellied like the fig's fruit" upon the distractions of the flesh; but though "Lord, I am not worthy," he persists.

In the fourth movement, he has made his way to the Earthly Paradise of Mount Purgatory. The Lady, now the "silent sister," in her purity by the undying yew trees, gives a sign; and the fountain springs up. "Redeem the time, redeem the dream . . ."

The Word, the Logos, which the world has denied, is sought in the fifth movement. The "veiled sister" between the yew trees is entreated to pray—

> For children at the gate
> Who will not go away and cannot pray:
> Pray for those who chose and oppose . . .

The Seeker recognizes, as Leonard Unger puts it, "that the condition of the modern world is prohibitive of the experience which he desires."[30] Those who have climbed up to the Logos have reached the last desert of the Waste Land.

Finally, in the sixth movement, Eros and Agape have been transcended, and so remorse and shame have been.[31] Upon this height, the dreams of past and present and future intersect. As yet, the peace of God is not attained; but as we sit here, the Rose may be perceived in the distance.

This poem, or these poems, may be read many times, with growing sympathy and wonder. Max Eastman (the least humorous man who ever wrote a book about humor) was outraged by it, calling *Ash-Wednesday* "an oily puddle of emotional noises." But Eliot's power of moral imagination at last had found its source in faith; and if Eliot could find it possible to believe, minds previously closed to the possibility of transcendence would begin to ask the tremendous questions.

By 1930, Eliot's reputation would have been sufficient to have made many consider seriously whatever he might have had to say, odd though it might seem. Had Eliot written a devotional poem of the conventional sort, nevertheless, it could have made no lasting impression upon his public. Christian symbolism signified little to the intelligent public of 1930: it was taken to be archaic, a survival (fragmentarily evocative) from the childhood of the race. To that public, the Bible was only a confused collection of Hebrew and Greek writings, brought into doubt by the Higher Criticism of the nineteenth century and by eminent theologians of the twentieth; the Church seemed mostly moralism and sociability; "science" (not that the public really understood much natural science) was said to have exploded myth.

Many of that public knew religion only in the form that Coleridge had called bibliolatry; for others, it was sabbatarianism, agreeable or disagreeable; for such advanced thinkers as still condescended to utilize some of the old symbols, it might be the Social Gospel—the Great Commandment with its first clause excised. Revelation was remote in time. Could these dry bones speak?

Now symbols always have been a means for conveying a truth experienced. That truth must be experienced by a mortal man; and when the man is distant or dead, the symbols must be reduced, ordinarily, to words. Eric Voegelin puts this well: "As a consequence, when the experience engendering the symbols ceases to be a presence located in the man who has it, the reality from which the symbols derive their meaning has disappeared. The symbols in the sense of a spoken or written word, it is true, are left as traces in the world of sense perception, but their meaning can be understood only if they evoke, and through evocation reconstitute, the engendering reality in the listener or reader."

Those traces of an experience of transcendence had been nearly erased in the twentieth century: the symbols no longer evoked the transcendent experience. The ideologue would find it to his advantage to speak of a "post-Christian world"; and no one desires to be regarded as an antiquarian survival. Only by experiencing afresh the reality that once brought forth the old symbols can modern man regain faith, "the substance of things hoped for, and the evidence of things unseen."

Just that expression anew of transcendent experience was Eliot's achievement in *Ash-Wednesday*. He was not refurbishing old formulas merely: what mattered to those who understood or half-understood him, he was relating his own *experience* of "the higher dream," reality perceived by the moral imagination. Although he did not assume the prophetic afflatus, he spoke as one having authority: in the mind's eye, he had seen; in profound emotion, he had felt. Employing the ancient symbols, he had renewed their connection with living man. Through contrition, guilt might be washed or burned away; the "deceitful face of hope and of despair" might be left behind; the Word still might be heard in the world; renouncing lusts, Gerontion might become Gerontius; high above Grishkin with her promise of pneumatic bliss, there could be detected truly a glimmer of immortality, for to the humbled the Lady makes a sign.

Eliot's infernal visions had been accepted as valid descriptions of twentieth-century reality; it might follow that his purgatorial visions ought to be taken seriously. He had accomplished what eminent churchmen of his age could not achieve: he had reminded his time that myth may be true, a symbolic expression of the permanent things of experienced reality in every age. In Voegelin's words, "a truth whose symbols have become opaque and suspect cannot be saved by doctrinal concessions to the *Zeitgeist* but only by a return to the reality of experience which originally has engendered the symbols. The return will engender its own exegesis . . . and the exegetic language will make the older symbols translucent again."[32]

From 1932 to the present moment, exegesis of *Ash-Wednesday* has been in progress. A man of genuine intellectual power and broad learning might believe in dogma, it was clear; more important, he might experience something of the transcendent, and might express that experience in a mingling of old symbols and new. The intellectual public, or some part of that public, was moved.

George Santayana, in his little essay on Americanism, later would suggest that the liberal classes were uncertain of their own liberal assumptions: "Modern civilization has an immense momentum, not only physically irresistible but morally and socially dominant in the press, politics, and literature of the liberal classes; yet the voice of a dispossessed and forlorn orthodoxy, prophesying evil, cannot be silenced, and what renders that voice the more disquieting is that it can no longer be understood."

In Eliot, that forlorn and dispossessed orthodoxy had found a voice which might be understood by some men of the twentieth century. Although the voice might startle their ears, they would listen.

VI

The Poet, the Statesman, and the Rock

❖

Commentaries on a Time of Troubles

At the age of forty-two, T. S. Eliot was not much changed outwardly from what he had been when, in 1917, Prufrock and the Hippopotamus had captivated London. Photographs show this; and Wyndham Lewis remarks that there had not yet appeared "the haggard and exhausted mask" of Eliot's face late in the 1930's. True, the Gioconda or Lamia smile of his Harvard and early London years was to be seen no longer: "the saturnine vein was strongly fed with the harsh spectacle of the times . . . the spectacle of Europe committing suicide."[1]

By 1931, Eliot had made himself the most interesting poet of his day, the most formidable critic, the most respected serious editor; he was even something of a power in publishing. The author of *Ash-Wednesday* remained quite capable of fun: on the Wednesday nearest the Fourth of July, he and Frank Morley and Morley Kennerley would set off giant firecrackers under the table in the board room of Faber & Faber, to the annual astonishment of the directors at luncheon.[2]

Some faint hope lingered, perhaps, that withered love might blossom again. Vivienne Eliot was far gone: by 1930, when young Wynyard Browne had called at the Eliots' flat in Marylebone, "A lady opened the front door, asked him what he wanted, and on hearing 'Mr. Eliot' wailed, 'why, oh why, do they all want to see my husband!' and slammed the door in his face." Yet Vivienne still would remain with Eliot for another year, and as late as August, 1932, she would go down with him to Pike's Farm, Frank Morley's country place, for a christening.

The effort of *Ash-Wednesday* may have drawn heavily upon his resources as pure poet, for the time being; but he was waking to an interest in writing for the theater. From 1931 through 1934, he would publish two important new poems; an enduring volume of criticism (his Charles Eliot Norton lectures at Harvard); a long essay (his Page-Barbour lectures at the University of Virgina) touching on literature and theology and politics, which would bring him difficulties; the choruses of *The Rock;* and more than fifty contributions to periodicals.

Demon Ideology was beginning to diminish old friendships, though Eliot continued to publish in *The Criterion* the writings of associates with whom he disagreed. John Middleton Murry—one of those rare creatures, the genuine heretics, Eliot had written—drifted far into warm sympathy with Communism, believing that the medieval synthesis was impossible to restore and that modern man must find a new philosophical foundation. Ezra Pound, now established in Italy, had written to *Hound & Horn,* at the end of 1930, a letter assailing "Criterionism" and declaring that Eliot was interested in "dead and moribund writing"; late in 1931, Pound began to date his letters according to the Fascist calendar. George Bernard Shaw (never a friend) had gone off to Soviet Russia, where Czar Stalin granted him an audience. Wyndham Lewis, crossgrained and always opposed to whatever seemed to be the popular temper of the hour, published in April, 1931, his book commending Adolf Hitler as a friend to an aristocracy of intellect, a champion against Communism, and a force for peace. In his letters about this time, Lewis sneers at Eliot; and Eliot's admiration for Lewis was diminished. The approach of a new time of international troubles was setting literary men at loggerheads.

This was the year when the Japanese marched into Manchuria, and when the Spanish monarchy fell. It was the year of the German election in which the Nazis won a hundred and seven seats in the Reichstag, and the Communists seventy-seven.

It was the year of a bewildering financial crisis for Britain. By Easter, nearly three million men were unemployed, and the unemployment-insurance fund was more than a hundred million pounds in debt; the budget suffered from a deficit of more than thirty million pounds, though one-third of Britain's income was being spent upon taxes and rates; the Bank of England was drained of forty-five million pounds in gold during July alone; there occurred a near-mutiny in the North Sea fleet, because of pay reductions. The Labour government surrendered office that summer to a National government—four Labour ministers, four Conservative, two Liberal—though still with Ramsay MacDonald as prime minister. In September, Britain abandoned the gold standard. George Orwell was out with the tramps and hop-pickers; presently he would take the road to Wigan Pier.

At the general election, in October, Labour was smashed: the National coalition candidates received fourteen and a half million votes, against six and a half million for the Socialists. The National government would continue in office, growing steadily more Conservative (and Baldwin succeeding MacDonald as prime minister in 1935), until 1940.

These circumstances and events are the background for the two poems that make up *Coriolan*: "Triumphal March" (first published as an Ariel Poem, in October, 1931) and "Difficulties of a Statesman" (published in *Commerce* at the end of the year). In Eliot's *Collected Poems,* these are joined under the general title *Coriolan;* they were intended, in 1931, to be parts of a much longer poem or series of poems. These are Eliot's only political poems—though by no means wholly political—and they will be better understood if, before examining them, we look at Eliot's *Criterion* Commentaries during that year.

In his Commentary of January, 1931, Eliot attacked the shallow understanding of politics promulgated by the daily newspapers. The London *Times,* and the press generally, disseminated a baneful fallacy about "political education," and the papers' meaning of that phrase was clear enough:

"It means that if we keep the Socialist Party in office until by practical experience, which means getting into plenty of hot water, and running heads against stone walls, and generally by having their minds addled by overwork and worry, the wretched Ministers are reduced to complete incompetence and harmlessness, then the Government will be wiser and sadder and exactly like any other Government," Eliot wrote. "And it also means that during this period we shall keep pointing out all the Government's mistakes to the People; so that the People, also sadder and wiser, will install by acclamation a really good sound Government. Both these assumptions appear to me to be wholly wrong, wrong both as principles and predictions. As principle, they imply that there is no principle except Caution; they deny that there are any fundamental moral divisions in politics, on which men are willing to fight to the end and to suffer and make

(*184*)

others suffer. The ideal is the ideal of two parties, or even three, so far as all parties are exactly of the same practice in regard to everything that matters; they must however differ completely on a number of showy points that don't matter; otherwise the newspapers would have nothing to write leading articles about, and the public would lose the fun of that most costly of sports—the Sport of Democrats—the General Election. It implies, in the end, a theory of politics which is by no means patented by *The Times;* which is now-adays the common property of most papers and most politicians of every stripe; which is indeed, by democratic blessing, the common property of every common subject and citizen; the view that politics has nothing whatever to do with private morals, and that national prosperity and the greatest happiness of the greatest number depend entirely upon the difference between good and bad economic theories. It is further more and more the opinion of the common man that his private morals, except when they infringe criminal law, are nobody's business but his own—unless they bring him within the clutches of the scandal press. Private morals are not only private, but wholly negative. And on the other hand, so far as they are not private, they are made contingent upon economic conditions: so that we may conceivably have, in time, legislation framed to enforce limitation of families (by the usual methods) upon certain parts of the population, and to enforce progenitiveness upon others. With the applause of some of the clergy."

We need another Ruskin, he continued, and more thorough study of economics; the City men did not really understand political economy; and the genuine sciences of theology and ethics are fallen to low estate. Economics must recognize the higher authority of ethics:

"I cannot but believe that there are a few simple ideas at bottom, upon which I and the rest of the unlearned are competent to decide according to our several complexions;

but I cannot for the life of me ever get to the bottom. I cannot, for instance, believe in over-population so long as there is room in the world for everyone to move about without suffocation; I cannot understand the concurrence of over-production with destitution and I cannot help feeling that this has something to do with people wanting—so far as they are in a position to want anything more than food and shelter—the wrong things, and cultivating the wrong passions. So that we need Economists who will not merely demand of us enough wit to appreciate their own intellectual brilliance, who will not aim to dazzle us by their technical accomplishments, but who can descend to show us the relation between the financial cures that they advocate and our simple human principles and convictions."

John Middleton Murry had been advocating "a new asceticism"; Edgar Mowrer had written a book arguing for the application of scientific principles to politics; Sigmund Freud and Bertrand Russell had been recommending the *menus plaisirs* of life. What the time really needs, Eliot concluded, is something in which to believe:

" 'The need of a new asceticism is upon us,' indeed; but a cloistered or solitary asceticism is not enough to save us at the present juncture, unless the world is wholly (and well) lost; so that the few are left *redeeming the time, because the days are evil,* yet perpetually pestered with Income Tax Applications. I am afraid that the new asceticism should not only be practiced by the few, but imposed upon the many; else new asceticism will be merely, as it is already for some, old necessity writ large. In other words, whilst the new economists hope to improve the new world for the old Adam, the new psychologists hope to improve the old Adam for the new world; where an impulse capable of disciplining the individual and at the same time increasing his possibilities of development as an independent member of society is needed. Instead of liberty, which most people can hardly appreciate anyway, we are offered license; instead of order, we are offered mass-production of everything; including art and religion."

In *The Criterion*'s April number, Eliot published Thomas Mann's Berlin speech, "An Appeal to Reason," in which Mann exposed the menace of National Socialism and entreated the French to permit revision of the Versailles settlement. In his Commentary, Eliot rejected proposals for a National government, or indeed any emergency or coalition government for Britain. Something more stable must be thought of; political imagination was needed urgently. "We are not convinced that a combination of old gangsters will be a great improvement on the old gangs separately."

"Tiding over" or "weathering" or "stemming" would not suffice; for world conditions were altering rapidly. "It is very depressing to find that the Labour party in office has proved not only conservative but reactionary. The one most rational form of representation in the House of Commons, the representation of the Universities, is, if the Labour party has its way, to be destroyed. It is amazing stupidity, for the sake of perhaps a slight temporary numerical advantage, to remove just those men who do actually represent something. Far from abolishing this form of representation, we ought to increase it; and to have more members responsible to genuine interests with which they are acquainted rather than to mixed constituencies which they may hardly know."

Eliot then glanced at a political program published by the followers of Sir Oswald Mosley. In 1930, Mosley had been the hero of the rank and file of the Labour party; he almost had defeated the party leadership at that year's Annual Conference. Impatient, however, Mosley had departed to form his own party, and was in passage then (all his candidates being defeated in the general election of 1931) toward the leadership of the British Fascist party. Eliot found the Mosley program to contain some germs of intelligence, although in general vague or feeble; but it was lacking in "evidence of profound moral conviction. . . . *Politique d'abord,* certainly; but *politique* means more than prosperity and comfort, if it is to mean even that; it means the social aspect of the Good Life."

In the Southern Agrarians' book *I'll Take My Stand,* published in 1930, Eliot did find minds akin to his own; two of the contributors to that symposium, John Gould Fletcher and Allen Tate, had been frequent contributors to *The Criterion.* It was not the Southern states alone, however, that had been ravaged by modernity; no longer is the contrast in America between North and South merely:

"It is a conflict between all of the local and spiritually living districts or *enclaves* and the dominant uniform mode of existence which is New York and the monotony of the Middle West," Eliot remarked. "A New Englander cannot read the book without admitting that his own country was ruined as the South is ruined, and that New England was ruined first. . . . cannot but feel that in that isolated, cantankerous, often narrow, bigoted and heretical society there was more intellectual and spiritual flowering, more beauty of manners, architecture, painting, and decorative art—and a local and peculiar beauty at that—than is possible in New England today, when Boston is five hours from New York by train, and no distance at all by air. And the contrast and sometimes conflict, between the different and complementary types of New England and Virginia, gives the late Colonial and the early Republican history of America (to 1829) an interest and an urbanity which American history has not had since. The American intellectual of today has almost no chance of continuous development upon his own soil, and in the environment which his ancestors, however humble, helped to form. He must be an expatriate: either to languish in a provincial university, or abroad, or, the most complete expatriation of all, in New York. And he is merely a more manifest example of what *tends* to happen in all countries.

"Unrestrained industrialism, then (with its attendant evils of over-production, excessive 'wealth,' an irrelevance and lack of relation of production to consumption which it attempts vainly to overcome by the nightmare expedient of 'advertisement'), destroys the upper classes first. You cannot make an aristocrat out of a company chairman, though you can make him a peer; and in a thoroughly industrial society the only artist left will be the international film producer." Regionalism, he concluded, in its American or its Scottish form, "is something of which politicians ought to take thought, if they are capable of thinking in any terms except 'emergencies.'"

A world consolidated, standardized, grimly industrialized, obsessed by the great producer-consumer equation, managed ineffectually by feeble politicians, menaced by ideologues and political predators: that was the probable future— indeed, the present—Eliot believed; a new Toryism, better founded than the old Toryism, might yet save a society with some degree of variety and freedom and beauty. In his Commentary for July, 1931, the editor of *The Criterion* flayed J. Beaumont Pease of the British Bankers' Association and Lord Sankey, then Lord Chancellor in the MacDonald government. He was harder still upon George Bernard Shaw and the latest *Fabian Essays in Socialism;* this Commentary is a fine exercise in political wit.* Neither the platitudes and the facetiae of the Bankers' Association, nor the socialists' pompous plan ("a Ten Year Plan, perhaps") of "a model for the reconstruction of all modern societies," could redeem the time:

"What Mr. Shaw and his friends do not seem to un-

---

* Shaw, earlier that year, had informed a gathering of librarians at Letchworth that "I will remain a Communist until I die." He did not so remain.

derstand, in spite of the highly cultivated changeability of their human nature, is that the old contrast between Capitalism and Socialism is hardly going to suffice for the next forty years. It is not true that everyone will be born into the world either a little Capitalist or a little Socialist; and some persons even suspect that Socialism is merely a variant of Capitalism, or vice versa; and that the combat of Tweedledum and Tweedledee is not likely to lead to any millennium. Certainly, there are many people, and there will be more, who are seeking some alternative to both. There are many who suspect that Socialism is not radical enough, in the sense that its roots penetrate no deeper than the blue-book stratum of human nature. It seems to have moral enthusiasm without moral profundity. Mr. Shaw might know more about the changeability of human nature if he knew more about its permanence. And there are a great many hungry sheep who look up, and down, and all around them, and are not fed by the orations of Mr. Shaw, or Mr. Lansbury, any more satisfyingly than by those of Mr. Pease and Lord Sankey."[3]

At the time when these Commentaries were written, invoking a plague upon all parties, Eliot was polishing the two poems that make up *Coriolan*. He was seeking for leaders with imagination and courage—men like Maurras, perhaps (though Maurras, a most talented writer, actually was a most impractical politician); but men distinctly unlike Mussolini or Hitler—or unlike Churchill, for that matter. And more than strong leaders, Eliot was saying, the world stood in need of religious and moral principle upon which to renew the civil social order. The two poems of *Coriolan* were as far as Eliot ever proceeded to express this aspiration in verse; but years later, he would give it systematic shape in the prose of *The Idea of a Christian Society* and *Notes towards the Definition of Culture*. If *Coriolan* ever had been finished—

though some technical difficulties stood in the way—it might have exerted an influence more enduring, if more subtle, than have those two books.

Enfeebled Heroism
and Small Dusty Creatures

The past being in the present, the soldier-statesman Coriolan is both ancient and modern. Coriolan is Gaius Marcius Coriolanus, the Roman patrician of the fifth century before Christ, betrayer and savior of his people; also he is a barracks-emperor of Roman imperial times (Eliot having said that our age is analogous to the Roman decadence); also he is the tragic hero of Shakespeare, contemptuous of the rabble; also he is a Man on Horseback of the 1930's; finally he is a modern chief of state, bewildered and entangled in bureaucracy, his resignation demanded by those who cheered him yesterday.

Although *Coriolan* is not one of Eliot's more difficult poems, critical interpretations of it vary widely. The early analysis (1935) by F. O. Matthiessen probably remains the best.[4] But to mention other readings will suggest the intricacy of Eliot's thought and style: in every poem of Eliot's, even the careful reader must beware of confounding his own principles and experiences and prejudices with Eliot's.

There is the interpretation of the doctrinaire Left, which is simple and silly: this is a "Fascist poem," glorifying a successful dictator. The ironic recitation, in "Triumphal March," of the captured armaments trundled through the streets by the conqueror (the inventory being Ludendorff's list of German weapons forfeited after Versailles) is anything but celebration of militant imperialism. And, of course, Eliot had been writing against Fascism ever since 1928.

There is the interpretation of the majority of friendly critics—who, in substance, argue that Eliot is exposing the false pretensions of dictators (looking on Mussolini at the moment, and foreseeing Hitler), and is contrasting the secular pomp of the hour with the moral foundations of true authority. This is not false, but neither is it the whole truth: *Coriolan* means more than that.

There is the interpretation of a few commentators (notably D. E. S. Maxwell) that Eliot's Coriolan "is not any one earthly leader, but a transfigured version of the composite Coriolanus in *The Waste Land* . . ."; perhaps "he represents even the law of God," and is related to "the common idea of Christ as the light of the world . . ."[5] If "Triumphal March" stood solitary, this surmise might be tenable; but it is undone by the leader's frustration in "Difficulties of a Statesman."

Yet *Coriolan* has more contrived corridors than these several interpretations allow. Eliot gave some account of what he had meant the poem to become, had he ever finished it: the central character would be Cyril (a little boy in "Triumphal March," a young telephone operator in "Difficulties of a Statesman"), in whose person would be represented the obscure citizen, perceiving only dimly the public events (let alone their significance) of his time—swept along by the currents of ego and circumstance, a passive observer of tremendous happenings. This intention raised difficulties for the poet quite as perplexing as the difficulties of the statesman: for how could Eliot's perceptions of reality be made known through the eyes or voice or mind of a young Cockney? (Similar problems with Sweeney as a medium may have discouraged Eliot from completing *Sweeney Agonistes*.) That obstacle to expression, combining with Eliot's months in America during 1932 and 1933, presumably sufficed to terminate *Coriolan* after only two parts had been written.

As I understand it, this poem is neither a deification of the Leader, nor yet a denunciation of strong leadership. It contains some mockery of the vainglorious great captain, and also a reproach against the shallow and passive multitude. It is an appeal to true principles of public order, rooted in religion and in historical consciousness, against ideology, against the cult of personality, against the indifference or irresponsibility of the crowd, against the "servile state" described by Hilaire Belloc, and against captivity to a moment in time. Eliot is saying, in part, what Yeats had said a decade earlier, in "The Leaders of the Crowd":

> They have loud music, hope every day renewed
>
> And heartier loves; that lamp is from the tomb.

The image of Coriolan had occurred twice before in Eliot's poetry: in "A Cooking Egg" (1920), where Coriolanus, Sir Philip Sidney, and "other heroes of that kidney" enjoy honor in Heaven; and in *The Waste Land,* where "a broken Coriolanus" is revived by aethereal rumors at nightfall—an heroic exemplar who momentarily liberates the disheartened from the prison of self. Coriolan of "Triumphal March" has the hero's mien:

> There is no interrogation in his eyes
>
> Or in the hands, quiet over the horse's neck,
>
> And the eyes watchful, waiting, perceiving, indifferent.

This is no political charlatan; and the final line of the poem, taken from a passage by Maurras, suggests his power.

This is Shakespeare's Coriolanus, resolved not to tolerate the mob's plundering of public stores, a corruption of Roman virtue by Greek example:

> Though there the people had more absolute power,
>
> I say, they nourish'd disobedience, fed
>
> The ruin of the state.

> Let deeds express
>
> What's like to be their words:—"We did request it;
>
> We are the greater poll, and in true fear
>
> They gave us our demands":—Thus we debase

The nature of our seats, and make the rabble
Call our cares, fears: which will in time
Break ope the locks o' the senate, and bring in
The crows to peck the eagles.

The degradation of the democratic dogma has made
necessary the ascendancy of Coriolan: the crowd that admires his spoils and his trumpets and his eagles is out to make
a Roman holiday—a modern mob after the old Roman fashion, thoughtless and fickle, greedy and ignorant. Whatever
Coriolan may perceive of a moral order, "under the palmtree
at noon, under the running water"—why, the crowd perceives nothing of that sort. Interested in sausages and crum-
pets, the crowd goes to church only when it cannot get to
the country; and young Cyril mistakes the bell during the
Eucharist for a costermonger's tinkle. Cyril's parents ask for
a light—for a cigarette; but the Light they need is of another order. What wonder that the soldiers form ranks, face
to face, shutting off Coriolan from view?

The Roman crowd betrayed Coriolanus, and in turn
Coriolanus betrayed them—though in the end, at his mother's
urging, he went to his ruin for the sake of the republic.
Upon what popular support can a modern Coriolanus rely?
In his triumphal procession there march feeble adherents
—the Scouts, the gymnastic society, the "golf club Captains."* Legitimate authority is of God, "hidden under the
dove's wing, hidden in the turtle's breast": that authority

---

* These "golf club Captains" are such gentlemen as Mr. J. Beaumont
Pease, "the presiding sprite" of the British Bankers' Association dinner
at the Fishmongers' Hall, whose "exhibition of penguin frigidity" was
described by Eliot in his *Criterion* Commentary of July, 1931. In a
footnote, Eliot informed his readers that "Mr. Beaumont Pease has
recently been elected to the captaincy of the Royal & Ancient Golf
Club of St. Andrews. He is also captain of the Royal St. George's Golf
Club, and therefore will hold the two offices concurrently, a distinction
only achieved previously, I believe, by Lord Forster and Captain Angus
V. Hambro. Mr. Pease is also, I believe, distantly connected with
Andrew Marvell."

lacking, Coriolan must rest uneasy, despite his "5,800,000 rifles and carbines."

Young Cyril's prospects are dim, though "he's artful." His view of the triumphal march has been imperfect; and the sacrifice at the temple, where the maidens bore urns containing the dust of antiquity, has meant nothing to him. Some years later, Arthur Edward Cyril Parker will be a telephone operator, at a maximum salary of two pounds ten a week, with a bonus of thirty shillings at Christmas— and one week's leave a year. (Eliot himself, in London, had two weeks' leave to begin with, and three weeks in later years.) Cyril will be a proletarian in the Roman meaning of that ugly word, giving to the commonwealth nothing but his body and his progeny. He will have a ballot, of course, but he will employ it to no good purpose.

And what of Coriolan's prospects? Those difficulties of a statesman descend upon him: he discovers that truly, as Isaiah proclaimed, "All flesh is grass." He is submerged in committees and commissions: the funds must go for rebuilding the fortifications. There will be held a conference about peace, with a commission from the Volscians; but at that disagreeable possibility of disarmament, the armorers appoint their own committee to protest against the reduction of orders. The peace is an unquiet lull between disasters, the croaking frogs and the fireflies of the Pontine marshes being most ominous. "What shall I cry?" Ancestral busts, thick-necked in their high old Roman virtue, do not answer him: the file affords no precedent. He is deathly tired. For solace and counsel, perhaps, his mother's ghost may come to him "with the sweep of the little bat's wing . . ." Small dusty creatures importune him. "What shall I cry?" And the voice of the leaders of the crowd is heard, demanding an investigation: "RESIGN RESIGN RESIGN."*

---

* In 1931, that demand was being pressed upon Ramsay MacDonald by the radical wing of his party. Baldwin's resignation as Conservative

"Very subtly, and entirely in poetic image and association, Eliot contrasts a world structure focussed finally on the visible Hero as the centre of a vast organization of force, with that hidden point which is the central light of another world," Elizabeth Drew says of *Coriolan*.[6] The spirit of Virgil broods over this poem; and perhaps there occurs an echo of Cicero—who inquired whether men or laws had failed the Republic, and answered that, corrupted and corrupting, the two had sunk together. "At the still point of the turning world" may be found abiding wisdom and justice. But People and Leader, prisoners of time and ego, do not perceive that still point.

A civilization deserves the Coriolans by whom the people are led—perhaps to the slaughter. A democracy of appetites soon has a dictator crammed down its throat. When the state is expected to do all things, soon its interminable committees do nothing tolerable; and even the strong man at the summit is dragged down by the unwieldy system. He falls —and is supplanted by another of the same stamp.

For a commonwealth, Eliot is saying, endures in order and justice and freedom only so long as it is united by love.

---

leader was demanded by a faction, too, in the national financial crisis and during the controversy over Indian reform. It may be noted that Eliot exempted Stanley Baldwin from his list of wretched political rhetoricians whose policies reflected their language: Baldwin might possess no high imagination, but he was an honest man who spoke well, and his adversaries were Eliot's adversaries. Winston Churchill had resigned from the Conservatives' shadow-cabinet when a "naked fakir," Mahatma Gandhi, was permitted to negotiate with the Indian Viceroy. Baldwin's leadership was in peril then; but he recovered by a speech as forthright as that by which he had overthrown Lloyd George. At Queen's Hall, Westminster, in March, 1931, he replied to the "insolent plutocracy" that had intended to undo him. Paraphrasing Disraeli, he struck out at the press lords, Beaverbrook and Rothermere, who had defamed him in their papers: "What the proprietorship of these papers is aiming at is power, and power without responsibility, the prerogative of the harlot throughout the ages." For those words, Eliot could forgive Baldwin many deficiencies. See G. M. Young, *Stanley Baldwin* (1952), pp. 157–163.

The alternative to the aristocrat is the oligarch; the alternative to a democracy with limits is tyranny unlimited. Thou shalt love the Lord thy God with all thy heart and soul, and thy neighbor as thyself: upon this commandment is true community founded. That forgotten, ruled and rulers betray one another—and worse than Coriolan will be raised up.

These are the political premises not of Mussolini or Maurras or Hitler or Stalin, or of the party leaders then contending for office in befuddled Britain; but they are the premises of Johnson and Burke and Coleridge. In his *Criterion* Commentary of October, 1931, Eliot drubbed both the materialistic socialism of Harold Laski and the materialistic conservatism of Lord Lymington (who would have expelled the bishops from the House of Lords).

"Unless Toryism maintains a definite and uncompromising theory of Church and State," Eliot wrote, "Toryism is merely a fasces of experiments." The thread of Toryism had run through the inarticulate and instinctive; practical Toryism has to be invented. "Lord Lymington, like Mr. Laski, wants a state in which government shall be designed for the happiness of the governed; but as alternatives to Communism, both outlines seem to me drearily incapable of arousing enthusiasm." British criticism of the Soviet experiment had been founded on the argument that Communism was not succeeding materially. But suppose that the Soviet government should succeed, after all?

"What matters is not whether they have carried out the programme of Marx, or whether they have betrayed it, or whether they have improved upon it; the point is that their philosophy is equally repugnant whether it fails or succeeds. And we can only oppose it with another which shall be correspondingly dear to us whether it succeeds or fails. The Bolsheviks at any rate believe in something which has what is equivalent for them to a supernatural sanction: and it is only with a genuine supernatural sanction that we can oppose it. . . . The theory of nationalism, as advanced in Italy, is not good enough; it becomes both artificial and ridiculous. . . . The only hope is in a Toryism which, though not necessarily distinct for Parliamentary purposes, should refuse to identify itself philosophically with that 'Conservatism' which has been overrun first by deserters from Whiggism and later by business men. And for such a Toryism not only a doctrine of the relation of the temporal and spiritual in matters of Church and State is essential, but even a religious foundation for the whole of its political philosophy. Nothing less can engage enough respect to be a worthy adversary for Communism."[7]

Those are Eliot's principles of social order reflected—or perhaps best expressed—in *Coriolan*. Eliot had an air of writing *ex cathedra*, doubtless: it was not necessary for him to make compromises, but practical politicians could not hold office long in the British democracy without a multitude of concessions to the appetites and the opinions of the moment. Yet the theorist and the essayist detached from party have their duties, not identical with those of the practical politician. Specific remedies, as expressed in parliamentary bills, Eliot did not offer, then or later. Specific remedies were the business of the political economist and the master of diplomacy. Until the practical politicians should wake to awareness of an enduring moral order, Eliot believed, their specifics would cure no social affliction.

His labor was diagnosis. But in Britain and America, general ideas seem to require about three decades, after being expressed in such a publication as *The Criterion*, before they are accepted (if ever accepted at all) and given effect by popular opinion. The filtering of theorists' notions is slow, and that has helped to insulate Britain and America against ideological rashness; also, on occasion, that deliberateness has permitted mischief to be worked. Some fifteen months after Eliot wrote his final Commentary for 1931, Hitler became Chancellor of Germany. "But how many eagles! And how many trumpets!"

No Man Is Saved by Poetry

Probably Eliot would not have completed *Coriolan*, even had he refused Harvard University's invitation to be Charles Eliot Norton Professor of Poetry during the academic year of 1932–33. He accepted the invitation; one of his motives may have been that London life with Vivienne was growing unendurable. In any event, these months in America—the first time he had set foot in the United States since 1914—interrupted his train of thought; while after his return to England, first sorrow and then new literary interests gave the quietus to what, conceivably, might have become a long poem equal to *The Waste Land* or *Ash-Wednesday* or *Four Quartets*.

His *Selected Essays, 1917–1932*, were published simultaneously in England (three thousand copies) and in America (thirty-seven hundred copies) just about the time when Eliot arrived at Harvard. That collection has gone through many printings since then; it has become the most influential volume of criticism of the century. Included in it were much from *The Sacred Wood* (1920), the whole of *Homage to John Dryden* (1924), *Shakespeare and the Stoicism of Seneca* (1927), most of *For Lancelot Andrewes* (1928), his *Dante* (1929), *Thoughts after Lambeth* (1931), his English Association pamphlet on Charles Whibley (1931), and a few of his better periodical essays previously uncollected: thirty-three long critical essays, in all. Many good pieces he omitted—perhaps only for lack of space, this being a fat book already; several people, including myself, have been sorry that he did not include in this volume, or in any later collection, his preface to an edition of Samuel Johnson's *London* and *The Vanity of Human Wishes,* published in 1930. However that may be, his *Select Essays* have Johnsonian strength and authority.

That is less true of his Harvard lectures, published in 1933 as *The Use of Poetry and the Use of Criticism* (twenty-five hundred copies in Faber & Faber's printing, fifteen hundred in the printing of the Harvard University Press). In his preface to the first edition, Eliot apologizes that at Harvard, such success as his lectures had "was largely dramatic"; but in his preface to the second edition (1964), he thinks better of these lecture essays, and hopes that some of them may be printed in new anthologies, as relief from his "Tradition and the Individual Talent"— the darling of every Eliot anthologist, as "The Lake Isle of Innisfree" has been included (though scarcely representative) by every anthologist seeking a specimen of Yeats.

These Harvard lectures surely remain worth printing in anthologies; yet, in general, these essays on Sidney, Dryden, Wordsworth and Coleridge, Shelley and Keats, and Matthew Arnold are not Eliot at his strongest. He cast them in sequence as a loose historical survey—a method not congenial to him. The assurance and bite of *The Sacred Wood* are diminished; Eliot professes some shame at his early enthusiasm—although he does not repudiate his principles of "Tradition and the Individual Talent." He examines Coleridge's distinction between "imagination" and "fancy"; but his treatment of that interesting subject, despite some memorable suggestions of his own, remains incomplete. (It does, however, furnish information about the way in which early observation and reading fed Eliot's later poetic imagination.) Often discouragement may be read between the lines of these lectures.

Possibly Eliot was asking himself, just then, whether the criticism of poetry was the way in which he ought to be spending his time in the year 1932. In his introduction and in his lecture on Arnold, he quotes a kindred mind—that of Charles Eliot Norton; and not Norton on poetry, but Norton on the state of society. In 1869, the future of Europe had been dark: "I wonder whether our civilization can maintain itself against the forces which are banding together for the destruction of many of the institutions in which it is embodied, or whether we are not to have another period of decline, fall, and ruin and revival, like that of the first thirteen hundred years of our era," Norton had written. To Leslie Stephen, in 1896, Norton had commented: "The rise of the democracy to power in America and Europe is not, as has been hoped, to be a safeguard of peace and civilization. It is a rise of the uncivilized, whom no school education can suffice to provide with intelligence and reason. It looks as if the world were entering upon a new stage of experience, unlike anything heretofore, in which there must be a new discipline of suffering to fit men for the new condition."

A few days after Eliot delivered his first Norton lecture, Franklin Delano Roosevelt (steadily disliked and distrusted by Eliot) was elected president of the United States. Before the fifth lecture was delivered, Adolf Hitler had made himself chancellor of Germany. Eliot's private preoccupation during those months was with political questions; and though Dryden and Wordsworth and Coleridge and Shelley touched on the principles of politics, still Eliot's attention was distracted. His *Criterion* Commentary of January, 1932, had been an essay in economics; that of April had been an attack on Communism, Nationalism, and "the mystical belief in herd-feeling"; the Commentary of July, before he sailed for America, had discussed the degrading of literature by Communism and other ideologies. In his introductory lecture, Eliot praised Norton for having been able "even at an early age, to look upon the passing order without regret, and towards the coming order without hope." Doubtless Eliot wished that he might muster resignation enough to do as much in his own time.

These Harvard lectures contain, besides, several strong hints that Eliot thought his own literary gifts might be failing. He had been unable to finish *Coriolan:* now he thought of Coleridge, "drugged by metaphysics." From metaphysics, true, Eliot had emancipated himself before his first poems were published—but not from burning concern with politics. "It was better for Coleridge, as poet, to read books of travel and exploration than to read books of metaphysics and political economy"—even though Coleridge genuinely wished to read the latter sort of book. The Muse had visited Coleridge (in his instance, this being no mere hackneyed metaphor), and thereafter Coleridge was a haunted man and a ruined man. So Eliot thought of himself: the implication is clear enough. "Sometimes, however, to be a 'ruined man' is itself a vocation."[8]

He saw something of himself in Wordsworth, too, one gathers: "Those who speak of Wordsworth as the original Lost Leader . . . should make pause and consider that when a man takes politics and social affairs seriously the difference between revolution and reaction may be by the breadth of a hair, and that Wordsworth may possibly have been no renegade but a man who thought, so far as he thought at all, for himself. But it is Wordsworth's social interest that inspires his own novelty of form in verse, and backs up his explicit remarks upon poetic diction; and it is really this social interest which (consciously or not) the fuss was all about."[9]

Eliot knew that he was undertaking, as best he could, the task at which Coleridge and Wordsworth had succeeded (so far as there can be practical influence by a poet upon his own time): "a profound spiritual revival." Yet those Romantic poets' attachment to questions of faith and of social order had been the undoing of their poetic talents. Upon Eliot, the state of society, by 1932, weighed terribly; what he could do to redeem the time, he must do; he was not doing it in these lectures, and he had begun to wonder whether he ever would find time or imagination again to write anything comparable to "Gerontion" or "The Hollow Men," let alone his longer poems. This dread glowers out of the concluding sentences of his final lecture (March 31, 1933). In those lectures he had trespassed too far beyond his proper frontier, Eliot said: "If, as James Thomson observed, 'lips only sing when they cannot kiss,' it may be also that poets only talk when they cannot sing. I am content to leave my theorizing about poetry at this point. The sad ghost of Coleridge beckons to me from the shadows."[10]

Except for "Dejection: an Ode," all of Coleridge's important poetry had been written during a brief period early in his life; after that enthusiastic time had come "the long dissipation and stupefaction of his powers in transcendental metaphysics." Eliot's powers as a poet might be swallowed up by political necessity. But there is a double meaning—as Frank Morley suggests—to this evocation of the sad ghost of Coleridge. The marriage of Coleridge with Sarah Fricker —ill sorted, those two, from the first—had been a disaster: they had lived together only fifteen years, and Coleridge had seen as little as he might of his wife after the first nine years; later in life, though nominally still man and wife, they never met.

Eliot's marriage, by 1933, had endured (in spite of suffering on either side) for eighteen years; now parting was at hand. To another sort of man, this would have been an order of release; to Eliot, even though he had experienced and written *Ash-Wednesday*, it was death's dream kingdom. This weight hung upon him as he lectured at Harvard.

The most important aspect of these lectures is Eliot's argument that poetry cannot become a substitute for religion. In the time of Wordsworth and Coleridge and Shelley and Keats, "the decay of religion, and the attrition of political institutions, left dubious frontiers upon which the poet encroached." Those debatable lands still are ravaged by the heretics of poetry-as-religion, and there remain people "who imagine that they draw religious aliment from Browning or Meredith."[11] Into this delusion fell Matthew Arnold—as Eliot already had written elsewhere. In his lecture on "The Modern Mind," Eliot gave the subject his most systematic treatment.

Although Eliot had become the most admired Christian poet of his age, finding his way to that faith with much travail, he agreed with Jacques Maritain's declaration that "It is a deadly error to expect poetry to provide the super-substantial nourishment of man." By "deadly" error, Maritain (in his *Art and Scholasticism*) meant, quite truly, damning error. Faith may suffuse poetry; a poem may lead men toward faith; but verse is not theology, and poetic sentiments cannot do duty for belief and religious knowledge.* Poetry expresses many things, and it may express religious insights; yet it is as foolish to say that "Poetry teaches us" certain

---

* In this, as in so much else, Eliot is the disciple or the coadjutor of Samuel Johnson. Consider the following passage from Johnson's "Edmund Waller," in his *Lives of the Poets:*

"Let no pious ear be offended if I advance, in opposition to many authorities, that poetical devotion cannot often please. The doctrines of religion may indeed be defended in a didactic poem; and he who has the happy power of arguing in verse will not lose it because his subject is sacred. A poet may describe the beauty and the grandeur of Nature, the flowers of the spring and the harvest of autumn, the vicissitudes of the tide and the revolutions of the sky, and praise the Maker for his works, in lines which no reader shall lay aside. The subject of the disputation is not piety, but the motives to piety; that of the description is not God, but the works of God.

"Contemplative piety, or the intercourse between God and the human soul, cannot be poetical. Man, admitted to implore the mercy of his Creator, and plead the merits of his Redeemer, is already in a higher state than poetry can confer."

ultimate truths as it has been to say that "Science teaches us" such permanent things. One encounters many poets and many scientists, and they do not teach with a single voice: "Any theory which relates poetry very closely to a religious or a social scheme of things aims, probably, to *explain poetry* by discovering its natural laws; but it is in danger of *binding* poetry by legislation to be observed—and poetry can recognize no such laws."[12]

In I. A. Richards, Eliot encountered "a modern emotional attitude" akin to that of Bertrand Russell in *A Free Man's Worship* (which Eliot had reviewed in *The Criterion*). Richards' attitude toward poetry was that of "intense religious seriousness"; but Richards was proposing a regimen of spiritual exercises for a pagan world, with poetry as a new Holy Writ; Richards wrote that "poetry is capable of saving us." Some critics have objected to Eliot's interpretation of Richards' views on such matters; but perhaps they miss the point that Eliot deliberately was caricaturing the analysis of a fellow-critic with whom he always was on friendly terms; in the 1964 edition of this book, Eliot found no reason to modify his remarks on Richards.

By Richards, poetry would be employed to alleviate modern man's loneliness; to reconcile him to the facts of birth and death, "in their inexplicable oddity" (Richards' phrase); to console him for "the inconceivable immensity of the Universe"; to show him his place in the perspective of time; to diminish the "enormity" (Richards' word) of man's ignorance. But poetry cannot properly accomplish any of these ends, Eliot replied—just as pure metaphysics cannot. (Eliot might have noted, though he does not mention it, the similarity between Richards' aspiration for Poetry and Sir Robert Peel's aspiration for Science—"a consolation in death," and much more—expressed by Peel in his speech at the Tamworth Reading Room; Eliot replies to Richards as Newman answered Peel in 1841.)

Loneliness? "In what sense is Man in general isolated, and from what?" How can one conceive of an "isolation" that is "not a separation from anything in particular?" There is isolation as described by Diotima, in Plato, and there is "the Christian sense of the separation of Man from God." But Richards does not have Plato and Christ in mind; so he would have poetry fill a vacuum that he cannot bound.

Inexplicably odd facts of birth and death? Poetry does not alter those: "I cannot see why the facts of birth and death should appear odd in themselves," Eliot commented in his terse smiling way, "unless we have a conception of some other way of coming into the world and of leaving it, which strikes us as more natural."

The immensity of the universe? Why, Pascal was terrified not by the immense spaces, but by their eternal silence. That silence can be understood only by those who possess a religious sense. And is not vast space, like the vastness of an ocean, insignificant enough for a living man?

The perspective of time? That question certainly had roused Eliot's imagination often, and he would attain his best expression of time and the timeless in his *Four Quartets*. But this inquiry is unedifying, unless one believes that human history has meaning—and that meaning, Eliot implied, cannot be derived from pure poetry. "I fear that in many people this subject of meditation can only stimulate the idle wonder and greed for facts which are satisfied by Mr. Wells's compendia."

The enormousness of man's ignorance? Ignorance of *what*? And what definite information can the whole body of poetry give? Poetry is not right reason, although right reason may be acquired by the poet. If people like second-rate poetry, will that make them wise?

Richards was engaged in "a rear-guard religious action," after the fashion of Julian Huxley—and of one greater than Huxley, Immanuel Kant—Eliot wrote: Richards sought to "preserve emotions without the beliefs with which their history has been involved."[13] Poetry may preserve emotion—for a time; yet poetry cannot convert emotion into a substitute for wisdom. The force of this judgment was the greater because Eliot himself, more than any other poet of his age, had reinvigorated the moral imagination, and had expressed in poetry an experience of transcendence.

Richards maintained, in effect, that art is the savior; Leon Trotsky, in *Literature and Revolution,* maintained that art is the handmaiden of social environment. Art should be neither, Eliot insisted. But as things are moving, "we may expect to find quite different literatures existing in the same language and the same country," produced by fallacies about the functions of poetry and of criticism.[14] One powerful form of this new literature, as Maritain had suggested, is the diabolical. Since Eliot wrote, the literature of abnormity has become a major branch of publishing. That is what happens to literature when it is severed from the moral imagination and from religious understanding, Eliot wrote repeatedly: the writer discovers the perverse.

Eliot saw a few familiar faces at Harvard, but the America to which he had returned briefly was alien to him. His parents were dead; Eliot had not seen them since he went abroad in 1914, though he had dedicated *For Lancelot Andrewes* to his mother; true, he had sisters living in New England, and would visit them from time to time, in later years. But with the triumph of Franklin Roosevelt, American society would move in a direction abhorrent to him—another step in the progress that had commenced in 1829. He went home to England in June, 1933; yet even there he had no home.

For he did not return to his wife in London: like the Hyacinth Girl, Vivienne Eliot could be to him now only a forlorn memory—or, beyond time, in some manner the Lady of *Ash-Wednesday.* Hysterical psychosis had mastered Vivienne; friends and relations would look after her; she would be confined to a nursing-home; she would live, unknowable, until 1947. Eliot now entered a solitude for which incessant work was a palliative.

For the time being, he went to the Morleys at Pike's Farm. There—all alone for three weeks of the summer, and feeling "as if he had come to pieces, and at the same time . . . standing in the road inspecting the parts, and wondering what sort of machine it will make if he can put it together again"—Eliot remained until November, when he made a trip with friends to Scotland. After Christmas, he took lodgings in London, where he could be near to the theater. At Pike's Farm, that summer—while he did chores and learned to bake bread—he had begun to write the choruses of *The Rock*.[15]

The years of "the haggard and exhausted mask" were settling upon Eliot. There is Wyndham Lewis' description: "Appearing at one's front door, or arriving at a dinner-rendezvous . . . his face would be haggard, he would seem at last gasp. . . . However, when he had taken his place at a table, given his face a dry wash with his hands, and having had a little refreshment, Mr. Eliot would rapidly shed all resemblance to the harassed and exhausted refugee, in flight from some Scourge of God. Apparently a modest reserve of power, prudently set aside, would be drawn on."[16]

During his months at Harvard, in 1932 and 1933, Eliot may have feared that he had exhausted his reserves of poetic and critical talent. Yet less than a year after his return to England, he would publish the choruses of *The Rock*—a successful application, in verse, of Christian teaching to the troubles of the time. This was the commencement of a whole new field for him: the drama. He was tired, in 1933; yet more than half his accomplishment as man of letters and as critic of society was still to come.

Claims of Strange Gods

Eliot's expedition to America resulted in a second book: his
Page-Barbour Lectures at Charlottesville in 1933, published
early in 1934 as *After Strange Gods: a Primer of Modern
Heresy* (three thousand copies of the London edition, fifteen
hundred of the New York edition). This long essay, now
difficult to obtain, never was reprinted—Eliot being discouraged, it appears, by hostile criticism. One finds it mentioned, here and there, as a prop of bigotry. But today
the reader of *After Strange Gods* may find that the little
book can be more sympathetically understood in the 'seven-
ties than it was in the 'thirties.

A few sentences—really an aside—in the first of these
lectures account for most of the denunciation of the book
by liberals and radicals. Eliot had expressed his sympathy
with the Southern Agrarians and his hope that Virginia
might be able to preserve or restore her own culture better
than had his ancestral New England. For tradition to endure,
he wrote, stability is necessary:

"You are hardly likely to develop tradition except where
the bulk of the population is relatively so well off where it
is that it has no incentive or pressure to move about. The
population should be homogeneous; where two or more
cultures exist in the same place they are likely to be fiercely
self-conscious or both to become adulterate." (Or else, he
added in a footnote, a caste system would develop, very
different from classes, "which pre-suppose homogeneity of
race and a fundamental equality"; doubtless this is a veiled
reference to the condition of the Negro in the South.)
"What is still more important is unity of religious background;
and reasons of race and religion combine to make any large

number of free-thinking Jews undesirable. There must be a proper balance between urban and rural, industrial and agricultural development. And a spirit of excessive toleration is to be deprecated. We must also remember that—in spite of every means of transport that can be devised—the local community must always be the most permanent, and that the concept of the nation is by no means fixed and invariable."[17]

What later happened to the Jews of Germany and central Europe was to make Eliot a target for those zealous to hunt down "anti-Semites." But, as Eliot told newspaper reporters, he could not be anti-Semitic, because he was a Christian. Eliot said to William Turner Levy, years later: "I am grieved and sometimes angered by this matter. . . . I am not an anti-Semite and never have been. It seems to me unfortunate that persons give that odious term such a broad and ill-defined definition. American Jews are sensitive in a way you never find is true of their counterparts in England, although I can realize that there are several reasons for this." Those who so slandered him, he said, "do not know, as you and I do, that in the eyes of the Church, to be anti-Semitic is a sin."[18]

"Bleistein with a Cigar" and other unattractive characters with Jewish names, here and there in Eliot's poems, do suggest some prejudice against Jews—or rather, against "free-thinking Jews," secularized and adrift between two worlds. (One thinks of Samuel Johnson's observation that when a Catholic falls away, he falls into nothing; so Eliot looked upon the Jew who had forsaken Moses, but who had not forgotten the Golden Calf.) These allusions in the poems, nevertheless, employ the Jew as a symbol of a crass commercialism: a convention of English literature, from Marlowe to Dickens and later, but unhappily encountered in many writers of the 1920's and 1930's. Anti-Jewish feeling is much less conspicuous in Eliot's work than it is in the writings

of Chesterton and Belloc, say; for that matter, one encounters such denigratory expressions, used almost unconsciously,
in the correspondence of writers so liberal as Bertrand Russell.
All this would change, especially in Eliot, when the doom
of the Jews under the Nazis transformed literary suspicion
into horror and compassion.

Sir Herbert Read writes that Eliot never used anti-Jewish
expressions in his conversation, to his knowledge; everyone
suffers from a certain xenophobia, however: "It is an in-
stinct that the educated man controls or eradicates, and in
this respect Eliot was as controlled as the best of us."[19] For
all that, Eliot's sorrow at "the shame of motives late revealed,
and the awareness of things ill done and done to others'
harm," in "Little Gidding," probably reflects—as some critics
have suggested—remorse at having set down, in his early
writings, phrases of prejudice. He was harshly—but tardily—
attacked for such occasional early expressions by some writers
who may have entertained their own prejudices—if not the
same sort of prejudices, precisely.*

* With his accustomed candor, George Orwell took up this accusation
in a letter to Julian Symonds (29 October 1948). F. R. Fyvel, a friend
of Orwell's, and then literary editor of *Tribune,* had revived charges
of "anti-Semitism" against Eliot, at a very late date. "It is nonsense
what Fyvel said about Eliot being antisemitic," Orwell wrote. "Of
course you can find what would now be called antisemitic remarks in
his early work, but who didn't say such things at that time? One has to
draw a distinction between what was said before and what after 1934.
Of course all these nationalistic prejudices are ridiculous, but disliking
Jews isn't intrinsically worse than disliking Negroes or Americans or
any other block of people. In the early 'twenties, Eliot's antisemitic
remarks were about on a par with the automatic sneer one casts at
Anglo-Indian colonels in boarding houses. On the other hand if they
had been written after the persecutions began they would have meant
something quite different. . . . Some people go round smelling after
antisemitism all the time." See *The Collected Essays, Journalism and
Letters of George Orwell,* Vol. IV, p. 450.
   What with the anti-Jewish virulence of Hitler and his supporters
in the early 'thirties, nevertheless, Eliot was strangely insensitive to
the drift of affairs when he referred slightingly to "free-thinking Jews"
in *After Strange Gods.*

Those who read *After Strange Gods* unaffected by the prejudices of ideology should find this essay courageous and lively. "In a society like ours, worm-eaten with Liberalism," Eliot writes in his preface, "the only thing possible for a person with strong convictions is to state a point of view and leave it at that." He refuses to submit to the doctrine of economic determinism: good traditions may be regained, if they are what people desire. These lectures are a vindication of tradition and orthodoxy against innovation and heresy.

Genuine tradition is not hostile to all change; and it should not be accepted unexamined. "Nor should we cling to traditions as a way of asserting our superiority over less favored peoples. What we can do is to use our minds, remembering that a tradition without intelligence is not worth having, to discover what is the best life for us not as a political abstraction, but as a particular people in a particular place; what in the past is worth preserving and what should be rejected; and what conditions, within our power to bring about, would foster the society that we desire."[20]

Eliot stood firm on the ground he had taken in "Tradition and the Individual Talent"; but he now discouraged too rigorous classification of writers as "classical" or "romantic," and he pointed out that his own principles of catholicism, royalism, and classicism were not to be taken as peers: religious faith had primacy. A tradition is "a way of feeling and acting," often unconscious; while orthodoxy requires the exercise of conscious intelligence. The writer ought not to yield to the seductions of "individuality"; it is disastrous when readers "cherish the author of genius, not in spite of his deviations from the inherited wisdom of the race, but because of them."[21]

His "Strange Gods" are the clay-footed idols of certain modern authors. (The most ethically orthodox of writers, Eliot says, in this century, is James Joyce.) These literary

ELIOT AND HIS AGE

heresies generally are products of latter-day Protestantism.* The vague "hymn-singing pietism" of Lawrence's mother did not help her son; and Eliot's teacher Irving Babbitt had been prejudiced against Christianity by lacking emotional acquaintance "with any but some debased and uncultured form" of that faith.[22]

To search for theological and ethical guidance outside one's own cultural tradition often leads literary people into confusion: it has been so with Babbitt, Lawrence, Pound, and (in his earlier phase) Yeats. What does most mischief is the loss of the sense of Original Sin: this gone, the characters of literature become less real. "If you do away with this struggle, and maintain that by tolerance, benevolence, inoffensiveness, and a redistribution or increase of purchasing power, combined with a devotion, on the part of an élite, to Art, the world will be as good as anyone could require, then you must expect human beings to become more and more vaporous." So it is with Ezra Pound's concept of Hell, "a hell for the *other people*, the people we read about in the newspapers, not for oneself and one's friends."[23]

In his concluding lecture, Eliot discussed heresy—fanatic belief in one isolated truth—and exposure to the diabolic influence. Orthodoxy (that is, acceptance of what mankind has learnt from revelations, from the insights of genius, and from historic experience) nourishes the moral imagination; but heresy may lead a writer beyond the idyllic imagination to the diabolic imagination.

It is not blasphemy that afflicts modern man: "Where blasphemy might once have been a sign of spiritual corruption, it might now be taken rather as a symptom that the soul is still alive, or even that it is recovering animation:

---

* Like Chesterton earlier, Eliot points out that the heretic is not an unbeliever (far from it) but rather a man who emphasizes some point of doctrine too strongly and obsessively.

for the perception of Good and Evil—whatever choice we may make—is the first requisite of spiritual life."[24] No, the curse of modern novelists is obsession with "their own *personal view of life*"—the cult of *personality*. Thomas Hardy wrote for self-expression, and wrote well; he used man as a vehicle for emotion only, scorning reason. *The Mayor of Casterbridge* is "a refined form of torture on the part of the writer, and a refined form of self-torture on the part of the reader." Hardy's story "Barbara of the House of Grebe" introduces us to a world of pure evil, "solely to provide a satisfaction for some morbid emotion."

For a positive power for evil may work through men of genius whose private character is good enough. D. H. Lawrence, emancipated from tradition and institutions, incapable of self-criticism, was unable to discriminate between spiritual forces for good and spiritual forces for evil: "The man's vision is spiritual, but spiritually sick." Lawrence tells us not to reconcile ourselves to Liberalism, Progress, and Modern Civilization; Eliot happens to hold the same conviction, but for different reasons: "It matters a good deal in what name we condemn . . ."* Despite his genius, Lawrence appeals not to the discriminating, but "to the sick and debile and confused," increasing their affliction.

Eliot's use of the word "heresy" was not hyperbolical.

* A very different interpretation of *The Mayor of Casterbridge*, however, is offered by a Southern writer of the school praised by Eliot in *After Strange Gods:* Donald Davidson. See the essays "The Traditional Basis of Thomas Hardy's Fiction" and "Futurism and Archaism in Toynbee and Hardy" in Davidson's *Still Rebels, Still Yankees, and Other Essays* (1957). "Like Swift in 'A Modest Proposal,'" Davidson writes, "Hardy reveals the false pretensions of modernism by dramatizing its logical extreme. Henchard's will is the parallel, in prose fiction, of the heap of broken images in T. S. Eliot's *The Waste Land*."

Eliot himself had published some of Lawrence's fiction that has its "capering redskins" who "seem to represent Life. So they do; but that is not the last word, only the first." For Lawrence's "The Woman Who Rode Away" first appeared, in two parts, in *The Criterion* for July, 1925, and for January, 1926.

For Lawrence truly was a heretic, Eliseo Vivas remarks, because Lawrence denied Christ. "Lawrence denied Him, and he denied Him because he hated Him," Vivas writes in his close analysis. "To acknowledge Him would have meant acknowledging the role of love—not eros but agape—in our Western world. And to make this acknowledgement would have involved a repudiation of his deepest feelings, his radical alienation and his radical misanthropy."[25]

If one denies the divine incarnation, Eliot believed, one must affirm a different though inferior power. The diabolical enters into literature, and into society, when we grow fascinated with "the *unregenerate* personality, partly self-deceived and partly irresponsible, and because of its freedom, terribly *limited* by prejudice and self-conceit, capable of much good or great mischief according to the natural goodness or impurity of the man; and we are all, naturally, impure." Such was the influence of the modern heretic in literature. We need to repair, Eliot concluded, to those standards of criticism which distinguish between "the permanent and the temporary, the essential and the accidental."[26]

As Eliot lectured in America, such an unregenerate personality rose to power in Germany. And ideology, rushing in to fill the vacuum created by the loss of tradition and orthodoxy, would demonstrate through its operation upon society those ancient hard truths which the ideologue denied.

While Eliot was at Harvard and Charlottesville, many pages of The Criterion were addressed to ideology—but to discussions of Communism and Fascism, rather than the ideology (or ideology in embryo) of National Socialism, for as yet the character of Hitler's domination was not fully visible. During this period, the defense of tradition and orthodoxy was conducted chiefly by the editor himself, who throughout his years of editorship stood in opposition to the political and economic interests that dominated Britain and the West generally—a self-proclaimed reactionary, in Roy

Campbell's sense that "a body without reaction is a corpse; so is any social body without tradition."* Eliot wrote against the concentration of wealth and power in "capitalist" societies, and was dismayed by the apathy of the democracies; but there could be social systems still more distasteful.

In his Commentary for October, 1932, Eliot singled out the fundamental error in all ideologies: the notion of a changeless perfection upon earth. Eliot defended permanence; but he went on to point out that the progressivists, the ideologues of Progress, though they love the idea of change, actually advocate the static:

"But the believer in the values only of this world can only offer himself a dilemma. If the progress of mankind is to continue as long as man survives upon this earth, then . . . progress becomes merely change; for the values of man will change, and a world of changed values is valueless to us— just as we, being a part of the past, will be valueless to *it*. Or if the progress of mankind is to continue only until a 'perfect' state of society is reached, then this state of society will be valueless simply because of its perfection. It will be, at best, a smooth-running machine with no meaning; and this it might well become. Does the bee in the efficient bee-hive find anything about it abhorrent or repulsive?"

In *The Criterion* of January, 1933, Eliot published his own "Five-Finger Exercises"—lines addressed chiefly to cats, dogs, and a duck, pleasantly remote from National Socialism and Communism. But in the same number, he took up Leon Trotsky and V. F. Calverton in his Commentary. The Marxist concept of literature he pulled to pieces—especially its humorlessness:

---

* One encounters now and again the odd notion that Eliot, because opposed to political collectivism, was (in the phrase of Robert McAlmon) subject to "the sterile cant of a vested interest." (See Robert McAlmon and Kay Boyle, *Being Geniuses Together* [1968], pp. 7–10.) It was against the material "vested interests" of his age that Eliot reacted.

"In matters of aesthetics the Christian theorist is in a position of unfair terms with the communist, of which he is not slow to take advantage. He is able to recognize an inconsistency in the affairs of this world, even to admitting the possibility that a man might be a communist, an orthodox Marxian dialectician, in our time, in this very year and month, and yet write decent English prose; even that such a one might be a great poet. He might even derive pleasure and instruction from the man's poetry. But the Marxian is compelled to scorn delights, even such moderate ecstasies as may be provoked by the reading of Emerson's Essays, and live laborious days in deciding what art ought to be. For this knowledge of literature he is obliged to apply himself, not to the furtive and facile pleasures of Homer and Virgil—the former a person of doubtful identity and citizenship, the latter a sycophantic supporter of a middle-class imperialist dynasty—but to the arduous study of Ernest Hemingway and John Dos Passos. . . ."

In his April number, Eliot recognized the appeal of Communism to the rising intellectual generation. Communism is a substitute for religious faith, essentially:

"Communism—I mean the ideas of communism, not the reality, which would be of no use in this way—has come as a godsend (so to speak) to these young people who would like to grow up and believe in something. Once they have committed themselves, they must find (if they are honest, and really growing) that they have let themselves in for all the troubles that beset those who believe in something. . . . They have joined that bitter fraternity which lives on a higher level of doubt; no longer the doubting which is just play with ideas, on the level of a France or a Gide, but that which is a daily battle. . . ."

Eliot acknowledged having "much sympathy with communists of the type with which I am here concerned; I would even say that, as it is the faith of the day, there are only a small number of people living who have achieved the right *not* to be communists. My only objection to it is the same as my objection to the cult of the Golden Calf. It is better to worship a golden calf than to worship nothing; but that, after all, is not, in the circumstances, an adequate excuse. My objection to it is just that it happens to be mistaken."

In July, the editor of *The Criterion* declared (in contradiction of the American liberal magazine *The Symposium*) that the Communists are right in believing spiritual and moral questions to be bound up with politics. Like the Catholic Church, Communism has something in it "which minds on every level can grasp." At least in its revolutionary stage, Communism is exciting; and mankind can endure anything but boredom. The editors of *The Symposium* maintained that the political activities of the Communists in Russia were impeded by ideology—to which Eliot replied, "I am inclined to believe that the 'cluttering ideology' holds the whole thing together; and that it is this which has attracted most converts of an intellectual and pseudo-intellectual kind." It is not adjustment to economic conditions that the modern world requires:

"The system which the intelligent economist discovers or invents must immediately be related to a moral system. I hold that it is ultimately the moralists and philosophers who must supply the foundations of statesmanship, even though they never appear in the forum. We are constantly being told that the economic problems cannot wait. It is equally true that the moral and spiritual problems cannot wait: they have already waited far too long."[27]

Before the altars of the Strange Gods of ideology, sacrifice was being made at that hour. Yet there endured one obstruction to the new commandments of the terrible simplifiers: the Rock.

(218)

Do Lions Need Keepers?

The Rock is a good church pageant, on the lines of a music-hall revue, with heavily invested worshipers, in the chorus, supplanting thoroughly divested girls. But Eliot did well to include in his *Collected Poems* only his choruses from *The Rock*. For many cooks stirred that ecclesiastical broth, and in general the pageant or revue was not really Eliot's. These choruses, nevertheless, are important poetry, and the whole undertaking was a new stage in Eliot's recovery of the moral imagination.

To raise money for building churches in London's sprawling fringes, the Forty-Five Churches Fund engaged E. Martin Browne, in 1933, to direct a pageant dramatizing the history of the Church. Browne persuaded the Fund to ask Eliot to write the script—along lines already drawn up. Long active in the cause of preserving old churches, and in various other concerns of the Church of England, Eliot consented: at that time he had no other important writing in immediate prospect, and his solitude may have been lightened by this task.[28]

Soliciting funds for church-building was a difficult undertaking in 1934. One encounters in the correspondence of Bishop Herbert Hensley Henson, during January of that year, a letter to a canon of Norwich that touches on the matter: "I think that, in fairness to our own generation, we must not forget that our altruistic expenditure—woefully inadequate as it is—ought to be seen in connexion with the new, vast, and ever waxing expenditure on 'Social Services' by the State. *Heavy taxation has laid the axe to the root of voluntary benevolence;* and, I am sure, we are by no means yet in sight of the full magnitude of that disastrous fact."[29]

A church established and endowed was not, of course, a church subsidized by the state. During these years, Eliot was gloomy about prospects for voluntary and church-associated charities—perhaps more melancholy than he needed to be, since nearly four decades later the English cathedrals, at least, continue to raise restoration funds by private subscription, and the National Trust for Places of Historic Interest or Natural Beauty endures—despite Eliot's prediction in his *Criterion* Commentary of October, 1934, that probably the state eventually would assume the trust's duties.

At first glance, one may wonder why it was thought necessary to build any new churches. From 1900 to 1934, it appears, church attendance in urban Britain had declined about 25 per cent, despite a 50 per cent increase of population in many cities. The number of Nonconformist communicants had shrunk more rapidly than had active participants in the Church of England, but within the Anglican communion the spectacle of beautiful old churches ill-attended and decayed, or perhaps altogether derelict, had become common. This decline would continue unchecked throughout Eliot's lifetime: the Rock seemed to be eroding away.

In the new suburbs of England, and along the web of roads that the automobile had caused to be built (mostly since Eliot had settled in London), there lived a twentieth-century population ill-provided with parish churches. These, usually, were the people most ignorant of, and indifferent to, the Church Visible. What the Archbishop of York would write of the English population generally, eighteen years later, already was true of suburban London and the ribbon-developments: "The majority of men and women neither say their prayers, except in some terrifying emergency, nor read their Bibles, unless to look for help in a crossword puzzle, or enter a church from one end of the year to the other, except for baptisms, marriages or funerals."[30] Might it be possible to build churches for them? And if new parish

churches could be erected, would it be possible to interest
these people in the Rock? In the nineteenth century, and
indeed until the First World War, the Church of England
had been described as "the Tory party on its knees": a
church for gentlefolk, with gentlemen-parsons. Could this
Church speak to the inhabitants of the monotonous county-
council houses ("like goods-waggons on a siding," in Aneurin
Bevan's description of two decades later) and the little ugly
bungalows of the urban sprawl?

Eliot scarcely was a popular evangelist: the converts
he won were converts, most of them, to the God of the
philosophers. Yet in *The Rock*—though handicapped by the
scenario and by the interference of several hands—he contrived to simplify his verse enough to appeal to an audience
considerably larger than that which he usually reached. The
pageant itself—which has been adequately described by
several writers—did not endure much beyond the occasion
that produced it.[31] Its scenes were at once historical and contemporary: Fascists and Communists derided the Rock,
and the Plutocrat set up the Calf of Gold—which really is
Power.

Some of Eliot's concepts and imagery that may be found
in *The Rock* are better studied in connection with *Murder
in the Cathedral* and *Four Quartets;* and the sweep of these
choruses can be appreciated only by an attentive reading.*

---

* "The ten-syllable line of 'blank verse,' which was almost uniform in
Shakespeare's early plays, came to vary from eight to fourteen syllables
in his later ones; but still the ten-syllable basis was at the back of the
mind of both writer and hearers. Eliot has broken this 'blank verse'
tradition of syllables by going at once back and forward. He has gone
back to the basis established by the medieval poets, of a fixed number
of *stresses* in the line without any fixed number of syllables. He has
gone forward to meet the development of prose-rhythms by the inclu-
sion of a very long, sweepingly rhythmic line having six or eight
stresses, but still a part of the verse-structure. Thus a form of verse
much more varied than any before is placed at the service of the
theatre; and this Chorus of *The Rock*, which in its half-masks is so
forbiddingly impersonal to look at, is able by its poet's voice to rouse

But comment upon Eliot's endeavor toward renewal of the Church may be useful here.

In his first chorus, Eliot looks upon an age that finds no place for the Church in the City, in the industrial towns, in the countryside, or in the suburb. We know words, but not the Word.

> Where is the Life we have lost in living?
> Where is the wisdom we have lost in knowledge?

The Rock—which is Saint Peter, and is also the Church—is led in by a boy. One thing, the Rock says, does not change: the perpetual struggle of Good and Evil. Shrines are neglected, and the desert in the heart is neglected. The unemployed "shiver in unlit rooms." What the time needs is a Church for all and "each man to his work."

In our building of recent years, the cornerstone has been forgotten—this is the burden of the second chorus.

> "Our citizenship is in Heaven"; yes, but that is the model and
> Type for our citizenship upon earth.

Imperial expansion and industrial development have been too much with us. Truly the sins of the fathers are visited upon the sons, here on earth; but expiation is possible. Forever decaying, forever attacked, the Church must be forever rebuilding.

> What life have you if you have not life together?
> There is no life that is not in community,
> And no community not lived in praise of GOD.

Forgetting community, we dash about in automobiles—"and daughters ride away on casual pillions"; verily, we "live dispersed on ribbon roads."

In the third chorus, the Lord reproaches modern man, who alternates between "futile speculation and unconsidered

---

great audiences to exaltation or to laughter . . ." (E. Martin Browne, "The Dramatic Verse of T. S. Eliot," in March and Tambimuttu, *Eliot, op. cit.,* p. 198.)

action." Modern civilization will fall desolate if the Word is unspoken. We conquer physical nature; we weary ourselves by our inventions; we embrace ideologies of nationalism or race or humanitarianism; but—

There is one who remembers the way to your door:
Life you may evade, but Death you shall not.

We are told in the fourth and fifth choruses how Nehemiah rebuilt Jerusalem. The enemies of Christianity write innumerable books. (Here Eliot means, doubtless, adversaries like Russell and Wells and Shaw, "seeking every one after his own elevation, and dodging his emptiness.") While some of us labor to rebuild the Church, others must stand guard against the enemy.

Modern complacency will terminate in blood, if the Faith is betrayed: so runs the sixth chorus. Martyrs and saints rise in every age, and the blood of martyrs will flow on the steps of the Temple in our time. There is no escape in dreaming "of systems so perfect that no one will need to be good."*

At a moment in what we call history, Christ intervened: man was given Light. Yet there has occurred in modern times what never happened before: men have left God without seeking new gods—or rather, really they have whored after abstractions which they refuse to acknowledge as their gods—Reason, Money, Power, Life, Race, Dialectic; our age "advances progressively backwards." The unemployed cry out again, in this seventh chorus; they are among the victims of a nation that has forgotten all gods but Usury, Lust, and Power.

* There come to mind John Betjeman's lines in "The Planster's Vision," written a decade later:
"I have a Vision of The Future, chum,
    The workers' flats in fields of soya beans
        Tower up like silver pencils, score on score:
And Surging Millions hear the Challenge come
    From microphones in communal canteens
        'No Right! No Wrong! All's perfect, evermore.'"

Time was when men went on crusade, we are reminded in the eighth chorus; it is otherwise with us:

Our age is an age of moderate virtue
And of moderate vice
When men will not lay down the Cross
Because they will never assume it.

But let us make perfect our *will*: faith and conviction may be ours again.

The House of God is no House of Sorrow, the ninth chorus declares. Those gifts which today we employ for our vanity, we must bring to the service of the Lord.

At the conclusion of this pageant, one church has been built: the tenth chorus exhorts modern man to build the Church Visible throughout the world. Linger not in Attalus his garden: we have been given light enough to guide our steps. Honoring the Light Invisible, we set our little lights upon altars.

For a fortnight during the spring of 1934, *The Rock* was performed at Sadler's Wells Theatre; its comic passages probably were more popular than the solemnity in the choruses. This pageant play could accomplish little enough to diminish the smug secularism of readers of *The New Statesman,* or to alter the ways of the denizens of suburban sprawl. What it might do, nevertheless, was to hearten those who still believed, or who clung to some rag of belief. It was sufficiently prophetic:

It is hard for those who have never known persecution,
And who have never known a Christian,
To believe those tales of Christian persecution.

It is hard for those who live near a Police Station
To believe in the triumph of violence.
Do you think that the Faith has conquered the World
And that lions no longer need keepers?

So intoned the chorus. On the second day of August, that

year, Marshal von Hindenburg, President of Germany, gave up the ghost. Chancellor Hitler made himself Führer; the Republic was abolished. Now the politics of revived paganism would be felt in Europe: having forgotten the Rock, modern man would encounter the gods of the copybook headings. Life and Race would be worshiped in Germany, Dialectic in Russia. "The Son of Man is crucified always."

Seventeen years after Eliot wrote *The Rock*, the Mystery Plays were revived, for the first time since the Reformation, in old York. In that year, I made my way through a tangle of medieval streets on the west bank of the Ouse to the church of St. Mary, Bishophill Senior. It is hard to say precisely how old any church in York may be; perhaps the foundations of this one were oldest of all; certainly much Norman work could be seen still, and the tower was of Roman stones. Within this century, St. Mary's, Bishophill Senior, still had a large congregation, and the neighboring parish church of Bishophill Junior (also very old) was equally well attended.

But in 1951, when I came there, Bishophill Senior was derelict, its services having ceased long before, and Bishophill Junior was struggling along with a very scanty congregation. The venerable square tower of Bishophill Senior loomed abruptly from a graveyard grown up to weeds, the tombstones chalked with drawings by children; the lock on the churchyard gate was broken, and the lock on the church door, too; one hesitated, somehow, to enter the shadowy porch. I went in, nevertheless, and found people: two tramps, male and female, who seemed to be squatting permanently in the church, and a teen-age couple apparently ready to violate the Seventh Commandment. This congregation watched me apathetically as I paced the ruinous aisles, and while I looked at slates fallen from the sagging roof, at monuments stripped from the walls; while I climbed over benches smashed to kindling, to inspect the few fragments of stained glass still dangling forlornly in the broken windows. As I left the churchyard, small boys and girls were amusing themselves by throwing pebbles at the surviving panes—now a tinkle, now a crash.

To that estate the Rock had fallen. Since then, Bishophill Senior has been demolished, and the ancient tower has been taken down and re-erected as part of a new suburban church. Neither T. S. Eliot nor anyone else was able to arrest the decline of the Church of England, or of other churches in Britain, throughout this century. Yet some continuity survives, and it has been in part the work of Eliot that some people persist in endeavoring to redeem the time. If men reject the authority of the Rock, Eliot knew, they will not enter upon an earthly paradise in the style of H. G. Wells; they will be lucky, indeed, if they sink merely to the condition of humankind in Betjeman's "The Planster's Vision"; most of them will succumb to the pseudo-authority of oligarchs or enthusiasts who, though unable to make heaven upon earth, are quite competent to erect a terrestrial hell. Architecture of the latter sort was making swift progress, under the direction of Stalin and of Hitler, in the year 1934.

VII

Christians and Ideologues in Heartbreak House

❖

The Ideologue Against the Person

At the end of twenty years in London, Eliot loomed head and shoulders—as poet and as critic—above everyone else. The rising poets, notably W. H. Auden and Stephen Spender, were his admirers; and literary criticism, chiefly through his accomplishment, had grown in stature since the time of Gosse.

His reputation was not unchallenged, even by his early friends. In a letter to *The Spectator*, late in 1934, Wyndham Lewis took up questions of originality and imitation, and implied that Eliot had returned poetry to the Academy (an opinion shared, with regret, by William Carlos Williams). "Mr. T. S. Eliot has even made a virtue of developing himself into an incarnate Echo, as it were (though an *original* Echo, if one can say that). This imitation method, of the *creator-as-scholar*—which may be traced ultimately to the habits of the American university, spellbound by 'culture'— and which academic *un-originality* it was Mr. Ezra Pound's

(227)

particular originality to import into the adult practice of imaginative literature—does not appeal to me extremely, I confess. But at least no amateurish touchiness on the score of 'originality' is involved in it."[1]

Yet such fulminations as those that had issued, during Eliot's early years of writing, from the old *Dial* and from Arthur Waugh and from Paul Elmer More were heard no longer. The older generation of literary people, by the middle 'thirties, still might be puzzled by Eliot's ascendancy, and vexed; but even they had begun to yield to the critics' verdict that Eliot was an impressive poet—perhaps a great one.

His *Collected Poems, 1909–1935,* would be published early in 1936 (six thousand copies in London, nearly five thousand in New York), with his new "Burnt Norton" included. He was passing through a six-year period in which he would publish only one major poem—this "Burnt Norton," first of his *Four Quartets*—aside from the verse-dramas *Murder in the Cathedral* and *The Family Reunion;* but his domination was secure. (As he had told William Empson about 1930, soberly enough, the most important thing for many poets to do "is to write as little as possible.")[2] Though his reputation was not yet quite at its summit, already it was unsurpassed. His *Elizabethan Essays* were published late in 1934 (four thousand copies); his *Essays Ancient and Modern* would appear (two thousand, five hundred copies in London, the same number in New York) early in 1936; together, these volumes contained only six essays that had not been collected earlier, but now they were accepted as an enduring contribution to the select shelf of English criticism.

In his office at the top of Faber & Faber's, he was becoming the Pope of Russell Square. "There cannot be many writers of my generation who were not equally intense in their veneration of Eliot, and not many of our seniors who were not astounded by it," Desmond Hawkins says of Eliot about this time. "Eliot was championed by us, discussed, quoted, idolized (and inevitably imitated) with a partisan fervour which even Shaw or Lawrence might have envied. And yet he had no intoxicating 'message,' no angry polemic, no crusading banner. Everything was an incongruity—the Royalism, the incense-swinging, the correct bank-manager look, pervading a High Bohemia of armchair communists. Absurd! But it happened. It happened because the poetry got into your head like a song-hit, because the essays acquired imperceptibly the momentum of authority: the ifs and buts, the cautious buttressing, are reminders that this was an unpopular popularity. After all, the tide wasn't running that way."[3]

In those years, the tide of ideology came near to drowning Eliot's order of the soul. Eliot's literary triumph had not been paralleled by any discernible influence upon the course of twentieth-century society. *The Criterion* was much respected, but Eliot had begun to doubt whether a quarterly review still could work upon the minds of the movers and the shakers. Christopher Dawson, Stephen Spender, Dylan Thomas, Montgomery Belgion, W. B. Yeats, William Empson, and Martin D'Arcy were eminent among the contributors to that quarterly in 1934 and 1935; A. L. Rowse, Geoffrey Grigson, George Scott Moncrieff, Michael Roberts, Janet Adam Smith, and other able writers frequently reviewed for it; there still were some American contributors.

Yet the international character of this periodical had diminished, as braggart nationalist and ravening ideology tore apart that unity of European culture which Eliot the editor had advocated. The younger writers on the Continent, in Britain, and in America were drawn toward political poles—most of them toward the Communist arm of the ideological magnet.

Already, as George Orwell would write, to be more or less

"left" had become orthodox in English literary circles. By 1936 or 1937, the doctrine was spread that only men of the Left could be good writers: "Between 1935 and 1939," according to the passionate but impartial Orwell, "the Communist Party had an almost irresistible fascination for any writer under forty. It became as normal to hear that so-and-so had 'joined' as it had been a few years earlier, when Roman Catholicism was fashionable, to hear that so-and-so had 'been received.' For about three years, in fact, the central stream of English literature was more or less directly under Communist control."[4]

In style and imagery, Eliot worked upon Auden and Spender and their set—but not in politics. Nor, despite the fact that more and more friends of things established saw in Eliot an ally, did the poet and his quarterly move the politicians. In the British government, ministers and members of parliament clung timorously to a raft that must break up; unsure of themselves, they professed confidence in the League of Nations. *The Criterion* had not been read—or if read, had not been accepted—by Coriolan.

In this political ferment, Eliot moved outwardly unperturbed; he was to poetry what Henry James had been to the novel. "One learnt by degrees that genius didn't necessarily wear a beard and have neurotic love-affairs," Desmond Hawkins goes on, "but might be found in a Kensington churchwarden who discussed cheese with the scholarly taste of a connoisseur. . . . You might have met him any morning in the Park, elegant, the rolled umbrella in position, the uncommonly handsome head a trifle bowed as if to escape the notice of the Eumenides; on his way perhaps to Lady Ottoline's where Yeats and A. E. would be eloquent . . . And Mr. Eliot would bow ceremoniously and demonstrate his intellectual invulnerability with the faintly dandified good breeding that made one inquisitive."[5]

The Eumenides were seeking other prey than Eliot; they

were about to seize upon those who had cut the ties of European kinship. The shoddy fabric woven at Versailles would be torn to pieces by their nails. At sun-blasted Wal Wal, in the Ogaden, on December 5, 1934, Italian and Abyssinian forces came to blows: the Italian armored car killed a hundred of the Ethiopians who had tried to overturn it, and broke the swords of the rest. Mussolini would invade Ethiopia in force; the League of Nations would hesitate, act equivocally, and then fall apart. A train of events had been set in motion—from proximate causes more petty than those of Sarajevo—that would parch the Waste Land more terribly than it had been stricken in the year when Eliot had come to London.

Universal compulsory education and universal military service—so Christopher Dawson wrote in *The Criterion* of October, 1934—had made possible the totalitarian state. From the same soil there arose the Communist and Fascist systems; indeed, all the world was overgrown with rank ideology. "How far does this new political development threaten the spiritual liberty which is essential to religion?" Dawson asked. "Ought the Church to condemn the Totalitarian State in itself and prepare itself for resistance to the secular power and for persecution? Should the Church ally itself with the political and social forces that are hostile to the new state? Or should it limit its resistance to cases of state interference in ecclesiastical matters or in theological questions? Or finally are the new forms of authority and political organization reconcilable in principle with Christian ideas and are the issues that divide Church and State accidental and temporary ones which are extraneous to the essential nature of the new political development?"

Those questions raised by Dawson filled Eliot's mind as he wrote *Murder in the Cathedral;* then and thereafter, Christopher Dawson, the most perceptive Christian historian of the age, worked upon Eliot's moral imagination, reinforcing Eliot's own convictions long held. And Eliot's reply to these questions, in *Murder in the Cathedral* and in his two books on society and culture, would be very like Dawson's concluding affirmation:

"The state is steadily annexing all that territory that was formerly the domain of individual freedom; it has already taken more than anyone would have conceived possible a century ago," Dawson argued. "It has taken economics, it has taken science, it has taken ethics. But there is one thing it can never take, because to quote Karl Barth . . . 'Theology and the Church are the natural frontiers of everything—even of the Totalitarian State.' Only it is necessary that Christians should themselves recognize this frontier: that they should remember that it is not the business of the Church to do the same thing as the State—to build a Kingdom like the other kingdoms of men, only better; nor to create a reign of earthly peace and justice. The Church exists to be the light of the world, and if it fulfils its function, the world is transformed in spite of all the obstacles that human powers place in the way. A secularist culture can only exist, so to speak, in the dark. It is a prison in which the human spirit confines itself when it is shut out of the wider world of reality. But as soon as the light comes, all the elaborate mechanism that has been constructed for living in the dark becomes useless. The recovery of spiritual vision gives man back his spiritual freedom. And hence the freedom of the Church is in the faith of the Church and the freedom of man is in the knowledge of God."[6]

The dark was closing down upon Europe; T. S. Eliot—no politician, no economist, no mover of the masses of men—would do what he might to restore spiritual vision in that prison. In his tribute, a few months later, to the dead A. R. Orage, Eliot reaffirmed his principle that the inner order of the soul and the outer order of society cannot be separated:

"We are really, you see, up against the very difficult problem of the *spiritual* and the *temporal,* the problem of which the problem of Church and State is a derivative. The danger, for those who start from the temporal end, is Utopianism; settle the problem of distribution—of wheat, coffee, aspirin or wireless sets—and all the problems of evil will disappear. The danger, for those who start from the spiritual end, is Indifferentism; neglect the affairs of the world and save as many souls out of the wreckage as possible. Sudden in this difficulty, and in pity at our distress, appears no one but the divine Sophia. She tells us that we have to begin from both ends at once. She tells us that if we devote ourselves too unreservedly to particular economic remedies, we may only separate into minute and negligible chirping sects; sects which will have nothing in common except the unexamined values of contemporary barbarism. And she tells us, that if we devote our attention, as do some of our French friends, to *le spirituel,* we may attain only a feeble approximation to catholicism, and a feeble approximation to Guild Socialism."[7]

It cannot be said that Eliot himself offered much that was new toward the diminishing of those economic perplexities and national rivalries which tormented the world in the middle 'thirties; nor did *The Criterion* publish much that might help directly—Eliot believing that practical political and economic measures were beyond the proper scope of such a journal as his. The editor and many of the Criterion group, for years, had put considerable trust in a "chirping sect," the Social Credit concepts of Major C. H. Douglas: Pound, Lewis, Aldington, Eliot himself, and others were in danger of becoming "money cranks"—though Eliot less in peril than were his associates, for his years as a banker had made him aware at least of the complexities of the credit mechanism, even if contemptuous of bankers' narrow views.

The Criterion group sympathized, too, with the Distributism of Chesterton and Belloc. Property and purchasing power must be restored to the average citizen: economic concentration, setting up a vulgar oligarchy in a nominal democracy, lay at the root of economic confusion and social discontent, they believed; Marxism was the bastard child of Benthamism.

Social Credit promised to work that salutary transformation of the economy. Pound became an ideologue of Social Credit: the scheme intruded upon his poetry, and he reproached Eliot for fretting about theological questions, when money was the root of all evil and Social Credit was the way, the truth, and the light. This hypnotizing of the Criterion group by the lantern of Major Douglas may seem odd enough half a century later, but it occurred in a time of economic eccentricity: it was less odd, surely, than the cult of Technocracy, then seriously discussed in the United States. A Social Credit party would achieve political power only upon the gaunt prairies of Alberta—and even there, on a provincial scale, enthusiasts would find it impossible to give flesh to a scheme meant for the centers of finance and industry; Social Credit in Alberta was as great a paradox as was Marxism in Russia.

Ten years earlier, the ablest succinct demolition of the notion of Social Credit had been published in *The Criterion* itself—a review by J. MacAlpin, who shared Hulme's and Eliot's attachment to classicism. "Major Douglas is the inventor of a scheme for the granting of credit to *consumers* instead of to producers, and it is apparent that his analysis of the economic system has been inspired by the ardour of propagating this scheme," MacAlpin had written. "It is, therefore, not surprising that he arrives at fantastic conclusions: behind the schemes of High Finance in London, Frankfurt, Paris, and New York lies the 'Invisible Government'—the hidden hand of some few financiers utilising a money power under which a misguided world approaches its doom. The

'Invisible Government' derives its power from the exploitation of the doctrine of rewards and punishments, a doctrine which Major Douglas maintains not only supplies a machinery which imposes on the world the policy of limitation and inhibition dictated by the classical attitude toward life— his conception of classicism is commonplace, the classical and moral mind, he asserts, is characterized by a devastating rigidity of thought—but also the doctrine which Labour nurtures through the conviction that work alone gives title to the fruits of production. . . .

"The chaos and dislocation of trade which accompany inflation and deflation have their chief cause in money becoming an unreliable measure of value, and, in assuming that the problem of value measurement is illusory, Major Douglas has based his proposals on a fallacy which renders them wholly inflationist in character. . . . *Social Credit* is an extravagant and pretentious book."

Too true; yet Eliot clung for years thereafter, if hesitantly, to Social Credit, much as Henry Adams and Brooks Adams (despite their powers of insight into many matters) had developed out of monetary theories resembling those of William Jennings Bryan a gloomy economic determinism. Replying, in 1933, to Pound's attack on his "conception of the good life," Eliot still expressed his hope "that Major Douglas is right from top to bottom and copper-plated; but whether he is right or wrong does not matter a fig to my argument for the priority of ethics over politics."* One will

* "Economics are about as complicated as a gasoline engine and ignorance of them is not excusable even in prime ministers and other irresponsible relics of a disreputable era," Pound had written to the editor of *The Criterion*, in "The Eleventh Year of the Fascist Revolution." See also an exchange between F. S. Flint and Pound on this subject: "Correspondence," *The Criterion*, Vol. XIV, No. 55 (January, 1935), pp. 292–304.

By 1938, Eliot remarked a certain ideological tendency in the Social Credit movement: "Social Credit, for instance, seems to me constantly in danger of petrifying in a form fifteen or twenty years old."

not find economic realism in *The Criterion* of this period. It may be said for Eliot, nevertheless, that his economic specifics were no stranger than various economic experiments then being undertaken in great states by a diversity of Coriolans. What one does encounter in Eliot's Commentaries about this time is a defense of the human person against collectivism, and a ringing expression of the moral basis of politics.

At a time when the intellectuals were infatuated with the abstract charms of collectivism, Eliot defended the claims of the person and of true community. By 1935, Middleton Murry (forever seeking a revelation, but not the one experienced already) had become a thoroughgoing theoretical Communist. To him, Eliot replied that he was not enchanted by the magic adjectives "organic" and "dynamic." Christianity is dualistic:

"The City of God is at best only realizable on earth under an imperfect likeness. . . . It is true that some forms of government, of social and economic organization, are incompatible with Christianity; it is not true that Christianity dictates any particular form of organization." John Middleton Murry's Marxism "is a very different thing from any government we should ever see in practice. I should be more interested to see Communism advocated as a workable scheme for eliminating a great deal of ordinary suffering and injustice, than as a means for experiencing the mystical ecstacies of depersonalization."

To rest the case for Communism upon the abstractions of Hegel was like resting the whole case for Christianity upon the system of Aquinas. "Marxism may be, for a few philos-

---

In his quarterly's final number (January, 1939), Eliot regretted that "the tendency of concentration upon technical economics has been to divide rather than to unite." See *The Criterion*, Vol. XVII, p. 484; and Vol. XVIII, p. 273.

ophers, a religious experience: for the man of action it will only be another style of the art of ruling men."[8]

While the debate about political and economic theory filled the English reviews, in Africa, Coriolan marched. In October, 1935, Italian divisions thrust into Abyssinia from Eritrea and Somaliland. Confronted by this war in the horn of Africa (which would not end in Africa, Eliot feared), the editor of *The Criterion* endeavored to maintain some standard of equity against the ideologues of the Left and the ideologues of the Right.

In the October number of his quarterly, Eliot set himself in opposition to the sort of imperialism represented by the *Daily Express*—or, in another fashion, by the *Times*. The newly discovered Tari Furora people of Papua might be ruined by having modern technological and commercial influences thrust upon them; they might be destroyed, for that matter, by the mentality of the London *Times* (in which one writer had expressed concern for those Papuans' future). The authors of other leading articles in the same newspaper were willing—nay, eager—to "civilize" Abyssinia; they cried up the virtues of gadgets, and recognized that Italy had "some title" to transform Ethiopia.

The concept of Empire is not necessarily ignoble, Eliot wrote (thinking, doubtless, of Virgil)—not "the notion of extending law, justice, humanity, and civilization—with no other interest than glory, and no other motive than a sense of vocation. But in the present state of things, the glory of the administrators is quickly followed, if not accompanied, by the ignominy of exploiters. How many lower peoples have been, on balance, really helped by our European intervention? And until we set in order our own crazy economic and financial systems, to say nothing of our philosophy of life, can we be sure that our helping hands to the barbarian and the savage will be any more desirable than the embrace of the leper?"

Eliot's opposition to the Italian invasion of the lands of
the Negus Negusti was very different from the attitude of
such friends of his as Ezra Pound and Roy Campbell (although later, in the Second World War, Campbell would
lead a company of the King's African Rifles against the
Italian garrisons of the Ogaden). His stand carried him, too,
into grave misgivings about the French Right, for which
he had long felt sympathy. The Abyssinian war had provoked
manifestoes from three groups of intellectuals: from the
Right, from the Left, from the Catholics. With the last, Eliot
took his stand.

About the time when *The Criterion* for January, 1936,
was published, Marshal Badoglio was bombing the Tembien
with high explosives and mustard gas. The French Right
was arguing that any inteference with the Italians in Abyssinia would be "an attack upon the civilization of the West."
This case Eliot found flimsy—except so far as it was a veil
for French interests. Even the statement of the Left (though
it, too, was a veil—for Soviet interests) came nearer to
Christian teaching, Eliot wrote.

Races, like individuals, remain unequal in condition.
"But the fundamental identity in *humanity* must always be
asserted; as must the equal sanctity of moral obligation to
people of every race. All men are equal before God; if they
cannot all be equal in this world, yet our moral obligation
towards inferiors is exactly the same as that towards our
equals," Eliot said. "And to say that to maintain Christian
principles, in a crisis such as that which has called forth
these various declarations, is to weaken our defences against
communism, is a confession of cowardice. It is an admission
that the truth is not strong enough to prevail against its
imitations; it is to fight the devil with the powers of evil.
That is not to deny that between the Christian and the Communist there is a great gulf fixed, and that in this country we
are in danger from amiable bridge-builders."[9]

In 1935, the total state—Communist or Fascist—was striking down the permanent things. When reasons of state are
given precedence over everything, including the first principles of morality; when Coriolan demands the total obedience
of his subjects—what shall the Christian do? Although the
totalitarian state is a modern creation, that general difficulty
has been encountered for many centuries. And that question,
to which martyrs have given their answer, is asked in *Murder in the Cathedral.*

The Witness of Blood

Early in 1935, Eliot was invited to write a play for the Can-
terbury Festival, to be performed that June; E. Martin
Browne would direct it. The success of *The Rock* had brought
about this invitation, and (being given a freer hand for the
Canterbury Festival than he had been given by the Forty-
Five Churches Fund) Eliot accepted. At first he meant to
call his drama about Saint Thomas à Becket "Fear in the
Way"; he even thought (having been an occasional reviewer
of thrillers) of "The Archbishop Murder Case"; but Mrs.
Browne suggested *Murder in the Cathedral.*

In the medieval chapter house of Canterbury cathedral,
the play was presented for a few afternoons, with Robert
Speaight in the role of Becket; then Ashley Dukes carried
off the drama to London, where (beginning November 1,
1935) it ran for a year at the Mercury Theatre, and for several months thereafter at the Duchess. In the United States,
the Federal Theater of the Works Progress Administration
took *Murder* on tour; the Dukes production later made its
way to Boston and New York.

Murder in the Cathedral has been produced many times
since then, in several countries, with especial success in ecclesiastical buildings. It would be made into a film sixteen

years later, with some changes in the script, the first contemporary verse-drama adapted to the screen.[10] The various English and American editions and printings of the play, between 1935 and 1965, ran to a total of nearly seventy-five thousand copies.

The first performance of this drama, in the chapter house with its door opening upon Canterbury's cloisters, occurred within a few yards of that spot in the north transept where the masterful Archbishop had fallen beneath the swords of Henry's knights, in the year 1170; and hard by the violated site of Becket's shrine in Trinity Chapel, erected in 1220 and destroyed by Henry VIII in 1538. To Canterbury, Chaucer's pilgrims, and Piers Plowman's and countless others, had made their progress for centuries, "the holy blisful martir for to seke," multitudes along the Old Road from Winchester, the Pilgrims' Way that had existed before history was written. Thomas à Becket, the "Cheapside brat," the towering martyr, spoke through Eliot to the twentieth century.

In the quarrel "between the Soul and the State: that is, between things eternal, personal, inward, and things civic, communal . . ." as Hilaire Belloc had written of the murder of Becket, "violence, our modern method, attempted to cut the knot. At once, and as it always must, fool violence produced the opposite of what it had desired. All the West suddenly began to stream to Canterbury, and à Becket's tomb became, after Rome, the chief shrine of Christendom."[11]

Eliot's drama has to do with things personal—the triumph of Becket over temptation; and with things communal—the resistance of the Church against political absolutism. Eliot's Archbishop is the primate of Daniel-Rops' description: "a man of culture, high intelligence, and subtle pride, a minister experienced in business and of unlimited devotion to duty . . . " who "underwent a psychological transformation by the promptings of divine grace."[12] He is the saint of the hagiography by Guernes de Pont-Saint-Maxence, of the painted windows in the cathedrals at Paris, Sens, and Coutances, of the popular cult that chastened English royal power for three centuries and a half. And, so far as one can determine historical fact, Eliot's Becket is truer than Tennyson's or Anouilh's.

Grover Smith calls Eliot's Becket "novel and peculiarly unhistorical . . . Instead of assuming the common judgment of Becket as overwhelmingly arrogant, waging a battle of personal and ecclesiastical spleen with a foe hardly more impoverished in spiritual attributes, Eliot depicts him as humbly submissive, accepting death, not resisting it."[13]

But this portrait scarcely is novel: Chaucer's pilgrims never doubted it. And unhistorical? That depends upon whether one has been brought up to accept, uncritically, the "Whig interpretation of history" and the sketch of Becket in Dickens' *Child's History of England* (as, indeed, many in Eliot's audiences had been brought up).

Henry VIII and the Reformation annihilated Becket's cult, dear to the Old Profession and to the poor; Whiggery and Rationalism meant to lay Becket's ghost forever. Becket had demanded the canonizing of Archbishop Anselm, who had defied King Rufus; he had defended clerics, even criminous ones, against suffering two penalties for one offense; he had stood up for appeals to Rome, for the Church's privileges and jurisdictions, for Christian asceticism, for the Rock. By dying, Becket had defeated the monarch who had hoped to make his power absolute. Would none among those cowards who ate his bread, Henry had asked, rid him of this pestilent priest? Thinking to please the king, four knights had made their way to Canterbury; and by striking down Becket, they had undone Henry and (what endured longer, quite against their intention) they had buttressed the Church.

Unlike historians in the line of Macaulay, Eliot did not

entertain what Leslie Stephen had called the Whigs' "invincible suspicion of parsons"; nor did he assume that reasons of state always should prevail over the voice of the Church. "Two there are by whom this world is ruled," Saint Gelasius had declared at the end of the fifth century: by church, by state. A champion of the claims of the Church need not be a bladder of pride and vanity. Because we cannot know the heart, we must judge men by their actions, and so Eliot judged Becket. Recognition of our sins may transform us; grace does operate upon some men.

The Becket whose magnificence had been the wonder of London, the Becket who (standing six feet four in his mail) had directed the Toulouse campaign of 1159—this Becket gave way to Becket of the hair shirt, washing in secret the feet of the poor. Why assume that the early Becket was the true man, and the martyr false? Eliot's Archbishop was the hero purged by grace, not the rash adventurer of the eleventh edition of the *Britannica*, the ultramontanist whose name the Reformers rightly had expunged from the Anglican calendar. "It is evident that in the course of his long struggle with the state he fell more and more under the domination of personal motives," the *Britannica* said of Becket. But can even the *Encyclopaedia Britannica* know the heart? One recalls Eliot's "Animula":

> The pain of living and the drug of dreams
> Curl up the small soul in the window seat
> Behind the *Encyclopaedia Britannica*.

Grace does not operate through the Benthamite *Britannica*; had Eliot thought that any encyclopaedia might rouse the moral imagination, it would have been such an encyclopaedia as Coleridge had projected but never completed. So Eliot's Becket is a man imprudent, perhaps, as the *Britannica* had assayed him; but a man redeemed, who knows that in his end is his beginning.

More perhaps than any other drama that has got out the closet, *Murder in the Cathedral* has been the subject of critical essays out of all proportion to the theater audiences it has attracted; so a new minute analysis is not required here. What I attempt is an examination of *Murder in the Cathedral* as an expression of the two aspects of order—the order personal, and the order civic. In 1935, as in 1922, the inner order and the outer lay supine in the Waste Land.

It is the chorus of the poor Women of Canterbury that regains the inward order through this drama; for Becket already is saved, and the four Tempters that assail him are foredoomed to defeat as was the Satan who tempted Jesus in the wilderness. By witnessing the Archbishop's suffering and his transcendence of that agony in a moment of time, the Women learn to praise God anew:

For the blood of Thy martyrs and saints
Shall enrich the earth, shall create the holy places.

In his "strife with shadows," Becket encounters first the temptation of self-seeking prudence: "The easy man lives to eat the best dinners." Return to the pleasures of this world, the kissing below stairs, the First Tempter counsels him, and the king's friendship will be restored; Becket has done no more than to exchange low vices for high vices. But the Archbishop knows that no man steps in the same river twice. From generation to generation, the same things occur repeatedly, a chronicle of folly; yet no man "can turn the wheel on which he turns." This temptation Becket repels easily enough, though the impossible still is tempting; the only mischief done by such "voices under sleep" is to distract the mind in the present.

Offering the prize of secular power, the Second Tempter is more subtle. Power can promote the common good:

Disarm the ruffian, strengthen the laws,
Rule for the good of the better cause . . .

Power must be purchased, this Tempter admits—at the price of submission to the princes of this world. What then? "Private policy is public profit." Yet Becket will not take this, either:

> Those who put their faith in worldly order
> Not controlled by the order of God,
> In confident ignorance, but arrest disorder
> Make it fast, breed fatal disease,
> Degrade what they exalt.

Representing himself as a hearty Norman proprietor, "a rough straightforward Englishman," John Bull, the Third Tempter, offers an alliance between the Archbishop and the barons, making common cause against the Angevin throne. As Thomas made Henry, so might he break him; at worst, he might be Samson in Gaza. But Becket will not betray his king, to run "a wolf among wolves."

The Fourth Tempter (invisible in the later film version) surprises Becket, who does not know his face or expect him: he is an evil angel—or perhaps (as Eliot suggested to Martin Browne in 1956) a good angel in disguise, "leading Becket on to his sudden resolution and simplification of his difficulties." This visitor holds in contempt the earlier temptations: wantonness is despicable, the King will not forgive, and the barons cannot unseat Henry. What counsel? Why, "Fare forward to the end."

Let Thomas seize enduring supremacy: think of glory after death. "Saint and Martyr rule from the tomb." What does a sword-thrust matter? Martyred, Becket will be venerated by generations of pilgrims at his miracle-working shrine, while kings and other enemies suffer the torment eternal. True, the wheel of existence turns ceaselessly, so that nothing endures forever; the future shrine will be pillaged at last:

> When miracles cease, and the faithful desert you.
> And men shall only do their best to forget you.
> And later is worse, when men will not hate you

> Enough to defame or to execrate you,
> But pondering the qualities that you lacked
> Will only try to find the historical fact.

So be it: there exists an enduring crown, worn by the saint in the presence of God. Martyred, Becket will stand high in heaven, beholding far below in the gulf his persecutors' "parched passion, beyond expiation." Choose eternal grandeur.

But Becket recognizes this prize, in truth, for the damning sin of pride, his own vice, once overmastering.

> Can I neither act nor suffer
> Without perdition?

The Fourth Tempter replies in mystical phrases: the wheel turns and yet is forever still; action is suffering, and suffering action; we must submit in patience to the divine will. These final counsels are not diabolical.

Though the Tempters have worked upon Becket as they might, he remains unmoved. He pulls down his vanity—even the vanity of action. All four Tempters join to mock him, now employing terror in place of promise—the terror of unreality and insubstantiality, of the vanity of human wishes, of the Self adrift in a nightmare:

> This man is obstinate, blind, intent
> On self-destruction,
> Passing from deception to deception,
> From grandeur to grandeur to final illusion,
> Lost in the wonder of his own greatness,
> The enemy of society, enemy of himself.

The priests implore the Archbishop to equivocate, awaiting a better hour; the Chorus entreat him to save himself, that they may be saved. Yet Thomas is resolute:

> The last temptation is the greatest treason:
> To do the right deed for the wrong reason.

As the unwilling servant of God ("You have not chosen Me: I have chosen you") he has run greater chance of sin and sorrow than when he was the king's good servant. In the greater cause, being feeble as all men are, God's servant may make that cause political merely. But that's done with: now Becket will submit himself passively to the will of God. He has restored order in his soul.

There follows the Archbishop's Christmas sermon—in simple and moving twentieth-century prose. "A Christian martyrdom is never an accident," Thomas says, "for Saints are not made by accident. Still less is a Christian martyrdom the effect of a man's will to become a Saint, as a man by willing and contriving may become a ruler of men. A martyrdom is always the design of God, for His love of men, to warn them and to lead them, to bring them back to His ways."

The Knights, now come to murder Becket, are the Tempters transmuted into powers of violence. The Archbishop refuses to absolve the bishops—servile to Henry—whom he had suspended; he will not return to France; he asserts the authority of the Rock. The Chorus scents the bestial under the skin of man: when moral authority is rejected, there emerges "the horror of the ape." But the Women will forget the terrors of the impending moment, the Archbishop tells them; mercifully, memory is feeble; Eliot says here, as he had written before and would write again, "Human kind cannot bear very much reality."

Against "beasts with the souls of damned men," the Archbishop will not bar Canterbury's doors: the Church is not a fortress of oak and stone. We conquer by suffering; and Thomas will repay by his blood the blood that Christ shed. The Knights hew him down.

"Hitler had been long enough in power to ensure that the four knightly murderers of Becket would be recognized as figures of the day, four perfect Nazis defending their act on the most orthodox totalitarian grounds," Ashley Dukes writes.[14] But also these knights are modern Englishmen, speaking in the tones of members of the House of Commons or of a leading article in the *Times*; they make it clear that past and present are one. Their speeches to the audience are mumblings in the Waste Land. Becket was "well qualified for the highest rank of the Civil Service," says Hugh de Morville; if only Becket had done the king's will, spiritual and temporal administration might have been united perfectly.

At "a just subordination of the pretensions of the Church to the welfare of the State," modern society has arrived. Becket's murderers know they deserve the applause of a modern audience—if one approves this condition of the commonwealth. The Fourth Knight (who has been silent during most of the action, and may be a diabolical power working upon the intellect, rather than a creature of flesh) offers a psychiatric analysis of Becket, whose death really amounted to suicide while of unsound mind: "a charitable verdict." With their appeals to the English way of looking at both sides, their commonsensical phrases, and their "charitable verdict" upon alleged disturbance of the brain, these Knights of Eliot's irony are more clearly liberal than they are National Socialist.

By Becket's martyrdom, the Chorus—the common men and women—have been awakened to consciousness of sin; and upon that consciousness, redemption may follow. Upon their heads is the sin of the world, for they are those—
Who fear the blessing of God, the loneliness of the night of God,
    the surrender required, the deprivation inflicted;
Who fear the injustice of men less than the justice of God . . .
In that fear is the beginning of wisdom.

In the days that were crowding upon the modern Waste Land, there would be found martyrs—bishops among them. The total state would demand obedience to "the final utter uttermost death of spirit"; and while most men and women would consent to the last humiliation, some would offer to faith the witness of blood. By martyrdom, even in the hour of the death-bringers, "grey necks twisting, rat tails twining," the time might be redeemed.

To cultivate the spirit alone would be to abandon the Women of Canterbury to violence; to cultivate the secular alone would be to reduce humankind to the horror of the ape. In the Terrestrial City, Coriolan will represent one power always; but always Becket will represent another power; in that tension, justice is possible.

The Loss of a Standard

Over *The Criterion*, during the last three years of its existence, there hung a cloud of weariness. Beyond denying, now, things were in the saddle, and rode mankind: Waldo the Guardian had been right enough in that. And the worst were full of passionate intensity—the line of Yeats, who died in the year of *The Criterion*'s end. While the totalist powers paraded toward Armageddon, the democracies lacked all conviction. Nothing that would alter events could be said in such a quarterly as Eliot's.

From 1935 to 1939, those events broke down what remained of the comity of nations. The Hoare-Laval pact for the partition of Abyssinia; the Italian conquest of that barbaric realm, in defiance of the League; Hitler's reoccupation and fortification of the Rhineland, uncontested; the eruption of civil war in Spain; the Nazi seizure of Austria; Neville Chamberlain's ruinous missions to Hitler at Berchtesgaden and Godesberg; the terrible blunder at Munich; the abandoning of Czechoslovakia to Hitler's mercy—these disasters, Eliot knew, smothered what hopes he had entertained when he had begun to publish his review.

And Eliot understood, too, that this descent of Europe could not now be arrested by men of letters—certainly not by "intellectuals," themselves servile to ideology. (Eliot would have concurred with Bertrand Russell in that aristocratic liberal's later definition of an "intellectual": a person who thinks he knows more than he knows.) Even the humane scholar cannot sit long in the statesman's Siege Perilous. All that Eliot and his friends could do was to occupy an intellectual redoubt between the strongholds of ideology, and to say what they might in the cause of international order. In his Commentary of July, 1936, Eliot objected to the Bishop of Durham's remarks on "just wars"; little militant justice was in prospect:

"I cannot agree with those who maintain that no war can be just: for a just war seems to me perfectly conceivable," the editor of *The Criterion* wrote. "But in practice, if we refuse to consider the causes, and consider a war only at the moment when it breaks out, there is likely to be a good deal of justice on both sides: and if we do consider its causes, we are likely to find a good deal of injustice on both sides. The believer in just war is in danger of inferring, at the moment when war is seen to be inevitable, that the war is necessarily just; on the other hand the person who sees clearly the injustice behind the war may be equally in error in assuming that because the war is unjust, he is justified in refusing to take part in it. And it is almost impossible to say anything about the subject without being misunderstood by one or both parties of *simplifiers*. . . . If we gave enough thought and effort to the institution of justice during the condition of 'peace,' we might not need to exercise our consciences so violently in anticipation of war."

The revolutionaries of the age, with their enthusiasm for the total state, were bringing on war and injustice and destroying freedom, Eliot continued; the reactionaries (reacting against the drift toward the Total State) were attached to the concept of order, which makes peace possible. "The only reactionaries today are those who object to the dictatorship of finance and the dictatorship of a bureaucracy under whatever political name it is assembled; and those who would have some law and some ideal not purely of this world." But there were revolutions of the Right, as of the Left; and the Right revolution of that sort, already triumphant in Germany and Italy, was "a symptom of the desolation of secularism, of that loss of vitality, through the lack of replenishment from spiritual sources, which we have witnessed elsewhere, and which becomes ready for the application of the artificial stimulants of nationalism and class."[15]

It was possible also, Eliot perceived, to become an impractical ideologue of "peace"—to assume a pose of pacifism which actually might encourage aggressors. By the autumn of 1936—when Hitler commenced his four-year plans, guns instead of butter, to prepare the German economy for war— England was aflutter with petitions for peace: a peace through a militant League of Nations, a peace through disarmament, perhaps a peace at any price. Eliot refused to subscribe his name to the petitions of the International Peace Campaign or similar appeals to "artists and writers" and "scientists and other intellectual workers." Only the Christian pacifists, he wrote, held a position logically consistent, and they were few in numbers. No one in Britain, and few elsewhere, advocated (at that moment) war on principle, or professed hostility toward civilization—though such attitudes might come later, possibly among the very folk now circulating "peace" petitions. The actual line of demarcation was not between the advocates of peace and the advocates of war:

"The real issue is between the secularists—whatever political or moral philosophy they support—and the anti-secularists; between those who believe only in values realizable in time and on earth, and those who believe also in values realized out of time. Here again the frontiers are vague, but for a different reason: only because of vague thinking and the human tendency to think that we believe in one philosophy, while we are really living according to another."[16]

While Eliot wrote these sentences, Socialists and Liberals were demanding action of some sort against Nazis and Facists —and yet opposing, simultaneously, any effective rearmament of Britain, which had lost parity in the air with Germany not long before. Stanley Baldwin and Neville Chamberlain still put their trust in the League of Nations, in part because they knew that Britain was unprepared to fight; but just who was to fight the League Militant's battles, if Britain could not, no one suggested. The war, indeed, already had begun— in Spain, where Roy Campbell had been trapped in Toledo by the Communist terrorists, to escape during the siege of the Alcazar. Wyndham Lewis' best novel, *The Revenge for Love*, published in 1937, describes with grim derision the climate of opinion among London's intellectuals at that hour.* Eliot retained some faint hope that the great powers still might be dissuaded from entering upon a general conflict in which the passions of ideology, nationalism, and economic interest would be joined; and through his Commentaries ran an urgent concern for Britain's neutrality. Though nearly everyone prated of peace, very few intellectuals really shared that concern for neutrality.

Their concern, as a class, during these years, was for power. No one perceived this appetite of the intellectuals better than did Wyndham Lewis (who had recovered abruptly in 1932, as befitted an iconoclast, from his passing infatuation with Hitler during 1931). *The Revenge for Love*

---

* "It shows how contemporary politics, like contemporary art, of the fashionable order, have been unobtrusively commandeered by an exceedingly unpleasant and unscrupulous gang of racketeers," Hugh Gordon Porteus would write of *The Revenge for Love*, in *The Criterion* of October, 1937. "These fictions certainly stand for realities: they reveal the contemporary scene-behind-the-scenes in all its shoddiness."

(written in 1935, but published only after many difficulties, two years later) has for its backdrop Spain on the eve of explosion, but most of its scenes occur in the literary-radical circles of London, exposed by Lewis as repellent combinations of inverted snobbery, appetite for power, muddled humanitarianism, private interest, and conspiratorial malice —a novel discerning as Conrad's *Under Western Eyes*. The only decent people in Lewis' book are dupes, Victor and Margot Stamp, a poverty-stricken painter of small talents and his dreamy wife; they are used as bait by the London Communists, and go over a cliff in the Pyrenees. Margot, who reads Ruskin, sees the whole set for what they are— though this does not save her; she senses the inhumanity of these reformers, sufficiently represented by Gillian Phipps, the young woman with the boarding-school tones who likes to be kissed by men of the lower orders:

"Margot understood that no bridge existed across which she could pass to commune as an equal with this Communist 'lady'—living in a rat-infested cellar out of swank (as it appeared to her from her painfully constructed gimcrack pagoda of gentility). Nor did she wish to very much, because—for Victor's sake—she dreaded and disliked all these false politics, of the sham underdogs (as she felt them to be), politics which made such a lavish use of the poor and unfortunate, of the 'proletariat'—as they called her class—to advertise injustice to the profit of a predatory Party, of sham underdogs athirst for power: whose doctrine was a universal Sicilian Vespers, and which yet treated the real poor, when they were encountered, with such overweening contempt, and even derision."

Such ears, in the late 'thirties, were deaf to Eliot's genuine plea for peace. Yet the inner circle of the Criterion group (Montgomery Belgion writing regularly from Paris, for one), among them some recent recruits to that standard, refused to submit themselves to Giant Ideology. In *The*

Criterion for January, 1937, William G. Peck's essay on
"Divine Democracy" paralleled Eliot's convictions. "The failure of what has passed for democracy in the modern world,"
Peck wrote, "the rise of the totalitarian State, whether communist or fascist, must not be allowed to confuse Christian
thought. The conclusion is not that democracy is incongruous
with Christianity, but that the only true, indeed the only
possible, democracy must be Christian." In the same number, Eliot himself refused to accept either *The New Statesman's* argument that the Spanish "Loyalist" government
"represented an enlightened and progressive liberalism," or
the *Tablet's* declaration that the Spanish Nationalists took
up arms only in defense of Christianity and civilization:

"Political fanaticism in releasing generous passions will
release evil ones too," Eliot remarked. "Whichever side wins
will not be the better for having had to fight for its victory.
The victory of the Right will be the victory of a secular
Right, not of a spiritual Right, which is a very different thing;
the victory of the Left will be the victory of the worst rather
than of the best features; and if it ends in something called
Communism, that will be a travesty of the humanitarian
ideals which have led so many people in that direction. And
those who have at heart the interests of Christianity in the
long run—which is not quite the same thing as a nominal
respect paid to an ecclesiastical hierarchy with a freedom
circumscribed by the interests of a secular State—have especial reason for suspending judgment."[17]

In the next issue of his review, Eliot took to task C. Day
Lewis, as representative of the Popular Front mentality then
dominant among the intellectuals. For Lewis, Soviet Russia
could do no wrong; to obtain peace, one should lend a hand
to Communists everywhere. "He is the opposite of a Jingo;
for though he *does* want to fight, he is not so sure about
wanting the ships, the men, the money too," Eliot wrote of
Day Lewis. The time might come, Eliot suggested, when

Russia would aspire to an imperialism more grandiose than the "imperialist powers" ever had dreamed about:

"The great danger at the moment seems to me to be the delusion of the 'Popular Front,' which is so seductive to the intelligentsia of every country. Our Liberal practitioners have so hypnotized themselves with the bogey of fascism that they seem to be like Tibetan initiates, in a fair way to give it form and activity. Those professed 'realists,' who so far surrender principles as to join in a Popular Front which is meaningless unless it is an extreme Left Front, will have only themselves to thank if they find that they have conjured up a spirit which will not go back into the bottle, and which will be an Unpopular Front."[18]

The Unpopular Front, indeed—the pact between Hitler and Mussolini—was only a few months distant. Britain ought to do everything in her power to pour oil upon the waters, Eliot continued to insist. In his Commentary of July, 1937, he wrote (in support of Edmund Blunden) that Oxford University's refusal to send representatives to the University of Göttingen's bicentenary celebration might be interpreted as formal disapproval of the German government—to the exacerbation of diplomatic tempers. Herbert Read replied, in the next number of *The Criterion*, that the rejection of Göttingen's invitation was a protest against the loss of academic freedom in German universities; but Eliot was not reassured. His was truly a "correct," if not a blinkered, neutrality.[19]

As it became clear, however, that Hitler was bent upon conquest of central Europe, regardless of British opinion or action, Eliot abandoned his defense of British neutrality; indeed, he ceased almost wholly to comment upon international affairs. Hitler's annexation of Austria, and then the Chamberlain government's pusillanimity at Munich, made Eliot despair of averting war. Two decades later, he told William Turner Levy of his admiration for Anthony Eden when that foreign secretary resigned from the cabinet, on the eve of the fall of Austria, in February, 1938.

"I felt a deep personal guilt and shame for my country and for myself as a part of the country," Eliot said of Britain's desertion of Austria and Czechoslovakia. "Our whole national life seemed fraudulent. If our culture led to an act of betrayal of that kind, then such a culture was worthless, worthless because it was bankrupt. It had no morality because it did not finally believe in anything. We were concerned with safety, with our possessions, with money, not with right and wrong. We had forgot Goethe's advice: 'The dangers of life are infinite and *safety* is among them.' "[20]

So it is that editorial Commentaries for the last two volumes of *The Criterion* contain no reference to diplomacy and war—except for that of October, 1938. In devastated Spain, the Nationalists then were about to launch their counter-offensive along the Ebro; clearly General Franco was close to victory. But Eliot was not heartened much by the triumph of one set of ideologues over another. He took his stand with Jacques Maritain, recently denounced by Serrano Suñer, Nationalist minister of the interior. Eliot could not accept the propaganda of the Left, which had represented the Communists and Anarchists as champions of liberty; he could not accept the propaganda of the Right, which represented the campaign of Franco's forces as a "holy war." The heirs of liberalism, Eliot wrote, found "an emotional outlet in denouncing the iniquity of something called 'fascism.' If the intellectual is a person of philosophical mind philosophically trained, who thinks things out for himself, then there are very few intellectuals about, and indeed the position of M. Maritain is as 'intellectual' a position (as well as being Christian) as anyone could adopt.

"The irresponsible 'anti-fascist,' the patron of mass-meetings and manifestoes, is a danger in several ways. His activities, when exploited by a foreign press, are capable of nourishing abroad the very ideas which he so vehemently repudiates; they confuse the issues of real politics with misplaced religious fanaticism; and they distract attention from the true evils in their own society."

The genuine difficulties of England, Eliot wrote, were not to be remedied by ideological slogans. "Urbanization of mind" lay at the root of much of the evil—in agriculture, in finance, in education, in the whole outlook upon life. "One sees no hope either in the Labour Party or in the equally unimaginative dominant section of the Conservative Party. There seems no hope in contemporary politics at all. Meanwhile the supposed progressive and enlightened 'intellectuals' shout themselves hoarse in denunciations of foreign systems of life which they have not taken the trouble to comprehend; having never considered that the preliminary to criticizing anything must be an attempt to understand how it came about, and that criticism involves discerning the good from which we might profit, as a qualification for condemning the evil which we wish to avoid. Another characteristic of the type of mind which is doctrinaire without being truly philosophic, is to assume that *all* problems are soluble: which leads to an ignoring of those which are of such large compass as to appear to present insuperable difficulties."[21]

As this number of *The Criterion* had gone to the printer, Neville Chamberlain had given Hitler what he desired, at Munich, on September 30; and Czechoslovakia had submitted that day. Eliot had despaired of Chamberlain's diplomacy, and of peace in Europe, at least eight months earlier. The Anschluss had been *The Criterion*'s deathwound, and that review's grave was dug—alongside many other graves—at Munich. In the quarterly's concluding numbers, what could be said about things civic? Why, fragments might be shored against ruin; and Britain, like the Fisher King of the Waste Land, might set her lands in order.

So the Commentaries of *The Criterion*'s last six numbers

are concerned with the decay of culture and with the decline of community in Britain. Britain's two most serious problems, apart from religion, were Education and the Land, Eliot wrote: neither was being studied intelligently. Ideologues ignored these afflictions, or else plastered them over with slogans; people in power did nothing effective to reduce them. Education was regarded as a quantitative and utilitarian matter, "the old liberal panacea of more education for everybody"; the attempt was being made to create a mass culture by governmental direction—but it would fail. Centralized planning does not build a public for poetry, or make happier those upon whom approved poetry is thrust. Schemes like that for a National Theatre would stifle artistic freedom: "It seems to me possible that, once the Government takes an active and overt part in the cultivation of the Arts, such confusion will ensure that in time there will be a call for a 'dictator of the arts' (will it, by that time, be Mr. Hore-Belisha or Mr. Duff Cooper?) to put things to rights."

With dismaying speed, the countryside was being depopulated and its old leadership drained away, by taxation or by the false attractions of London. (Here Eliot reminds one of George Gissing in *The Private Papers of Henry Ryecroft*.) "I believe that the real and spontaneous country life—not *legislated* country life—is the right life for the great majority in any nation."[22] Britain may be left with swollen cities, sprawling suburbs, and a few preserved "beauty spots."

The body of intellectuals, fascinated by grandiose declarations and universal schemes, neglect these vital particulars. Eliot discussed the dangers of ideological domination of arts and letters in a criticism of the Exhibition of the "Unity of Artists for Peace, Democracy and Cultural Development." Artistic talents do not confer authority in social concerns. "I fear that the groups of 'artists' who engage in political affirmations may bring about for themselves just the opposite of what they intend: instead of influencing political directions they may merely be cutting themselves off from the world of events."[23]

In this Britain, its imagination parched, those publications which help to form intelligent public opinon were wilting; increased costs of publication, including the price of paper, told against them. The newspaper press was mostly mischievous: "It helps, surely, to affirm them [the general public] as a complacent, prejudiced and unthinking mass, suggestible to head-lines and photographs, ready to be inflamed to enthusiasm or soothed to passivity, perhaps more easily bamboozled than any previous generation upon earth."

Britain, and every country, needed a considerable number of small independent periodicals, not run for profit, with two thousand to five thousand purchasers: the means of communication among cultivated people. But the days of such publications might be numbered. "Independent opinion finds greater and greater obstacles to expression. We assume that we have 'freedom' of the Press so long as we have violent differences of opinion finding their way into print; so long as a silly official position on any matter can be attacked by an opposition with a policy still sillier. This is the freedom of two mobs. It is a higher degree of freedom when thoughtful and independent individuals have the opportunity of addressing each other. If they have no vehicles by which they can express their opinion, then for them the freedom of the press does not exist."[24]

In January, 1939, the best of such publications in Britain came to an end—about the time when Chamberlain and Halifax were paying a visit to Mussolini. That Coriolan, we learn from Count Ciano's diary, looked upon the British statesmen with contempt. "These men," said Mussolini, "are not made of the same stuff as Francis Drake and the other magnificent adventurers who created the Empire. They are after all the tired sons of a long line of rich men."

For the preceding two years, Eliot had thought of terminating his editorship. As war became virtually certain, he made plans for suspending publication; even though it still was possible to bring out *The Criterion* early in 1939, he was too disheartened to carry on. "A stale editor cannot do his contributors justice."

That renewal of the unity of European culture, *The Criterion's* principal end during the first half of its existence, now seemed to Eliot a hopeless undertaking. "Gradually communications became more difficult, contributions more uncertain, and new and important foreign contributors more difficult to discover. The 'European mind,' which one had mistakenly thought might be renewed and fortified, disappeared from view: there were fewer writers in any country who seemed to have anything to say to the intellectual public of another. Divisions of political theory became more important; alien minds took alien ways, and Britain and France appeared to be progressing nowhere."

In this new age, Eliot continued, his attention had turned increasingly to political theory. "For myself, a right political philosophy came more and more to imply a right theology—and right economics to depend upon right ethics: leading to emphases which somewhat stretched the original framework of a literary review." He had come to wonder whether it might have been better, from the beginning, to have paid less attention to literary standards and instead "to have endeavoured to rally intellectual effort to affirm those principles of life and policy from the lack of which we are suffering disastrous consequences."

Small and obscure reviews, perhaps for a long time to come, must be depended upon to maintain the continuity of culture, under painful handicaps. It would be well if these could be sold cheaply: "I suspect that the price at which *The Criterion* has had to be published is prohibitive to most of the readers who are qualified to appreciate what is good in it, and to criticize what is faulty." (Although Eliot did not know it, George Orwell, in 1935, had written to a friend that he could not afford to buy *The Criterion,* which cost seven shillings and sixpence.) However that might be, Eliot's quarterly would appear no more. "In the present state of public affairs—which has induced in myself a depression of spirits so different from any other experience of fifty years as to be a new emotion—I no longer feel the enthusiasm necessary to make a literary review what it should be."25

In the years after the Second World War, although many long-established magazines would go under, some periodicals intended to sustain the continuity of culture would arise—among them, the one nearest to Eliot's *Criterion* in character and tendency being *The Cambridge Journal,* edited by Michael Oakeshott, but not destined to endure so long as had *The Criterion.* Despite the rapid increase of population, the number and circulation of serious journals have diminished; and in the surviving reviews (with the partial exception of some American literary quarterlies, university-supported) concern for the moral imagination has given ground before sociological interests.

The times having been what they were, it is surprising not that *The Criterion* perished, but that it lived so long. Eliot knew this; also he knew that though he had addressed a small Remnant, in subtle ways his review may have quickened the minds of people whom he never would meet, but who might make their mark during the next thirty years or longer. Yet *The Criterion* ended upon a dying fall, with the lights of Europe going out again. That review had consumed a great part of his time during fruitful years; editorial labors may have been one reason why Eliot never wrote, in maturity, a concerted book so long as his Harvard dissertation. He found none of his Commentaries and few of his reviews for his own quarterly enduring enough to include in his several volumes of collected essays. Yet anyone who can afford to acquire the eighteen reprinted bound volumes of

The Criterion will encounter there some of the best writing and some of the more seminal thought of the twentieth century.

Reunion at Heartbreak House

Two months after the final number of *The Criterion* was published, there was performed in London the first of Eliot's four verse-plays about modern life: *The Family Reunion.* Faber & Faber brought out their first edition of the play (more than six thousand copies) in the same month, and a few days later, in New York, Harcourt Brace came out with the American edition of two thousand, five hundred copies. Early audiences of *The Family Reunion* would have done well to read and discuss that drama before going to the theater; as it was, many people left the theater thoroughly puzzled.

For the play was almost as innovating as *The Waste Land* had been, and as subtle. It could be understood, if apprehended at all, on several levels of meaning. On the stage, though not a failure, neither was it a grand success; later, radio presentations of this play were well received, for it is not at all necessary to *see* the characters of *The Family Reunion.* Eliot, who had begun to write this play not long after *Murder in the Cathedral* had been applauded at Canterbury, had here two objects, the first declared, the second somewhat veiled: to revive the verse-play in a prosaic time; and to restore an awareness of the spiritual and the transcendent among a people who dismissed Christianity as an incredible body of doctrine. It was meant for an audience much more heterodox (or ignorant of religion) than that which had attended performances of *Murder in the Cathedral,* and more numerous than the readers of his poems.

Eliot's critics are divided on the merits of this experimental play—some dismissing it as a mistake, others finding both remarkable virtues and remarkable vices in it, and a number declaring that it stands with the best of Eliot's work. However that may be, I believe that Eliot's plays of the twentieth-century drawing room can be better examined by a thorough analysis of *The Cocktail Party*, in a later chapter. For one thing, the severest criticism of *The Family Reunion* came from its author himself, in his lecture on "Poetry and the Drama," twelve years later—reprinted in *On Poetry and Poets* (1957); and that essay, being Eliot's only lengthy disquisition on any of his own writings, is more worth reading than anything I could set down here. So I confine myself to an inquiry into what convictions Eliot endeavored to convey to his time through *The Family Reunion*.

Bernard Shaw had begun to write *Heartbreak House* on the eve of the First World War; a quarter of a century later, Eliot wrote *The Family Reunion* in an hour of crisis grimmer still. Wishwood, the country house of Eliot's play, has its similarities to Heartbreak House; certainly Wishwood always had been a "cold house," a heart-breaker. The afflictions of the inhabitants of Heartbreak House were levity and selfishness (from neither of which vices Shaw was exempt); the people of Wishwood House suffer from self-delusion and dullness; both of these country-house sets in some degree are what Matthew Arnold had called Philistine, though not so Philistine as the folk of Horseback Hall. In both plays, there stirs a yearning for the life of the spirit. "Life with a blessing! that is what I want," says Shaw's young Ellie. Eliot's Harry Monchensey is near to obtaining that blessing, though not in a manner that Shaw would have chosen.

What Shaw desires is a revolution; what Eliot seeks is a rediscovery. Neither Heartbreak House nor Wishwood House can stand much longer. Upon the ruins of Heartbreak, Shaw would build "Utopia for the common people." Upon the site of Wishwood, Eliot would restore the City of God. The inmates of both houses are the upper classes of England, vacant rather than truly leisured. War will disintegrate their fabric of security; in part, war is the result of their lack of belief in anything worth believing. In Heartbreak House, life is flirtation; in Wishwood, life is conformity to ephemeral convention. Is there nothing more satisfying than these follies of the time?

To Wishwood, there returns—after seven years of aimless wandering—a modern Orestes: Harry, Lord Monchensey, haunted by the Furies. Attempting to escape from the domination of his dowager mother, Harry had fallen into a miserable marriage; but the wench is dead. She had become unendurable, and Harry had pushed her over a liner's rail—or so it appears, and so he says. Yet did he? May it not have been accident or suicide? Sometimes Harry fancies that he is a character in someone else's dream. Morally, in any event, he is his wife's slayer, for he desired her death; and as a man who lusts after a woman commits adultery in his heart, so a husband who desires his wife's destruction breaks the Sixth Commandment.

For three hours only, Lord Monchensey returns to the house of his youth, Wishwood—to his mother, Amy, who would reduce him to servitude again; who is a prisoner of time, unable to accept death, vainly bent upon keeping unchanged what by nature must be mutable. He returns to Mary, the cousin that Amy meant to become his wife, and for the first time is drawn to her—until the Furies intervene. He returns to dull uncles and feckless brother; to a haunted house of childhood memories that is no sanctuary, for the Furies are visible to him even there.

And he returns to his Aunt Agatha—who, he discovers after all these years, has been his mother in spirit. What Agatha reveals to Harry is the source of the curse that has lain upon him. Harry's father had come, suddenly, to love Agatha, a few months before Harry was born; the older Lord

Monchensey would have murdered Amy to gain Agatha, but
Agatha prevented him for the sake of the baby in her sister's
womb. The sins of the fathers are visited upon the sons:
Harry's unrest is the product of his father's sin and its effect
upon all the family. There must be expiation.

So far, the frame of this play is that of Aeschylus. But
Eliot's Hellenic legend is a mask; or Eliot rows with muffled
oars. For Eliot knew that his audiences would refuse assent—
in an era soon to be called "post-Christian"—to a drama
openly drawn from what they would call the Christian
Myth. A classical myth, nevertheless, they might tolerate as
remote, harmless, and undemanding. Let Christ or Saint
Paul never be mentioned, and those audiences might listen.
Eliot will be all things to all men.

By enlightenment of his plight, by coming to understand
the causes—deep-rooted in the past—of his misery, Harry is
redeemed. The remainder of *The Family Reunion* is Christian teaching in the riddle of a mirror—though the words of
theology and faith are not uttered explicitly. Harry will
expiate his father's sin and his own; he will renounce the
love of created beings, in the sense of attachment to Wishwood and its tenants, though his departure will bring about
the death of his time-captive mother. The Furies become
the Eumenides, no longer dreadful, and Harry no longer
flees from staring eyes, for they will be the eyes of God.
He will seek "a stony sanctuary and a primitive altar," perhaps like Charles de Foucauld, "a care over the lives of
humble people." His destination remains uncertain, but no
longer is he in flight from the past or from the nature of
things. (Michael Redgrave, who played Monchensey in the
first production, asked Eliot "What *does* happen to this young
man at the end of the play?" Eliot replied that he thought
Harry and his servant would work in the East End of London—and even provided Redgrave with lines to make clear
this intention of good works, though those lines are not in-

cluded in the printed version of the play.) By coming to
understand the continuity of his family, Harry had found
it possible to live; more, he had found it possible to live with
purpose and hope.

The preceding bald summary may reduce everything to
bathos; for that matter, *The Family Reunion* is easily burlesqued; but one must see or read the play, which has many
lines of power and beauty, close enough to twentieth-century speech for an audience to find reality in this fable. Although all the commentators upon this play recognize the
Christian symbolism, still several of the better-known glosses
on *The Family Reunion* are oddly naïve—perhaps because,
as Eliot had expected, the critics retain a smattering of Christian knowledge, yet only as a congeries of abstractions; they
do not perceive how Christian faith permeates the play.

Some critics object, for instance, that Harry (ignoring
his own crime of act or of intention) endeavors only to efface
the family curse, of his father's bringing. But really, Eliot is
not writing about the house of Atreus. This "curse" is Original
Sin, and Eliot's lesson is the first one in the New England
Primer: "In Adam's fall we sinned all." There is more of
Baudelaire than of Aeschylus in this drama. All fathers and
all sons are sinners in some way: by faith and works we
redeem the past and our own time.

The same critics, or others—among them ardent admirers
of Eliot—are scandalized that Harry expresses no remorse for
the death of his wife. But the blessing of the regenerate is
that sins are washed away. Remorse—subconscious remorse,
at least, symbolized by the Furies—is precisely what Harry
has been tormented by; now that he enters upon the life of
grace, and has purgatorial hope, the horror of relentless
memory is removed. Penance and atonement may be Harry's
lifelong; but that is different from brooding remorse. "Let
the dead bury the dead," according to Saint Matthew.

Another complaint of certain critics is that Harry abandons his mother to death. Yet why is Harry's departure from Wishwood inconsonant with his purgation? Jesus of Nazareth told his disciples to leave parents and to follow Him. Amy, as she says herself, is "an old woman in a damned house"; for Harry to submit to her afresh would be to fall into her own error that time can have a stop. Whether Harry stays or goes, death must take her soon; and deferential sons who linger to the last beside hard domineering mothers, after all, are not the highest type of humanity. Life is for moral action, not for apron-strings.

So the play is internally consistent, I believe—which is not to say that it is strong at all points. A dozen years later, Eliot picked his own play almost to pieces. He had given attention to versifying, at the expense of plot and character, he said; old Lady Monchensey alone was fully delineated. His use of the Family as chorus had not been really successful; he had introduced poetic passages that could not be justified dramatically. Worse, he had used up too much time in presenting the situation, which had left him short of time for development. Worse still, he had not adequately reconciled the Greek legend and the modern situation; the Furies should have been invisible, not members of the cast: "I should either have stuck closer to Aeschylus or else taken a great deal more liberty with his myth." Worst of all, "we are left in a divided frame of mind, not knowing whether to consider the play the tragedy of the mother or the salvation of the son." Finally, "my hero now strikes me as an insufferable prig."

These strictures by the author are harsh, but concede them: still, Eliot succeeded in two things with *The Family Reunion*. First, he opened the way for a reinvigorated verse-drama that could assert meaning and dignity on the stage again, without the archaic language or the shallow prettiness of the Georgian poets and playwrights. "What we have to do is to bring poetry into the world in which the audience lives and to which it returns when it leaves the theatre; not to transport the audience into some imaginary world totally unlike its own, an unreal world in which poetry is tolerated." Let the audience know that they, too, can talk in poetry; then "our own sordid, dreary daily world would be suddenly illuminated and transfigured."

Second, Eliot in this play unbarred a gate to the realm of spirit. "For it is ultimately the function of art, in imposing a credible order upon ordinary reality, and thereby eliciting some perception of an order *in* reality, to bring us to a condition of serenity, stillness, and reconciliation; and then leave us, as Virgil left Dante, to proceed toward a region where that guide can avail us no farther."[26] Eliot's moral imagination, working through the drama, made possible emancipation from the prison of a moment in time and from the obsessions of the ego. The Greek drama had been meant to order the soul; Eliot returned to that purpose. With Harry Monchensey, some hereafter might follow the bright angels.

Not a few are repelled by Eliot's search for the spiritual, in this play and in *The Cocktail Party*. (It was one of Eliot's recurrent regrets for the modern British and Americans that they dreaded the word and concept "spiritual," although a French writer would not hesitate to employ *spirituel*.) If "spiritual" implies a touch of the supernatural or of the preternatural, as in these plays, it is doubly rejected. "That kind of resort to the 'supernatural' in such a context is both indefensible and betraying: it reveals in Eliot an inner pressure towards the worst kind of insincerity, that which is unconscious," F. R. Leavis writes.

In some ways, Leavis is the most interesting critic of Eliot, because his strong praise repeatedly is modified by acerbic dissent. For Leavis, much as for Irving Babbitt, the "spiritual"—if one must use that term at all—is the apprehension of an enduring human nature, with needs that the technologist and the Benthamite cannot know. Leavis would have the literary critic leave Christian theology quite out of any discussion of Eliot's achievement.[27]

But that would be very like omitting any mention of Stoic philosophy from a criticism of Seneca; or forbidding any reference to Jewish theology in an examination of Maimonides; or taking the gods away from classical authors. If Eliot can be perceived only in the light of the humanists (strong though that light often is), then one must ignore Eliot's steady development and ruling beliefs—including his conviction that we are worked upon by powers of light and powers of darkness, above our nature and below it. If the literary critic can have no truck with theology, must the theologian have no truck with literature? Life and letters cannot endure in little coffin-like compartments. How could one criticize Pascal or Coleridge, say, without taking into account their religion? How, then, Eliot?

Dr. Leavis find Eliot's poetry heroically sincere, but his four drawing-room plays evasive or cheap in some respects: a spiritual shoddiness here, produced by Eliot's alleged incapacity to "take full cognizance of full human love between the sexes." In "Marina," Eliot is most tender—but it is the love of father for daughter. With Eliot, Leavis continues, "in general, the relations between man and woman implied by the 'daughter' don't, for the poet, exist. . . . The fact is that his inner disorder and his disability remained grievous and tell to its disadvantage on his concern for the spiritual."[28]

In *The Family Reunion*, Harry Monchensey detests and destroys his wife (who appears to have been detestable), and rejects Mary for a life of asceticism—which latter choice is Pauline, and scarcely peculiar to Eliot. Throughout all of Eliot's poems and plays, until late in his life, there does run a renunciation of the physical union of the sexes, which most critics were reluctant to analyze candidly while Eliot lived. Does this seeming aversion to the flesh, or difficulty in responding to the claims of the flesh, affect and distort Eliot's "concern for the spiritual"? The point may as well be considered here, as we look at Eliot in 1939.

There exists a blunt but sympathetic essay on this subject of Eliot's sexual asceticism by Arthur M. Sampley. A good woman is hard to find in Eliot's poems and plays, Sampley remarks; as the Fisher King was wounded, so perhaps Eliot:

"His shyness and reserve . . . perhaps inhibited him in one of the most difficult areas of communication. His critical spirit . . . perhaps kept him from the full experience of love which his later poems eloquently praise. Certainly involved was the element of chance or fate which brings or does not bring to a man the woman with whom he can fully communicate." Dismay at sexual misadventures looms disproportionately large in *The Waste Land* and elsewhere in Eliot's work: "the failure of marital love seems hardly an adequate and certainly not complete cause of the threat of chaos which does indeed seem to overhang the world."[29]

Sexual impotence (whether or not Eliot himself ever so suffered) clearly has afflicted not a few literary men during the past century: the names come to mind, among others, of writers so various as John Ruskin, Henry James, J. M. Barrie, Lionel Johnson, and (for a considerable part of his life) George Bernard Shaw; there is the old Yeats, too. But no common pattern of thought or writing emerges from the impotence of these men. Nor does it follow that because a writer may not enjoy Amaryllis or Campaspe, he must embrace a phantom, in a debased supernaturalism. One might as well deduce from the notorious concupiscence of Bertrand Russell or H. G. Wells or C. E. M. Joad the principal tendencies of their thought. Freudian analysis of Eliot's work—particularly *The Family Reunion*—has been ingenious but unconvincing.* A shy man is not necessarily a neurotic.

* Notably, C. L. Barber, "Strange Gods at T. S. Eliot's 'The Family Reunion,'" in *The Southern Review*, Vol. VI, pp. 387–416; reprinted in Leonard Unger (ed.), *T. S. Eliot: a Selected Critique* (1966), pp. 415–443.

So I find it easier far to believe that the touches of the supernatural or the preternatural in Eliot's plays, encountered now and again in his poems, too ("Difficulties of a Statesman," for example), are *not* connected with the disability of sexual deprivation; that the Furies are not surrogates for Doris and Dusty, and that the One-Eyed Reilly's hints of occult power are not a substitute for the love of woman. With mysticism after the fashion of Yeats or Orage, indeed, Eliot often expressed uneasiness at best, and sometimes disgust. The "supernatural world" of Yeats was "the wrong supernatural world," Eliot said in *After Strange Gods*. "It was not a world of spiritual significance, not a world of real Good and Evil, of holiness or sin, but a highly sophisticated lower mythology summoned, like a physician, to supply the fading pulse of poetry with some transient stimulant so that the dying patient may utter his last words."[30]

I find it much easier to believe that Eliot perceived, as he said, operations of the Evil Spirit; and was convinced that there existed Bright Angels, too; and an everlasting Rose Garden. He knew that we are enveloped in mysteries, including the mysteries of the Self and of Time; but that we are not the sport of Hardy's Immortals; that religion, Christianity in particular, is an endeavor to communicate with transcendent being—which, its nature not copying man's nature, we call supernatural. If this understanding, and Eliot's expression of love, seem somewhat less refined in the drawing-room plays than in the poems—why, that is not the consequence of any betraying unconscious insincerity, but because (as he declared) Eliot was trying to reach through those plays an audience broader and less educated than the public which read his poems. The more widely one seeks a following, the less abstract one's images must be.

Finally, I suspect that even had Eliot been idyllically coupled, most of his years, with a Hyacinth Girl of infinite variety, or even with uncorseted Grishkin of the friendly bust, still he would have heard whispers of immortality; still he would have lamented over the bent world and sought the intersection of time with the timeless; still he would have encountered the devil of the stair. Others, your servant among them, have kept their metaphysics warm even in the company of Cupid and Campaspe.

The fullness of love would be Eliot's reward, the crown of life, toward the end; but in 1939, despite the healthy humor that relieves *The Family Reunion*, his solitude is painful to think of. In effect a widower, though Vivienne still lived, to be visited in a place of retreat on Sundays; childless; his quarterly review brought to a melancholy end; ideological infatuation swallowing up the new crowd of writers; public disorder inducing that "depression of spirits so different from any other experience of fifty years"—this was existence in Heartbreak House or Wishwood.

F. R. Leavis says that this condition had the effects of starvation on Eliot's spirituality. "But we have to recognize, I think," Leavis writes, "that one of those effects was intensity, and without the intensity . . . —I won't develop that consideration further than to say that the distinctive Eliotic intensity was a necessary condition of that astonishing feat of sustained creative intensity, *Four Quartets*."[31]

This makes Eliot sound desperate as Gerontion; but it was not quite so. The comical side to his nature was not extinguished, even in 1939. That October, Eliot published *Old Possum's Book of Practical Cats* (some three thousand copies), full of fun, acknowledging the help of little Fabers and Morleys and other children. Children liked him; so did cats; so, apparently, did mice.* In the autumn of 1939, it

---

* When Wyndham Lewis painted his portrait of Eliot in 1938, Lewis' studio was infested by swaggering mice, startling Lewis' sitters. "At last, when Tom Eliot was sitting to him," Edith Sitwell writes, "their behaviour became intolerable. They climbed on to his knee, and would sit staring up at his face. So Lewis bought a large gong which he placed near the mouse-hole, and, when matters reached a certain limit,

was as well to laugh with Democritus as to weep with Heraclitus.

For Britain had declared war upon Germany on the third day of September. On October 14, the battleship *Royal Oak*, in Scapa Flow, was torpedoed by a German submarine, and carried down with her nearly eight hundred officers and men: death by water. For this nightmare of the time, one could wake only through the life of spirit.

---

he would strike this loudly, and the mice would retreat." See *Edith Sitwell: Selected Letters, 1919–1964*, edited by John Lehmann and Derek Parker (1970), p. 231.

VIII

The Communication
of the Dead

✥

Is a Christian Society Conceivable?

The Twilight War (Neville Chamberlain's phrase, borrowed by Winston Churchill) lasted from September 3, 1939, to May 10, 1940; after that, with the German invasion of the Low Countries, the enormous war of frightfulness burst out. It was during the Twilight War that Eliot published *The Idea of a Christian Society* and finished two of the *Four Quartets.*

Philip Mairet, then editor of *The New English Weekly,* tells of colloquies with Eliot in a milk-bar near Victoria Station, during those gloomy months, after meetings of the members of the board of *The Christian News-Letter* (of which whole numbers were written by Eliot, who also was active in the direction of *The New English Weekly*). Eliot was weighed down by the imminent ruin of Europe: "Yet something he said to me here, in reply to an unconsidered expression of mine about patriotism, gave me a sudden realization that he, while fully sharing the emotional involve-

(273)

ment in the political situation, did so with a detachment of spirit I could not maintain, so that his response pierced me like a rebuke."[1] Eliot could not assent to Stephen Decatur's doctrine of "my country, right or wrong."

It was not patriotism alone that could save order in the world. Within three weeks, Poland was overrun by the Germans and the Russians; then, and for months thereafter, the British and the French seemed nerveless. Late in October, 1939, Eliot's little book on a Christian society was published (two thousand copies in London, and three thousand in New York at the beginning of January), while London lay under the blackout. Could Christian doctrine still be the light of the world?

The ideological materialists were declaring that Christianity was an exploded fable, in which no one could believe honestly: through political action would man be saved. There had just been published David Daiches' influential book *The Novel and the Modern World*, permeated by the assumptions of dialectical materialism. Eliot, and Aldous Huxley, were dismissed by Daiches as writers who avoided the real issue, "which is not personal compensation but the alteration of the environment which has produced the necessity for that compensation—the evolution and stabilisation of a standard in which society can believe and with reference to which its activities can be given purpose and meaning and value." Daiches implied that Eliot had affected a sham-religion, when he should have identified himself with the proletariat— rather a comical notion, in Eliot's case—and have submitted to the current of historical determinism.

To Daiches, there replied Edwin Muir: "To believe such things is ultimately to believe that we have no personal relations and no personal difficulties in living, but merely the public duty to change our environment, a duty which will bring us allies and enemies and nothing else. Mr. Daiches

thinks that Mr. Eliot's religion is merely an avoidance of
the issue and a compensation for his real duty; yet how he
can believe that after reading *The Waste Land, Ash-Wednesday* and *The Family Reunion* is past imagining, unless he
has read them without believing that they deal with anything
real. . . . Words like 'compensation' are two-edged; Mr.
Daiches' interpretation of Mr. Eliot's experience may be a
compensation for not understanding it. The first condition
of any genuine criticism of Mr. Eliot's religion is that it
should be understood; the critic may then decide that it contains truth or contains nothing but error; but he is not
entitled to transform it into something else and then assess
it as something else."[2]

Daiches' persuasion that political dogmas should supplant
religious dogmas was precisely what Eliot had been criticizing for years in *The Criterion* and elsewhere; it was a more
polished form of the quasi-professional "anti-Fascism" that
Eliot had found as repugnant, and as dangerous, as Fascism
itself. The most biting contempt for fanatic "anti-Fascism"
was expressed by a veteran of the P.O.U.M. militia in
Catalonia—George Orwell, whose *Coming up for Air* was
published in June, 1939.

"You know the line of talk," says Orwell's George Bowl-
ing, who has been listening to a "well-known anti-Fascist"
lecturer. "These chaps can churn it out by the hour. Just like
a gramophone. Turn the handle, press the button and it
starts. Democracy, Fascism, Democracy. . . . What's he
doing? Quite deliberately, and quite openly, he's stirring up
hatred. Doing his damndest to make you hate certain foreign-
ers called Fascists. It's a queer thing, I thought, to be known
as 'Mr. So-and-so, the well-known anti-Fascist.' A queer
trade, anti-Fascism. This fellow, I suppose, makes his living
by writing books against Hitler. But what did he do before
Hitler came along? . . . He's trying to work up hatred in the

audience, but that's nothing to the hatred he feels himself. Every slogan's gospel truth to him. . . . Perhaps even his dreams are slogans."[3]

Orwell and Eliot shared a detestation of the ideologue. (In 1940, Orwell would list Eliot as one of his four favorite living authors.) But what could restrain ideologues, Orwell's men "who think in slogans and talk in bullets"? Orwell, in the end, saw little hope for restraining them; he could not bring himself to share Eliot's religious understanding of society. Eliot's remedy was the recovery of Christian community, expressed in *The Idea of a Christian Society*.

To this little book (the core of which was his Boutwood lectures at Corpus Christi College, Cambridge, in March, 1939) Eliot appended his radio talk of February, 1937, "The Church's Message to the World"—perhaps his best brief political statement. "We need not assume that our form of constitutional democracy is the only one suitable for a Christian people, or that it is itself a guarantee against an anti-Christian world," he had told his B.B.C. audience. "Instead of merely condemning Fascism and Communism, therefore, we might do well to consider that we also live in a mass-civilisation following many wrong ambitions and wrong desires, and that if our society renounces completely its obedience to God, it will become no better, and possibly worse, than some of those abroad which are popularly execrated. . . .

"For most people, the actual constitution of Society, or that which their more generous passions wish to bring about, is right, and Christianity must be adapted to it. But the Church cannot be, in any political sense, either conservative, or liberal, or revolutionary. Conservatism is too often conservation of the wrong things; liberalism a relaxation of discipline; revolution a denial of the permanent things."[4]

A Neutral Society cannot long endure; a Pagan Society rightly is abominated by the upholders of democracy. There remains the possibility of recovering the idea of a Christian Society, much decayed in the twentieth century. Whatever is positive in modern society still is Christian, or derived from Christian belief; but the culture of negation looms before us, Eliot said.

Liberalism and Democracy cannot stand unsupported. Liberalism is "something which tends to release energy rather than accumulate it, to relax, rather than to fortify.... By destroying traditional social habits of the people, by dissolving their natural collective consciousness into individual constituents, by licensing the opinions of the most foolish, by substituting instruction for education, by encouraging cleverness rather than wisdom, the upstart rather than the qualified, by fostering a notion of *getting on* to which the alternative is a hopeless apathy, Liberalism can prepare the way for that which is its own negation: the artificial, mechanised or brutalised control which is a desperate remedy for its chaos." Already Liberalism is dissolving.[5]

As for Democracy, that state of society has been enfeebled by materialism; and a democracy without religious faith must be "a state of affairs in which we shall have regimentation and conformity, without respect for the needs of the individual soul . . ." Too often, what we call democracy is either financial oligarchy manipulating the mass of people, or else the regime of the demagogue. "The term 'democracy' . . . does not contain enough positive content to stand alone against the forces that you dislike—it can easily be transformed by them. If you will not have God (and He is a jealous God) you should pay your respects to Hitler or Stalin."[6]

Christianity prescribes no especial form of government. Yet the source of any political order is a religious creed—or else the inverted religion of ideology. A principal function of the state is the maintenance of justice; and justice can be defined only upon ethical assumptions, ultimately derived from religious insights. If the state is in opposition to the religious principles of a society, or indifferent to those principles, then either the state or the society is not long for this world. For our civilization, Christianity has provided both the principles of personal order and the principles of social order. If we repudiate or ignore those principles, our only alternative is the Pagan State, obeying the commandments of the Savage God. So it is that we must labor to restore the Christian State. It is not necessary that all statesmen be good Christians; nor is it necessary that dissent be discouraged among the citizens; but it is necessary that the state should recognize the moral order which Christianity outlines, and should conform the public order, so far as possible in this imperfect world, to that ethical understanding. (It will be understood that throughout this exposition, I am paraphrasing Eliot's arguments, not advancing some novel theories of my own.)

For a Christian State to come into being, there must exist a Christian Community, or a society in which most people are strongly influenced by Christian teaching. That community is given direction by a "much smaller number of conscious human beings," the Community of Christians. These men and women, somewhat resembling Coleridge's "clerisy" but not confined to clergymen and teachers, are the minority whose faith is founded upon right reason, and who by their example and their leadership consciously and conscientiously guide the mass of citizens whose acceptance of Christian belief is passive only.

The Community of Christians, and the Church itself, must recognize, and work within, the social condition of the modern world—but should not be totally immersed in that world, or conform Christian doctrine to the follies of the time. They may revise the parish structure; they may not revise the Sermon on the Mount. "However bigoted the announcement may sound, the Christian can be satisfied with nothing less than a Christian organisation of society—which is not the same thing as a society consisting exclusively of devout Christians. It would be a society in which the natural end of man—virtue and well-being in community—is acknowledged for all, and the supernatural end—beatitude— for those who have the eyes to see it."[7]

That is not the society and the state which "the West" enjoys today. The war against the Fascist powers was not a struggle of Christendom against Paganism, for Britain and her allies were not genuinely Christian powers. As Lincoln had said during the Civil War in America, he did not know that God was on "our side"; he only hoped that we were on His. Much denunciation of the Axis powers, Eliot believed, was no better than a device for ignoring or concealing similar vices in one's own society (another point on which he was in agreement with George Orwell).

As Peter Kirk writes of *The Idea of a Christian Society,* "The theme that it states is not one which was popular at the time, when the air was full of the voices of politicians and parsons informing the world that we were fighting for Christianity against paganism, nor would it be overpopular now, when many politicians and parsons are using the same phrases, having merely moved the pagans a little further East. Not that Eliot was prepared to condone in any way what Nazis or Communists are doing; he is merely pointing out that, whatever we are doing, and however right it may be—and it is astonishing how relevant the book still is to our times—we are not defending Christian society against paganism, because we are not living in a Christian society."[8]

A nation must have a political philosophy, Eliot continues —something more than the programs of parties. A vestigial Christianity still provides a tattered rag of political principle for the western democracies, but expediency counts for more nowadays. For political theory, as for morals, there is needed the visible and recognized Church, of which the Church of

England has been a form. Yet Church and State must not be a unity—of that Erastian error, the ruin of the Russian church stands as a dread warning. "Two there are by whom this world is ruled."

Nor should Christianity be advocated because it is socially beneficial; what matters is truth, not immediate material advantage. Benefits may flow from faith, but not faith from benefits. Eliot detested endeavors to employ religion as a moral stimulant or police-force: the man who advocates a vague generalized religiosity as a means to national invigoration is living a lie, for no one believes in a "socially expedient" religion. With the Bishop of Durham, Eliot condemned movements like Frank Buchman's "Moral Rearmament," which "may engender nothing better than a disguised and peculiarly sanctimonious nationalism, accelerating our progress towards the paganism which we say we abhor."*

The Kingdom of Christ on earth never will come to pass in history, literally, though in a sense we realize that Kingdom in daily acts of good. "We must remember that whatever reform or revolution we carry out, the result will always be a sordid travesty of what human society should be—though the world is never left wholly without glory."[9] Even were we to recover the Christian Community and the Chris-

---

* Buchman's "Moral Rearmament" movement, active in 1939, became more influential (or more extravagant in its claims to influence) in the years after the Second World War, and did not expire as a coherent organization until 1970, when its American center at Mackinac Island, in Michigan, was closed. Although in 1939 the Buchmanites professed zeal for democracy, earlier Buchman had admired the Nazi leaders—Heinrich Himmler in particular. Originally Buchman had called his movement the "Oxford Group"—surely a far cry from the Oxford Movement of Keble and Pusey and Newman. Eliot was closely acquainted with the writings of Herbert Hensley Henson, who as Bishop of Durham had smitten the Buchmanites hip and thigh. See Bishop Hensley Henson, *The Group Movement, being the first part of the charge delivered at the third quadrennial visitation of his diocese* . . . (1933), particularly the Introduction.

tian State, we would not be purged of original sin, and decay would recommence at once. But if we ignore the very *idea* of such a society, only force can make it possible for us to live in community. Then, of necessity, the totalitarian state fills the vacuum left by the disappearance of the Church.

Even if the democracies do not slide into their own variety of totalitarianism, Eliot argues, still they are irreligious in many ways already, particularly in their economic measures. To organize society merely on the principle of private profit leads to a rejection of nature—including the exhaustion of natural resources by unregulated industrialism, and ending in "dearth and desert." Utilitarian "progress," so closely connected with the ideology of liberalism, breaks the contract of eternal society, despoiling the soil itself. "For a long enough time we have believed in nothing but the values arising in a mechanised, commercialised, urbanised way of life: it would be as well for us to face the permanent conditions upon which God allows us to live upon this planet."[10]

Here, as elsewhere in this treatise, Eliot is close to Samuel Taylor Coleridge. It is worth remarking that Eliot's aside concerning nature's resources—the impiety of ravaging the earth to satisfy immediate material appetites and the desire for quick profit—was echoed precisely thirty years later by many people of different moral and social principles.

"As political philosophy derives its sanction from ethics," Eliot wrote, "and ethics from the truth of religion, it is only by returning to the eternal source of truth that we can hope for any social organisation which will not, to its ultimate destruction, ignore some essential aspect of reality." The events of September, 1938, had awakened many people, Eliot among them, to the need for contrition, humility, repentance, and amendment; to the need for ideas with which to withstand totalist ideology. "Was our society, which had always been so assured of its superiority and rectitude, so confident of its unexamined premisses, assembled round anything more permanent than a congeries of banks, insurance companies and industries, and had it any beliefs more essential than a belief in compound interest and the maintenance of dividends?"[11]

Almost twelve months after the disgrace of Munich, the war—brought on in part by Britain's lack of moral firmness— fell upon Europe. On September 6, 1939—when Polish lancers were charging German tanks—Eliot had just time to add a final paragraph to his book. The world must choose either Christianity or Paganism, he said; and thought must not be deferred until the war should end.

Like much of Eliot's work, *The Idea of a Christian Society* seems a fragment; one wishes he had written more. Nine years later, however, he would resume much of his argument in *Notes towards the Definition of Culture*. Even so, this annotated essay of 1939—sneered at by many reviewers, still unread by most people who might sympathize with Eliot's convictions—has gained in meaning with the elapse of three decades.

Most of Eliot's essays and reviews during the war years remain uncollected: they must be tracked down in old numbers of the *Times, The Listener, The New English Weekly, The Christian News-Letter, Partisan Review,* and other periodicals. To the war itself, his references were incidental. Living much of that time with friends at Guildford, he did his work in London as the great city was bombed almost out of recognition.

W. H. Auden and Christopher Isherwood—like Hobbes, "the first of all that fled," despite their zealous anti-Fascism— already had sailed for the United States, and many British writers would emulate them. Wyndham Lewis would go to Canada; Pound would broadcast in Italy for the Fascist regime; Roy Campbell would shoulder his Flowering Rifle against the Italians in Africa. The German bombing of London commenced on August 24, 1940. As a fire-warden in

Russell Square, Eliot looked upon the perfection of technology in the German robot-bombs, and saw Wren's churches burn. "O City, City!"

He had cast his lot deliberately with England long years before, and he would not withdraw in the hour of agony. Urbane as ever, he published "The Dry Salvages" and "Little Gidding"; he lectured to the Classical Association, of which he had been chosen president, on "The Classics and the Man of Letters"; to the Virgil Society, on "What Is a Classic?" He endured while death undid so many. In the middle of the war there appeared his *Four Quartets*, through which the dead spoke to the living.

The Pleasing Dreadful Thought

Except for the terror of bombed and burning London, in the second part of "Little Gidding," the *Four Quartets* have to do with things more enduring than wars and rumors of wars. Eliot's greatest philosophical poem (for *Four Quartets* form a unity, rather than a series of poems) was published as a book in New York in the spring of 1943, and in London in the autumn of 1944; but all four poems had appeared earlier—"Burnt Norton" in his *Collected Poems* of 1936; the the other three originally in *The New English Weekly*, during 1940, 1941, and 1942, and also in separate editions. Although *Four Quartets* mystified the common reader even more than had Eliot's earlier long poems, its critical success and its sales were larger: like *Prufrock*, to some *Four Quartets* came as relief from slaughter and war propaganda.

By this time, also, nearly all literate people knew that if they made any claim to intellectuality, they must read Eliot. In a broadcast talk for the BBC's Eastern Service, in 1942, George Orwell (despite his differences with such writers as Eliot and Joyce) declared that these men of the early nineteen-twenties mattered mightily: "They broke the cultural circle in which England had existed for something like a century. They re-established contact with Europe, and they brought back the sense of history and the possibility of tragedy. On that basis all subsequent English literature that matters twopence has rested, and the development that Eliot and the others started, back in the closing years of the last war, has not yet run its course."[12]

Yet Orwell was no admirer of *Four Quartets*. A few months later, reviewing "Burnt Norton," "East Coker," and "The Dry Salvages," Orwell wrote that Eliot's later work made no deep impression upon him: "It is clear that something has departed, some kind of current has been switched off, the later verse does not *contain* the earlier, even if it is claimed as an improvement upon it." What was wrong? Why, Eliot's subject matter, Orwell wrote: Eliot had become an orthodox Christian, and "the Christian churches still demanded assent to doctrines which no one seriously believes in." Eliot, he concluded, "does not really *feel* his faith, but merely assents to it for complex reasons. It does not in itself give him any fresh literary impulse."[13]

In Orwell's preference for Eliot's earlier poetry over his later, I happen to concur, to some degree; it is true, as Orwell says, that not so many lines of *Four Quartets* stick in the reader's head. The immediate effect of "Gerontion" or *The Waste Land* or "The Hollow Men" is more awakening than that of *Ash-Wednesday* or the *Quartets*. But the greater wisdom is found in the later poems, and that serenity which was Dante's and Virgil's.

I cannot agree with Orwell that Eliot gave no more than a melancholy assent to doctrines now quite unbelievable. Over the past quarter of a century, most serious critics— whether or not they find Christian faith impossible—have found in the *Quartets* the greatest twentieth-century achievements in the poetry of philosophy and religion. *Four Quar-*

tets, as Vincent Buckley writes, "presuppose certain values as necessary for their very structure as poems yet devote that structure to questioning their meaning and relevance. The whole work is, in fact, the most authentic example I know in modern poetry of a satisfying religio-poetic meditation. We sense throughout it not merely a building-up of an intricate poetic form on the foundation of experiences already over and done with, but a constant energy, an ever-present activity, of thinking and feeling."[14]

In the following examination of these four connected poems, or this long poem, I take it for granted that readers of this book have studied, or will read attentively, the poem itself. The "lemon-squeezer school of criticism," disliked by Eliot, is too fond of lengthy indolent quoting from the poet, extracting drops of juice that these drops may be inspected briefly through the critic's microscope. Carried to excess, this technique bewilders the common reader and bores the man who has read Eliot several times over. I endeavor here to get at Eliot's larger meanings, rather than to dissect *Four Quartets* upon a literary anatomist's slab.

As Orwell remarked, the *Quartets* profess Christian resignation; but what Orwell did not see, or could not believe, also they are visions of Paradise. "Prufrock," "Gerontion," *The Waste Land,* and "The Hollow Men" are delineations of Hell; *Ash-Wednesday* leads us up Mount Purgatory; and *Four Quartets* point out the way to the Rose Garden that endures beyond time, where seeming opposites are reconciled. Freed from Time, Sin, and Ego, modern man may know God and enjoy Him forever—if man does not presume to try to understand Him. With *Four Quartets,* Eliot at last achieves that ordering of the emotions, or of the soul, which had been his aspiration for three decades.

In a subtle fashion well described by Denis Donoghue, Eliot's undertaking in *Four Quartets* is strategic: it has ties with the War and with his lectures on a Christian society.

Eliot is evacuating metaphysical and theological positions that no longer can be held, so that man may build anew upon the fastness of the Rock. "The critique is religious, dogmatic, and Christian," in Donoghue's words. "Eliot's hope is to clear a space, or if necessary to take over a bombed-out area, and there to build a new life of the spirit; to realize 'the idea of Christian society.' He will approach the Meaning from several experimental directions, making several fresh starts, because he can hardly hope—the conditions being unpropitious—that one will suffice. The redemption of time will be his theme, his case, but he will have to resist a Manichean force within himself which is notoriously subversive; it doesn't really believe that time can be redeemed, it fears that the human scale of action is puny beyond or beneath redemption. . . . And therefore an 'ideal' strategy for a secular age would consist in persuading one's reader to void his allegiances by showing up his daily preoccupations as mere 'fancies'; and then to translate this voiding into renunciation, a positive sacrifice which he is encouraged to make to a God now certified by the quality of the sacrifice itself."[15]

So, as Orwell saw, the concluding passage of "The Dry Salvages" counsels resignation to the grave beneath the yew-trees; but what Orwell missed, that resignation is not the significance of life and death. Resignation is only a means to redemption and to that eternity for which the soul is intended. We renounce vanities and errors that we may redeem the time and transcend the time: that we may pass, purged, beyond death to the vision of the multifoliate rose and to the peace which surpasses all understanding. Despite its strategy of evacuation, the parts of the *Four Quartets* form a *Paradiso* of the twentieth century.

In each Quartet, a discovery is made; and, as Helen Gardner suggests, it is the same discovery in all four poems, but a discovery expressed through a variety of images and settings. The *Four Quartets* constitute both certain fragmentary descriptions of experience of transcendence, and certain criticisms of the modern temper. The central discovery, the meaning, is this: through the transcendent consciousness, it is possible to know God, and through Him to know immortality.

"Eternity! Thou pleasing dreadful thought!" So Addison's Cato exclaims, about to fling himself upon his sword. Although Eliot knows the terror and the promise of Eternity, he knows that thought as a Christian must, not as did the Stoic who died at Utica. The simple soul in "Animula," issuing from the hand of time, "irresolute and selfish, misshapen, lame," after its hard trial of the world, is restored—to the eternity of Love.

From the limits and the powers of his art, the true poet cannot employ the methods of discursive reason. The poet must offer images that wake emotions; his way toward truth is the leaping vision. He does not impart theology; rather, he makes it possible for his readers to understand religious belief. As Eliot was to say at Concord in 1947, "If we learn to read poetry properly, the poet never persuades us to believe anything. . . . What we learn from Dante, or the *Bhagavad-Gita*, or any other religious poetry is what it *feels* like to believe that religion."[16]

To demand that Dante be didactic after the system of Aquinas would be to efface *The Divine Comedy*; to demand that Eliot, in little more than a thousand lines of verse, should refute modern rationalism—that would be to deny the function of poetry. So it is through a diversity of questing insights, through abstractions illustrated by concrete representations, that Eliot renews the moral imagination. The rest must be left to theological studies, and to one's own experiences of reality.

All that such a poem as *Four Quartets* may accomplish is

to relate one remarkable man's vision of time, self, reality, and eternity: to describe one person's experience of transcendence. Because there does exist a community of souls, it is possible for some other human beings to apprehend the poet's symbols of transcendence; and to draw analogies between those symbolic images and their own fleeting glimpses, in the journey of this life, of permanent things not knowable through the ordinary restricted operation of five senses. Phenomenology notwithstanding, it is possible for a conscience to speak to a conscience, and for the interior perceptions of a man of genius to quicken and order another man's moral imagination.

One cannot understand *Four Quartets* if one reads with the eyes of ignorance or the eyes of prejudice. If one assumes, for instance, that Eliot is trying to revive some simplistic catechism, or if one knows the genius of Christianity only through early unhappy experience with the dissidence of dissent—why, then such a reader concludes that Eliot either was insincere or self-deluding.

T. S. Eliot was very well aware that the natural sciences had worked a new Reformation. He is not defending medieval superstitions, or the pietism of the nineteenth century; still less the twentieth-century chaos of cults or the pseudo-religious "ethos of sociability." Instead, Eliot is doing this: he is endeavoring honestly, and with a high talent for penetration, to renew a type of perception from which the natural sciences, by their nature, are barred. Readers who desire a lucid and systematic explanation of the Christian doctrines Eliot expresses in *Four Quartets*—but an explanation little encumbered by the complex vocabulary of modern theology—will do well to consult Father Martin D'Arcy's little book *Death and Life*, published in 1942. The doctrine of Heaven, as D'Arcy writes, belongs to the *disciplina arcani*; so if there are mysteries in Eliot's poem, that is because no subject is more difficult to communicate.[17]

Nor is it possible to appreciate Eliot—whether or not one agrees with him—if one comes to *Four Quartets* with ideological blinders. Ideology, it must be remembered, is the attempt to supplant religious dogmas by political and scientistic dogmas. If one's first premise is that religion must be a snare and a delusion, for instance, then it follows that Eliot becomes an enemy to be assaulted, rather than a pilgrim whose journey one may admire—even if one does not believe in the goal of that quest. Truly there exists such a state as the invincible ignorance of the learned. If Liberalism, or Socialism, or Communism, has become a god-word, not to be questioned; if Science has become an uncritical faith, amounting really to Scientism—then the captive of ideology will be unable to read with understanding what Eliot wrote painfully and carefully.

Eliot was not ignorant of the strength of convictions contrary to his own; nor did he commence with prejudices. In *Four Quartets,* he does not assume the prophetic afflatus: instead, he opens to inspection all the doubts and difficulties of his position, with a candor seldom encountered. Over a quarter of a century, he had been searching; he had come to certain beliefs by experience of life, by reading of books, and by much exchange with other minds of his time. What Eliot offers in this last and most meditated of his long poems is a picture of the insights he had obtained.

These insights may be accepted or rejected; but it is not well to reject or to accept them from ignorance or prejudice. Here a powerful intellect and an earnest conscience regard ultimate questions. Of course one may sweep aside all such questions as irrelevant to this life of the senses. But such an unexamined life is not worth living; and besides, while an individual may survive in disregard of all such questions, any society that ignores ultimate questions must find its tenure nasty and short.

Still Point and Numinous Depths

Each of the Quartets is connected with (and in some measure, evoked by) a particular place. "Burnt Norton" commences in the garden of a country place in the Cotswolds. In that unspoilt district about Chipping Campden and Chipping Norton, Eliot spent some time during the summer of 1934, after the twelve months that had been the loneliest of his life.

There is a country house called Burnt Norton (set afire by its owner in the eighteenth century). But the formal garden and shadowy house of this poem are composites, doubtless. In Chipping Campden, the shell of a ruined manor-house of the sixteenth century stands near the church; Hidcote Manor, three miles away, has a famous garden, open to the public; at Great Tew, five miles from Chipping Norton, there had lived Lord Falkland, gathering about him in that house the scholars and poets whose company Eliot might have relished more than he enjoyed the communication of twentieth-century intellectuals. All these scenes and memories lie back of "Burnt Norton."

The sweet slopes of the Cotswolds, and the old cottages of warm stone, stood for rustic England and for a long historical continuity. Otherwise, Burnt Norton (or the composite called Burnt Norton) is not known to have had any especial significance, as a place, for Eliot. Except that the poet may have experienced some insight there in the Cotswolds (akin, perhaps, to Carlyle's experience in Leith Walk, though less dramatic), the Cotswold garden might have been any English garden. Written long before its companion poems, "Burnt Norton" is less a poem of place than are the others; it incorporates fragments left over from *Ash-Wednesday* and from *Murder in the Cathedral*, and when Eliot included this new poem in his *Collected Poems* of 1936 (where it complemented the choruses of *The Rock*), he had not yet thought through the scheme of *Four Quartets*. So though the places of the other Quartets were deeply rooted in Eliot's experience and memory, it would be profitless to dig for biographical shards at Burnt Norton.

The Incarnation has made it possible for us to enter into an abiding order of the soul, and so not to perish as beasts perish: that is the general expression of *Four Quartets*. In "Burnt Norton," however, this apprehension is latent or implicit only.[18] This first poem begins with reflections upon Time—drawn from Saint Augustine's *Confessions*, rather than from those lectures of Henri Bergson which the young Eliot had attended in Paris. Only the present moment really signifies for us, Eliot says: we cannot undo the past or foresee the future; yet our past has determined our present, and our decisions of this moment will endure for good or ill throughout our remaining years of this life. It is the exertion of the will *now* that matters: a moment may partake of eternity.

In this rose garden at Burnt Norton, memories enchant us. There are touches of the garden in *Ash-Wednesday*, and of the earlier Hyacinth Garden, and—far stronger—of the door not opened to the rose garden at Wishwood, in *The Family Reunion*—written just after "Burnt Norton." This garden is Eden; also it is our private lost hopes and loves. We are lured into vain speculations upon what might have been, had we taken another path, opened another door.

Children's voices cry from the leaves, joyful; but those children are only children that might have been, as in Kipling's story "They"; perhaps they are the children that Old Possum never fathered. Stately presences, too, walk in this garden, as once they walked in the gardens of Great Tew; possibilities unrealized, talents neglected, whisper all round us. It will not do to linger here in illusion, for full knowledge

(*291*)

of what might have been, but was cast away, would be unbearable: mankind cannot bear to look steadfastly upon reality. And the meaning of existence must be found in the present.

In the second movement of this musical poem "Burnt Norton," we transcend memory and regret, that we may discern (as in *Coriolan* and in *Murder in the Cathedral*) "the still point of the turning world"—the axle upon which the wheel of life revolves, permanence in the midst of change. Existence is an order, a dance of measures; human existence is possible only because of that still point, where time and the timeless intersect.[19]

True consciousness is not to be found within what we call time; consciousness—awareness of Self and of abiding order—is transcendence of time. Yet from time we cannot escape long; prolonged simultaneous awareness of past and present and future would destroy us; brief moments of genuine consciousness, of suffusing vision, are all that we can endure in this life. "Only through time time is conquered"—that is, only in the confused experience of this life of ours can we encounter, "by a grace of sense," that inner freedom which is release from inner and outer compulsion.

From the rose garden, in the third movement of "Burnt Norton," we are swept abruptly to the London Underground, neither daylight nor darkness, a place like Death's dream kingdom. These passengers in the wilderness of technology —time-ridden, "distracted from distraction by distraction," apathetic and purposeless—are modern people who do not know the Logos, the Word, the source of order; who exist unaware of an enduring and transcendent truth. "Burnt Norton" has for epigraphs two passages from Heraclitus. "Although the Logos is common to all, most men live as if each had a private wisdom of his own," is the first. "The way up and the way down are the same," runs the other. These

Underground passengers live by their myopic private judgment and by their appetites; by those are they betrayed.
If one would be more than a Hollow Man, he must descend
into the depths of the soul, or else ascend the purgatorial stair
of *Ash-Wednesday*. By either route, he may find his way to
that still point which is divine love and wisdom.*

Deep underground indeed lie the numinous depths,
the Dark Night of Saint John of the Cross. By evacuation of
the world of fancy, renunciation of the love of created beings,
destitution and denial of the senses, one may attain to a
glimpse of the Love that does not change. This renunciation
of the Ego makes possible recognition of the Self; few walk
that way.

With the ten lines of the fourth movement of "Burnt
Norton," we return from the depths of the *via negativa*
to vegetal nature—but to a country churchyard, rather than
to the rose garden. Do we end altogether in the grave, "fingers of yew . . . curled down on us?" We are answered in
the fifth movement: by participation in the timeless pattern
of transcendent reality, we may escape desire and dissolution. We may know, through a discipline, the Self and the
Other to whom the Self is drawn.

Eternity may be experienced in those rare moments of
true consciousness when one escapes from the clutch of
Time—such moments as are suggested by C. S. Lewis' phrase
"surprised by joy." The world being too much with us, we

---

* Although Eliot does not employ the word "numinous," there exists
no better term for expressing this sense of dependence upon God which
is found in the mystical Night of the Soul. The word "numinous" was
coined by Rudolf Otto, in 1923, to describe the Object of the religious
experience called "creature-feeling"—that is, dependence upon a
presence other than the Self, resulting from "submergence into noth-
ingness before an overpowering, absolute might of some kind." See
Rudolf Otto, *The Idea of the Holy: An Inquiry into the non-rational
factor in the idea of the divine and its relation to the rational* (1923),
Chapter I.

enter upon those moments seldom, though they alone make
life worth living:

> Ridiculous the waste sad time
> Stretching before and after.

If "Burnt Norton" stood alone, it would be the most
puzzling poem in the English language. What could the
reader make of this, from a poet who would·redeem the time?

> If all time is eternally present
> All time is irredeemable.

But this, Eliot makes clear later, is only the *apparent*
nature of time. (As Helen Gardner remarks, one finds in
Four Quartets a literal meaning, a moral meaning, and a
mystical meaning.)[20] In truth, only to God is all time eternally
present; and to God there are known also all intentions un-
fulfilled, all possibilities not realized. From man, mercifully,
the total awareness of simultaneity is kept back, together
with knowledge of what might have been. And by the grace
of God (which grace is the half-hidden theme of "Burnt
Norton") indeed man may be redeemed and may redeem the
time. The rose garden need ñot be the wistful garden of
Wishwood or Burnt Norton merely: much we have lost
through sin or negligence, but much do we retain.

In "Burnt Norton," Eliot is haunted by wasted possibilities, and grace is only glimpsed. The possibility of grace
might not of itself efface remorse for "the waste sad time";
but Eliot had come to believe in more dogmas than the dogma
of grace. The later Quartets have to do with the dogmas
of faith, hope, and charity, and through them many of the
seeming omissions of "Burnt Norton" are made up. And
throughout them all, one must bear in mind that Eliot is
not describing a religious "experience," except incidentally:
his intention is to describe, as he put it, "the experience of
believing a dogma." He affirms the poetic vision as a means to
the apprehension of a transcendent order, and he offers a

(294)

criticism both of blinkered unbelief and of the illusion that poetry can do duty for religion.

On the Edge of a Grimpen

"Burnt Norton" is a poem of early summer, and of air; "East Coker," a poem of late summer, and of earth. The subject of "Burnt Norton" is grace; of East Coker, faith.

From East Coker, in 1667, Andrew Eliot had gone out to Massachusetts Bay Colony. In that Somerset village, two centuries earlier, had been born Simon Elyot, the grandfather of Sir Thomas Elyot, and the family connection is renewed in Eliot's poem.* In the poem's first movement, Eliot's ghostly dancing villagers were put into his mind by Friedrich Gerstärker's story "Germelshausen," set in a parish long under the Interdict, neither living nor dead, which rises from beneath the earth once in a century, for a single day of joy, only to sink back. Anyone who visits East Coker must perceive the parallel: for the tooth of time scarcely has gnawed at that village.

Eliot first saw the place in August, 1937, and came to love it; there, in the thirteenth-century church of St. Michael, his ashes lie now. East Coker is an easy walk from the market-town of Yeovil—a pleasant town, Yeovil, like one of Hardy's Wessex towns, when Eliot first visited Somerset, but now disfigured by grim economic processes. East Coker, nevertheless, still is a "beauty spot": almost perfect, with charming farmhouses and cottages (of a golden stone, rather than the "grey stone" in the poem), many of them thatched,

---

* Most glossators on T. S. Eliot state erroneously that Thomas Elyot was born at East Coker. But that was his ancestral hamlet only; the author of *The Boke named the Gouvernour* probably was born in Wiltshire.

and the newer houses built of that stone much in the same style. On a ridge above the straggling hamlet stands St. Michael's, with its graveyard ("old stones that cannot be deciphered") and the massive ancient house of Coker's Court, once an ecclesiastical building. (The wind has not broken the loosened pane of Coker's Court, really: this manor-house is inhabited and in good repair.) By what Eliot called "a loop in time," East Coker has remained much as it appeared in the day of Andrew Eliot, and earlier.

In St. Michael's (with a vicar, a curate, and perhaps twenty-five worshipers, when I attended a Sunday service there), a tablet in memory of William Dampier is fixed high on a wall—Dampier, great navigator and lively writer, but less happy as buccaneer, who contrived to intercept the Manila galleon in the vastness of the Pacific and then failed to take her. (He was born in this parish, but died in London, and no one knows where his bones lie.) The other chief memorial, to a very different sort of voyager, is the oval stone tablet, in the wall at the west end of an aisle, with this inscription: "In my beginning is my end. Of your kindness, pray for the soul of Thomas Stearns Eliot, poet. In my end is my beginning." By an intellectual voyage—dogmatic rather than enthusiastic, as Eliot wrote in *The Idea of a Christian Society*—the poet found his way to faith and to eternity; he took his galleon.

Eliot's survey of his age, in "East Coker," is gloomy as that in *The Waste Land*. Houses live and die, we are told in the first movement; they were dying throughout Europe as he wrote. "In my beginning is my end"—this inversion of Mary Stuart's motto dominates this poem, until at its close we are reminded that what the Queen of Scots had embroidered on her chair of state was no less true in its original expression: "In my end is my beginning." In the cycle of material life, everything passes to dust and ashes. A passage extracted from *The Boke named the Gouvernour*, with dancing as a symbol of ordered matrimony, suggests a model of community now perishing. The order of the sixteenth century, after all, was captive to time, and its aspirations have gone to the bonfire: life always has been Sweeney's "birth, and copulation, and death," a slow weary rhythm—if this life is all. Here at East Coker, Eliot's family had its beginning; here Eliot looks toward the end.

That material end may not be far distant, the first strophe of the second movement informs us: in our time, nature is disrupted, and we—whirled in a vortex—may be consumed in that destructive fire "which burns before the ice-cap reigns." But are these poetic images adequate? Words are tools that break in the hand. Are not the notions of the Renaissance, like that age's images, hollow today? Empirical knowledge cannot of itself suffice: the "quiet-voiced elders" bequeath to us "merely a receipt for deceit." Nowadays we abjure some of those elders' errors, committed in a time of arrogant optimism; yet our disillusion itself is superficial, for what notions we have exploded were past harming us. We retain the more damning errors, and to them add our own delusions; our own elder statesmen, Eliot implies, brought the Wars upon us, by trusting in practical experience only.

We blunder "on the edge of a grimpen" (the Grimpen Mere of *The Hound of the Baskervilles*), astray in thickets still; another step or two, and we end in slime. It is not old men, boasting of wisdom in their time, fearful "of belonging to another, or to others, or to God" who can guide us. Only in humility do we find true wisdom, as houses fall and dancers vanish beneath the hill.

Darkness falls upon the captains and the kings, in the third movement—upon the financiers and the industrialists, too, of our purblind materialistic age, and upon all who, with Coriolan, have paraded their vain ambitions for an hour. Again we glimpse the Underground, with the empty faces of passengers succumbing to "the growing terror of nothing to think about." We wait without thought, and even without hope, upon the coming of God. There is left to us faith alone, and trust in providential purpose. Again, the *via negativa* is our only path to wisdom—a way without ecstasy.

The motto of the Eliot family, the "silent motto" woven upon the tattered arras of "East Coker," was *tace et fac*— "be silent and act," or "be still and still moving."[21] The only action possible for us is the act of faith. Wait upon the coming of God, for no man is autonomous. The false dawn of Renaissance humanism was hubristic, and for that pride we pay now. If we renounce the ego, we may achieve consciousness. So in the fourth movement we are reminded that in Adam's fall, we sinned all. Christ, the wounded surgeon, operates upon us; this world is a spiritual hospital; the Church, our dying nurse; we cannot be hale until we have passed through purgatorial fires. Here, as so often in Eliot's writings, the critic with a smattering only of theology and church history begins to debate with himself and his colleagues about whether Eliot was really a Catholic, or really a Puritan. This tedious debate is unnecessary: for Eliot, here and elsewhere, is the disciple of Saint Augustine of Hippo, whose patrimony Catholic and Calvinist share. There ring echoes of Sir Thomas Browne and of Saint John of the Cross in his fourth movement, but within the encompassing orthodoxy of Augustine. Man and society suffer from a wasting disease of spirit, never to be cured wholly in this world. Eliot's cry is Augustine's: "There is in God, some say, a deep but dazzling dark. . . . O for that night, that I in Him might lie invisible and dim."

For the twenty years between the wars, Eliot says in the final movement of "East Coker," he had been a guerrilla of the mind, trying to recover what had been lost: a fight waged over and over again, through the ages, by men better than himself. "For us, there is only the trying. The rest is not our business." We wait upon the coming of God, but meanwhile we hold or retake what ground we can.

Those intense moments of perception, when we glimpse transcendent reality, do not stand isolated. We are part of a great continuity and essence; and in every moment a lifetime can burn, if we know love:

> There is a time for the evening under starlight,
> A time for the evening under lamplight
> (The evening with the photograph album).

Having been granted a glimpse of the truth of things, that is, we can be redeemed from the "waste sad time"; we can taste eternity in humble acts; it is not too late, however blind and slave to appetite we have been heretofore. Every moment of love counts, and makes up our immortality. Still and still moving, however old we are, exploration of reality through love and the higher dream remains possible for us— even in "the dark cold and empty desolation" of our time, so like Saint Augustine's time. "In my end is my beginning." Keep faith in that dogma, and faith will set us free from servitude to time.

A man's "end" is his aim, his purpose, his destination— not his destruction. So, at East Coker or wherever one's home lies, at a man's beginning his end may be discerned. That end, for those who apprehend a reality superior to "birth, copulation, and death"—a reality transcending the rhythms of physical nature—is to know God and enjoy Him forever. Or, as Christopher Dawson put it, this is true of a community's culture also. To achieve anything, a people must begin with a recognition of divine transcendence; this cultural beginning becomes that culture's end, its means of progress. In civilization, we commence with "the highest type of knowledge—the intuition of pure being." For man to become more than brute, there must exist a community of spirit:

"For a culture even of the most rudimentary kind is never simply a material unity," Dawson had written in 1929.

"It involves not only a certain uniformity in social organization and in the way of life, but also a continuous and conscious social discipline. . . . It must be remembered that intellectually, at least, man's development is not so much from the lower to the higher as from the confused to the distinct."[22] Of social thinkers in his own time, none influenced Eliot more than Dawson.

In the person and in the commonwealth, then, the end lies potent in the beginning. The end is not dissolution. For what we call the "end," the termination, of life is only a fresh beginning—though troubled as the Dream of Gerontius—for those who have submitted themselves to a discipline of spirit. What proofs have we of this? Platonic speculations, of course; but far greater than those, the Incarnation. "Were it not so, I would not have told you"; it is a proof, too, that without faith in the promise of life eternal, we become the most miserable of creatures.

Upon our momentary acts, here and now, union with the divine depends: through Christ, we participate in eternity. That lacking, we are ghosts performing a ritual dance; that lacking, we have only the knowledge of private experience and social empiricism, which fails us at need. Let us believe what we have been told, that we are spirits in prison, to be freed only through love of God and love of one another. "In the draughty church at smokefall," experiencing perhaps a moment out of consciousness which is a moment of reality, pray for the soul of Everyman.

Fare Forward, Voyagers

"The Dry Salvages" is a poem of water, and a poem of hope. Almost to a man, the critics assign it a dignity of style well below that of the other Quartets; some of its lines are perilously close to prose. But it serves as a transition from the somber passivity of "East Coker" to the high affirmation of "Little Gidding," and it promises liberation from the cycles of nature.

If this poem's imagery is less compelling, perhaps that is because Eliot evokes only distant memories of his boyhood beside the Mississippi and off the Massachusetts coast. Under Eads' Bridge (built fourteen years before Eliot was born), at St. Louis, the river bears toward the Gulf "its cargo of dead negroes, cows and chicken coops"; off Cape Ann, where the Eliots had their summer place, the ocean gnaws endlessly at the Dry Salvages, the beacon upon those rocks a warning against man's *hubris*. "The river is within us, the sea is all about us." In man's blood runs the continuity of mankind, and we are adrift upon the sea of time.

That bell upon the rocks tolls for us; but also it is the bell of the Annunciation. If we resign ourselves to immersion in time, "to the drift of the sea and the drifting wreckage," we end broken upon the Dry Salvages. I believe that no one has pointed out how closely Eliot's images here, of the fishing vessels and the bell upon the treacherous shoals, resemble the language of Paul Elmer More's essay on William James, who stood "entranced in the illusion of the present," resigned to the flux of time and change.[23]

Like More, T. S. Eliot could not accept James's preoccupation with the present moment, except as that moment was bound up with time past and time future; nor could they accept either the time-concept of Kant or the time-concept of Bergson. Like More, Eliot came to believe that only through Annunciation and Incarnation was the tyranny of time undone.

Without the hope that the Annunciation proclaimed to the world, twentieth-century man awaits his end "in a drifting boat with a slow leakage." Our hope does not lie in the present moment, even though right action in the present is our means to immortality. If we lack understanding of our personal past and of the historical past, the present moment is meaningless. The past has not been mere sequence of chance events; still less has it been the "evolution" of a vulgarized social Darwinism. Truly understood, the past has a pattern: those moments of sudden illumination held a meaning which we missed—

> And approach to the meaning restores the experience
> In a different form, beyond any meaning
> We can assign to happiness.

Not an ephemeral pleasure, but a taste of eternity, is the meaning of those moments of transcendence. Those illuminating moments occur to many of us, though infrequently; yet what matters more, we learn (as Eliot had written in "East Coker") not from "the lifetime of one man only," not from our private moments merely, but from such moments experienced by men of vision who have preceded us in time. What we call revelation is such experience of transcendence; we inherit a patrimony of vision from prophet and philosopher and poet. Those moments of ecstasy of spirit are permanent. And so are the moments of terrible vision— better understood through sympathy, by looking upon the agony of others:

> For our own past is covered by the currents of action,
> But the torment of others remains an experience
> Unqualified, unworn by subsequent attrition.

Mercifully, we forget our private terrors; we could not endure life if we were fully aware of the terror that our species has known; yet the fearsome "ragged rock in the restless waters" lies there always, awaiting our acts of arrogance. We are denied full awareness of the meaning of ecstatic vision because such understanding would bring with it a concomitant ruinous power to know fully the agonized moments.

Here, briefly—as if to rescue us from the vertigo of a

ship's pitching and rolling—in the third movement of "The Dry Salvages," Eliot shifts to the image of a train departing from a station (paralleling the third movements of the two preceding Quartets). The train's passengers are "not escaping from the past into different lives, or into any future." Yet those passengers are changing with every moment that passes; they cannot step into the same river twice.

So it is "on the deck of the drumming liner," as we watch the wake: when we disembark, we will not be the same people that we were when we went aboard. This truth is drawn from the *Bhagavad-Gita;* and so is the truth which follows—

> At the moment which is not of action or inaction
> You can receive this: "on whatever sphere of being
> The mind of a man may be intent
> At the time of death"—that is the one action
> (And the time of death is every moment)
> Which shall fructify in the lives of others:
> And do not think of the fruit of action.
> Fare forward.

To us (though not to God) the future is unknowable; the result of present action is unpredictable; all we can know is our past, and the past of mankind. Upon that knowledge of what has been—recognizing, at last, the meaning in previous experience—we must act to redeem the time. If we act in the light of the moral imagination, obtained from meditation upon experience, that reflective action joins us with God and may fructify in time to come.

If we pray for voyagers, living and dead, we may hear the ominous bell upon the rocks; but we may know it for an angelus. It is not through notions of interplanetary communication, through calling up spirits in the seance, through astrology, the Tarot cards, or other superstitions, that we can apprehend the intersection of time with the timeless. Nor will psychoanalysis redeem us—not exploration of "the womb, or tomb, or dreams." Only the saint transcends time and mortality. But what hope exists for those who are not saintly?

> For most of us, there is only the unattended
>
> Moment, the moment in and out of time,
>
> The distraction fit, lost in a shaft of sunlight . . .

Most of us must turn to prayer, observance, discipline, thought, and right action. Incarnation, the Logos made flesh, gives us the possibility of conquering past and future. If we do not know the divine, we are driven by the diabolical impulses of the underworld. Although our bodies must be sown in corruption, we pass on to our successors the life of spirit; beside the yew-tree, the verdant symbol of resurrection and immortality, we are part of an eternal continuity.[24] The drowned sailor rises on another shore, and the moral order joins the dead, the living, and those yet unborn.

Did Eliot genuinely believe in the Christian doctrine of the life eternal, including the resurrection of the body? Is this the hope of which he writes in "The Dry Salvages"? Orwell took Eliot's meaning to be merely that we resign ourselves to pushing up the crocuses beside the yew-tree, while the life of others goes on; and many commentators upon Eliot glide over the question with uneasy obscurity. But the question cannot be ignored: the answer to it makes, literally, a world of difference—the difference between the ethical Humanism which Eliot found insufficient and the Christian dogma which he came to affirm. It is the question that tormented Miguel de Unamuno, the most interesting philosopher of Eliot's age. In *The Tragic Sense of Life* (written about 1912), Unamuno—as notorious, in Spain, for his heretical opinions, as Eliot was notorious in England for his orthodox opinions—went to the heart of the matter: "The man who does not long passionately, and with a passion that triumphs over all the dictates of reason, for his own immortality, is the man who does not deserve it, and because he does not deserve it he does not long for it. . . . and perhaps the sin against the Holy Ghost—for which, according to the Evangelist, there is no remission—is none other than that of not desiring God, not longing to be made eternal."[25]

It was not Bradley's Absolute, but Unamuno's God, for which Eliot came to hope. Eliot hoped to pull down the vanity of the Ego, yet to save that aspect of the Self which we call the Soul. For Eliot's chain of reasoning, one does well to turn to the arguments of Father Martin D'Arcy in *Death and Life*. Through the Incarnation, the life eternal in Christ becomes a great deal more than pushing up the crocuses. In that "after-life" (which really is not "after," because it transcends time and attains simultaneity), the person endures, perfected. "All experience would be at the tip of the fingers of mind," D'Arcy writes, "and so alive that the past could be counted as real as the present. . . . Nor need there be anything fantastic in supposing a body which is adapted to the new condition of the soul, a body which is a work of art of the soul and alive with its new supernatural energy and loveliness." Past time will be redeemed truly: "Memories will give up their dead and the past will live again in this fullness of life."[26] What might have been in the earthly rose garden or hyacinth garden, but was not realized in time, will be known beyond time in the garden of the multifoliate rose. In "The Dry Salvages," Eliot does not demonstrate the reality of this hope, of course; no poet can do that, and no philosopher. What Eliot does accomplish is to make his readers feel how it is possible to accept the dogma of hope, which Eliot had learned to accept.

Redeemed from Fire by Fire

Remote in the seventeenth century, Little Gidding remains obscure today. One goes up to the Giddings, afoot or by hired car, from the little county town of Huntingdon, where

Oliver Cromwell was born and where, in 1612, at the church of All Saints, still jutting into the Great North Road, the body of Mary Queen of Scots rested on the way to Westminster Abbey. Those two now are symbols "perfected in death."

Even in 1625, when Nicholas Ferrar bought the place, Little Gidding was depopulated. Of three hamlets—Great Gidding, Little Gidding, Steeple Gidding, each with its church—Little Gidding is the least. The Hall where Ferrar's community of thirty or forty souls resided has vanished: there remains the little church (restored by Ferrar, and rebuilt in 1714), with its brass lectern of Ferrar's day—a spot "where prayer has been valid." To Little Gidding, Eliot found his way in the "midwinter spring" of 1936, turning "behind the pig-sty to the dull façade/ And the tombstone." Out of that visit came this poem of fire, and this poem of charity.

At Little Gidding, a man of genius founded what the Puritans called "the Arminian Nunnery," a retreat of Anglican piety that the Cromwellians would sack not long after Ferrar's death. The best brief description of that community, beloved by George Herbert and influencing Richard Crashaw, is Izaak Walton's, in his life of Herbert. Ferrar knew everything, and could have been anything; but in 1625, great in Parliament, he renounced preferment to lead a life of prayer and contemplation and religious discipline at Little Gidding.

"Professorships lay open to him," T. O. Beachcroft wrote of Ferrar, in *The Criterion*; "he was marked out for high office; every parliament man courted his acquaintance; he was even offered an heiress with ten thousand pounds. It is hard to find a parallel to his double mastery of the world of thought and action, save among the world's greatest men."[27] Yet with his kinsfolk, Ferrar withdrew to Little Gidding, there to undertake the life of spirit, most austerely. An apparent similarity of character may have attracted Eliot to

Ferrar's grave and church; there may be said of Eliot what
Bernard Blackstone wrote of Ferrar: "The restraint, the quiet
dignity, and the objectivity of Ferrar's writing proceed rather
from a continuous inner tension than from habitual serenity."
Upon the young Ferrar, the consciousness of sin lay heavy—
particularly of the sin of unbelief. And Ferrar had been a
religious poet, though Roundhead troopers roasted sheep over
their bonfire made of Ferrar's manuscripts and his organ's
fragments.

Charles I, Charles the Martyr, visited Little Gidding
thrice, they say—the last time just after his defeat at Naseby,
a broken Coriolanus at nightfall. So Eliot followed an antique
drum to Little Gidding, where in the end had been the beginning. During a time of destruction more ruinous still,
Eliot chose Little Gidding as the paradigm of the charity of
God that passes all understanding.

After a fashion, Little Gidding lies at the world's end.
Eliot might have chosen to kneel at other places, remoter:
Iona of Saint Columba, or Lindisfarne of Saint Cuthbert, or
Glendalough, or the Thebaid, or Padua of Saint Anthony—
all at the modern world's end, in their way, and all (except
the Thebaid) places he had seen. But rustic and humble
Little Gidding, disrupted in 1646, would do as well for the
offering of solitary prayer: Little Gidding, where

> Water and fire shall rot
> The marred foundations we forgot,
> Of sanctuary and choir.

The dead mystical Nicholas Ferrar, buried there—a kind-
lier spirit than the dead wizard of the Chapel Perilous—
might inform the poet, in a timeless moment of prayer: thus,
in the first movement of "Little Gidding," we come to the
burning lines that are graven upon Eliot's stone in the pavement of Westminster Abbey—

> And what the dead had no speech for, when living,
> They can tell you, being dead: the communication

Of the dead is tongued with fire beyond the language of the
living.

Uninhibited by our own hesitations and ambiguities, the
dead speak to us every hour: through history, through poetry,
through their surviving descriptions of moments of transcendent consciousness, through our memories of them—indeed, through our very flesh. We are full of ghosts, Lafcadio
Hearn had written: our genetic inheritance fills us with the
appetites and wishes and hopes and dreads of countless
ancestors. Past experience, as Eliot had written in "The
Dry Salvages," is the experience of many generations. Living
in us and in God's cognizance, those dead speak with a
clarity and a candor we cannot obtain from the people of
our own moment in time.

This being so, we must dwell, and find true consciousness,
among a community of souls, Eliot believed, joining past and
present and future. Our acts and our very thoughts at this
moment in time must reverberate unpredictably in time future—and in a sense at once larger and more subtle than
the genetic legacy that is the subject of Ibsen's *Ghosts*. This
awareness that the dead survive in us, and that we shall
survive in future generations, runs through the *Four Quartets.**

So, in the second movement of "Little Gidding," a dead
man is heard. In flaming London, at the hour between the
homeward wheeling of the night's last German bomber and
the horn of the all-clear signal, dust rises from old houses
annihilated in a moment—not left to the creeping decay

---

* There is a hint of surviving Buddhist doctrine, as well as Christian
belief, in this insight of *Four Quartets*. Eliot's reflections here on the
Self and its participation in "the sensations and ideas and desires of
other folk, mostly of dead people"—Lafcadio Hearn's phrase—parallel
fairly closely a passage in Hearn's essay "Dust," in his *Gleanings from
Buddha-Fields* (1897). Whether or not Eliot had read this piece by
Hearn, he was familiar with Paul Elmer More's essay on Hearn, which
refers to Hearn on cells and souls.

of the house in "East Coker." Theirs is "the death of hope
and despair"; they are reduced to "ash on an old man's
sleeve." The destroyer has passed overhead, and so has the
Dove, the Holy Ghost. Through the waning dusk there comes
"some dead master . . . a familiar compound ghost"—com-
pounded of Dante, Swift, Yeats, and (what the commentators
on Eliot generally ignore) perhaps Nicholas Ferrar, so like
Eliot himself. These two, dead master and living poet, meet
in a moment of true consciousness, out of time, and the narrator is compelled to take a double part: "Knowing myself
yet being someone other." Time and the timeless intersect;
personalities intertwine and yet discourse; there is imparted
the communication of the dead.

The language of this communication, "words I never
thought to speak," has a dread grandeur unexcelled elsewhere in Eliot's poetry. To the narrator this dead master
imparts a warning. Yesteryear's concern with critical theory
must be buried by the dead, as decay and dissolution draw
near. The senses atrophy; rage grows impotent; there come
remorse for actions once thought virtuous, disgust with
"fools' approval," and distaste for honors. What remains?*

> From wrong to wrong the exasperated spirit
>
> Proceeds, unless restored by that refining fire
>
> Where you must move in measure, like a dancer.

That saving, refining fire is the discipline of spirit. In this
poem's third movement, Eliot praises again that detachment
from self and things and persons which Saint John of the

---

* Although the better-known exegetists remark that this splendid
dismaying passage on the prospect of senility owes something to Swift,
Yeats, and Milton, only one of them—Grover Smith—mentions the
influence of *The Vanity of Human Wishes*. Yet surely the tone of
Samuel Johnson is strong here:

> In life's last scene what prodigies surprize,
>
> Fears of the brave, and follies of the wise!
>
> From Marlb'rough's eyes the streams of dotage flow,
>
> And Swift expires a driv'ler and a show.

Cross sought: not indifference, "between the live and the dead nettle," but renunciation of passion and ambition. Memory can liberate, teaching us how to pass beyond eros to agape—beyond desire to a purged love. Faces, places, and the self itself must be transfigured, "in another pattern," if aught is to endure. The knowledge of history, so often chaining one to old feuds and passions, can become an emancipating power.

Eliot weaves into this movement the perceptions of the medieval mystic Juliana of Norwich: "Sin is Behovely," and "All manner of thing shall be well." Much must be left to Providence, for even seeming evil is part of a divine pattern obscure to our eyes.* The church at Little Gidding evokes memories of opponents now "folded in a single party": King Charles, Cromwell, Archbishop Laud (whose friend Nicholas Ferrar had been), the forsaken Strafford, Ferrar, John Milton. What we are taught by these dead men, "all touched by a common genius," is the mystery of Providence and the continuity of society; we cannot ring the bell backward to raise them and their times:

> We cannot restore old policies
> Or follow an antique drum.

These lines may reflect Eliot's renunciation of his early hopes for a reinvigorated royalism, and his powerlessness to arrest the degradation of the democratic dogma. The devastation of the War weighed Eliot down. Yet it is our motives that God takes into account, not the success or

---

* Juliana's "Sin is Behovely," and Eliot's acceptance of the historical part played by men whose beliefs he opposed, is best explained in the words of Eliot's skeptical contemporary Unamuno: "Yes, everything deserves to be eternalized, absolutely everything, even evil itself, for that which we call evil would lose its evilness in being eternalized, because it would lose its temporal nature. For the essence of evil consists in its temporal nature, in its not applying itself to any ultimate and permanent end." (*The Tragic Sense of Life*, Chapter XI.)

failure of our actions; and those who seem to die desolate may move men's minds and consciences, centuries later:

> All manner of thing shall be well
> By the purification of the motive
> In the ground of our beseeching.

By fire we are consumed, the fourth movement of "Little Gidding" declares: our choice is the "incandescent terror" of the bombers, or else the descent of the Holy Ghost. The human will is free—to enter a hell terrestrial and spiritual, or to take the path of penitence. By divine love is this choice thrust upon us, by that primal love of which Hell itself is a necessary creation. We wear the burning shirt of Nessus, and only by passing through purgatorial fire can we escape our agony, "to be redeemed from fire by fire." Like the human person, the realm of England can be redeemed through repentance and a reawakening of the higher love.

For thirty years, Eliot had endeavored to restore the grammarian's order of the sentence and to refurbish words. What he had done as poet and critic—so he suggests in the final movement of "Little Gidding"—is analogous to the task of restoring order in the soul and in the commonwealth. Here he draws together the meanings and symbols of all the Quartets. From our beginning, we move by actions toward our end—actions that may lead "to the block, to the fire, down the sea's throat." History is no tale told by an idiot, signifying nothing: instead, history is a Providential pattern, discerned in certain timeless moments. The meaning of history is here and now, not in some misty future—here, indeed, in the chapel at Little Gidding, where the meaning of thought and action has survived dissolution and the passage of three centuries.

After all our vagrant days, we return to the rose garden—to Eden. Through right action, undertaken in humility, truly we may redeem the waste sad time. It is not "the spectre of a Rose" (the vain endeavor to conjure up what Time has devoured) that we should seek; for the Rose itself may be attained, blooming eternally in the love of God. Love like fire consumes our dross, and our essence is warmed in that flame.

These *Four Quartets* form the testament of a man of intellect and vision who, like Nicholas Ferrar, had found his way from early agonizing incertitudes to acceptance of dogma and discipline. Eliot had not demonstrated by his poems the truth of a creed; but he had shown, through imagery, how the believer comes to his belief. Although what Eliot had described was the experience and the reflection of one man only, others in the community of souls might draw parallels; they might discern the possibility of a similar journey of spirit, leading to order in the soul and to love in the commonwealth.

Perhaps, however, this is to claim too much: perhaps, as some critics have suggested, Eliot intended and accomplished no more than an approach to the meaning of the world of poetic insight. Even so, that was an achievement of high power. In Eliot's age, no poet could expect to accomplish more.

As Eliot had written in "Shakespeare and the Stoicism of Seneca" (1927), every poet starts from his own emotions. In that essay, Eliot mentions Dante's "nostalgia, his bitter regrets for past happiness—or for what seems happiness when it is past—and his brave attempts to fabricate something permanent and holy out of his personal animal feelings . . ." Those phrases may be applied to Eliot himself. Dante and Shakespeare, said Eliot, make "gigantic attempts to metamorphose private failures and disappointments. The great poet, in writing himself, writes his time."

Just so; and what Dante was to the fourteenth century, or Shakespeare to the sixteenth, Eliot became to the twentieth century. "Poetry is not a substitute for philosophy or theology or religion," Eliot concluded in 1927; "it has its own function. But as this function is not intellectual but emotional, it cannot be defined adequately in intellectual terms."

One does not look to Eliot—or to Dante, or to Shakespeare —for irrefragable demonstration of dogma or for an ingenious philosophical system. All that poetry of Eliot's kind can attain is to express one man's understanding through emotion, and to criticize a culture which rejects the theological virtues. Even that attempt strained poetry to its limits, especially in *Four Quartets;* sometimes Eliot doubted whether in the future poetry would be written at all.

"When the traditional form of even our central belief has become a problem of intellectual analysis," Anthony Thorlby says of *Four Quartets,* "what should we expect of our lesser forms, the conventions of art and poetry? The critical answer, if it is only this we are able to understand, and must insist on for our understanding at all, leaves the formal truth still *questioned,* however right our answer shows it to be. . . . Perhaps in our unhappy age the traditional happiness of poetry is no longer possible."[28]

Be that as it may, in the midst of frightful disruption, a poet had affirmed the enduring order of things. His achievement was the more remarkable in that Eliot's progress had not been "enthusiastic" in the sense that the eighteenth century spoke of religious enthusiasm, but rather what Eliot called "dogmatic." That is, having decided from reflection and experience that there is truth in Christian teaching, he had proceeded to find his way *inside* those dogmas, so to speak, by putting into poetry his honest religious feelings. He had sought for images that could express emotional experience of a dogma. The way had been painful for him. Like John Henry Newman, he had begun with certain theological and philosophical assumptions; and he had sought to describe through poetry his search for a fuller understanding. This may not seem a promising method for writing great poetry; yet Dante had succeeded so in the fourteenth century, and so did Eliot in the twentieth.

As champion of the moral imagination, Eliot had begun by describing the abyss into which we fall if we reject the inner order and the outer; he had concluded by suggesting that it is not impossible to recover the order of the soul and the order of the commonwealth. After "Little Gidding," though two more decades of life remained to him, he would write no more major poems. He had answered his own ultimate questions, so far as such inquiries may be pursued by poetic vision; the pilgrimage from certain half-deserted streets to Little Gidding had been fulfilled; and others might take heart and direction from those momentary glimpses of Eliot's ascent.

IX

Culture and
Cocktail Parties

❖

All Hallows' Eve, 1948

By the Second World War, the unity of European culture
had been smashed—perhaps irreparably. Eastern Europe
had fallen to Communism and Soviet imperialism; western
Europe was preserved from that servitude only by American
garrisons. Nineteenth-century optimism was undone: H. G.
Wells had died in 1946, after writing his testament of despair,
The World at the End of Its Tether; George Bernard Shaw
would die in 1950, in a bewildered England that really had
become Heartbreak House.

Winston Churchill—whom Eliot so little admired, most of
that ebullient statesman's career—had won the war; he lost
the peace, Clement Attlee and the Socialists shouldering him
aside. Aneurin Bevan and the radical wing of Labour were
promising the people that with Labour in power, such things
would be done that never again might the "spivs and drones,"
the "vermin" of Heartbreak House, rise up. A despoiling and
dismantling like that of the sixteenth-century Reformation

(315)

had commenced: nationalization of coal, of transport, of steel, of the cotton exchange, of the Bank of England, went on almost unresisted; nationalization of the land was advocated; the parliamentary seats of the universities were swept away; the old public schools must go soon, the Socialists said—and much more of the old order, to clear the ground for the New Jerusalem.

Round St. Paul's lay rubble and ashes; cathedral cities and county towns had been laid waste by the "Baedeker raids," never to regain their beauty; of the four hundred splendid country houses listed as most worthy of preservation, half at least stood derelict. The remnant of the old upper classes sank under what even a Labour minister called "savage taxation"; the middle classes were ground between upper and nether millstones; the mood of the working classes was photographed later—not caricatured—in the film "I'm All Right, Jack." ("When 'working men' began to be called 'workers,'" a Rugby contractor told me during those years, "they ceased to work.")

Churchill notwithstanding, the Empire was being liquidated speedily; in India, more people would be slaughtered during that liquidation than had died in Europe during the whole of the War. In great regions of Europe and Asia, whole populations that had dwelt for centuries in a territory, rooted like trees, were forcibly transplanted—when not extirpated. What had occurred after the First World War had been trifling, almost, by the side of the catastrophic events which occurred between 1944 and 1948.

The two literary men closest to Eliot in the formative years from 1914 to 1917, Ezra Pound and Wyndham Lewis, had been cast into the outer darkness. Back from America, impoverished and sick, Lewis ("the most fascinating personality of our time," Eliot had written of him in 1918) was going blind at the top of a house in decaying Notting

Hill. Captured in Italy, Pound was shut into a massive iron cage in the yard of a prison for military criminals, as if he had been taken by some Renaissance tyrant; having nearly died of exposure there, he was transported to Washington and confined to the "hell hole" of a lunatic asylum, it being uncertain that this expatriate could be convicted of treason: victors' justice.

The end of Charles Maurras, whom Eliot had admired, with reservations, ever since his Parisian year, was worse still. France's *épurateurs*, after the fall of the Vichy regime, accused Maurras of having collaborated with the Germans—though actually Maurras had detested everything German, had removed his paper *Action Française* to the unoccupied zone of France, had refused even to mention the name of Laval, and had accepted no subsidies from the Vichy government. His real crime was his royalism; and so Maurras, "the oldest prisoner in the world" except for Marshal Pétain, was condemned to life imprisonment; he did not long survive that travesty of justice.*

After his fashion, Eliot had been as harsh a critic of his society as ever had been Pound or Lewis or Maurras. From them he had been distinguished early, however, by a temperance of thought and utterance—and distinguished latterly by a faith in transcendent order that these other writers could not

---

* Some of Maurras' views were exasperating, and others deplorable, Eliot would say in 1955; nevertheless, Maurras had been a great writer and a great lover of France; he had deserved a better fate. "I have sometimes thought that if Charles Maurras had confined himself to literature, and to the literature of political theory, and had never attempted to found a political party, a *movement*—engaging in, and increasing the acrimony of the political struggle—if he had not given his support to the restoration of the Monarchy in such a way as to strengthen instead of reducing animosities—then those of his ideas which were sound and strong might have spread more widely, and penetrated more deeply, and affected more sensibly the contemporary mind." See Eliot's talk "The Literature of Politics," reprinted in *To Criticize the Critic* (1965), pp. 142–143.

accept. So it had come about that (James Joyce being dead), of the "Men of 1914," only Eliot, three decades later, stood high in reputation and influence.

Making his way from Italy to shattered London, Emilio Cecchi called on the Pope of Russell Square about this time, finding him very unlike most poets and artists. "He might have been a chemist or a philologist with the kind of intellectual aristocracy and aloneness that goes with that kind of discipline." They talked of David Rousset's book about the concentration camps. "And Eliot wondered whether the gates of such hells, in the spiritual and material order, can really be considered to be closed for ever. Or whether mankind, now capable of reaching such extremes of frightfulness, has a weaker resistance to new and infernal suggestions; whether the wheel of bloodshed can stop at last or will follow its murderous course. These things were said lightly so as in some way to mitigate their frightfulness. But I felt that with the man I was speaking to, as with myself, the dread was almost stronger than the hope."[1]

What Eliot had aspired to say as a poet, he already had said: this second war was followed by no such burst of writing as Eliot had produced after the earlier war. It no longer was necessary for him to keep at his typewriter for subsistence; but also will and inspiration were lacking. During 1945, 1946, and 1947, he published only a score of essays and reviews, and most of those were tracts for the times. His reflections on the meaning of culture and the unity of European civilization appeared in *The New English Weekly, Adam*, the *Times*, and other periodicals, to be incorporated in 1948 into *Notes towards the Definition of Culture;* he found only a few other pieces of his during this period worth reprinting. *The Waste Land* could be written only once.

In those years, England seemed illuminated only by owl-light: this impression was subtly reinforced by continuing shortages of electrical power and by the blanket-draperies

left over from the black-outs of the war. In this crepuscular
land, memory of the dead and fear for the future, joining
(as the Festival of Britain approached) with an official
simulated joviality, conjured up an atmosphere of Hallowe'en
—more readily sensed by the visitor to Britain than by all
those millions who, during the long years of the war, had
become inured to an arcane existence. One fancied that more
than one countenance was a mask, really, and might dissolve at the blowing of a horn. The Hollow Men took on
substance of a sort: this was a land of guisers—some of whom
talked with hollow enthusiasm of Planning.

When I came up the Mersey on a foggy morning in the
autumn of 1948, the hulks of sunken ships still protruded
corpse-like on either side of the channel. Pigeons flew in and
out of Liverpool's roofless public library. One lunched at a
fashionable restaurant, musicians playing, the napery and the
china and the silver plate and the black-jacketed waiters all
correct, as if enclosed in amber ever since King Edward's
reign; but one got very little food. Rural Lancashire and
much of the North might have come out of nineteenth-
century prints—until one noticed that the great house within
the park walls stood tenantless, and reflected that it might
never be occupied again; otherwise, a resurrected Nathaniel
Hawthorne would have found himself in familiar surround-
ings. The Waverley Novels and *The Fortnightly* still were
sold at railway kiosks; but C. E. M. Joad, strolling through
a long train from Edinburgh to London, found only one man
reading a book—and that *No Orchids for Miss Blandish*—
which loathly best-seller George Orwell, too, singled out as
an illustration of the decline of culture.

In Eliot's London, reconstruction scarcely had commenced: business was carried on in the stumps of buildings.
Many of the City churches that Eliot knew so well had
been gutted; others that he and his friends had tried to save,
throughout England, stood perpetually locked, left to dry

rot and death-watch beetle. Although the life of club and pub had revived as if nothing had intervened, still this surviving Britain was eerie as the City of Charles Williams' romance *All Hallows' Eve*, for which Eliot supplied an introduction, in 1948. It was W. H. Auden's Age of Anxiety, this time, lights burning late at police stations, passports expiring, ports watched, in most of the world. The Empire was falling apart altogether, and the statutes of the Welfare State took effect that year. Windsor and Westminster had withstood the robot bombs; in the City, one did well to acquire shares in Woolworth's and Vickers'—gewgaws and armaments. In that London, nevertheless, the spectator was tempted to surmise that when the fog should lift, all might be ash on an old man's sleeve.

Everywhere one encountered the marks of social fatigue. Under Lord Beveridge's welfare state, poverty of the old nineteenth-century sort was said to be verging upon extinction. Yet the rates of criminality moved upward as rapidly as the indices of deprivation diminished, so that some eight years after the war, crimes of violence were estimated to have increased by 250 per cent. To a comparatively detached observer, it appeared that the old motives to private and public integrity were decaying rapidly, and that the welfare state—so young, yet already showing symptoms of decrepitude—had provided no substitute for those traditional motives.

Much of this dissolution had been predicted by Eliot in *The Criterion* and in *The Idea of a Christian Society*. In this dim postwar England, still suffering from shock, the vestiges of old custom and old confidence disappearing before one's eyes, T. S. Eliot wrote those reflections which he was to call (with characteristic restraint) *Notes towards the Definition of Culture*. The book was published in November, 1948—six thousand copies; the New York edition, next year, was of seven thousand, five hundred copies; later it had a fairly wide distribution in paperback. Eliot might well have set upon his title page a sentence that James Fitzjames Stephen had written in 1873: "The waters are out and no human force can turn them back, but I do not see why as we go with the stream we need sing Hallelujah to the river god."

Culture and Class

If culture had been beset by difficulties in Arnold's day, a fiercer anarchy assailed the culture of which Eliot was so conspicuous a representative in 1948. During 1914, Bertrand Russell had written to Lady Ottoline Morrell of his Harvard pupil Eliot—"the only one who is civilized, and he is ultra-civilized, knows his classics very well, is familiar with all French literature from Villon to Vildrac, and is altogether impeccable in his taste but has no vigour or life—or enthusiasm."[2] In the intervening thirty-four years, through suffering and purgation, Eliot's vitality may have increased; certainly his culture was undiminished; and in his urbane way, Eliot now struck a hard blow in defense of culture.

Twenty years earlier, there had occurred a literary flurry about culture and civilization. "Public opinion," John Cowper Powys had written then, "is always trying to democratize culture—in other words to prostitute it and change it. Public opinion—led by affected rhetoricians—is always seeking to encourage the latest fashions and obsessions in art, the latest fashions and obsessions in thought, religion and taste. Against all this, culture stands firm; grounding itself upon the eternal elements of Nature and human nature."[3]

Clive Bell had declared that civilization, or high culture, was menaced by "plutocracy tempered by trade-unionism," the British political order of the day. "I am led to suspect that the British working man likes his barbarism well enough. . . . Who gets the cars and the cocktails is a matter of complete indifference to anyone who cares for civilization and things of that sort. The trade-unionist is as good as the profiteer; and the profiteer is as good as the trade-unionist. Both are silly, vulgar, good-natured, sentimental, greedy and insensitive; and as both are very well pleased to be what they are neither is likely to become anything better. A will to civilization may exist amongst the Veddahs of Ceylon or the Megé of the Gold Coast, but no sign of it appears on the Stock Exchange or in the Trade-Union Congress."[4]

To such voices there had replied R. H. Tawney, Christian social reformer, seeking to reconcile traditional culture with the growing equality of condition: "If civilization is not the product of the kitchen garden, neither is it an exotic to be grown in a hot-house. . . . Culture is not an assortment of aesthetic sugar-plums for fastidious palates, but an energy of the soul. It can win no victories, if it risks no defeats. When it feeds on itself, instead of drawing nourishment from the common life, it ceases to grow, and, when it ceases to grow, it ceases to live."[5]

In the years that followed immediately upon the Second World War, this debate about the prospects for culture (which always, down the centuries, had been closely connected with church and class), during an age increasingly secular and egalitarian, took on urgency; the questions considered by Eliot have become more pressing still, a quarter of a century later. Between 1945 and 1948, the customs and conventions and institutions of the old culture seemed almost whole, if one glanced at them only casually; but the axe had been laid to their roots. After 1948 came the deluge of the anti-culture, wave upon wave: the inanities of television, the "democratizing" of universities and schools, the triumph of sensationalism and pornography in letters, and all the other phenomena of an intellectual degradation of the democratic dogma.

Certain misuses of the word "culture" 'by the authors of the draft constitution of the United Nations Educational, Scientific, and Cultural Organization, and by the minister of education in the Attlee government, roused Eliot to write the essays which make up his cultural *Notes*. For a high civilization to thrive, Eliot argued in his introduction, there must exist an organic structure, necessitating social classes, for the hereditary transmission of culture; there must be local or regional cultures; and there must survive "unity and diversity in religion."

What a totally new culture, as distinguished from the continuing growth of cultural tradition, might be, no man can say; so all that the friend of culture can do is to renew and improve the culture into which he has been born. "A new civilization is, in fact, coming into being all the time: the civilization of the present day would seem very new indeed to any civilized man of the eighteenth century, and I cannot imagine the most ardent or radical reformer of that age taking much pleasure in the civilization that would meet his eye now." But it is possible to distinguish between high and low cultures: "We can assert with some confidence that our own period is one of decline; that the standards of culture are lower than they were fifty years ago, and that the evidences of this decline are visible in every department of human activity."[6] It has become conceivable that society may enter upon a period in which *no* higher culture may be discernible.

One may distinguish the culture of an individual; of a group or class; and of a whole society. Matthew Arnold's concept of culture now seems thin, because he did not relate personal culture to class, and because he did not take into account some of the various aspects of culture—which has such facets as urbanity, learning, philosophy, and the arts.

Modern specialization and fragmentation do mischief not to the culture of the higher levels only, but to a whole people. In our time, classes tend to separate, living in different quarters, not blending imperceptibly as once they did; at the same time, classes are disintegrating, in the sense that mere wealth, rather than manners and culture, more and more becomes the line of demarcation. "The artistic sensibility is impoverished by its divorce from religious sensibility, the religious by its separation from the artistic; and the vestige of *manners* may be left to a few survivors of a vanishing class who, their sensibility untrained by either religion or art and their minds unfurnished with the materials for witty conversation, will have no context in their lives to give value to their behavior."[7]

Culture is that which makes life worth living. All culture arises out of religion. When religious faith decays, culture must decline, though often seeming to flourish for a space after the religion which nurtured it has sunk into unbelief. But neither can religion subsist if severed from a healthy culture; no cultured person should remain indifferent to erosion of apprehension of the transcendent.

We must not fall into the error of thinking that religion and culture are identical—although culture may be the incarnation of a people's religion, and although in primitive societies the two are blended almost indistinguishably. Below the level of consciousness, even in the most fully developed societies, a seemingly autonomous high culture continues to draw nourishment from its religious roots. If ours were a really Christian society, then our culture, all its phases considered, could be proclaimed the highest culture ever known.

Then Eliot turns to the relationship between culture and class. In the emerging order of society, some say, classes will disappear, to be supplanted by élites: "These groups, formed of individuals apt for powers of government and administration, will direct the public life of the nation; the individuals composing them will be spoken of as 'leaders.'" Whatever the deficiencies of particular individuals within existing classes, Eliot sets his face against the concept of a new élite (though he often has been charged, by those who have not really read him, with "elitism"); for the doctrine of élites goes beyond an endeavor to find for every man the station in society for which he is suited by his talents: "It posits an atomic view of society."[8]

At this point, Eliot cudgels Karl Mannheim, on whose writings he had commented often, over the years, in *The Criterion* and elsewhere. In Mannheim, as a critic of society, Eliot encountered an adversary intellectually more systematic and formidable than Eliot's old foes Wells and Shaw and Russell. (Mannheim had died not long before Eliot wrote this chapter; his reputation, what with the post-war hankering after *Plannwirtschaft*, was then tremendous.) This is like the contest between the poetic vision of Coleridge and the corrosive rationalism of Bentham; had Eliot developed his criticism of Mannheim more fully, we might consider this clash so important in twentieth-century intellectual controversy as, according to John Stuart Mill, the contest between Coleridge and Bentham had been for the nineteenth century.

Eliot believed society to be organic, so far as one may employ a biological term to describe a community of souls: society is Burke's "great mysterious incorporation of the human race," cohering and surviving through an intricate continuity—far more like a great ancient tree than like a new machine. Mannheim and his school thought of society as a conglomeration of social atoms, an ephemeral mingling of individuals—the perils of which view Eliot had come to know, early, through his studies in Idealism and his admiration for Bradley. For Eliot, culture was created by society as a whole; for Mannheim, it was manufactured by talented individuals. Eliot's understanding of culture was more "democratic," if one may resort to a term of politics, than was Mannheim's—even though, about the time when E. M. Forster gave his two cheers for democracy, Eliot would have uttered only one cheer.

Élites are composed of the enterprising talents of a rising generation. But modern élites, through specialization, are isolated one from another, and so tend to lack a general culture. Moreover, the very constitution of élites damages their efficacy as transmitters of culture from past to present and to future: in a system of élites, there exists no continuity —through family, institution, or local community—enabling generation to link with generation; Mannheim confesses as much. It is a dominant *class*, not the élite, which nurtures a broader culture and passes on that culture, unimpaired, to posterity.[9] And more than one class within a society contributes to the general culture, although at different, if equally necessary, levels of that culture.

Commenting on Eliot's criticisms of Mannheim, Raymond Williams, who disagrees with Eliot in much, remarks that Eliot "has left the ordinary social-democratic case without many relevant answers. As a conservative thinker, he has succeeded in exposing the limitations of an orthodox 'liberalism' which has been all too generally and too complacently accepted."[10] Williams notes certain similarities between the stand of Burke and the stand of Eliot, a hundred and sixty years later; indeed, Eliot's direct debt to Burke, in the understanding of class and élite, is larger than Williams admits. This passage of Eliot's on the cultural continuity of family is a paraphrase, in part, of a passage from *Reflections on the Revolution in France*: "I have in mind," Eliot writes, a bond embracing a longer period than a generation or two: "a piety towards the dead, however obscure, and a solicitude for the unborn, however remote. Unless this reverence for past and future is cultivated in the home, it can never be more than a verbal convention in the community."[11]

A vigorous society needs both class and élite, Eliot continues. Any society long dominated by élites would fall victim to the presumption of those élites—although rule by élites may be inescapable in a time of crisis. A planned society of the sort advocated by Mannheim might be harsh, and positively hostile towards high culture; certainly it would provide of itself no criterion for excellence. With notable fairness and gentleness, Eliot refrains from mentioning the Fascist and Nazi élites—or the host of squalid oligarchs constituting what Milovan Djilas later would call "the New Class," in the Communist states.

Formal schooling may create élites, but it can neither form a class or, unaided, provide society with an enduring high culture. Class structure is natural to society: aristocracy and democracy are not antithetical; for true democracy requires different levels of culture, "a continuous gradation of cultural levels." (Class is quite different from caste.) "A democracy in which everybody had an equal responsibility in everything would be oppressive for the conscientious and licentious for the rest." Through the existence of class, groups of families ("the primary vehicle for the transmission of culture") are able to persist over several generations; without such continuity, élites lose purpose and grow arrogant.[12]

In all this argument, Eliot is close to Edmund Burke's exposition of "actual virtue" and "presumptive virtue," found most clearly in Burke's *Letter to a Noble Lord*. The men of ability, the new men of "actual virtue," are equivalent to an élite; the men of "presumptive virtue," the aristocracy, the settled great families, constitute a class. For Eliot, as for Burke, a high civilization exhibits a commingling of these elements, checking and reinforcing each other. For the sake of culture, and for the sake of a tolerable civil social order, that balance or tension of class and élite should not be overthrown.[13] In a fortunate nation, then, the political élite, or body of leaders—both those who happen to occupy office and those who happen to oppose them—will be a blending of men who have inherited special advantage and affluence, "a stake in the country," with rising men of unusual talents. It is desirable that both these elements of leadership should enjoy a high common culture, emphasizing particularly history and political theory; they should be something better than technicians and specialists, cut off from broad understanding of society by concentration within the narrow compass of political administration.

The dissolution of classes has continued, since Eliot wrote; so has the decline of culture, in Britain as in most of the world. What has been occurring since 1948, it appears, is not the wider diffusion of the inherited culture (the hope of Tawney), but the rise of an anti-culture, most notoriously —though perhaps not most ominously—among college and university students in democratic states, with their demand for "relevance"—that is, for obsession with the superficial and the ephemeral, with becoming rather than with being, with what D. H. Lawrence called "chewing the newspapers."

This recent social experience, fulfilling Eliot's vaticinations, has produced some intellectual reaction in favor of Eliot's analysis of culture and social order. In the spirit of Eliot, Rowland Berthoff, for example, writes that any society which is a mere congeries of atoms must be violent and unhappy; it is quite possible, even here in America, that we may come round again to an organic society, bound together by true class, church, family, and community. A stable social structure is part of a hierarchy of values; it stands above economic values, and is a foundation for "loftier values of mind and spirit—aesthetic and intellectual achievement of some excellence and perhaps even what is variously called self-fulfillment, redemption from sin, or salvation of the soul."[14] Those "loftier values" are what Eliot meant by a "high culture," and the survival or reinvigoration of class is to be sought as a means to such cultural ends.

It was from such an American class—his family having transmitted a high culture, from generation to generation, since the seventeenth century—that Eliot himself came. He saw in Britain a multitude of instances of such continuity of culture maintained through family, within different classes: the Huxleys and Sitwells of his own generation may illustrate sufficiently, in their different backgrounds, this nourishing power of continuity; for that matter, the inherited radical Whiggery of the Russells demonstrates his point.*

That cultural continuity ensured by class was being terminated—by crushing taxation, among other forces—in Eliot's age. In Wyndham Lewis' novel *Self Condemned,* one encounters a specimen of a dying breed—Rotter, the scholar of modest private means, whom taxation and inflation soon will annihilate; Rotter's good private library will be unknown by 1984, perhaps. The grander libraries of the great country houses were being sold up to pay death-duties as Eliot wrote, and with them would depart more than a collection of folios.

A few years later, when Eliot accepted an honorary degree from St. Andrews University, he would be a guest at a great Scottish house that embodied precisely what he meant by continuity of class and family: seven centuries of con-

---

* "A class can preserve a culture because it is itself an organic and changing thing," George Orwell wrote in his review of *Notes.* "But here, curiously enough, Mr. Eliot misses what might have been the strongest argument in his case. That is, that a classless society directed by élites may ossify very rapidly, simply because its rulers are able to choose their successors, and will always tend to choose people resembling themselves." See *The Collected Essays, Journalism and Letters of George Orwell,* Vol. IV, *In Front of Your Nose* (1968), pp. 455–457.

tinuity in the family, and four centuries in the house itself. The library of rare books remained splendid, though but "the shadow of a shade"—kept back from the sale of the immense family library, one of the finest systematic collections of learning in the world, which for generations had been made available to any serious scholar; that house's paintings and other works of art were the accumulation of generations of cultivated taste. What mattered more, the many members of that old family, over the centuries, had been participants in what Burke called "the unbought grace of life," able leaders in the public order and more effective guardians of culture than were Arnold and Emerson. Far from diminishing, the talents of that family had proliferated down through Eliot's generation: Eliot's host was the rector of St. Andrews, and much else besides in the domain of culture.

I had known that family and that country house before Eliot was made a doctor of St. Andrews; it was neither Heartbreak House nor Horseback Hall. Among the great trees of their rolling park, family and house had survived the unrests of centuries. Once I happened to remark to the head of this family that, our times considered, it .could not be cheerful in this house to think overmuch of prospects for continuity.

"There is no prospect of continuity here," he said, with a faint smile.

Just that truth was what Eliot expresses in the first part of his *Notes*. A society led by Mannheim's élite—"shaped and brought together by the barren world of monopoly industry and centralized government," as Orwell would put it in *1984*—would not know beauty, or tranquility, or manners of this sort. And such a society would not endure for seven centuries; or even for one century.

The Blessings of Cultural Diversity

From the defense of class as a bulwark of culture, Eliot moves to the need for diversity in unity. He discusses regional culture—returning to a theme upon which he had touched in *After Strange Gods*. It is well that there should be minority cultures, or coordinate cultures, or subcultures, within a political unity; it is well, indeed, that, within limits, there should be friction among cultural groups: civilization is invigorated by such competition, by attraction and repulsion of cultures. Zealots for world government notwithstanding, independence of culture should enjoy precedence over unity of organization. Any world culture "which was simply a *uniform* culture would be no culture at all. We should have a humanity de-humanized. It would be a nightmare."[15]

In the aspiration for truth, nevertheless, we should desire a world culture, or rather a catholic interest in true shared civilization; but any attempt to impose culture, whether by imperial power or by some future global authority, must destroy an existing culture without bringing into being a satisfactory new or transplanted culture; just that had happened in British India. Any imposed uniform culture for the whole world necessarily would be a culture ignoring or repressing religious differences—and therefore an anti-culture.

It is to Christianity that Eliot looks for a unifying power: to Christian culture, within which much diversity is possible. Within Christendom, there should continue an endless conflict between ideas, enlarging the truth, and giving expression to local and national differences. In cult and sect, "As in the relation between the social classes, and as in the relation of the several regions of a country to each other and to the central power, it would seem that a constant struggle between the centripetal and the centrifugal forces is desirable. For without the struggle no balance can be maintained; and if either force won the result would be deplorable." Here Eliot expresses again the idea of healthful tensions, frequently encountered in his work. Great freedom, he argues in this book, brings the danger of deliquescence; strict order, the danger of petrification.[16] As we endeavor to maintain political tension, in this sense, so we benefit from a cultural tension—supposing that a common faith prevents that tension from becoming a baneful hostility.

Modern political theory and practice often tend to diminish both the diversity and the depth of culture, Eliot believed. In a society of gradations, with several levels of culture; in a decentralized society; in a society where political leaders, as a class, know one another, and mingle with people of high culture—there it becomes possible for the benefits of true cuture to affect beneficially the tone of public life. But we have been moving in the opposite direction, doing mischief to both politics and culture. With Mannheim and his school in mind, Eliot writes that much modern political theory has been baneful: "Being occupied with humanity only in the mass, it tends to separate itself from ethics; being occupied only with that recent period of history during which humanity can most easily be shown to have been ruled by impersonal forces, it reduces the proper study of mankind to the last two or three hundred years of man. It too often inculcates a belief in a future inflexibly determined and at the same time a future which we are wholly free to shape as we like."[17]

What Mannheim and his disciples were inflicting upon political theory, Karl Popper and his associates were doing with philosophy in general—divorcing philosophy from the moral imagination, and so from true proliferating culture with its religious roots. As Eliot would write four years later, in his introduction to Josef Pieper's Leisure, the Basis of

Culture, "Certainly, logical positivism is not a very nourishing diet for more than the small minority which has been conditioned to it. When the time of its exhaustion arrives, it will probably appear, in retrospect, to have been for our age the counterpart of surrealism: for as surrealism seemed to provide a method of producing works of art without imagination so logical positivism seems to provide a method of philosophizing without insight and wisdom." But then, philosophy had been sick for a long time; logical positivism was only the latest phase of that decline.[18]

Although dismal social phenomena and fallacious theories give us reason to work for the better understanding of our cultural roots, nevertheless an obsessive "culture-consciousness"—if misdirected—may nourish totalitarian ideologies and a belligerent nationalism. Also such an obsession may breed a supercilious contempt for "inferior" or "archaic" cultures—as in the later stage of British administration in India; or it may take the more subtle way of Soviet imperialism, preserving the outward forms of local cultures but really subordinating everything to political dogmas (and, half-consciously, subordinating everything to Mother Russia as the model for all the world). Liberal anti-imperialists often have been serious offenders in this disastrous culture-snobbery, on humanitarian principles: "According to such enthusiasts, we do well to intrude ourselves upon another civilization, equip the members of it with our mechanical contrivances, our systems of government, education, law, medicine, and finance, inspire them with a contempt for their own customs and with an enlightened attitude towards religious superstition—and then leave them to stew in the the broth which we have brewed for them."[19] Eliot refrained from mentioning that America, even while he wrote, was proceeding to just that operation in vacuums left by the departure of the old "colonial powers" execrated by American liberals.

Culture cannot really be planned by political authority. For much of culture is unconscious; and politics grows out of culture, not culture out of politics; and political planning itself is a product of culture. The practical effect of state direction of "cultural activities" is to narrow or debase our cultural patrimony. "For one thing to avoid is a *universalized* planning; one thing to ascertain is the limits of the plannable."[20]

What we need is the unity of nature, not the unity of organization; the spiritual organism of Europe is far more important than the material organization of Europe. The culture of Europe could not survive a disappearance of Christian faith: "Then you must start painfully again, and you cannot put on a new culture ready made. You must wait for the grass to grow to feed the sheep to give the wool out of which your new coat will be made. You must live through many centuries of barbarism. We should not live to see the new culture, nor would our great-great-great-grandchildren: and if we did, not one of us would be happy in it."[21]

As the decay of religious belief has enfeebled our culture, so has the lowering of standards of formal education (not that "education" and "culture" are synonymous). Here it may be remarked that Arnold's intended substitute for religious dogma, his quasi-religion of humane studies, by 1948 was giving at the seams quite as rapidly as was the faith of Abraham, Isaac, and Jacob.

Eliot wrote the essays and lectures of *Notes towards the Definition of Culture* at a low ebb of social vitality, when ideological sloganizing had vanquished reasonable discussion in many quarters; when it was more difficult to maintain intellectual communication among different countries than it had been for centuries past; when talk of a total "planning" of society had not been chastened by the failure of many such experiments after 1948 (most immediately, so far as

British public opinion went, by the collapse of John Strachey's grandiose "ground-nuts scheme" in East Africa). But the processes of cultural disintegration that he described have not ceased to erode the common cultural patrimony.

It is a mark of the increasing fragmentation of culture that Eliot's book, written deliberately as a sociological treatise, rather than as a piece of apologetics or of literary criticism, has not been more seriously weighed outside literary circles. As Eliot might have become an academic philosopher, had he chosen, so might he have been a professor of social studies. Eliot's criticism of the fashionable sociology and political science of his age, though expressed so succinctly, hit its target with force. Yet most professors of the social sciences have chosen to ignore that criticism—if aware of its existence; while some literary critics, whether applauding or deriding the *Notes,* possess so feeble a command of social theory that their comments upon this slim book of Eliot's amount to little more than the reaffirmation of prejudices.

Still, Eliot was understood by a public much larger than he ever had attracted to the pages of *The Criterion,* where there had germinated many of the concepts expressed in *Notes.* Of recent books on culture, none has been received more respectfully. It is not that such books have been few in number; there have appeared many, some of these neglected unjustly.*

But it was Eliot's words that the serious public weighed. For by 1948, Eliot had come to possess more cultural *authority* than anyone else could claim in a world then repudiating authority generally. In 1948, he was awarded the

---

* Here it is well to mention a book by Eliot's friend Michael Roberts, *The Recovery of the West,* which Faber & Faber published in 1941. And in the year when *Notes* appeared, Faber & Faber also published C. E. M. Joad's *Decadence: a Philosophical Inquiry*—a book covering much of the ground of Eliot's *Notes,* but more systematic, full of arresting instances, and lively.

Nobel Prize for Literature; in 1948, the King presented to him ("in a very simple way in a very short audience") the cross of the Order of Merit. The age against whose powers Eliot had contended so steadfastly now recognized him, in its paradoxical fashion, as intellectual master.*

Eight years before, in his lecture on Yeats,[22] Eliot had remarked the peril, escaped by Yeats, which famous poets encounter late in life—"of becoming dignified, of becoming public figures with only a public existence—coat-racks hung with decorations and distinction, doing, saying, and even thinking and feeling only what they believe the public expects of them." With some hesitation, doubtless bearing in mind his own admonition, Eliot had published this little book on culture. But there was more to his *Notes* than elderly dignity.

With *Notes towards the Definition of Culture,* Eliot had made his longest successful raid across that debatable land which runs between the realm of poetry and the realm of politics. Poetry does have a social function, Eliot had declared in lectures during 1943 and 1945; he wished that politicians would cross more often the frontier separating them from those realities of spirit which lie under poets' sway. "On my side of the line one is concerned with living things which have their own laws of growth, which are not always reasonable, but must just be accepted by the reason: things which cannot be neatly planned and put into order any more than the winds and the rains and the seasons can be disciplined."

Without some apprehension of the poetic, those concerned with political questions, like everybody else, must

* "I had never hoped to see the greatest poet of our time properly honored and reverenced," Edith Sitwell wrote to Eliot, January 1, 1948, on learning that he had been appointed to the Order of Merit in the New Year's Honours. "Well, I have." See *Edith Sitwell: Selected Letters, 1919–1964,* edited by John Lehmann and Derek Parker (1970), pp. 155–156.

fail to express—or even to feel—"the emotions of civilized beings"; therefore they must tend to leave the emotions out of account in their political reckoning, a neglect that has unpleasant prosaic consequences for grand political schemes. Inability to *feel* deeply is perhaps the greatest affliction of our time; more damage is done by the disappearance of religious *feeling* than by the dwindling of religious belief. Should the heart's reasons be ignored by the statist, Eliot concluded, he would be apprehensive of cultural and social death: "the feeling for poetry, and the feelings which are the materials of poetry, may disappear everywhere: which might perhaps help to facilitate that unification of the world which some people consider desirable for its own sake."[23]

The spectre of a colossal planned boredom—classless, faithless, frontierless, rootless, deprived of poetry, of historical consciousness, of imagination, and even of emotion; a Waste Land governed, if governable at all, by an "élite" of dull positivists and behaviorists and technicians, knowing no standards or aspirations but those of their own narrow trade; a world utterly impoverished in spirit, and therefore soon to be impoverished in flesh—this apparition stalks through the calm admonitory pages of *Notes*. Only here and there does Eliot permit a denunciatory image to emerge: by our educational policies, we are "destroying our ancient edifices to make ready the ground upon which the barbarian nomads of the future will encamp in their mechanized caravans."[24] Meanwhile, one still can go round to cocktail parties.

The Mystery of the Guardians

At the Edinburgh Festival, in 1949—ten years after *The Family Reunion*—T. S. Eliot resumed his endeavor to restore poetic drama as a power among thinking people. As his instrument, he chose West End drawing-room comedy, blending that popular form with the scheme of a classical drama—this latter device undetected by the early critics. He succeeded famously, for the first time penetrating to the big theaters and a kind of audience he had not reached before. *The Cocktail Party* swept out of its Edinburgh triumph to London and New York, and has been revived several times; more than two decades later, its relevance to the condition of modern man is undiminished. In 1950, about forty thousand copies of this play were printed in England, and ten thousand in America; there have been several cheap reprints. It has been the most thoroughly criticized play of the past thirty years or more.[25]

This is a play of atonement and fulfillment. Its audiences were lured into easy appreciation of a fashionable fast-moving comedy, suggestive at first of Noel Coward—and then, as the drama developed, many in those audiences grew uncomfortable at the probing of its moral imagination and its challenge to their lives and their culture. It was not altogether reassuring, in 1949, to be told that if one would live even a "normal" life of private order, one must strip away shams of personality; still less was it agreeable to be reminded that the highest end of mankind is sanctity, to be achieved through renunciation, suffering, and grace in death —that whoever would save his life must lose it.

Artistically, Eliot achieved his purpose of showing that a verse-drama can be better understood than a prose play. It was a startling accomplishment to make poetry of what seemed to be ordinary conversation. Indeed he had almost perfected what he had commenced in *The Family Reunion*, though he would fall away somewhat in his two later comedies: he had forged "a loose, flexible, and accentual line instead of a heroic line"; he had emancipated the verse-drama from the iambic pentameter that had become unreal and oppressive to twentieth-century audiences. "It may be that the norm of English versification is iambic pentameter, but that the only way to refresh it from one time to another will be to get away from it in a curve which will gradually return—having freed itself from the stiffness of previous generations," Eliot told Leslie Paul, in 1958. He would be happy beyond the grave, he said, if he should have helped future dramatists to return to iambic pentameter as "a fresh instrument."[26] The metric of *The Cocktail Party*, its seemingly light chatter made ominous by the three heavy stresses in every line, possesses a rhythm that changes an audience's mood without that audience's conscious participation in a movement from triviality to martyrdom.

Yet the Eliot of 1949, this high ingenuity notwithstanding, was less interested in metric and style than the Eliot of 1917 had been. He was bent, now, upon communicating certain truths perceived; literary techniques were means only to that end. How are we to live this imperfect life of ours and transcend the body of this death? How do we escape from the prison of ego, and from our old servitude to time? How do we redeem, at once, the self and the time? These are the concerns of *The Cocktail Party*.

Like *The Family Reunion*, this second drawing-room play may be apprehended at different levels. At first, one may take *The Cocktail Party* for a clever account of how several people are given new direction in their lives by a "great doctor" and his friends. Then one comes to perceive a deeper moral significance, redemption achieved through acceptance of one's true self. And presently, perhaps—though several critics prefer to glide away from this—one glimpses the intrusion into ordinary lives of an Other, a Power from which we flee to our ruin, or which we welcome as deliverer.

It is a bent world, the setting of this cocktail party, anxious and bored, its modish culture the froth of gossip, everybody standing, as if ready for flight. A supper is communion; a cocktail party is evasion of thought and feeling.

Heartbreak House is nowhere to be seen: these people gather, for an hour or less, in Heartbreak Flat, built yesterday, to be demolished tomorrow, in this London that has forgotten tradition. (The only great house mentioned, and that near the end of the play, is Boltwell, the most decayed—though still inhabited—noble mansion in England: useful chiefly as model for a pseudo-decayed pseudo-Boltwell to be erected as a Hollywood set.) There is no family to reunite—only a quarreling couple, ill sorted, and their guests of the fleeting moment.

Or rather, of this host-couple only Edward Chamber-layne, a dry stick of a barrister, is present to receive the guests; his wife, Lavinia, has left him, to his passing humilia-tion; the Unidentified Guest will restore her (as Hercules, in Euripides' *Alcestis,* restores the dead wife) to her husband —who can neither live with her nor live without her; but that will be no glad reunion. This is a little circle of frustrated and self-deceived modern people: Edward, unable to love; Lavinia, unlovable; Celia Coplestone, a girl adrift and quest-ing, involved in a delusory affair with Edward; Peter Quilpe, Lavinia's former lover, now in visionary pursuit of an unreal Celia-figure. They are false to themselves; except for Celia, they are false to one another. One meets them at cocktail parties every day.

Then there are three more guests, rather troublesome. Old Julia Shuttlethwaite seems to be a type described by C. S. Lewis—"one of those who likes living for others; you can tell the others by the hunted expressions on their faces." Alexander MacColgie Gibbs, equally meddlesome, may be taken for a globe-circling butterfly, dropping hints of in-fluence. Finally, there is a stranger, too fond of gin and water, and of indecent song, at first known only as Riley but presently revealed as that eminent psychiatric practi-tioner Sir Henry Harcourt-Reilly. But these are guests only incidentally: in reality, these three are Guardians, and their intervention in the lives of the other four people produces recovery in the soul.

Through the contrivance of the Guardians, and through their own acts of will, Edward and Lavinia Chamberlayne are brought to recognize their own failings, to accept their past, and to complement each other, in amity if not in love; if the best thing they can do with their lives is to hold cocktail parties, at least they learn to hold them well. Peter Quilpe, though left at loose ends, comes to perceive existence with clearer eyes. And Celia Coplestone, passionate and oppressed by a sense of sin? Why, Celia, after having obtained a discipline of spirit, is crucified by savages, very near an ant-hill: in her end is her beginning.

The Chamberlaynes recover order in the soul through painful self-recognition, atonement to each other, and the performance of responsibilities: the ordinary ways in which ordinary folk must learn to walk, if they are to find peace and purpose in life. It was perilous, Harcourt-Reilly confesses, for him to have stripped them naked to their souls; they might have put on new disguises, rather than proper costumes. Like Gregers Werle in *The Wild Duck*, one may add, Harcourt-Reilly might have destroyed the Chamberlaynes by making clear to them the truth about themselves:

It's not the knowledge of the mutual treachery
But the knowledge that the other understands the motive—
Mirror to mirror, reflecting vanity.
I have taken a great risk.

Yet this doctor's—or doctor-priest's—bitter dose does purge the Chamberlaynes, and they come to recognize the claims of others.

Celia's way is very different: the *via negativa*, the dark night of the soul, the renunciation of the love of created beings, the path of sanctity. To resign private ties is not to renounce humankind: she dies in agony so that she may comfort doomed hospital patients in their last hours. And Harcourt-Reilly shows his exultation when he hears how Celia died; she has worked out her salvation; and he has seen a vision, long before, of Celia's astonished face five minutes after her violent death.

The Cocktail Party, one scarcely need remark, is not a play wholly consonant with the modern temper; and yet it has moved many, and disturbed more. To get at the meaning of this play, it is well to try to understand what the Guardians are, and what Celia's martyrdom signifies. Eliot himself said that it would be no more wise for him to respond at length to questions about this play than it would have been for Shakespeare to have set down written responses in detail to the curious after the first performance of *Hamlet.* The lessons of *The Cocktail Party* must be extracted by those who are in quest of purpose; and not all of those possible teachings necessarily were in the forefront of Eliot's own mind.

Superficially, the three Guardians may be taken for sensible people whose understanding of human nature is far deeper than one might surmise from a meeting at a cocktail party: the sort of people who, out of good will, unobtrusively correct the courses of acquaintances fallen into private confusion. Indeed they are this; but Eliot makes it sufficiently clear that also the Guardians have greater power than any ordinary well-intentioned friend might possess.

In some sense, these Guardians are members of that Community of Christians which Eliot had described in *The Idea of a Christian Society*—people whose faith and insight are strong, and who engage actively in the imitation of Christ, seeking to fulfill the Great Commandment. They are involved in a benevolent conspiracy to open eyes, to suggest alternative courses, to make possible for others the ordering of the soul—though they do not buttonhole victims to inquire, "Are you saved?" Now and again, in this time dubiously called the post-Christian era, one encounters some such, and through them a conscience speaks to a conscience.

But also Eliot offers strong hints that these three Guardians, although operating with human powers—more by suggestion than by direction—upon human wills, in essence are other than human. Is Harcourt-Reilly, as Celia murmurs early in the play, perhaps the devil? Surely not, we find presently—yet possibly a different sort of angel. The doctor does not know what he means by his own exhortation to his patients, "Work out your salvation with diligence"; one recalls that angels, not knowing good and evil, do not enjoy human free will: they are forever changeless. And Julia, talking with Harcourt-Reilly of Celia's choice to enter the "sanatorium" where she will learn the *via negativa*, confesses her ignorance of the terrors of that journey:

You and I don't know the process by which the human is
Transhumanized: what do we know
Of the kind of suffering they must undergo
On the way of illumination?

To Celia, projected spirits will appear; these are not ordinary alienists who have undertaken to guard and guide her. No Christian belief is more tender—or more neglected today— than the concept of guardian angels.

The doctrine of angels—Jewish, Stoic, Mithraic, and Christian in its origins—is no less credible than many other dogmas which Eliot had learned to accept. (This idea took another form with Yeats, who believed that some great dead man watches over every passionate living man of talents.) Imperfect though it may be, evidence for the existence of intermediary spiritual beings is no less intelligible than the proofs for various theories in natural science. It is a mark of democratic ages, Alexis de Tocqueville mentions, that the common man denies or ignores any invisible hierarchy separating him from direct relationship with God.

Now Eliot was anything but a doctrinaire democrat: for him, as for C. S. Lewis or G. K. Chesterton, there was nothing repugnant or incredible in conceiving of tutelary beings of another order than human. We are not required to believe that the Guardians of *The Cocktail Party* come from the heavenly hosts; yet neither is it indispensable to explain away the Guardians as a kind of playful device of Eliot's.

Finally, it is possible to regard these Guardians as symbolic figures, representing incarnate the inner will of the person to order and righteousness. It is upon the better self of the character that the Guardians work; they exert no magical powers. They are not merely the "inner check" of Irving Babbitt or the "inner voice" of John Middleton Murry, long before rejected by Eliot as insufficient; they are not untutored conscience. But they may stand for a divine providential impulse working upon intellect and feeling, in arcane ways: the Guardians may enter into the soul, so that Harcourt-Reilly, Alex, and Julia may stand for a power originating elsewhere, intervening through less tangible means than cocktail talk and psychiatric consultation.

His own inner self, Edward Chamberlayne tells Celia, is nothing but an "indomitable spirit of mediocrity"; yet it is otherwise with some men:

The self that can say "I want this—or want that"—
The self that wills—he is a feeble creature;
He has to come to terms in the end
With the obstinate, the tougher self; who does not speak,
Who never talks, who cannot argue;
And who in some men may be the *guardian*—

The appetent self, that is, falls to blows with a restraining, guardian self, Sir Thomas Browne's "man within me who is angry with me." For that kind of guardianship, the voice of moral authority, the Guardians of *The Cocktail Party* conceivably may stand. "The Guardians are not at the centre of the action," Helen Gardner suggests. "At the true centre there is an unnamed Power who speaks within the heart and conscience of every man."[27]

All these avenues of approach to the Guardians, Eliot leaves unobstructed; his readers may accept what interpretation, or blending of interpretations, they choose. What can be affirmed confidently is this: Eliot believed that the person may be assisted in his endeavor to find meaning and order both by the living Community of Christians and by opening himself (through prayer, meditation, and atonement) to the Light.

In his introduction to Charles Williams' *All Hallows' Eve,* Eliot mentions "the kind of unexplainable experience which many of us have had, once or twice in our lives, and been unable to put into words." To what extent Eliot himself may have experienced a power of spirit operating upon him —within his consciousness or through the apparent agency of another person—one cannot learn clearly from his writings or, so far as I know, from his conversations. But impressions of that character are not altogether uncommon, even nowadays, among people of some intellectual strength and ability to discriminate. However this may be, *The Cocktail Party* declares—in the teeth of modern positivism—that powers of light and powers of darkness do move us, in one fashion or another; that there endures a mystery at the heart of human existence; and that if a person's will joins with such an impulse from outside, it may be possible to work out salvation with diligence.

The Mystery of Martyrdom

If the Guardians—and the Power that lies behind them— puzzled a large part of Eliot's audience, the martyrdom of Celia Coplestone seemed quite as strange to many. "What can be more hollow than this attempt to enforce the claims of transcendent goodness," Philip Rahv wrote in 1951, "by releasing the claimant from her dramatic obligations, so to speak, and packing her off to Africa to perform missionary work and die the death of a Christian martyr? . . . To substantiate Celia's choice of the 'second way' by immersing her in the experience of modern London is one thing; to send her off to Africa to be crucified is something else again."[28]

Since those sentences were published, many medical missionaries have been crucified in Africa, or done to death still more terribly: the Dark Continent has been anything but the "domain of abstraction pure and simple"—Rahv's description of Eliot's Africa. However diligently Harry Monchensey may have labored in the London slums, good works do not add up to martyrdom; and in *The Cocktail Party,* it was Eliot's purpose to remind his age that the testimony of blood did not end with Becket. In the concentration camps of the Nazis and the Communists, untold numbers of Christians and Jews had perished horribly for their faith during the war. But such folly distresses the complacent secularist: if only Celia had been assigned to play Lady Bountiful, Eliot might have been more readily forgiven his attachment to a creed outworn.

A martyr's death was Celia's reward for her yearning to be transfigured; for if any soul may be sure of redemption from the body of this death, it is the martyr's soul. A pretty girl with vague aspirations toward a film career, Celia comes to that first cocktail party full of amorous hope—her passion fixed upon Edward Chamberlayne, who, incapable of loving anyone, has used her to assuage the tedium of existence and the vacuum within him, and who now must have done with her to regain his detested, indispensable wife. Edward had been a phantom of Celia's high dream; now she finds only "a beetle the size of a man." What she had sought fondly in Edward must exist, must happen, somewhere— "but what, and where is it?"

Either there is something terribly wrong with the world,

Celia tells Harcourt-Reilly in the second act, or else there is something wrong with herself; and it is easier to believe the latter. She has come to understand that she always has been alone: "It no longer seems worth while to *speak* to anyone!" She suspects that this is the general condition of people:

> They make faces, and think they understand each other.
> And I'm sure that they don't.

This "delusion" is the first symptom of her sickness; the second is her sense of sin.

She does not feel immoral; indeed, people generally called immoral, she has found, are not afflicted by a sense of sin. In her affair with Edward, she was a fool, she knows now, but that does not oppress her. In the county family from which she came, she had learned to disbelieve in sin: anything wrong had been either "bad form" or "mental kinks." What torments her is this:

> It's not the feeling of anything I've ever *done*,
> Which I might get away from, or of anything in me
> I could get rid of—but of emptiness, of failure
> Towards someone, or something, outside of myself;
> And I feel I must . . . *atone*—is that the word?

She and Edward, Celia now knows, merely had been making use of each other, as if they had been fictions endowed with flesh: a horrible condition. Is everyone incapable of loving or being loved? Is every person totally isolated, as much dream-stuff as his own dreams? What she had sought in Edward had not been there, and perhaps could be found nowhere. "Why do I feel guilty at not having found it?"

Harcourt-Reilly (more a doctor of the Schools, really, than a doctor of psychiatry) tells her that he can reconcile her to the ordinary human condition experienced by most couples—with vision forgotten:

> Two people who know they do not understand each other,
> Breeding children whom they do not understand

And who will never understand them.
This is a good life, after all, in a world of lunacy, violence, stupidity, and greed.

But that way of routine, Celia does not accept: it would be surrender, or betrayal; she wishes to live with her vision —though a vision of what, she does not know. So Harcourt-Reilly offers her the second way, requiring blind faith, and she chooses the terror of that journey, in which she will not forget her loneliness. As Julia says, after Celia has left for the "sanatorium" that is the first way-station of her journey,

>She will pass between the scolding hills,
>
>Through the valley of derision, like a child sent on an errand
>
>In eagerness and patience. Yet she must suffer.

The Guardians drink a libation to Celia, beseeching that she may be protected from the Voices and the Visions, in the tumult and in the silence. She will not return: Harcourt-Reilly has known her for "a woman under sentence of death." Celia had swayed on the verge of the final desolation—

>Of solitude in the phantasmal world
>
>Of imagination, shuffling memories and desires.

But now she is safe from imprisonment in that hell, though in her final hour of trial she must endure such physical pain as passes ordinary imagining. To comfort dying folk, she will be translated in agony through the jaws of death. Entering that service which is perfect freedom, she will progress from despair to certitude; and having surrendered all, she will gain all. That something outside of herself, so futilely sought at first, she will come to possess beyond the confines of time.

Who knew Celia, while she lived? Not Peter Quilpe, adoring her; nor Edward Chamberlayne, making selfish use of someone in whom he glimpsed splendor; nor Lavinia, detesting her as a rival. In the end, it is Lavinia who understands Celia and her heroic sanctity best, and who says that they all have been living on false images of Celia.

For we cannot know another's heart, and we die to each other daily—so Harcourt-Reilly tells Edward, who had recognized that hard truth already. There is no permanence in this life of ours:
What we know of other people
Is only our memory of the moments
During which we knew them. And they have changed since then.
Captive to time and ego in this mundane journey of ours, we waste our days at cocktail parties, uttering trivialities, playing with shadows. "At every meeting we are meeting a stranger." As Eliot had said so often before, with Heraclitus, we never step in the same river twice. How can we endure this flux? How may we keep ourselves from madness and self-destruction? How may we attain to peace and permanence? Through *The Cocktail Party*, as through nearly the whole of Eliot's work, there echoes the entreaty of Lyte's hymn:

Change and decay in all around I see;
O Thou, who changest not, abide with me.

For most people who would be at peace with themselves, there is the way of custom and convention and regular performance of duty; love, however flawed, may be found in that obscure routine; and to such, much will be forgiven. But others feel a burning desire to find "someone, or something, outside" of themselves; and if they are willing to sacrifice, the grave will be denied victory over them. The mysterious path of sanctity does lead somewhere: those who persevere to the end will know God, and through Him immortality, which really is the resurrection of the body and the life everlasting. Their essence will endure always, they having escaped from bondage to Time.

That is what happens to Celia: through intense suffering of soul and body, she is freed, and will know forever her self, and abiding love, and the Source of all life and love. To that Platonic and Augustinian understanding of the transcendence of time, Eliot had attained. Celia (and, in inferior degree, even Edward and Lavinia) are redeemed from the curse of solipsism—that is, from the exclusive attention of a person to his own conscious experiences. Through acknowledgement of their individual feebleness, Edward and Lavinia learn to share experience—which is one aspect of true love. Through devotion to the Other, Celia is redeemed from emptiness and failure. These three characters are projections of their creator's experience of life. If one labors to redeem the time, and embraces the timeless moment, then one may be lifted out of time and caught up in eternity.[29]

In his long examination of the conundrums of Self and Time—in which quest, *The Cocktail Party* is a kind of climax —Eliot had not ignored the philosophical and scientific speculations of his age. To some critics, it seemed that Eliot, "reactionary" as he proclaimed himself, was engaged in a vain exercise of attempting to turn back the clock of knowledge. But it may come to pass that Eliot will be recognized, in the judgment of later generations, as a prophetic poet like Virgil and a precursor of an enlarged awareness of the human condition. There is relevant here an observation by an eminent scientific thinker of Eliot's age, Professor Michael Polanyi:

"Christianity is a progressive enterprise," Polanyi points out in his "Critique of Doubt." "Our vastly enlarged perspectives of knowledge should open up fresh vistas of religious faith. The Bible, and the Pauline doctrine in particular, may be still pregnant with unsuspected lessons; and the greater precision and more conscious flexibility of modern thought, shown by the new physics and the logico-philosophic movements of our age, may presently engender conceptual reforms which will renew and clarify, on the grounds of modern extra-religious experience, man's relation to God. An era of great religious discoveries may lie before us."[30]

(350)

Eliot did not lay claim, in *The Cocktail Party* or else-where, to any special inspiration. In writing *Four Quartets* —so he told Kristian Smidt—he had not been seeking a rev-elation; rather, he had been "seeking the verbal equivalents for small experiences he had had, and for knowledge derived from reading."[31] He was no martyr; but better than any other writer of his era, he touched upon the mystery of martyrdom. In the concerns of spirit, future critics may apply to Eliot what he would say in a broadcast talk of 1951 about Virgil:

"If a prophet were by definition a man who understood the full meaning of what he was saying, this would be for me the end of the matter. But if the word 'inspiration' is to have any meaning, it must mean just this, that the speaker or writer is uttering something which he does not wholly under-stand—or which he may even misinterpret when the inspira-tion has departed from him." Virgil, then, indeed may be the annunciator of Christ for whom Saint Augustine and the medieval scholars took him. "A poet may believe that he is expressing only his private experience," Eliot continued, in a passage that evoked his early rejoinder to I. A. Richards on the subject of a generation's disillusion; "his lines may be for him only a means of talking about himself without giving himself away; yet for his readers what he has written may come to be the expression both of their own secret feelings and of the exultation or despair of a generation."[32]

In the church of Santa Maria Aracoeli, on the Capitoline, friars show to visitors the stones in the pavement which, according to legend, were part of the altar, *Ara Primogeniti Dei,* erected by Augustus to the unknown god who would be born in the first emperor's reign. That prophecy, in Virgil's fourth *Eclogue,* is the nubbin of Eliot's talk on "Virgil and the Christian world." With a deprecating smile, the Fran-ciscan who points out this fragment of antiquity may tell strangers, "It is only a tradition, of course." Yet it is in

(*351*)

tradition, as Eliot reminded his age, that most truth may be unearthed. Drawing upon classical and Christian tradition, *The Cocktail Party* surely will be the most enduring of Eliot's plays. And like the fourth *Eclogue*, it may even acquire, with the passing of many generations, the prophetic afflatus.

X

Illusions and Affirmations

❖

Notes towards the Definition
of Educational Purpose

If the boredom and the glory of his age remained to Eliot
after 1950, the horror had passed out of his vision. After
The Cocktail Party, his writing is marked by an urbane
humor and resignation; later there would come serenity,
and even joy. Like Charles Eliot Norton, he was very nearly
able "to look upon the passing order without regret, and
towards the coming order without hope."

Vivienne Eliot, for fourteen years little more than a
phantom, had died in 1947. In his sixties, Eliot went his solitary way still, but no longer weighed down by that sense of
isolation of spirit which had descended upon him early and
had endured long: now he knew the community of souls.
After the end of the Second World War, he lectured at all
sorts of places—in western Europe, in America, even
in South Africa. (The American lectures had made it possible
for him to visit Pound in his asylum-prison—for he could
not have traveled without lecture fees during the austerity-

(353)

time of Clement Attlee and Stafford Cripps—and to do what
he might to effect Pound's release.) During seven years,
his only lengthy work was a gentle realistic play, *The Confidential Clerk:* poetic inspiration, though it had continued
with Eliot for nearly four decades, had departed at last; and
long before, he had made up his mind not to persist (as so
many injudicious poets had tried to continue) in writing
verses which could be no better than echoes of early talent.
And he labored under no necessity, now, of writing much
for money.

During these years, nevertheless, his essays on education,
his lectures on literature, and his excursion into political
theory were substantial accomplishments. They remained
essays only, these undertakings: as Eliot said of himself, he
was not so industrious as Coleridge (even though he took no
sort of opiate). Earlier, Eliot had lacked the time to put together any book that was more than a series of essays—often
loosely linked—except for his forgotten dissertation on
Bradley; now he lacked necessity or impulse for such prolonged writing. Intellect and feeling were strong as ever,
but the enthusiasm and the self-assertion of youth were
much diminished, as he confessed cheerfully enough; he
had encountered difficulty in recalling the affections and
the animosities that had produced some of his famous early
judgments or declarations of principle. He contented himself
with good-natured sniping against certain modern illusions
and with temperate affirmation of certain abiding convictions.

One strong cause, for all that, still moved Thomas
Stearns Eliot: the defense of an education meant to nurture
the moral imagination. This had been the subject of the
final chapter of *Notes towards the Definition of Culture,*
and in 1950 he enlarged upon it in a series of lectures, "The
Aims of Education."

Throughout his editing of *The Criterion,* Eliot had

touched repeatedly upon formal education. In his Commentary of October, 1931, discussing Harold Laski's little *Introduction to Politics*, he had taken Laski to task for unctuous vagueness about education—which Laski had asserted to be a right because it was "fundamental to citizenship." Eliot had written then, "Unless we mean by education that very modest amount of knowledge which can be imparted by mass-instruction, we have no more a right to education than we have to happiness, genius or beauty. So far as we have 'rights,' every man or woman has the right to be educated to *some* useful function in the community; but what is meant by education must differ greatly in kind." Laski would have reduced education to preparation for voting for the best candidate. "My own education was very defective," Eliot commented, "but I have known much better educated men than I to be completely baffled by the complexities of modern civilization." It would be better to try to reduce those complexities, than to force upon simple folk a "right" to be bewildered.[1]

In 1934, tearing to pieces in his Commentary the English Association's anthology *The Modern Muse* (of which the preface was "brainless balderdash"), Eliot had remarked that in the long run, education is the most important problem of society. "We seem nowadays to be committed to the task of giving some sort of education to everybody. Education is a training of the mind and of the sensibility, an intellectual and an emotional discipline. In a society in which this discipline is neglected, a society which uses words instead of thoughts and feelings, one may expect any sort of religious, moral, social and political aberration, and eventual decomposition or petrification. And we seem to have little to hope from the official representatives of education."[2]

In 1935, he had published in his quarterly Dr. Bernard Iddings Bell's "The Decay of Intelligence in America," an essay warm with that clergyman's bulldog vigor. "The degradation of intellectual function is nowhere more marked and nowhere more deadly than in our undergraduate colleges, which seem to many observers to be engaged in a sort of unwitting and blundering conspiracy to drown what potential human genius may be available in a sea of complacent mediocrity"—so wrote Bell, who not long before had been forced out of the presidency of his promising St. Stephen's College (later Bard College), on the Hudson, chiefly because he required young men to observe decent manners. American colleges were content, Bell said, "to 'orientate' brainy people to things as they are, lest perchance they hitch their wagons to a star; to pour out into the world graduates fitted only to earn their living, to buy and spend, to become paid slaves and potential consumers, in a world wherein labor becomes ever more dull and compensation ever less secure." Eliot had commented that the problems of education in England and in America were converging.[3] His continuing friendship with Dr. Bell did something to prompt Eliot's pungent remarks on education in *Notes towards the Definition of Culture* and in "The Aims of Education."

In his "Notes on Education and Culture," the concluding chapter of *Notes*, Eliot dealt with five vulgar fallacies promulgated by writers about education. (It is unnecessary here to go deeply into Eliot's educational principles in *Notes*, because Professor G. H. Bantock has written a penetrating little book about Eliot's educational ideas.)[4] He denied "That, before entering upon any discussion of Education, the purpose of Education must be stated"—that preface is prejudiced, confusing, and boring. He doubted "That Education makes people happier"—for either too much or too little education can make people miserable. He disagreed with the argument "That Education is something that everyone wants"—besides, "A high average of general education is perhaps less necessary for a civil society than is a respect for learning." He thought it impossible "That Education

should be organized so as to give 'equality of opportunity' "—
indeed, this misguided endeavor "would disorganize society,
by substituting for classes, élites of brains, or perhaps only
of sharp wits." He demolished the Mute Inglorious Milton
dogma—the notion that much first-rate ability is suppressed
by the absence of a systematic egalitarian educational apparatus.[5]

In our enthusiasm for Education as a means to the attainment of social ideals, Eliot wrote, we forget that true
education is supposed to lead toward wisdom; that it is
meant for the satisfaction of curiosity through knowledge;
that learning deserves respect for its own sake. His sentences
are in the spirit of John Henry Newman and Irving Babbitt.
By trying to force all young people into a common educational mold, regardless of their aptitudes or their class, we
may succeed only in destroying their real culture (which is
not identical with their schooling). "A 'mass-culture' will
always be a substitute-culture; and sooner or later the de-
ception will become apparent to the more intelligent of
those upon whom this culture has been palmed off."[6] A
quarter of a century later, the violent protest of university
students through the world would attest to this hard truth.

Dr. Robert Maynard Hutchins, then chancellor of the
University of Chicago, read this last chapter of Notes, and
in part disagreed; he replied in the first number of a new
quarterly, Measure, modeled somewhat after The Criterion,
and launched by the University of Chicago's Committee on
Social Thought. A strong-willed man, Hutchins dissented
(not altogether consistently, some of his own writings on
education considered) from Eliot's misgivings about educational egalitarianism. Hutchins had acquired some understanding of Aristotle and Aquinas from his friend Mortimer
Adler; also he had in him a kind of doctrinaire democratism,
often at odds with his own autocratic character and his own
educational inclinations. Replying to Eliot, Hutchins de-

fended the ideal of equality of educational opportunity: "In the United States, where the ideal of equality has been pursued longer than anywhere else, none of the consequences predicted by Mr. Eliot has appeared."[7]

This affirmation was difficult to reconcile with Hutchins' own earlier assaults on the school of John Dewey, and would be difficult to defend in the light of later developments in American college and university; in general, this essay was not one of Hutchins' happier productions. Hutchins appears to have been provoked by Eliot's quoting of Burke in his *Notes;* by a kind of accident, Hutchins had committed himself to a detestation of Burke. For in January, 1943, *The Thomist* had published a number dedicated to Jacques Maritain; Hutchins had been invited to contribute an essay; and he had set his name to a shallow article about Burke.[8] Thereafter, haunted by Emerson's hobgoblin of consistency, Hutchins found it necessary to assail the name of Edmund Burke wherever it should appear, even if he was somewhat less well acquainted with Burke's writings than he was with those of Aristotle and Aquinas.* "The difference between Burke and Mr. Eliot is that Mr. Eliot does not deny that democracy is the best form of society," Hutchins concluded his rejoinder in *Measure.* "Burke did. His favorite objects of satire were the sovereignty of the people and the rights of man. Though wrong, he was consistent. Mr. Eliot is both wrong and inconsistent."[9]

* While we were lunching together in London sometime in 1954, Eliot told me that during his Chicago lectures of 1950, Hutchins had attended a reception for the visitor. "I was puzzled by Dr. Hutchins' remarks, in his article in *Measure,* about Burke and me," Eliot told me. "So I went up to Hutchins and told him that I was grateful for his criticism of my ideas about education, but that I did not understand what he meant by saying that I am a democrat and Burke was not. Our times considered, I suppose that Burke was more of a democrat in his age than I am in ours. But Dr. Hutchins did not answer me; he walked away. Why do you suppose he did that?"

"The answer is simple enough," I replied. "Dr. Hutchins had not really read Burke."

This exchange between Eliot and Hutchins might not be worth noting, except that it was one reason why Eliot went to the University of Chicago, in the autumn of 1950, his lectures on "The Aims of Education" developing in greater detail the principles he had expressed in *Notes*. This series, his most lengthy discussion of education, was published in four successive numbers of *Measure*.° Although Eliot intended to make a little book of these lectures, after revision, he never found opportunity to improve his discourses, and fifteen years later they were printed unrevised in *To Criticize the Critic*.[10]

Canon Bernard Iddings Bell, then adviser to Episcopalian students at the University of Chicago, had published in 1949 his *Crisis in Education*, one of the more lively books of a number mordantly criticizing American schools and colleges which began to come from the press at that time. In education as in religion, Eliot and Bell were virtually of one mind; and Eliot commenced his lectures with a quotation from Bell's book. (This could not have endeared him to Chancellor Hutchins, who had refrained from speaking to Dr. Bell ever since that "well-known divine"—Eliot's phrase—had appeared at the University.)† In part, Eliot's lectures were a reply to Hutchins' criticisms in *Measure*.

Among the several writers on education with whom Eliot had differed in *Notes towards the Definition of Culture*, Dr. C. E. M. Joad had been eminent; and to Joad's readable (if "middle-brow intellectual") book *About Education*, Eliot gave renewed attention in his "Aims." There were many writers with whom Eliot disagreed more fundamentally than he did

---

° One of my early essays, "Beyond the Dreams of Avarice," was published next to Eliot's Part I of "Aims"; probably Eliot had not seen my name before that.
† Canon Bell told me, about 1954, that the coolness between him and Hutchins extended back to Bell's years as president of St. Stephen's College—when he had refused to appoint Hutchins to an instructorship in English, believing him to be too arrogant.

with Hutchins and Joad; presumably he singled them out because it is possible to reason with men whose first principles are not totally opposed to one's own. Joad had listed three ends of education: to enable a boy or girl to make his or her living; to equip him to play his part as a citizen of a democracy; to enable him to develop all the latent powers and faculties of his nature and so enjoy a good life. These ends beg the question, Eliot remarked, of what sort of society one hopes to have.

The word "democracy" is used nowadays in virtually every country—to describe "totally different institutions"; so it is suspect. We ought not to permit education to be interpreted as "educational adaptation to environment." The student must not be completely adapted to democracy "in the form in which he finds it around him; for that would be to train a generation to be completely incapable of any change or improvement, or to adapt itself to those changes which go on perpetually without anyone's having deliberately intended to bring them about." It is no simple affair, this "education for democracy." What if young people should be born into an evil society? Should they be educated for adjustment to that society? To define education, and the purpose of education, we must inquire, "What is Man?" and "What is Man for?"

In his second lecture, "The Interrelation of Aims," Eliot proceeded to assail the elective system (first adopted at Harvard by President Eliot), narrow specialization, obsessive vocationalism, and emphasis on "citizenship" almost to the exclusion of moral behavior and feeling—all this much after the fashion that had been Irving Babbitt's, half a century earlier. Only through improving the person can we improve the republic:

"Education for citizenship, then, seems to mean first of all the developing of social conscience; and I have already suggested that 'social' conscience can be only a development of 'conscience': the moment we talk about 'social conscience' and forget conscience, we are in moral danger—just as 'social justice' must be based upon 'justice.' The separation in our mind which results simply from dwelling constantly upon the adjective 'social' may lead to crimes as well as errors. In the name of social justice we can excuse, or justify to ourselves, or simply ignore, injustice: in the name of social conscience we can do the same by conscience. The same sort of substitutions can occur with the word 'democracy.' 'Social democracy' sounds at first a phrase to which no one could object; but the denotation can be so manipulated that it can be made to point to something which to most of us, I think, may be anything but 'democratic.'" As Eliot spoke, "social democracies" were extirpating whatever opposition remained within the countries of eastern Europe.

"The Conflict between Aims," Eliot's third lecture, begins with distinctions among the four phases of development in the term "education." At first, education meant the training of a few people for learned professions; next came the education of a gentleman, together with literacy for other classes; third, in the nineteenth century, educators were concerned with extending the supposed benefits of education to a large part of the population; and in this century, we have to deal with the vexing difficulty that nominal literacy has not sufficed: "There is an increasing proportion of the population which can read only headlines of any part of a newspaper not concerned with sport or crime." (Television had no more than begun its inroads, in 1950.)

Universal standardization in education looms before us; and this is no pleasant prospect, for there ought to be many different kinds of education for many different kinds of people. With standardization there marches the prospect of control of education by the state. The doctrine of "equality of opportunity" tends, in practice, toward mediocrity and boredom. And it will be employed by the state to advance the ends of those who control the state. "And we find that the principle of 'equal opportunity' is meaningless—that is, susceptible of being interpreted by everybody in terms of what he *desires,* instead of what he ought to desire—unless we answer the question 'opportunity for what?'"

Joad's aim of developing latent powers and faculties, too, has its perils; Joad "is leaving the area of latent powers and faculties uncontrolled. The danger of separation between the social and the private life—which has the corollary that the only criterion of morals is whether one's conduct is harmful to one's neighbors, and that every man should be free to do as he likes with *himself*—is that the social code, the code of citizenship, will become more and more constrictive, more and more exercising a pressure towards *conformity;* and that this public servitude to society will be compensated by extreme license in whatever conduct is supposed to be none of the state's business." When this license comes to hamper or threaten the ends of the state, however, the state will impose systematic controls. "Thus the individual may find his privacy, his opportunity for exercising his moral freedom and responsibility, gradually taken away from him in the name of society."

There exists a law of behavior that is more than duty to the state. We cannot develop the good citizen if we do not know what the good man is. And that leads to Eliot's concluding lecture, "The Issue of Religion."

Difficult though it is to impart religious knowledge in state schools, without injustice or distortion, still education with religious understanding omitted is no education at all, because it cannot touch upon ultimate questions. "The religious sense, and the sense of community, cannot be divorced from each other," Eliot said. "They are first formed, certainly, in the family; and when they are defective in the family, the defect cannot be supplied by the school and the university. But on the other hand, the contrast between a community

life in which religion has no place, and a family life for
which it is reserved, cannot be long endured; and the
weakening of it on the social side of religion in the outside
world will tend to weaken it in the family also; and the
weakening of the religious bond between members of the
same household, beginning at that early age at which we
first think that we are thinking for ourselves, will leave the
family reduced to the insecure bond of affection and sentiment. Thus, when religion comes to be more and more an
individual matter, and is no longer a family tie; . . . when it
ceases to inform the whole of life; then a vacuum is discovered, and the belief in religion will be gradually supplanted by a belief in the State. That part of the social
life which is independent of the State will be diminished to
the more trivial. The necessity will appear for a common
belief in *something* to fill the place of religion in the community; and the liberals will find themselves surrendering
more and more of the individual freedom which was the
basis of their doctrine." So there emerges totalist ideology,
the Savage God.

Neither church nor state is competent to undertake the
whole of education. We must consider the claims of both of
these—and of the self. "Was Thoreau a good citizen when
he retired to Walden? Many a man has pursued a course
which seemed folly to his family, or which appeared anti
social, or which meant pain and sacrifice for others, and
we denounce him or praise him according to results which
could never have been predicted. So I think we must allow
a place after all to individual choice in 'the development of
latent powers,' although with all the qualifications with
which we have now loaded the phrase."

Let us steer clear of standardization, then, and of omni-
competent state direction; let us beware the shoal of "contemporaneity," which since Eliot's time has come to be
called "relevance." The history and the literature of dead

ages emancipate us from immersion in the flood of our own hour. "We look to institutions of education to maintain a knowledge and understanding of the past," reinterpreted in every generation. "And to preserve the wisdom of the past, we need to value it for its own sake, not simply to defend it on the ground of its usefulness." What appears useless to one generation may be found very useful indeed in a later time. For the sake of wisdom and of a tolerable society—if we must choose—it is better "that a small number of people should be educated well, and others left with only a rudimentary education, than that everybody should receive a share of an inferior quality of education, whereby we delude ourselves into thinking that whatever there can be the most of, must be the best."

After all, education really cannot be defined, Eliot concludes, but we may become aware of education's purposes. Not to impose a theory, but to unsettle minds, had been Eliot's intention in this exercise. "I have not been thinking of convincing, though you may have been thinking of your next cocktail party."

To contend against secular dogmatism in education; to call attention to the peril that the state may subsitute ideology, through its control of schools, for religious understanding; to protest against a thoughtless leveling of minds and feelings through the degradation of the democratic dogma, applied to schooling; to argue, implicitly, for the primacy of the moral imagination in any truly educational undertaking—these had been Eliot's objects in these Chicago lectures. Like Demosthenes (quoted by Babbitt in the concluding paragraph of *Literature and the American College*), Eliot had implored his audience to *think*.

"The Aims of Education" may seem inconclusive; but Eliot's method was subtle. "Now, judged by current opinion and preoccupation, Eliot's answers were unusual," G. H. Bantock writes. "This is partly because his answer to the

ultimate question 'What is a man?' was also unusual. He saw
constant tension as characteristic of the human situation,
not harmony or adjustment. To put it another way, he saw
both the horror and the glory of human life; for he believed
that human existence was marked by qualitative discrimina-
tions. He was, in a word, not afraid to admit that he preferred one mode of life to another, and was, therefore,
prepared to judge and assess. He is typical of his age in that
his judgments and assessments have about them a mildness,
almost a scepticism, which readily offers the prospect of
disagreement. But at least he offers something to disagree
with . . . Eliot was an essentially urbane enemy; but he mani-
fested a firm repudiation and an equally firm alternative."[11]

Brief though his early experience as a teacher had been,
Eliot knew what the good teacher ought to be, and what—if
culture was to endure—ought to be taught. He derided the
notion that a new barbarism was spreading outward from
the United States (the disease being universal, not an in-
fection from America), but he recognized the power, for
good or ill, of American example. "I myself consider that
people in this country ought to pay more attention to the
history of education in America," he wrote to me from
London, on May 5, 1955, "as without doing so, they will almost inevitably repeat the same mistakes. But how is the
public for educational literature to be persuaded of this?"
He told me once that a sound journal of educational theory
would do much good in the United States—even if almost
no one should read it.*

* In a letter of January 13, 1956, Eliot would take up with me the
discouraging difficulties of serious periodicals. Before it ceased publication, *The Criterion*'s subscription list had diminished dismally; and it
had always been run at a loss, that quarterly. He had read an essay
of mine called "The Age of Discussion." "I think that one aspect of
the situation which is ignored in your article," he wrote to me, "is the
economic aspect. Here the situation, I imagine, is not quite so bad as
in your country, but still it is bad enough, I am afraid, to be extremely
dangerous. The fact is simply that the cost of production of materials,

Educational fallacies and social fallacies were closely intertwined, Eliot believed. He found an instance of this in
an address by Robert Hutchins (of which I had sent him a
copy) to the American College of Hospital Administrators
in September, 1955. Ever since he had left the University
of Chicago, Dr. Hutchins had been growing—as Alice
would have said—curiouser and curiouser in his opinions. To
the Hospital Administrators, he had made some remarks
with which Eliot and I agreed heartily. Also, in the latter
part of his speech, Hutchins fell into a strange chain of
reasoning. He suggested that there exist two great American
principles, now endangered: first, "that a man is to be judged
by what he does, not by what he thinks, not even by what
he says, certainly not by what his relatives think or say or
even by what they do . . ." and, second, "that the chief
qualification for a job is the ability to perform it." Educational institutions and foundations, Hutchins suggested,
need nowadays to reaffirm these two great American principles. (Hutchins was speaking at a time when Senator
Joseph McCarthy's influence was at its height, and when
many university and college people believed academic freedom to be endangered; had it not been for the heat of that
debate, Hutchins might have spoken more judiciously—
intemperance tending to breed intemperance.)

Eliot's comments on this speech will suggest the quick-
ness of his mind, burdened though he always was with much
correspondence and considerable editorial labors. "Hutchins'
address is a most curious combination of good sense and

---

and of labour, have increased to such an extent that a really serious
periodical must be either be subsidized or go out of existence. For a
magazine which within my memory, could have paid for itself, including contributors and editor, on, say, a circulation of 3,000, would now
barely make ends meet with a circulation of three or four times that
number; and it is a fact, generally ignored by the majority of people
who do not like unpleasant facts, that the number of educated readers
of the best type of periodicals, has not increased in proportion."

folly," he wrote to me on December 7, 1955. "I read it with a good deal of approval up to a certain point, but when I got to page 14, Hutchins' good sense seemed to have deserted him completely. But in any case, the moment I come across such a phrase as 'the great American principle' or 'the American idea' or 'the American way of life,' I begin to be suspicious. It would be exactly the same, I may add, if it was the British, or the French or the Indonesian 'way of life.' I do not like these phrases. And the two principles which Bob Hutchins selects as 'great American principles' both happen to be, in my opinion, wrong. If a man is not to be judged by what he says, but only by what he does, then no writer, however tendentious or corrupting, should be judged at all. Where is one to draw the line between doing and saying, between thinking and being? Is a man never to be judged by what he is? As for the other 'great American principle,' that the chief qualification for a job is the ability to perform it, that is a very dangerous half-truth. It ignores the moral qualifications which are of vital importance in selecting teachers. It leads to the view that so long as a man performs satisfactorily the work he is given to do, the rest of his life is his own business—a debilitating principle which ends by giving us in public life our Macleans and Burgesses."*

Despite Hutchins' vigor, his several books on education may be forgotten altogether when Eliot's brief discussions of such matters still attract serious discussion. The egalitarian concept of education which Hutchins defended soon would begin to dissolve in its hour of seeming victory.

In Britain, the Education Act of 1944, severely criticized by Eliot, would be succeeded by acts still more inimical to the traditions of grammar school and public school that he supported. The attempt to create a new élite, on the one

---

* Here Eliot refers to two British upper civil servants (and homosexuals), possessed of secret information, who had defected to Soviet Russia.

hand, by national standardized examinations aimed at narrow private rationality or mastery of "facts" (often swallowed
in special cram-schools) alone; the endeavor, on the other
hand, to level talents by sweeping away the old grammar
schools and supplanting them with "comprehensive" schools
in imitation of American high schools—these notions would
assail British education during the rest of Eliot's life, and
thereafter. As early as 1953, when I interviewed a good many
Englishmen and Scots about such matters, the damage was
conspicuous, and of the character that Eliot had predicted.

A Conservative M.P. expressed to me his thorough satisfaction with the intellectual state of the English people. If
they do not read good books nowadays, he said, still universal
education has served a more important purpose: it has enabled men and women to form political opinions more
readily than they had a hundred years earlier. There is
"education for citizenship"—which can be education for
servitude to demagogue or ideologue. But a lecturer in education at Sheffield University, a young Socialist, discussed
soberly the tendencies of the board schools. Standardized
examinations, he said, were discouraging independent
thought and even real literacy; they amounted to indoctrina-
tion, not education; and they tended to favor the more
cunning boys and girls, not the more imaginative or the more
honest. "The educationists' tests are calculated to make card-
sharps the masters of society?" I asked. He laughed, and
then sighed: "Just so."[12]

In America, the public schools slipped deeper into the
ethos of sociability; only the ascent of the Russians' Sputnik
would disturb Americans' complacency about education,
and that only temporarily and in the domain of applied
science. As for most American colleges and universities, they
progressively abandoned standards in favor of immense
numbers; and not long after Eliot had lectured at Chicago,
the president of one big Midwestern state university de-

clared with pride, "There is nothing to which this university will not stoop, if the public seems to desire it." From Behemoth University, it was a far cry to Eliot's old Harvard, or to Oxbridge. Nine years after "The Aims of Education," the superficialities of C. P. Snow, in *The Two Cultures and the Scientific Revolution* (at the antipodes from Eliot's convictions), would be taken, either side of the Atlantic, for the new gospel of the higher learning—at least until F. R. Leavis had replied ferociously.[13]

Only catastrophe, perhaps—discernible by the 1960's, in the riots of university and college and high school—would work reaction and reform; only adversity might revive the moral imagination. But what Eliot had said about education, in his even-tempered way, might take on more meaning by 1980 than it had given to most people in 1950.

The Virtue of Resignation

Except for his lecturing, Eliot's life was almost leisurely now. Between 1949 and 1958, he produced only one important creative work: a realistic verse-play, *The Confidential Clerk*, first performed at the Edinburgh Festival on August 25, 1953.* Although this play (in form a comedy, but not in substance) lacked the intensity of *The Cocktail Party*, twenty thousand copies were printed in England when the play was published the next year, and twenty-six thousand in America; later there came large paperbound editions. Its stage pro-

---

* Some students of Eliot have defined *The Confidential Clerk* as a farce—to his amusement. On October 28, 1953, having read my review of that play in *The Month*, he wrote to say that he was surprised to find I had been able to penetrate so far into his play, without a printed text available and after having seen only one performance. "I am wondering when or whether other critics will come to see the play from something like your point of view. It seems to be the impression of some intellectuals that *The Confidential Clerk* is a rather unsuccessful farce."

duction was good, and I saw Eliot—a little stiff in the joints, now—coming out of the Lyric Theater, the night of the first performance, looking pleased.

This is a play of resignation. Eliot's clerk is an ordinary man of business, and all the characters are people ordinary enough, with the partial exception of Colby, the new clerk. Their ordinariness is a cause of their unhappiness, and provides the play with its principal theme, a familiar one with Eliot: the prison of Self.

Sir Claude Mulhammer the financier, and his flighty wife Lady Elizabeth, and his protégés Lucasta Angel and Colby, and B. Kaghan the rising young broker, do not understand one another, or themselves, or even whence they came. The younger people know that they were born out of wedlock, and are quite rootless. Sir Claude, in the first act, declares that his principle of action is always to assume that he understands nothing about any man he meets; yet to assume that the other man understands *him* thoroughly. This premise betrays Mulhammer in the end, until he cries, his eyes shut, "Is Colby coming back?"—knowing now that even the presumed existence of his own son had been an illusion for twenty-five years.

These people, the wrack of broken families, specimens of a generation without certitudes and deprived of continuity with the past, are involved in the oldest of dramatic plots— mistaken identity, the missing son, and the classical comedy of errors; Eliot again turns to a Greek source, this time Euripides' *Ion*. Reviving these devices ingeniously, with some pleasure in his anachronisms, Eliot also writes whole speeches that could have been Shaw's, and others that could have been the work of Wilde, and others Ibsen's. Lady Elizabeth, with her "mind study," her Swiss clinics, and her intuitions, would have brought credit to Oscar Wilde; the bond between Lucasta and Colby, broken by Colby's discovery that they may be brother and sister, has a Shavian touch; while all through the acts, somberly, the spectre of *The Wild Duck* whispers that the truth we learn about ourselves may be our undoing. When all is over, Colby and Lucasta and Kaghan, at least, do know who they are, and in some degree realize their end in life, but they accept with resignation the discovery of their real nature—not with relief. Upon them all, though most heavily upon Mulhammer, descends a consciousness of the vanity of human wishes.

Everyone in this play (except, possibly, old Eggerson the retiring clerk, with his wife and garden and simple virtues) is haunted by loneliness and by regret for talents frustrated. Even accomplishment in the arts (Sir Claude wished to have been a praiseworthy potter, and Colby a talented organist and composer) is baffled by the spirit of the age. These people are unable to link with dead generations or with those yet unborn. They seek for continuity, status, faith; and, beyond all these, though only Colby senses this, they grope half-consciously for some assurance that their lives matter, and that the barriers which separate every man from his fellows may be transcended, ultimately, in a community of souls.

In structure, *The Confidential Clerk* is close to *The Importance of Being Earnest*, even to the revelation in the final act by the old nurse (or rather, here, Mrs. Guzzard, the foster-mother); and it is possible to laugh at certain lines and certain characters. But this is to laugh after the fashion of Democritus, at the pathos of evanescent things. In the second part, especially, occur lines of high tenderness and pathos, as when Lucasta comes to believe that she understands Colby and herself, and is on the brink of self-realization—and then is overwhelmed, the next instant, by disillusion, or rather by illusion of a different sort. Throughout the play, Eliot treats his people with mercy and sympathy; they become lovable, all of them. From Sir Claude to Mrs. Guzzard, they are men and women of kindly natures, honest inclinations, and generous hearts. But, being human and modern, they are heir to all the imperfections of spirit and flesh; they cannot escape the rootlessness of their time, nor the sense of talents run to waste, nor the prison of Self.

Lucasta thinks that Colby is different from the rest of them, for he can withdraw from their midst into his garden of the imagination, a sanctuary from the desolated material world. But Colby himself knows better: his garden of the mind is lonely as the sensate world without. If Colby were endowed with conviction of an abiding reality that transcends the Waste Land—why, then indeed he never would be solitary in his domain of fancy, for "God would walk in my garden." Wanting this faith, however, the man is left melancholy and unnerved, deprived of love, scarcely caring to learn the identity of his parents. We see him, near the end of the third act, groping toward a churchly vocation; yet only Eggerson, the practical old clerk, has come close to understanding Colby. Lucasta, turning back to Kaghan for some sense of affection and belonging, thinks that Colby needs no human company, being secure in the citadel of self-knowledge. She has not learned that a citadel besieged may be very like a prison.

Technically, *The Confidential Clerk* is a close-knit success. It is more easily apprehended than any other important work of Eliot's. Its verse is even closer to prose than that of *The Cocktail Party*—so close that Eliot's earlier purpose of reviving the verse-drama is almost indiscernible to an audience. A principal deficiency of this play, as of all Eliot's plays, is touched upon by Seán Lucy, who points out that Eliot's characters—quite unlike Shakespeare's— do not interact or truly share the action: "Eliot's heroes . . . are not only conscious of their isolation, but are also *isolated by the nature of the action which is necessary to them.* The pattern of realization, acceptance, choice and expiation, through which they must pass if they are to find themselves, means a with-drawal from all but gradual and isolated action—and with-drawal does not form a good dramatic theme."[14] Still, this is a play that touches movingly upon the sources of longing and the need for enduring love, and bears the mark of a man of genius.

Recognizing our limitations, we must resign ourselves to the possible in this life, and to the realities of self; then—especially if, like Colby, we look for an Other—we may find peace, if only the tranquility of routine. In *The Confidential Clerk*, the characters move slowly toward that peace—which Eliot himself already had attained.

By 1953, he had achieved, to all appearances, a serenity that most never know. During the years between *The Confidential Clerk* and *The Elder Statesman*, I corresponded with Eliot fairly often, and we met now and again. There were luncheons at the Garrick or the Authors' Club—sometimes with interesting companions, among them Bernard Iddings Bell, Frank Morley, and Herbert Agar; there were chats in Russell Square. He was thirty years older than I, but we had read the same books, knew the same places, were almost as one in literary preferences and social convictions, and had several old friends in common. I came from a family with a background, in a humbler way, rather like the Eliot family's; my own progress from doubt to acceptance had resembled Eliot's, though it was not half so tormenting as his. About the stage of life when he had settled in London, three decades later I had come to Britain for some years; we were comfortable together. (In September, 1953, I wrote to him that some day I would write a book to be called *The Age of Eliot*. It has taken me eighteen years to make good that intention.)

I came to understand Eliot better through talking with two old friends of his, whom I came to know, almost by accident, during 1953 and 1954: Roy Campbell and Wyndham Lewis. In personality, those three were wondrously disparate; yet a bond of affection subsisted. In November, 1954, on successive days, I called on all three. The Men of 1914 (if Campbell may be counted as a junior member of that band) still were livelier than anyone I knew of my own generation.

Full of cheerfulness and beer, Roy Campbell led his household and me from pub to restaurant and back to his flat. That rather desolate flat was in a house that had been gutted by a bomb during the war, on a night when all that street was ablaze; but it had been patched up tolerably. So had Roy, shot repeatedly in the Spanish civil war and in the Ogaden campaign of the King's African Rifles. His back was a mass of scar-tissue, and he had a length of plastic instead of a bone in one leg, but his tremendous body seemed indestructible. There revolved about this exuberant colossus his dark wife, his pretty daughter, the Marquesa (whose Spanish husband was wanted for counterfeiting), and intense Rob Lyle, who meant to be Roy's biographer. "This fellow," Roy said of Lyle, "is writing a book about me, and he's caught me in seven great whopping lies already."

Although he had translated Saint John of the Cross (translations much admired by Eliot), Roy Campbell was no traveler on the *via negativa*; and were martyrdom ever in prospect for him, he would have dispatched a number of adversaries first. Not long before, he had been made an honorary doctor of laws by the University of Natal. He had flown the length of Africa in company with Sir Alexander Carr-Saunders, director of the London School of Economics. That scholar, what with sterling-restrictions, had no money on his person, and Roy (as usual) little enough. At Khartoum, between planes, they went into a café to take coffee. When Carr-Saunders found he could not pay the reckoning, the Egyptian proprietor took him by the throat, uttering dreadful imprecations and promising the Director a thrashing at the hands of two stalwart porters. Then arose the massive smiling

Roy, throwing off his coat, and offering to fight every man in the station, if the proprietor would not be satisfied with a solitary piastre that Roy produced from a pocket. The Egyptian looked Roy up and down, bit the piastre—and thanked the kind gentlemen.*

He would like to live for ten thousand years, Roy told me, if only to watch from a Spanish hill the pigs rooting beneath the chestnut trees. Physically, he had suffered much; in soul, he had experienced nothing of Eliot's trials; he had taken life as he had found it, laughing and fighting. In the dark, we sauntered through the lanes of Notting Hill; when we came to Wyndham Lewis' back windows, Roy bellowed, "Wyndham Lewis, come out!" But no one answered. "If Wyndham asks you to lend him a hundred quid," said Roy, "don't do it: he'd never forgive you." Years before, Roy went on, Lewis had told him, "I never loved anybody— except perhaps you, Roy, a little."

Roy had been the model for Lewis' character Victor Stamp, in *The Revenge for Love*. In that novel and in others, Roy declared, "Wyndham Lewis is always trying to kill me off." Stamp had gone over a cliff in Spain; and just so, a few years later, Roy Campbell died. (Loving horses, he had detested automobiles, and in the end an automobile destroyed him.) He was the last of the skalds, as I had called him in an essay of mine, a lyric and satirical poet of peculiar talent. This swaggering adventurer understood Eliot's poetry, and Eliot's nature, better than did a score of sober academic critics all put together.

The next afternoon I spent with Wyndham Lewis and his wife, in their decrepit studio-flat high up an obscure staircase near Notting Hill Gate. Quite blind, deaf in one ear, and sick with a virulent cold, Lewis nevertheless was

---

* Did all this really happen quite as Roy told it? One could not be sure; Campbell was capable, almost simultaneously, of grand braggadocio and remarkable humility.

as kind to me as ordinarily he was insolent to most people. The world had not gone well with him: he could paint no longer, and his books never had brought him much money. (He bitterly distrusted all publishers.) Of his novel *Self Condemned*, recently published in London, about eleven thousand copies had been sold, bringing him perhaps six hundred pounds—his greatest success with a book. His originality of mind and conversation had not diminished. He detested doctors, and was forever consulting them. Years before, when Roy Campbell's daughter was a little girl—so the Marquesa had told me the previous evening—Lewis had given her a long, long balloon (a shape she detested), and it had burst in her face. He had treated the world that way.

Seated sardonically among his papers and books, contemptuous of the shabby city and the mechanized sprawling society round him, Lewis (like Coleridge at Highgate, long before) discoursed of the sunk condition of the world. There was no love in him, but there was manliness. The rising generation would not look to Lewis at Notting Hill as once young men had looked to Coleridge at Highgate, for Notting Hill is further down toward the river, and the dry rot worked there with malignant cunning. Yet some should have heard him.

With a hospitality that was unusual in him, Lewis pressed brandy upon me—until, talking, I had drunk nearly his whole bottle. (It might have gone otherwise if he had kept his sight.) Lewis himself drank champagne, for his latest doctor had told him he must drink nothing else, he said, and Eliot thoughtfully had brought him a whole case of little bottles of champagne, on returning from a lecture expedition to the Continent. From the beginning, Eliot had been Lewis' most admiring critic and most forgiving friend.

In 1937, Eliot had written that Lewis, in *The Lion and the Fox*, was defending the detached observer, which made Lewis unpopular with majorities: "The detached observer, by the way, is likely to be anything but a dispassionate observer; he probably suffers more acutely than the various apostles of immediate action. The detached observers are in theory the philosophers, the scientists, the artists, and the Christians. But most of the people who profess to represent one or another of these categories, are more or less implicated in the politics of their time and place. Philosophy has long since been suspect; and the kind that makes the most voluble pretensions to impartiality may be the most dangerous. The future of the detached observer does not seem to be very bright."[15]

Existence had not been bright for Lewis. William Butler Yeats had told the young Lewis that, as a satirist, he would be *stopped*—for that is what always had happened in England to satirists. Lewis kicked against the pricks, but at last he had been stopped. For the art of satire, as Lewis had argued in *Rude Assignment*, can endure only while the satirist stands firm upon a ground of moral principle, from which he can assail his victims with confidence: satire will be written, and read, and applauded, only when writers and the public acknowledge the existence of abiding moral standards. If no values exist, then follies and crimes are not follies and crimes at all, but merely phenomena of meaningless life; and no one will appreciate satire because no one will believe that the satirist attacks anything of importance. It was Lewis' misfortune to have written in the twentieth century.

At the age of seventy, Wyndham Lewis was a very crusty customer, and a very courageous one. His detestation of cant, and his half-reluctant concern for the future of the human race, had drawn him—no Christian, no nihilist—into the arena of controversy, where he had been as hacked and battered as any old gladiator, though he had given as good as he had got.

Love lacking, the inner life of nearly all of the characters in Lewis' novels had been dry and sour; faith lacking,

the civil social order seemed to be dissolving into its con-
stituent atoms. The world was becoming like the London
house described in *Self Condemned:* "The cellar was full of
dry leaves and a wild cat had established its home there, a
brood of wild kittens sprang about among the leaves. This
wild cat so terrorized the tenants that they dared not go
down to their trash bins just outside the cellar-door." Lewis
could not find his way to love and faith. Yet the society
scourged by Lewis might be driven at last to aspire to love
and faith once more, if only out of dread of the wild cat in
the cellar.

T. S. Eliot had nearly done with scourging his age—
though, like Lewis, he was too well aware of the wild cat
in the cellar. When I had some hours with him, shortly after
my visit to Lewis, I admired his unbroken patience. In a
quiet way, he gave precious time to helping people who
needed someone. Among these was John Hayward, a wretchedly crippled writer of talent with whom Eliot shared his
flat. (Hayward edited a useful little selection of Eliot's
prose, *Points of View,* published by Faber & Faber in 1941
but never distributed in America.) One conjectures that had
Eliot lived on a more commodious scale, with larger means,
he might have filled a house with dependents, as the widower
Samuel Johnson had done in Gough Square. About this time,
he was endeavoring to assist Wyndham Lewis—and in other
ways than by fetching him champagne. He encouraged
Henry Regnery, in Chicago, to bring out American editions
of several of Lewis' books, and went out of his way to attract
attention to Lewis in the literary quarterlies.*

---

* "I think *Rotting Hill* is a good book," he had written to Henry Regnery on June 17, 1952, after Regnery had decided to bring out an
American edition of Lewis' stories about postwar England, "perhaps
too good to be relished by the English reviewer. I wonder if you are
taking on any of Lewis' other works. I shall be glad if it has any sale,
because he is now in such a difficult position because of his blindness."

He still was the competent man of business, almost the confidential clerk, active at Faber & Faber—although he no longer turned out those discerning prefaces to the works of other writers, quick or dead, from Djuna Barnes to Rudyard Kipling, that for years he had written with ready versatility for his firm. As director there, he had been fairly cautious, as doubtless his colleagues had expected a banker to be: he had accepted eagerly, it is true, Robert Graves' *The White Goddess,* after it had been rejected by two other publishers; but he had decided not to publish George Orwell's *Down and Out in Paris and London* and (a more serious misjudgment) his *Animal Farm.* Wifeless and childless though he was, Eliot had been obstetrician or godfather to scores of good books; few of those he sponsored had fallen dead from the press.

If he never had shared greatly Roy Campbell's love of proliferating life, neither had he joined in Wyndham Lewis' sardonic defiance. He never showed anger or surprise: *nil admirari* might have been his motto. That elegant "aged eagle" profile of his seemed always in repose, though his body, never robust, had to be taken to the clinic now and again. (Friends, including Lewis, were concerned for his health; but he told Lewis that he was being treated for nothing worse than athlete's foot.)

Like Sir Claude in *The Confidential Clerk,* Eliot had accepted the terms that life imposes. He might have said, with Walter Scott, "Patience, cousin, and shuffle the cards." His glowing literary success had not puffed him up; the dark prospects for civilization had not made him despair. The age might make an end of its own culture; but the event was in the hand of God; what a man of letters might do to chasten the follies of the time, he had done already.

Carlyle had written of old Coleridge that the philosopher of Highgate had "escaped from the black materialisms and revolutionary deluges, with 'God, Freedom, and Immortality' still his." That seemed as true of Eliot in 1954. Through a discipline of spirit, he had acquired the theological virtue of hope: not confidence that his own time would be redeemed (though one must continue to labor for that), but rather hope for redemption beyond time, hope that in the ultimate judgment of God the sins of commission and omission would be forgiven.

A volume of poems, a volume of plays, a half-dozen volumes (some very slim) of literary and social criticism—his had been an achievement limited in quantity. (Donald Gallup's bibliography of Eliot's writings, published two years earlier, nevertheless required nearly a hundred and fifty closely printed pages to include the mass of his periodical essays and reviews, prefaces, and occasional pieces.) Yet in that compass, he had delineated with surpassing power the boredom, and the horror, and the glory of his age.

The oppression of horror, I have suggested, had departed from him by this time. In 1957, I would recommend to him the stories of Miss Flannery O'Connor, whose heart and conscience I had found akin to Eliot's. "I did see Flannery O'Connor's book of short stories when I was in New York," he replied (February 20, 1957), "and was quite horrified by those I read. She has certainly an uncanny talent of a high order but my nerves are just not strong enough to take much of a disturbance.

"Similarly with another book shown me in New York, a novel by Nelson Algren; that is terrifying too and I do not like being terrified. Apart from the general aversion to prose fiction which I share with Paul Valéry, I like pleasant, sunny comedies such as I write myself."

No doubt that last sentence was written with a smile; but it was true that his progress from "Preludes" to *The Confidential Clerk* had brought him to a certain serenity. No longer, for Eliot, did the worlds revolve like ancient women, gathering fuel in vacant lots. So far as a man may, he had conquered time; so far as such awareness is possible, he had apprehended the self. Like Don Quixote waked from illusion, he knew who he was.

The peril of solipsism had passed away from him years before. If he had not found wholehearted love here below— why, at least he had found it possible in himself, and that was relief. As Harcourt-Reilly says in *The Cocktail Party*:

> To men of a certain type
> The suspicion that they are incapable of loving
> Is as disturbing to their self-esteem
> As, in cruder men, the fear of impotence.

That suspicion was dimmed in Eliot or perhaps gone by this time.

So he was a good companion. Although sanguine of temperament myself, ordinarily, I always felt more cheerful after a conversation with him: the serenity did it, the serenity bred of resignation. Yes, Eliot knew who he was, and his convert's piety was not "tainted with a self-conceit."

That Christmas he sent to me—as to a good many others —his newly published Ariel Poem, "The Cultivation of Christmas Trees": an appropriate token of friendship in my case, for I had planted several thousands of pines and spruces on my ancestral acres, that year. He was a most faithful sender of Christmas cards—

> So that the reverence and the gaiety
> May not be forgotten in later experience,
> In the bored habituation, the fatigue, the tedium,
> The awareness of death, the consciousness of failure . . .

He had not forgotten the reverence and the gaiety; in his years of resignation and self-apprehension, truly, he had attained that power to affirm which Prufrock had despaired of. He had not measured out his life with coffee spoons.

The Literature of Politics

Five years after the publication of *Notes towards the Definition of Culture,* prospects for a tolerable civilization may have seemed better to T. S. Eliot than he had expected. Economically and politically, western Europe had recuperated well, handicaps considered; in Britain, the frame of society was not much altered by some years of Labour government.

It was now the Socialists' turn to be disheartened. Abandoning, in 1951, his attempt to govern with a parliamentary majority of only eight or nine votes, Clement Attlee had submitted to a general election; and the Conservatives had won, by a majority of twenty seats in the House of Commons. At the age of seventy-seven, Winston Churchill had kissed the Queen's hand again. Anthony Eden, whom Eliot liked, in time would succeed Churchill as prime minister. Political tradition in Britain, after all, was not nerveless.

Yet the Labour party had been defeated more by its own indecisiveness and lack of direction than by Tory vigor. In *New Fabian Essays* (1952), R. H. S. Crossman confessed that social reform had ended, rather than commenced, with the post-war Labour government: "The Labour Party was unsure where it was going."[16] Though immensely costly, the new welfare state had worked no political or social revolution: the old vices and the old virtues of the British civil social order that Eliot had known for four decades were not altered fundamentally; and Old School Tie still administered that order. Had *The Criterion* been revived during the 'fifties, Eliot's commentaries on men and measures doubtless would not have been very different from his criticisms of the 'twenties and the 'thirties. Neither great political party displayed much imagination, and further economic con-

(382)

solidation was paralleled by a continuing decline of the moral order. In an earlier chapter, I have quoted Professor W. L. Burn on Britain under the Conservatives, between the Wars; here it is appropriate to quote Burn on Britain under the Socialists, about 1949:

"It is a scene in which such things as football pools, amusement machinery, and cosmetics enjoy the place of honour. . . . Wine and spirits, turkeys, sausages, suits of clothes descend upon the fortunate recipients; there are dinners at Grosvenor House, at the Garter Club, at the Garrick Hotel; hospitality is generously offered and gratefully accepted. Yet, in spite of these apparent advantages, it is not a very happy or agreeable society. Perhaps the reason is that too many people want too many things too urgently. One wants sherry casks, one wants paper; others want to float companies, to build canteens or to enlarge hotels. . . . We may imagine the stage festooned with forms, applications for licenses, refusals of licenses, cheques that failed to command confidence and agreements that failed to produce the desired result. Music is supplied by the ringing of the telephone, the prelude to ambiguous and improbable conversations; and through this half-lit jungle, from public dinner to government department, from government department to sherry party, glides the contact-man, at once the product and the safety-valve of this grotesque civilization."[17]

Eliot thought that in this grotesque civilization, a philosophical conservatism was needed, that would transcend the expediency and the pragmatism and the corruption of parties. He found encouraging the progress of Reinhold Niebuhr's social ideas, and he paid attention to the writings of R. A. Nisbet and to my own books. On October 12, 1953, he wrote to me: "It would be interesting if the development of philosophical conservatism made its start first in the United States, which for half a century or more has hardly known anything except different shades of liberalism. It may well be that where the disease is further advanced, the antidote may be first discovered."

He was not altogether happy with the new weekly *National Review*, edited in New York by William Buckley. "It seems to me too consciously the vehicle of a defiant minority," he told me in a letter of January 13, 1956. "What I feel is that such a paper in the United States should, first of all, make a point of publishing facts, especially, of course, the facts played down or ignored in other papers. Second, it should put a good deal of emphasis on ideas and principles. Looking at American politics from this side of the water, it always seems as if there was far too much personal abuse and vituperation, and far too little discussion of politicians' principles, or lack of principles." Conservatives ought not to give the impression that all issues are decided in advance. "I think that it would be a great pity from the point of view of the need for a sane conservatism in American life, and the need for a dispassionate discussion of a number of current *idées reçues.*"

At the least, he wrote, it had been imprudent for *National Review* to have had Dean Acheson's recent book on foreign affairs reviewed by Senator Joseph McCarthy. "Such an article would carry more weight with a reader like myself, if written by almost anyone else." (In a conversation, he had asked me about that senator from Wisconsin; I had told him that the Senate had refrained from censuring McCarthy's conduct in accepting a fat honorarium from the Lustron Corporation—for writing a brochure for this firm, which obtained large contracts from the government—because too many other senators knew that their own sources of income might not endure close scrutiny.)

I had sent him some information about political contests in my state of Michigan. "I am most interested, and alarmed," he continued in the same letter, "by what you say about the labour intervention in the State of Michigan. It may be, it seems to me, that within a few years' time, as you suggest, the whole political life of America may be altered in ways in which it has been altered here, through the association of the Trades Unions Congress with the Labour Party. On the other hand, it must be admitted that the Trades Unions leaders represent, on the whole, the more conservative and responsible elements of the party. I am speaking of the officials of the Trades Unions Congress and of some unions. There are other unions, and important ones, which show little sign of responsibility. One trouble is that the vocabulary people use, and the thoughts they think they think, tend to lag far behind the actual situation. One reason why I like to keep in touch with my old friend Horace Kallen, is that he seems to me representative of a frame of mind which is a generation out of date."*

The slogans and vocabulary of most English Conservatives, too, had seemed out of date to Eliot, between the Wars; but now some new ideas appeared to be stirring among the Tories. The Conservative party had made a determined effort to attract young men of intellectual promise. The "One Nation" group of youngish members of the House of Commons, formed in 1950, was followed by the "Bow Group" of still younger Tory M.P.'s who believed that the welfare state would be transitory only, as the British economy recovered energy; these Conservative innovators participated in some of the aspirations that had worked upon the "Young England" Tories of Disraeli's early political years.

In April, 1955, Sir Winston Churchill submitted his resignation as First Lord of the Treasury to the Queen, and was

* Professor Horace Kallen, of the New School for Social Research, in New York, a liberal active in Jewish organizations and various humanitarian causes, was the author of *The Liberal Spirit, The Education of Free Men,* and *Secularism is the Will of God.* He was an able critic of art, and so had something in common with Eliot.

succeeded by Sir Anthony Eden. Eliot had admired Eden for withdrawing from the Chamberlain government after the appeasement of Hitler at Munich, and was favorably disposed toward him, doubtless also because Eden came from an old county family in Durham, with good repute for political integrity and cultural attainment. (Only a month later, nevertheless, Eliot was somewhat disappointed in Eden; and by the end of a year, he remarked that Eden had no verve.) [18]

The Tories were full of confidence—which was to be justified by the general election of that autumn, when the Conservatives would win a thumping majority in the House of Commons and a popular majority of the British electorate besides: the first occasion during ninety years in which a party holding office had increased both its popular vote and its parliamentary majority. Not long after that Tory triumph, Aneurin Bevan—the chief of the radical wing of Labour, long expected to be prime minister some day, but actually to die in opposition—would declare in the House of Commons that Labour had lost the election of 1955, like that of 1951, because Labour had lacked heart. The Socialists, he continued, had not known what way to turn. In office after the war, they had found no means for reconciling long-range social planning with democratic institutions; of the two, if compelled to choose, they had preferred democracy; and so, lacking self-confidence and direction, in effect they had abdicated. This, one may add, was a victory of sorts for Eliot's ideas over Mannheim's.

With Anthony Eden at Number Ten Downing Street, the Conservatives had been much buoyed up, and the London Conservative Union had asked Eliot to address a literary luncheon on April 19, 1955. He accepted: that party, whose leadership he had so acidly criticized between the Wars, at last seemed ready to entertain thought. This talk on "The

Literature of Politics" (first distributed as a pamphlet, with an introduction by Sir Anthony Eden, and years later reprinted in *To Criticize the Critic*) was his last detailed expression of political principles.

Political thinking and political movements may commence with a body of doctrine, ardently disseminated by men faithful to those political canons, Eliot said. Or, alternatively, a body of political ideas may arise out of the experience of a party that had arisen from common practical interests and necessities, but which gradually has acquired a set of beliefs. The latter sort of party corresponds to Edmund Burke's "organic" understanding of society.

Eliot briefly pointed out the dangers of historical determinism—which, curiously enough, often is embraced by the very people who swear by grandiose social planning. We all have learned from private experience "that there is no formula for infallible prediction; that everything we do will have some unforeseen consequences; . . . that every reform leads to new abuses . . . ; and that we move always, if not in the dark, in a twilight, with imperfect vision, constantly mistaking one object for another, imagining distant obstacles where none exists, and unaware of some fatal menace close at hand."

A party bound by political dogmas—an ideological party, that is, although Eliot does not use the term—discovers when in power that theory and circumstance often collide. Either that party then postpones or modifies its objectives, or else it ruins everything, in Jacobin rigidity. On the other hand, a non-doctrinaire party, always ready to compromise and adapt upon any strong pressure or inducement, may discredit itself by abandoning principle. "To know what to surrender, and what to hold firm, and indeed to recognize the situation of critical choice when it arises, is an art requiring such resources of experience, wisdom and insight, that I cannot envy those public men . . . who may in due course be censured by posterity, as either fanatics or as opportunists."

Thus the doctrinaire party must review its ideas after experience, and the party of organic development must repair now and again to its uniting principles. "For the permanent and the transitory have to be distinguished afresh by each generation."

Men of thought should mingle with men of action, and men of action should seek out writers and scholars. If the doctrinaire dominates the man of action, that is disastrous; it is no less ruinous if political philosophy becomes mere servant to ruling interests. There should exist gradations of types between thought and action:

"In an article which I read recently, on the subject of Conservatism in America, the author made the point, which struck me forcibly, that the true conservatives in that country in recent times had none of them been political figures: they had been the philosophic observers and moralists, often in academic positions; and the names he cited were nearly all of men I had known, or with whose work I was acquainted; such men as Paul More or Irving Babbitt in the last generation, and amongst those living, Canon B. I. Bell, and Professor Nisbet of California. If the writer, himself an American, is right, this is not a very healthy state of affairs, unless the views of such writers become more widely diffused and translated, modified, adapted, even adulterated, into action."*

It is not necessarily the more profound thinker, however, whose influence upon immediate political action is strongest. Shaw or Wells may have moved more men in their time than did Coleridge or Newman. (As for George Bernard Shaw,

* Here Eliot refers to my essay "The American Conservative Character," in *The Georgia Review*, Vol. VIII, No. 3 (Fall, 1954), pp. 249–260.

"one is compelled to admire a man of such verbal agility as not only to conceal from his readers and audiences the shallowness of his own thought, but to persuade them that in admiring his work they were giving evidence of their own intelligence as well.") What really matters is that some few serious writers should try sincerely to penetrate to the heart of things, seeking and expounding the truths of politics—not expecting to transform the civil social order immediately, and not despairing if their writings do not bear fruit at once: men of the "pre-political" area.

For in the pre-political soil of politics are the philosophical roots of social order; down there underground, too, lurk Kipling's grim Gods of the Copy Book Headings. If we would know politics, we must know ethics; and ethics must lead us to theology. "For the question of questions, which no political philosophy can escape, and by the right answer to which all political thinking must in the end be judged, is simply this: What is Man? what are his limitations? what is his misery and what his greatness? and what, finally, his destiny?"[19]

As was his way, in this address Eliot had raised more questions than he had answered. That was his intention: conservatives generally, and Conservatives especially, needed to think, if they would cast off John Stuart Mill's tag "the stupid party." They did not think enough, perhaps, during the years which were left to Eliot: the Eden government lacked energy, and the Macmillan government that followed it sometimes seemed ludicrous. ("Harold so *enjoys* being prime minister," a kinsman of Harold Macmillan said to me a few years later, with mild irony.) Yet in the long run, such minds as Eliot's work upon the general consciousness, even in practical politics.[20]

If Eliot had let cheerfulness break into his political expectations about 1955, that mood was not suffered to endure long. After my book *Beyond the Dreams of Avarice* had been published, he wrote to me (October 31, 1956) from Russell Square: "It pleased me to read your appreciation of Wyndham Lewis—a just and well-balanced one, I think. Much of what you say about this country supports my own gloomy views, and I think it is very true to say of any country, that a decline in private morality is certain to be followed in the long run, by a decline in public and political morality also." That last clause would be sufficiently illustrated, in 1963, by the Profumo affair, in which a cabinet minister, a peer, and a Soviet attaché were involved awkwardly with common prostitutes: two tarts nearly brought down the government. In the age of the contact-man, the idea of a Christian society seemed more remote than it had in 1939.

In 1956, when Leslie Paul interviewed Eliot for the European Service of the BBC, Eliot said that a pagan culture was no longer the most probable alternative to a renewed Christian society. That malign attempt had died with Hitler. Nor could the Communist version of a religion of humanity succeed: "I don't believe that any religion can survive which is not a religion of the supernatural and of life after death in some form." Rather, we may enter upon a society without any religion or culture. "I think that the end of a purely materialistic civilization with all its technical achievements and its mass amusement is—if, of course, there's no actual destruction by explosives—simply boredom. A people without religion will in the end find that it has nothing to live for."

He remained attached, ten years after the publication of *Notes towards the Definition of Culture*, to the concept of a society of classes—needed in our time, especially, as a shield against dictators and oligarchs. "Whenever one contemplates a stratified class society," he told Leslie Paul, "one is emotionally moved towards classlessness, and whenever one contemplates an actual, existing classless society—if there is

anything of the sort—one sees the faults of that and is moved
emotionally towards a class structure. In these matters one
is contrasting something actual and observed with an idea
or ideal preferable to the actuality one sees—because in
practice every society is very imperfect, and every society
commits social injustices of one kind or another. But today
it seems to me more important to argue the case for a class
society because the general accepted idea is one of equali-
tarianism. . . . Any healthy society will tend to facilitate
the transition from one class to another. It will be flexible;
it will somewhat blur the outlines of its classes."

The Community of Christians, the clerisy, transcend and
permeate a structure of classes; there is no inconsistency between *The Idea of a Christian Society* and *Notes towards the
Definition of Culture*. Conscious believers in religious truth
will labor within any society to achieve charity and justice;
classes will serve to maintain continuity and coherence in
the civil social order. "The fault, the evil, in a class society
is when privilege exists without responsibility and duty,"
Eliot said in this BBC interview. "The evil of the classless
society is that it tends to equalize the responsibility, to
atomize it into responsibility of the whole population—and
therefore everyone becomes equally irresponsible."[21] Brief
though his principal political writings are, with such ideas
as these Eliot had contributed something enduring to the
literature of politics.

If education is perverted to a process for socialization and
sociability merely; if isolation of the individual breaks up
the community of souls; if the art of politics declines into a
contest for power and place—why, there will survive no
Community of Christians, and no responsible classes. There
will endure no justice, and no culture; and even if physical
appetites are satisfied, boredom will reign. Those illusions
which betray twentieth-century man to such decadence,

Eliot had stripped naked, as at their birth—for such people as read him attentively. He had set against those illusions his affirmations of cultural continuity, community of spirit, and politics with principle. For comfort, he knew the parable of the sower and the seed.

XI

Age and Decrepitude
Have No Terrors

❖

The Elder Critic

Fifteen thousand people came to hear Eliot lecture on "The Frontiers of Criticism" at the University of Minnesota, April 30, 1956; he had not thought that in all the world there were so many folk interested in literary criticism. A fortnight later, I spoke on that campus, and found everyone still enthusiastically discussing Eliot. In defense of the twentieth century, at least it could be said that neither Johnson nor Coleridge, in the eighteenth century or the nineteenth, had found so immense a congregation to hear a critical sermon.

Eliot had been the Johnson or the Coleridge of his age. Thirty-three years before, in his essay "The Function of Criticism," he had belabored the impressionistic Georgian critics, then dominant. The function of criticism is a problem of order, he had declared in 1923, in the pages of *The Criterion:* "There is accordingly something outside of the artist to which he owes allegiance, a devotion to which he must

(393)

surrender and sacrifice himself in order to earn and obtain his unique position." This conviction made him a classicist, one of those who "believe that men cannot get on without giving allegiance to something outside themselves. . . . If, then, a man's interest is political, he must, I presume, profess an allegiance to principles, or to a form of government, or to a monarch; and if he is interested in religion, and has one, to a Church; and if he happens to be interested in literature, he must acknowledge, it seems to me, just that sort of allegiance . . ." The critic's allegiance is to our common inheritance of literature as an organic whole, a cultural patrimony, transcending time: the continuity of humane letters. The individual artist and the individual critic are significant only *within* this continuity, this tradition.

Through great toil one may enter upon this inheritance and contribute to its growth: literary muddling through, a "whiggery tendency," will not suffice; the great artist is not an unconscious artist, and he attains his stature only by coming to know the writings of his predecessors. If the critic, pulling down his vanity, participates in the timeless community of letters, possibly he may win through to what is called truth.[1]

Eliot had not deliberately constructed the imposing bulk of his literary criticism, for forty years, upon this framework of "The Function of Criticism": rather, he had written about books that had happened to come his way for review, or to which he had been asked to supply prefaces. Yet he had been faithful in his allegiance to tradition and continuity—to that something outside himself.

"One function of criticism is to act as a kind of cog regulating the rate of change of literary taste," Eliot had said in 1942, in his presidential address to the Classical Association. "When the cog sticks, and reviewers remain fast in the taste of a previous generation, the machine needs to be ruthlessly dismantled and reassembled; when it slips, and the reviewer accepts novelty as a sufficient criterion of excellence, the machine needs to be stopped and tightened up." Either fault places a premium upon ephemeral writing. In his early years, Eliot reassembled the critical machine; later, he would tighten it up. He defended "the more original literature of our time" against both conservatives and radicals; he renewed his generation's appreciation for that literature which is ancient but far from senile.

Unity in education, he told the Classical Association, is necessary for the survival of English literature. (As he remarked more than once, precisely what books ought to be read by the rising generation is not so important as the fact that young people ought to read the *same* books—for the sake of cultural coherence and community.) Literature keeps civilization from degenerating into barbarism. He appealed to "those who appreciate the need, if the present chaos is ever to be reduced to order, of something more than an administrative or an economic unification—the need for a cultural unification in the diversity of Europe; and who believe that a new unity can only grow on the old roots: the Christian Faith, and the classical languages which Europeans inherit in common."[2] Eliot had been as catholic in his regard for literature, from the first, as in time he came to be catholic in his religion.

He had opposed that provinciality which—as he had told the Virgil Society in 1945—is "a distortion of values, the exclusion of some, the exaggeration of others, which springs, not from lack of wide geographical perambulation, but from applying standards acquired within a limited area to the whole of human experience; which confounds the contingent with the essential, the ephemeral with the permanent." In criticism of literature, as in criticism of society, Eliot had asserted the claims of past generations and the prospects of future generations, against the modern intoxication with the ephemeral present hour.

"In our age, when men seem more than ever prone to confuse wisdom with knowledge, and knowledge with information, and try to solve problems of life in terms of engineering, there is coming into existence a new kind of provincialism which perhaps deserves a new name," Eliot had continued in his address to the Virgil Society on "What Is a Classic?" European literature is a whole, and if we strike out the Greek and the Roman classics, we wound terribly that organic whole.

This new provincialism is one of time—"one for which history is merely the chronicle of human devices which have served their turn and been scrapped, one for which the world is the property solely of the living, a property in which the dead hold no shares. The menace of this kind of provincialism is, that we can all, all the peoples of the globe, be provincials together; and those who are not content to be provincials, can only become hermits. If this kind of provincialism led to greater tolerance, in the sense of forbearance, there might be more to be said for it; but it seems more likely to lead to our becoming indifferent, in matters where we ought to maintain a distinctive dogma or standard, and to our becoming intolerant, in matters which might be left to local or personal preference."[3]

Against this new provincialism, Eliot's critical essays had been directed. Every generation must renew for itself its understanding of literature, Eliot had said and written repeatedly; new critical schools must arise from time to time; for in letters, as in politics, change is the means of our preservation. But renewal is not destruction: the "New Criticism," in the development of which Eliot had so large a part, ought not to be repudiation of our literary patrimony.

Today's criticism descends from Samuel Taylor Coleridge, Eliot told his Minneapolis audience in 1956; for Coleridge "established the relevance of philosophy, aesthetics and psychology" to literary criticism; and were Coleridge alive now, he would "take the same interest in the social sciences and in the study of language and semantics, that he took in the sciences available to him." Those studies which Coleridge introduced are one of the two principal causes of the rise of the New Criticism; the other cause, Eliot said, is the rise of the academic critic, writing in the shadow of the Ivory Tower—in consequence of the decay of serious literary journalism as a gainful occupation. This wealth of modern criticism has developed weaknesses. Losing sight of its object, it often has become overspecialized or pedantic. His own real contribution to the New Criticism had not been such terms as "the objective correlative"—now almost embarrassing to him, long later—but rather his "workshop criticism," the by-products of his "private poetry-workshop." His critical thinking had been a prolongation of thinking about his own verse. "In retrospect, I see that I wrote best about poets whose work had influenced my own, and with whose poetry I had become thoroughly familiar, long before I desired to write about them, or had found the occasion to do so."

He was speaking of the criticism of poetry, primarily; in the criticism of prose fiction, he claimed no authority.* Contemporary criticism of verse, as the New Criticism had spread in various directions, sometimes wandered down blind alleys. One of those illusory paths "may be characterized as the criticism of explanation by origins," which gives support to the error, "prevalent nowadays, of mistaking explanation for understanding." Eliot's own poems and plays

---

* At the offices of Faber & Faber, Eliot had as little as possible to do with manuscripts of prose fiction. "The only fiction they ever submit for my opinion," he wrote to me on February 3, 1958, "is anything that appears to be an imitation of James Joyce and these imitations seem now to have come to an end."

had been embraced by this critical set, not to his relish. (No other poet has been so much criticized and commented upon, in his own lifetime, as was Eliot; that is why I do not think of appending a critical bibliography to this book.) "After the production of my play *The Cocktail Party,* my mail was swollen for months with letters offering surprising solutions of what the writers believed to be the riddle of the play's meaning. And it was evident that the writers did not resent the puzzle they thought I had set them—they liked it."

Knowing something of a poet's images and ideas may contribute to the reader's understanding of that poet's work; but "explanation" cannot stand alone in criticism. It is far more important to "grasp what the poetry is aiming to be." One cannot be sure of understanding a poem by having read a biography of the poet, for "the critic or the biographer who, without being a trained and practising psychologist, brings to bear on his subject such analytical skill as he has acquired by reading books written by psychologists, may confuse the issues still further." One may add that such techniques, when applied to Eliot and his poetry, have been remarkably unfruitful.

"I am even prepared to suggest that there is, in all great poetry, something which must remain unaccountable however complete might be our knowledge of the poet, and that is what matters most," as Eliot put it. The poet does not merely draw upon obscure sources: he *creates.* And what the poet has added to the materials that fell into his imagination, the critic obsessed by "origins" is unable to discern.

Eliot had no more affection for "the lemon-squeezer school of criticism," which endeavors laboriously to extract juice from every line and stanza. On finishing one volume of lemon-squeezer essays, Eliot found it difficult to recover his love of the poems that had been subjected to this process: "It was as if someone had taken a machine to pieces and left me with the task of reassembling the parts."

Some energetic critics pass beyond the frontier of literary criticism and are lost in the social sciences or in a pointless contemporaneity. The test of the frontier is this: does literary criticism aim at understanding and enjoyment? "So the critic to whom I am most grateful is the one who can make me look at something I have never looked at before, or looked at only with eyes clouded by prejudice, set me face to face with it and then leave me alone with it."

So in literary criticism, as in education and in politics, Eliot affirmed the concept of necessary tensions. He had protested against one pressure in his youth; he objected to a different pressure as he grew old. What matters most is that literature should be a vigorous continuity, never wholly old and never wholly new, refreshed by the critic who is "the whole man, a man with convictions and principles, and of knowledge and experience of life."[4]

On poetry and Poets, Eliot's second most important collection of essays (after the *Selected Essays*), was published in September, 1957—about six thousand copies in London, fifteen thousand in New York. John Wain, reviewing this new volume, wrote the best criticism of Eliot as critic that I have encountered. It is not the duty of the critic, Wain pointed out, to bring about "massive readjustments" in the understanding of literature. "The real task is to convince each generation in turn that the great writers *are* great. Not merely to get them to accept it inertly—with some temperaments, that is easy enough—but to restate, in terms appropriate to the changed situation, the reasons for that greatness." Precisely this had been Eliot's critical achievement. He had made "literary history a living issue." Eliot's criticism had historicity for its gearbox, creative sensitivity for its engine.[*]

---

[*] Both Eliot's poetry and his criticism revived the historical sense among the rising generation of poets, joining this sense to the creative impulse. His understanding that past and present and future really are one: this has been apprehended, under Eliot's influence, by several

In our civilization, poetry finds it difficult to survive at all: this is a prosy age. A poet "has to be both vigilant and somnolent, both spontaneous and sophisticated, both complex and simple. Very few people have managed it with complete success. But Mr. Eliot is one of them; that is why his book is so important."[5]

Eliot would sum up his critical endeavor in what was to be his last major address or essay—delivered at the University of Leeds, in July, 1961. There he would acknowledge being a critic of the sort that Johnson and Coleridge, Dryden and Arnold, had been. These are critics whose criticism is a by-product of their creative activity.

Eliot's criticism grew out of his poetry; it had developed and changed as his poetry had developed and changed. Some of his early criticism, he had come to frown upon. "There are errors of judgment, and, what I regret more, there are errors of tone: the occasional note of arrogance, of vehemence, of cocksureness or rudeness, the braggadocio of the mild-mannered man safely entrenched behind his typewriter."

Like others, he had displayed the dogmatism of youth. "When we are young, we are confident in our opinions, sure that we possess the whole truth; we are enthusiastic, or indignant. And readers, even mature readers, are attracted to a writer who is quite sure of himself." Moreover, in his early years he had been a zealous advocate of the new sort of poetry that he and his friends had been writing.

In his early critical writing, Irving Babbitt and Ezra Pound had influenced him most, Eliot said: those two had

---

of the better poets now at the height of their powers. Consider, as example, these lines from Paul Roche's "The Spaces of Time":

The present is the future as it slips
Into the past and flings, oh, riotously,
Tomorrows into yesterdays and strips
Possible roses dragged from the air, rapaciously . . .

not seemed quite so far apart, then. (Maurras and Hulme had been infused into the classicism to which Babbitt had introduced him.) Of modern poets, Jules Laforgue had moved him most, not Baudelaire—though he had written essays on Baudelaire, and none on Laforgue, because no editor had asked him to criticize Laforgue; on several writers that he much admired, indeed, he had written nothing, no one caring to pay him for such an essay in the days when he had written steadily for money.

Marlowe, Webster, Tourneur, and Middleton and Ford, not Shakespeare, were the dramatic poets who had worked upon him early; Shakespeare is too grand to be an "influence." He had been devoted to Donne, he had reacted against Milton, on his own principle of the "dissociation of sensibility"—or rather, that Eliot principle had arisen from love for Donne and dislike for Milton. He had written best, he knew, about those authors who had influenced his own poetry. Of his three years of formal philosophy, when he was young, there remained to him "the style of three philosophers: Bradley's English, Spinoza's Latin and Plato's Greek."

His critical writings, Eliot went on, had done little enough to establish fashion, but he hoped that they might have helped to form taste: "Fashion, the love of change for its own sake, the desire for something new, is very transient; *taste* is something that springs from a deeper source. . . . It is the function of the critic to assist the literate public of his day to recognize its affinity with one poetry, or with one type of poetry, or one age of poetry, rather than with another." Taste cannot be created; if he had some part in reviving appreciation for the metaphysical poets, it was because his age had inclined naturally to that sort of poetry. "As the taste for my own poetry spread, so did the taste for the poets to whom I owed the greatest debt and about whom I had written. Their poetry, and mine, were congenial to that age. I sometimes wonder whether that age is not coming to an end."

He no longer turned often to the pages of Laforgue, Donne, or the seventeenth-century dramatic poets who had delighted his youth: Mallarmé, Herbert, and Shakespeare better satisfied his need in later years. From the age of twenty-two to the end, however, Eliot's "comfort and amazement" was Dante. And to the end, he felt a strong antipathy to D. H. Lawrence.

Moral, religious, and social judgments, Eliot concluded, necessarily influence even the purest literary criticism: "That literary merit can be estimated in complete isolation, is the illusion of those who believe that literary merit alone can justify the publication of a book which could otherwise be condemned on moral grounds." Like Johnson and Coleridge, Eliot never dissociated letters from ethics; and his fidelity to the cultural heritage of literature endured to the last. "But I hope," he ended, "that what I have said today may suggest reasons why, as the critic grows older, his critical writings may be less fired by enthusiasm, but informed by wider interest and, one hopes, by greater wisdom and humility."[6]

Whatever the decline of enthusiasm and the increase of wisdom, in essence a powerful continuity runs through Eliot's criticism, from his first review in a learned journal (when, in 1916, he criticized Arthur Balfour's *Theism and Humanism* in the pages of *The International Journal of Ethics*) down to his final preface (to *Selected Poems of Edwin Muir*), written in 1964. His differences with Matthew Arnold notwithstanding, his critical task had closely resembled Arnold's task. Whether he had been more successful in that labor than had Arnold, a later generation will judge.

The Last Act at Heartbreak Clinic

"It may be that from the beginning I aspired unconsciously to the theatre—or, unfriendly critics might say, to Shaftesbury Avenue and Broadway," Eliot had told the members of the National Book League, in 1953. Certainly he had developed what he called the third voice of poetry—"the voice of the poet when he attempts to create a dramatic character speaking in verse; when he is saying, not what he would say in his own person, but only what he can say within the limits of one imaginary character addressing another imaginary character."[7] Although he has had few successful emulators, Eliot did revive the verse-play; also he offered to modern drama the possibility of resuming its ancient ethical character. If he could not redeem the stage from Bernard Shaw, at least he might remind the public that there persist older views of the human condition than the Shavian.

In February, 1958, Eliot was trying to complete what would be his last play, *The Elder Statesman*. I had asked him to review, for a quarterly that I was editing, B. A. Smith's book about Dean Church; but he had no leisure for that. "I have to perfect a play which still has many defects," he replied to me, "but which has actually been accepted for production at Edinburgh this summer, so that I am working frantically against time."

Although *The Elder Statesman* shows some marks of haste, it is a moving play of self-recovery and redemption. Its verse, like that of *The Confidential Clerk*, is transparent to the point of invisibility; yet that verse-form makes possible a surviving power of expression which plain prose could not exert. Eliot's humor is successful in this play, and at the end he achieves catharsis. *The Elder Statesman* was first performed at the Edinburgh Festival during the last week of

August, 1958, and it was published (fifteen thousand copies in London, ten thousand in New York) in April, 1959.

The plot is close to that of Sophocles' *Oedipus at Colonus* —closer than is any of Eliot's other plays to its Greek model. An old man is redeemed by self-knowledge and by love; he escapes the fate against which the ghost in "Little Gidding" warns men who have stood high in the world:

> From wrong to wrong the exasperated spirit
>> Proceeds, unless restored by that refining fire
>> Where you must move in measure, like a dancer.

The same impulse that made Eliot write "Little Gidding," indeed, worked upon him in the development of *The Elder Statesman*. "It is likely, of course," he had mentioned in "The Three Voices of Poetry," "that it is in the beginning the pressure of some rude unknown *psychic material* that directs the poet to tell that particular story, to develop that particular situation."[8] Applied to *The Elder Statesman*, those words "psychic material" take on significance; for this is a play of ghosts.

Lord Claverton—formerly Mr. Richard Claverton-Ferry, and before that plain Dick Ferry—is a living ghost. He has been a cabinet minister, and after that a financier; one gathers that he had been remarkable neither for prudent judgment nor for honesty, but the world—so much with him —has admired Claverton. Now that he has retired (perhaps at urgent request from colleagues, perhaps because of impaired health), and is dying, he soon will be forgotten. He is a whited sepulchre, a Hollow Man.

Only one being loves him, or loves the man she thinks he is: his daughter Monica, generally agreed by the critics to be Eliot's only lovable dramatic character (though for my part, I am not repelled by Celia's fire and scorn, in *The Cocktail Party*). Claverton's marriage had failed when it began; his son, Michael, has been cosseted by Lady Claverton (now dead) and hypocritically exhorted to an impossible

rectitude by his father; that father's sins will be visited thrice-
fold upon his spoiled and resentful son. Monica is in love
with Charles Hemington, and that love is not delusory.
Then enter ghosts, in the form of living people—but they
must wait for a moment.

The second and third acts are set at Badgley Court, a
noble country house now made into a genteel clinic or con-
valescent home, its "amenities" glowingly described by Mrs.
Piggott, a delightful bore who refuses to let herself be addressed as "Matron." This is Heartbreak House, converted
into God's antechamber, a last earthly station for the senile
and the dying. A great beech tree stands near the house;
and beneath that tree, Claverton comes to sense, he must
die.

Like Gerontion, Claverton does not fear death itself, but
something more; he is eager enough for physical extinction.
He lives in terror of being alone, and in terror of strangers
(despite his long public career). For he is only a phantom if
deprived of his outward state; and now that he has retired,
he enjoys no pomp and circumstance. He is very like Lord
Mellifont, in Henry James' story "The Private Life": he does
not really exist except in the public eye. He clings desperately
to his daughter, trying to keep Charles Hemington at a distance, because only in Monica's sight (which still discerns
merely his public image) does he retain some scrap of reality.
Monica understands his fears well enough:

It's one thing meeting people
When you're in authority, with authority's costume,
When the man that people see when they meet you
Is not the private man, but the public personage.

Yes, he would face death gladly, he says; but he can only
wait, experiencing "a fear of the vacuum, and *no* desire to fill
it," as if he were in the empty waiting-room of a railway
station.

It makes me smile

To think that a man should be frightened of ghosts.

If they only knew how frightened a ghost can be of men!

When ghosts do appear, they terrify this Hollow Man, nevertheless: his sins have found him out. To his London house, there comes in the first act a being called Federico Gomez, now dishonestly wealthy as a citizen of a Central American republic, but formerly a young man named Fred Culverwell, the companion of Claverton's (or rather, Ferry's) youthful joys. Dick Ferry had led Fred Culverwell into dissipation, debt, and failure at the university; Culverwell then had turned forger; and money from Ferry's father had enabled him to go abroad, after serving his sentence. This grinning phantom from his youth has returned to haunt Claverton—demanding not his money, but his countenance and friendship, to obtain which he is ready to employ a form of blackmail. (After all, Dick Ferry had been driving the automobile that night they ran over the old man's body, and Dick in his cowardice had not told the police.) Why should Gomez not be countenanced? They are birds of a feather: Ferry had been worse than Culverwell, when they two ran side by side, and Gomez (or Culverwell) suggests that Claverton's course in the cabinet and in business has not been altogether straight.

From Gomez, Claverton flees (in company with Monica and Charles) to Badgley Court—an establishment so very like a good hotel that one scarcely notices the decayed condition of its guests. But there he is surprised by another ghost: Mrs. Carghill, formerly on the boards of Shaftesbury Avenue singing "It's Not Too Late for You to Love Me," under the name of Maisie Mountjoy—and before that, little Effie, whom Dick Ferry had seduced (without the least difficulty) when she was eighteen. Ferry's father had bought off Effie's breach-of-promise suit, as he had bought off Culverwell; but Mrs. Carghill retains love letters with which she, too, can attempt to blackmail Claverton. What does she want, being affluent now? Why, it's not too late for him to love her.

Gomez's purpose, and Mrs. Carghill's, is to torment Claverton more than man can bear: they cannot really expect to be taken to his bosom. If the Guardians of *The Cocktail Party* are angelic, these *revenants* of *The Elder Statesman* are diabolical. Mrs. Carghill hints broadly, and more than once, at a hellish union beyond the grave:

It's simply that I feel we belong together . . .
Now, don't get alarmed. But you touched my soul—
Pawed it, perhaps, and the touch still lingers.
And I've touched yours.
It's frightening to think that we're still together
And more frightening to think that we may *always* be together.
There's a phrase I seem to remember reading somewhere:
Where their fires are not quenched.

That phrase is from Saint Mark—but also from May Sinclair, the friend of Eliot during his early years in London, in whose short story "Where Their Fire Is Not Quenched" an adulterous couple are damned to embrace shamefully, loathing each other and themselves, for all eternity. Even the most degraded sexual union may bind a pair beyond death, so intimate and related to the springs of life is that connection; and Effie—a kind of Thames Maiden like the seduced girls of *The Waste Land*—may perform forever, with Dick Ferry, their burlesque of love.

Gomez and Mrs. Carghill are shades given flesh, conjured up by Claverton's "man within"; they join forces against him at Badgley Court. All his life, Claverton says, something deep within him has compelled him to seek justification—not merely justification to the world, but to himself:

What is this self inside us, this silent observer,
Severe and speechless critic, who can terrorize us
And urge us on to futile activity,
And in the end, judge us still more severely
For the errors into which his own reproaches drove us?

(*407*)

These two tormentors are spectres from his past, he tells Charles—malicious, petty, corrupting his son, clinging to Claverton as they have clung all his life, though not until now have they taken visible form. He will not flee from them; and yet they will not master him.

Of all the scholars who have dug among the fragments that Eliot had shored against his ruins, Mr. Grover Smith has dug deepest and most painstakingly. But Smith sits somewhat oddly in judgment upon Claverton—and upon Eliot. "The liberation of Gomez and Mrs. Carghill from ghostly torment forms no part of Eliot's dramatic design," he writes. "Claverton, troubled by his role in their past, is indifferent to their future, though neither has wronged him so much as he has wronged them. He makes no atoning gesture. The tardiness of his self-judgment banishes the quality of mercy which is said to bless both giver and taker."[9]

Yet how may a living man save ghosts or demons? If we are to take Gomez and Carghill for spectres, it is only the grace of God that can release them, not a gesture from Claverton; or perhaps, Claverton being redeemed in the hour of death, they will cease to walk when their victim is gone. If we are to take these two for real people, then there is nothing Claverton can give that will transform them: to spend one's days with a menacing swindler and one's nights with a faded demi-rep, for the sake of auld lang syne, would be a kind of martyrdom suffered by no saint in the calendar. We cannot redeem the time in any such way. No matter how much we may have sinned against others in the past, it is not in our power miraculously to transfigure other people in the form of what, conceivably, they *might* have become. All that Claverton can do is to cease trying to justify to himself his treatment of Gomez and Mrs. Carghill, and to confess his sins to Monica. As for the tardiness of his self-judgment— why, the unities of the play compel that.

(408)

Claverton's sins have not been grand or peculiar, but
they have been his own:

> It's harder to confess the sin that no one believes in
> Than the crime that everyone can appreciate.
> For the crime is in relation to the law
> And the sin is in relation to the sinner.

It is by confession that Claverton is saved: by confession to
the one person whom he loves, and who loves him—Monica.
At last he acknowledges to her, and to himself, what he really
is; and having pulled down his pretences, he is ready for
physical death. At the end, he knows himself, and knows
what love is, and peace.

> If a man has one person, just one in his life,
> To whom he is willing to confess everything—
> And that includes, mind you, not only things criminal,
> Not only turpitude, meanness and cowardice,
> But also situations which are simply ridiculous,
> When he has played the fool (as who has not?)—
> Then he loves that person, and his love will save him.

Monica can be his confessor because she is herself full
of love; because she walks innocent in the rose garden. Her
love for Charles has come upon her unaware:

> It crept so softly
> On quiet feet, and stood behind my back
> Quietly, a long time, a long long time
> Before I felt its presence.

Her love for her father is not destroyed by his confession;
she loves the real man even better than she had loved the
mask; she loves him in the hour of his death. When he has
died beneath the beech tree, alone (yet not isolated as
Gomez was, "when you come to see that you have lost *your-
self*"), Monica is bathed in her dead father's silent blessing,
and she knows the fullness of life:

> Age and decrepitude can have no terrors for me,

> Loss and vicissitude cannot appal me,
> Not even death can dismay or amaze me
> Fixed in the certainty of love unchanging.

The Elder Statesman is not obscure of meaning—except in the sense that most theater audiences, and most readers, have fallen into theological illiteracy in this century. It is ironic that Eliot, in *Murder in the Cathedral,* as D. E. Jones comments, "where he wrote at full stature. . . . succeeded magnificently in speaking to all sorts and conditions of men, whereas in the later plays, while deliberately simplifying his style for the benefit of the ordinary theatergoer, he has gained a reputation for 'obscurity.' This so-called obscurity is of course largely fictitious. Unable to reach an audience of the uneducated as he wished, Eliot has reached the half-educated and the ill-educated, whose sophistication will not allow them to rest content in simplicity of statement; they must always be searching frantically for hidden meanings."[10]

If *The Elder Statesman* has its shortcomings, they are the result chiefly of the limits imposed upon Eliot by his audiences' ignorance of the Christian understanding of the human condition, and by the general atrophy of the moral imagination in his century. If Eliot had written this tragedy (or melodrama, or even comedy—the critics differing in their categorizing) in 1917, say, and had contrived then to get it performed, it might have made his reputation as actually *Prufrock* did; his power had not diminished yet, though he was seventy years old in 1958. But probably no one could have been found to sponsor and produce it, in 1917.

For although Eliot's own ascent from tormenting doubt to the serenity of Monica's last lines had been slow and painful, still in some degree he had dragged his age after him up that stony slope. Whatever Eliot wrote, the literary public and even the theater public knew by this time, must be intellectually reputable, and worth talking about: even Christianity. It must have been some comfort to Eliot, at this last of his successes, that critics and audiences now found it necessary to grope for meaning (and to pretend to find meaning) in a drama that is a parable of orthodox Christian doctrine. To grope is better than to deride. Lord Claverton is Everyman: but Everyman, in this age, does not readily recognize his own face in a mirror.

Belonging to Another

"A Dedication to My Wife" is the last poem in Eliot's *Collected Poems, 1909-1962.** Miss Valerie Fletcher had been Eliot's secretary; to the world's surprise, she and Eliot were married in January, 1957, he being sixty-eight years old, she thirty. Real acts of love, if undertaken in mature judgment, are acts of wisdom: and this marriage became everything that Eliot's first marriage had not been. It undid Eliot's famous lines in "East Coker":

> Do not let me hear
> Of the wisdom of old men, but rather of their folly,
> Their fear of fear and frenzy, their fear of possession,
> Of belonging to another, or to others, or to God.

A few years before, a visitor to the Pope of Russell Square had found his business impeded by Eliot's secretary's inability to put her hand, at the moment, on some letter or document that was wanted. After she had left the room, Eliot said amiably to the visitor, "A very pretty girl, but perhaps not perfectly efficient." (Actually, she appears to have been a highly competent secretary.) For eight happy years they would be husband and wife. The duration of joy does not matter so much as its intensity.

"It is a wonderful thing, my dear William," Eliot wrote

---

* Of the first edition of the enlarged *Collected Poems* (1963), some fifteen thousand copies were printed in England, and eight thousand in America.

to William Turner Levy, "to be happily married, and a very blessed state for those who are called to it, even at my age. I have a very beautiful and good and sensitive wife, with a very good mind as well and a passionate love of poetry— she has everything to make me happy, and I am humbly thankful."[11] All this was true. Seek, and ye shall find. "Belief will follow action," Newman had written; Eliot had demonstrated that proposition in his religious progress. And now he had attained the crown of life: he having meditated long on love, love had been given to him.

After their marriage, the Eliots went to the south of France for some weeks. In the spring of 1958, during the course of an American lecture tour, Eliot took his wife to meet his Boston relatives. This union with Valerie (to whom Eliot dedicated both *On Poetry and Poets* and *The Elder Statesman*) in all respects was the fulfillment that Eliot, since his youth, had thought unattainable for himself. In the rose garden, at last someone walked with him:

No peevish winter wind shall chill
No sullen tropic sun shall wither
The roses in the rose-garden which is ours and ours only.[12]

To be surprised by joy at the age of sixty-eight is granted to few. No man had needed the full love of woman more than Eliot had needed it, ever since he had left St. Louis; he had struggled vainly, all during his first marriage, to hold together what men like Russell and Read had told him to abandon as hopeless; he had lived solitary at the height of his fame, Vivienne in the nursing-home. And now, in his late autumn, that long-denied fullness of love came to pass, and the multifoliate rose bloomed.*

Suppose that the seeming accident of that miserable early

* The three lines of "A Dedication to My Wife," quoted above, are Eliot's last employment of the rose-garden symbol that runs through his poetry. For apprehending this symbol, it is well to read Leonard Unger's chapter "The Rose-Garden," in his *T. S. Eliot: Moments and Patterns* (1956). All the essays in Unger's volume are illuminating.

marriage with Vivienne never had occurred: would we have Eliot's poems and plays? It had been sorrow, surely, that had given the man profundity of feeling and expression; it had been necessity that had kept him hard at his writing, during his years of poverty and private turmoil. By nature, he was not energetic: the seventh child of a bluestocking mother (middle-aged when he was conceived), Thomas Stearns Eliot was endowed with high intelligence but no great vigor. In the concluding eight years of his life, loved and loving, with money enough, he would write very little— even though his powers of mind were undiminished.

Suppose that Eliot had not married when he was too little experienced and too shy to choose well; suppose that he had not been compelled to scrape a meager literary living in London; suppose that he had obtained some professorial sinecure at Harvard or Oxford, and had published, perhaps, two or three more studies like that dissertation on Bradley; suppose that this gentle man, relishing good talk and leisurely travel, had enjoyed a competence and a placid wife—why, would there have been written *The Waste Land* and *Murder in the Cathedral* and *Four Quartets* and *The Cocktail Party*? No doubt his literary and social principles would have been the same, and his mind would have been as strong; but with Eliot, "feelings" provided the creative impulse, and his feelings would have been less intense, in brighter circumstances. What not many other men of intellect found it possible to believe, in his age, T. S. Eliot came to accept: the dogma that Providence moves in mysterious ways, vengeful or beneficent. That he should write what he did, suffering had been necessary; that he should obtain some compensation in his life, in the end all was made well.*

His long solitude of spirit, his sense of isolation from

---

* Although Professor Herbert Butterfield made a case for the workings of divine providence in history, Eliot was unfamiliar with Butterfield's books. "I have read with interest and some compunction," Eliot wrote to me on October 31, 1956, "your note on Herbert Butterfield—in fact,

others, had been the consequence of both constitution and reflection. "Live as if upon a mountain," had been the desolate injunction of Marcus Aurelius; that dwelling in the citadel of self had been encouraged, too, by the Idealist thought he had studied in his formative years. Although in time Eliot had passed beyond F. H. Bradley, he repeatedly acknowledged his debt to that dead master; perhaps Bradley had influenced him more subtly than he knew, and not altogether to his advantage. For Bradley had argued against any need for immortality of the soul, and had left out of his reckoning, the heart's reasons.

W. B. Yeats decided not to put Paul Valéry (another strong influence upon Eliot) among his "sacred books," because Valéry's rejection of personal immortality, in the *Cimetière Marin*, chilled him. Human life must *not* pass, Yeats knew. And Yeats added, in the third book of *A Vision*, a note on Bradley: "Professor Bradley believed also that he could stand by the death-bed of wife or mistress and not long for an immortality of body and soul. He found it difficult to reconcile personal immortality with his form of Absolute idealism, and besides he hated the common heart; an arrogant, sapless man."[13]

So the joy of life might have come upon Eliot earlier, conceivably, if he had not written that doctoral dissertation; if the barriers of Idealist metaphysics had fallen earlier. The longing for whole communion with another human being had been intense in Eliot, from his Harvard days, at least; the pale cast of thought had impeded that desire of spirit; but with Valerie, all manner of things shall be well, the fire and the rose becoming one.

I read it at the time, as the *Month* is one of the periodicals I take in. I say 'compunction' because I have so far read nothing of Butterfield's work." Here Eliot refers to my review-essay "The Achievement of Herbert Butterfield," in *The Month*, Vol. 15, No. 5 (May, 1956), pp. 267–273.

This man having attained his desire of spirit, the creative impulse diminished. He continued at Faber & Faber, the competent man of business still, but his letters less lengthy. Some letters to editors, obituary tributes to old friends (now passing away as if they had been dream-figures), and occasional lectures or radio interviews came from him—little more. Only the New English Bible—"vulgar, trivial, pedantic"—roused his wrath in print.

Aldous Huxley (long established in the mountains of California) had made a trip to London in 1958, and had seen Eliot, "who is now curiously dull—as a result, perhaps, of being, at last, happy in his second marriage. . . ."[14] Eliot had done his work, and in those last years his happiness was like that of the land which has no annals. He would live until January 4, 1965, full of years and honors, unafraid of the end.

In his last letter to me (dated August 25, 1964), he said that he hoped to see me when I would be on my way to Scotland, "the country whose nationality you appear to be adopting, no doubt with every right!" (I had restored a little ancient house at Pittenweem, on the Forth, and was about to be married—for the first time and the last—to a beauty even younger than Valerie Eliot.) But we would not meet again, this side of the grave; and not until 1969 would I find opportunity to say a prayer for him in Westminster Abbey, and another (at his graven request to all comers) before the oval stone set into the wall of the church at East Coker.

In My End Is My Beginning

In fifty years of writing, what had Eliot accomplished? He had endeavored consciously to redeem the time; at the end, he was under no illusion that he had succeeded. Self-censorious always—in this very like his ancestral connections, John Adams and John Quincy Adams—Eliot entertained no inflated opinion of his abilities or his achievements. His best poems had seemed only preludes to some splendor of concept that he never wholly contrived to voice; his best plays had been experiments, unperfected; his best essays had been challenging, rather than magisterial; his social criticism had been an exercise in definition, not a grand design. "These fragments I have shored against my ruins." Had he been meant, like Coleridge, for something greater? Like Coleridge, had he procrastinated and lingered in reverie, while time ran out? Were his the sins of omission?

There was some reason for these misgivings; yet only a man who had learned to practice the virtue of humility could have felt them, in Eliot's situation. He had won such a reputation as no other man of letters in his century acquired, and that in more realms than one.

As a poet, he had confronted hard reality with the armed vision: he had at once restored to poetry the nerve of sensibility and the matter of metaphysics. He had taken the measure of his age in verse, and he had renewed that age's moral imagination. Perhaps, as some critics have suggested, he had carried poetry to its furthest bounds; certainly no poetic school of comparable power has arisen since Eliot overthrew the Georgians and the American heirs of Whitman. When anthologists of future times—supposing that some high culture endures—deal with the twentieth century, Eliot's lines may cast into shadow all other verse of the age.

As a dramatist, he had reinvigorated the verse-play, and it may be that his influence upon the stage has not yet come to its height. What mattered more to Eliot, he had done something to revive the ethical and religious character of the drama, waking religious feelings as no prose apologist could.

As a critic of literature, he had rescued the critic's art

from personal impressionism, and had upheld the great continuity of humane letters, defending simultaneously the
permanent things and the claims of the renewing innovator.
He had taught the rising generation how to open their eyes
to the deeper meanings in a work of literary art. His range
had been tremendous: Virgil, Dante, the Elizabethans and
the Jacobeans, divines and metaphysical poets, Pascal and
Dryden, Milton and Johnson, Coleridge and Shelley, Arnold
and Baudelaire, Yeats and Lawrence, Kipling and Babbitt.
In 1920, replying to Sir Edmund Gosse, he had defined the
critic's function: "It is part of the business of the critic to
preserve tradition—where a good tradition exists. It is part
of his business to see literature steadily and to see it whole;
and this is eminently to see it *not* as consecrated by time, but
to see it beyond time; to see the best work of our time and
the best work of twenty-five hundred years ago with the
same eyes."[15] That function he had reanimated.

As a critic of society, he had stripped the follies of the
time. He had not spared the morals of his age, or its politics,
or its economics, or its notions of education, or its strange
gods. He had striven to renew modern man's understanding
of the norms of order and justice and freedom, in the person
and in the commonwealth. He had not offered the opiate of
ideology: he had pleaded for a return to enduring principle,
and for recognition of the tensions which are necessary to a
tolerable civil social order. "No scheme for a change of society
can be made to appear immediately palatable, except by
falsehood," he had said intrepidly, "until society has become
so desperate that it will accept any change." The alternative
to a totalist order, a social life-in-death, an existence without
culture or freedom—so he had told those who would listen—
is a social order founded upon religious truth. "That prospect
involves, at least, discipline, inconvenience and discomfort;
but here as hereafter the alternative to hell is purgatory."[16]
A Remnant had heard him.

The time remains unredeemed: prophets and saints fail in their generation at that labor, and no poet can prevail solitary against the pride and the passion of man. Yet Eliot, more than anyone else in his age, exposed smugness and illusion; he reminded many a conscience that, as Audrey Fawcett Cahill writes, "human existence is a challenging and perplexing and often painful experience; that it is fraught with contradictions and tensions; and that to live with any degree of consciousness is to be aware of unreconciled conflicts clamoring to be resolved." He did not hold out false hopes of a terrestrial paradise, but he affirmed that a man's life, and the life of society, can be endurable only if matter is moved by spirit. "The realities of evil, suffering, deprivation, and conflict are no less painful in their Christian context, and are faced by the poet with no less sensitivity," Miss Cahill continues. "They differ only in being subordinated to a redemptive pattern in which the human struggle is seen to have some purpose, and in which human power is understood in a new dimension, in relation to redemptive love . . ."[17] Eliot restored an awareness of that purpose and that love.

What the man believed in, he became. The gentle dignity of his life won over some who had denigrated his poetry and his prose; others, hostile at first to his writings, gradually found themselves persuaded by his honesty and his depth of feeling. And the seed of the spirit that he sowed, though falling among tares, may yet germinate in fields that have lain barren.

Eliot's words about Bradley apply better to Eliot himself: "We fight for lost causes because we know that our defeat and dismay may be the preface to our successors' victory, though that victory itself will be temporary; we fight rather to keep something alive than in the expectation that anything will triumph." Against the starving of their moral imagination, the rising generation blindly rebel, a few years after Eliot's death. Some of those who rise up against a domination of boredom and materialism may find in Eliot a mind and a conscience that endure.

Lifelong, Eliot had contended against the spirit of his age. He made the poet's voice heard again, and thereby triumphed; knowing the community of souls, he freed others from captivity to time and lonely ego; in the teeth of winds of doctrine, he attested the permanent things. And his communication is tongued with fire beyond the language of the living.

A NOTE OF THANKS

The writing of this book was made possible by a grant from Pepperdine College.

The first half of my manuscript was criticized perceptively by Professor Warren L. Fleischauer, my friend for some thirty-four years. Mr. William Odell prepared the index, and Mr. David Wolds helped me during the process of writing and revision.

I offer my thanks to the following publishers for permission to reprint passages from Eliot's poetry and prose:

To Faber & Faber for quotations from the British editions of Eliot's writings.

To Harcourt Brace Jovanovich for quotations from Eliot's *Collected Poems, 1909–1962; Selected Essays; Murder in the Cathedral; The Idea of a Christian Society; Notes towards the Definition of Culture; The Cocktail Party;* and *The Confidential Clerk.*

To Barnes and Noble for quotations from *The Criterion* and *The Use of Poetry and the Use of Criticism.*

To Farrar, Straus and Giroux for quotations from *On Poetry and Poets, The Elder Statesman, Knowledge and Experience in the Philosophy of F. H. Bradley, To Criticize the Critic,* and *The Cultivation of Christmas Trees.*

Henry Regnery Company permits me to quote from Eliot's

lectures published in *Measure*, and from their editions of the books of Wyndham Lewis and Roy Campbell.

Mrs. T. S. Eliot kindly authorizes me to quote both from Eliot's published works and from his unpublished letters to me—in which correspondence she retains copyright. Several friends and correspondents of Eliot—notably Dr. William Turner Levy—also permit quotation from their letters, or from their conversations. I profited much from discussing Eliot's poetry and thought with Roy Campbell and Wyndham Lewis.

This book has been written in a northern fastness that Eliot never visited, but which would have amused him and perhaps pleased him.

—RUSSELL KIRK

Piety Hill
Mecosta, Michigan

NOTES

❖

CHAPTER I

1 My own correspondence with Eliot, from which extracts appear
in this and later chapters, is deposited in The Clarke Historical Library at Central Michigan University.

2 One of the few critics to remark the intellectual connection
between Burke and Eliot is Northrop Frye, in his brief
T. S. Eliot (1963). Lionel Trilling, too, has reminded his readers of Burke on the moral imagination, recognizing the originality of Burke's concept.

3 James McAuley, "In Regard to T. S. Eliot," in his *Surprises of
the Sun* (1969), p. 55.

CHAPTER II

1 For an account of Eliot's relationships with Miss Weaver, *The
Egoist,* and The Egoist Press, see Jane Lidderdale and Mary
Nicholson, *Dear Miss Weaver: Harriet Shaw Weaver, 1876–
1961* (1970). Wyndham Lewis' quoted description of Eliot
will be found in his sketch "Early London Environment," in
Richard March and Tambimuttu (eds.), *T. S. Eliot: a*

Symposium (1948), pp. 24–32; see also his descriptions of the young Eliot in his *Blasting and Bombardiering* (1937).

2 Sir Osbert Sitwell, *Noble Essences* (1950), pp. 39–41.

3 Evelyn Waugh, *A Little Learning* (1964), pp. 65–66.

4 Sir Osbert Sitwell, *Laughter in the Next Room* (1949), pp. 32–33.

5 Aldous Huxley to Julian Huxley, December 13, 1917, in Grover Smith (ed.), *Letters of Aldous Huxley* (1969), p. 141.

6 Eliot, "A Commentary," *The Criterion*, Vol. X, No. 61 (July, 1931), pp. 715–716.

7 George Orwell, *Inside the Whale*, in Sonia Orwell and Ian Angus (eds.), *The Collected Essays, Journalism and Letters of George Orwell* (1968), Vol. I, pp. 524–525.

8 George Santayana, *Soliloquies in England and Later Soliloquies* (1922), pp. 177–178.

9 Eliot, "American Literature and the American Language," in *To Criticize the Critic* (1965), p. 44.

10 A good description of Eliot's family and of St. Louis at that time may be found in the first and second chapters of Herbert Howarth's *Notes on Some Figures behind T. S. Eliot* (1964).

11 See Eliot, preface to Edgar Ansel Mowrer's *This American World* (1928); and Eliot's letter to M. W. Childs, quoted in F. O. Matthiessen, *The Achievement of T. S. Eliot* (1947), p. 186.

12 Eliot, *To Criticize the Critic, op. cit.*, pp. 44–45.

13 *Ibid.*, p. 15; and Eliot's memoir of Babbitt in Frederick Manchester and Odell Shepard (eds.), *Irving Babbitt, Man and Teacher* (1941), p. 104.

14 Eliot, *After Strange Gods: a Primer of Modern Heresy* (1934), pp. 40–41.

15 Eliot, "A Commentary," *The Criterion*, Vol. XIII, No. 52 (April, 1934), pp. 451–454.

16 Conrad Aiken, "King Bolo and Others," in March and Tambimuttu, *Eliot, op. cit.*, pp. 20–23; and Aiken, *Ushant: an Essay* (1952), Meridian edition (1962), pp. 133, 137–138, 143, 156–157, 164, 168, 173, 186, 201–202, 205, 215–216, 231–233, 246, 249.

17 Charlotte C. Eliot to Bertrand Russell, May 23, 1916, in Russell, *The Middle Years, 1914–1944* (1968), Chapter I.

18 Eliot to Lytton Strachey, May, 1919, in Michael Holroyd, *Lytton Strachey* (1968), Vol. II, pp. 364–365.

19 Russell's account of his relationships with T. S. and Vivienne Eliot are to be found chiefly in the first chapter of the second volume of his autobiography, *The Middle Years, op. cit.*

20 Aldous Huxley to Julian Huxley, June 28, 1918, in Smith, *Letters of Aldous Huxley, op. cit.*, p. 156.

21 Eliot, *Knowledge and Experience in the Philosophy of F. H. Bradley* (1964), p. 10.

22 Hugh Kenner, *The Invisible Poet: T. S. Eliot* (1959), pp. 55–56.

23 Lewis Freed, *T. S. Eliot: Aesthetics and History* (1962), pp. 88–89.

24 Richard Wollheim, "Eliot and F. H. Bradley: An Account," in Graham Martin (ed.), *Eliot in Perspective* (1970), pp. 169–193.

25 Eliot, "Arnold and Pater," in *Selected Essays* (1932), p. 351.

26 Ian Gregor, "Eliot and Matthew Arnold," in Martin, *Eliot in Perspective, op. cit.*, pp. 267–268.

27 Eliot, "Matthew Arnold," in *The Use of Poetry and the Use of Criticism* (1933), edition of 1964, p. 114.

28 George Bernard Shaw, "Heartbreak House and Horseback Hall," preface to *Heartbreak House: a Fantasia in the Russian Manner on English Themes* (1919).

CHAPTER III

1 Donald McCormick, *The Mask of Merlin: a Critical Biography of David Lloyd George* (1964), p. 316.

2 Herbert Read, "T. S. E.—a Memoir," in Allen Tate (ed.), *T. S. Eliot: the Man and His Work* (1966), p. 23.

3 See Aldous Huxley to Julian Huxley (June 28, 1918), in Grover Smith (ed.), *Letters of Aldous Huxley* (1969), p. 154; also Stephen Spender, "Remembering Eliot," in Tate, *Eliot, op. cit.*, p. 63.

4 Clive Bell, "How Pleasant to Know Mr. Eliot," in Richard March and Tambimuttu (eds.), *T. S. Eliot: a Symposium* (1949), p. 18.

5 Frank Morley, "T. S. Eliot as a Publisher," in March and Tambimuttu, *Eliot, op. cit.*, p. 61.

6 *Letters of Aldous Huxley, op. cit.*, pp. 117, 123; and Huxley, quoted by Spender, in Tate, *Eliot, op. cit.*, pp. 58–59.

7 Eliot, "American Literature and Language," in *To Criticize the Critic* (1965), p. 58.

8 Eliot, quoted by Herbert Read, in Tate, *Eliot, op. cit.*, p. 15.

9 Eliot, "Francis Herbert Bradley," in *Selected Essays, 1917–1932* (1932), p. 363.

10 Kathleen Raine, "The Poet of Our Time," in March and Tambimuttu, *Eliot, op. cit.*, p. 78.

11 John Halverson, "Prufrock, Freud, and Others," in *The Sewanee Review*, Vol. LXXVI, No. 4 (Autumn, 1968), p. 578.

12 Kathleen Raine, *op. cit.*, p. 79.

13 See John Abbot Clark's amusing piece of detection, "On First Looking into Benson's FitzGerald," *The South Atlantic Quarterly*, April, 1949; reprinted in *Fifty Years of the South Atlantic Quarterly* (1952), pp. 344–355.

14 For some sensible, though not adulatory, criticism of Eliot's political inclinations, see J. M. Cameron, "T. S. Eliot As a Political Writer," in Neville Braybrooke (ed.), *T. S. Eliot: a Symposium for His Seventieth Birthday* (1958), pp. 138–151; and John Peter, "Eliot and the *Criterion*," in Graham Martin (ed.), *Eliot in Perspective* (1970), pp. 252–266.

15 For a more detailed examination of Eliot on this point, see Russell Kirk, "T. S. Eliot's Permanent Things," in his *Enemies of the Permanent Things* (1969), pp. 51–62.

16 Of many interesting essays concerned with "Gerontion," four may be mentioned here: Wolf Mankowitz, "Notes on Gerontion," in B. Rajan (ed.), *T. S. Eliot: a Study of His Writings by Several Hands* (1964); Hugh Kenner, "Gerontion," in his *Invisible Poet* (1959); John Crowe Ransom, "Gerontion," in Tate, *Eliot, op. cit.;* Elizabeth Drew, "Gerontion," in her *T. S. Eliot: the Design of His Poetry* (1949).

17 Marion Montgomery, *T. S. Eliot: an Essay on the American Magus* (1970), pp. 70–82; see also Hoxie Neale Fairchild, *Religious Trends in English Poetry*, Vol. V, *Gods of a Changing Poetry* (1962), pp. 566–568.

18 Spender, in Tate, *Eliot, op. cit.*, p. 59.

19 Noel Stock, *The Life of Ezra Pound* (1970), pp. 166–170.

20 *The Autobiography of William Carlos Williams* (1951), p. 217.

21 Montgomery, *op. cit.*, p. 89; and Graham Martin, "Language and Belief in Eliot's Poetry," in Martin, *Eliot, op. cit.*, pp. 127–130.

22 E. M. Forster, *Abinger Harvest* (1936), pp. 89–96.

23 Malcolm Cowley, "Readings from the Lives of the Saints," in his *Exile's Return* (1934), pp. 123–128.

24 Perhaps the most convincing examination is that of Cleanth Brooks, "The Waste Land: Critique of the Myth," in his *Modern Poetry and the Tradition* (1939), pp. 136–172. Another readable and intelligent treatment is that of C. M. Bowra, in his book *The Creative Experiment* (1948), pp. 159–188.

25 Williams, *Autobiography, op. cit.*, p. 174.

26 Hugh Kenner, *The Invisible Poet, op. cit.*, p. 171.

27 Rose Macaulay, "The First Impact of The Waste Land," in Braybrooke, *Eliot, op. cit.*, pp. 30–31.

CHAPTER IV

1 I. A. Richards, "On T. S. E.," in Tate (ed.), *T. S. Eliot: The Man and His Work* (1966), p. 5.

2 See William Wasserstrom, "T. S. Eliot and *The Dial*," *The Sewanee Review*, Vol. LXX, No. 1 (Winter, 1962), pp. 81–91.

3 R. C. K. Ensor, *England, 1870–1914* (1936), p. 311.

4 Hamilton Fyfe, *Northcliffe* (1930), p. 106.

5 Eliot to Read (October, 1924?), in Herbert Read, "T. S. E.—a Memoir," in Tate, *Eliot, op. cit.*, pp. 20–21.

6 J. M. Cameron, "T. S. Eliot As a Political Writer," in Neville Braybrooke (ed.), *T. S. Eliot: a Symposium for His Seventieth Birthday* (1958), p. 145.

7 Herbert Howarth, *Notes on Some Figures Behind T. S. Eliot* (1964), p. 3.

8 J. M. Cameron, *op. cit.*, p. 139.

9 W. L. Burn, "English Conservatism," *The Nineteenth Century and After*, February, 1949, p. 72.

10 *Letters of James Russell Lowell* (ed. by Charles Eliot Norton, 1894), II, p. 153.

NOTES

11 For Eliot on Samuel Johnson, see "Johnson as Critic and Poet," *on Poetry and Poets* (1957), pp. 184–222; and Eliot's introduction to Johnson's *London: a Poem,* and *The Vanity of Human Wishes* (1930).

12 For details of this political struggle, see Beatrice Webb, *Diaries 1912–1924* (1952), especially pp. 203–233.

13 D. C. Somervell, *British Politics since 1900* (1950), p. 161.

14 Frank Morley, "T. S. Eliot As a Publisher," in Richard March and Tambimuttu, *T. S. Eliot: a Symposium* (1949), p. 62.

15 Morley, in *ibid.,* p. 67.

16 *Frank Morley, "A Few Recollections of Eliot,"* in Tate (ed.), *Eliot, op. cit.,* pp. 100–101.

17 Keith Feiling, *A History of England* (1950), p. 1086.

18 Douglas Jerrold, *England: Past, Present, and Future* (1950), pp. 222–223.

19 Harold F. Brooks, "Between *The Waste Land* and the First Ariel Poems: 'The Hollow Men," in *English,* Vol. XVI, No. 93 (Autumn, 1966), pp. 89–93. This I believe to be the best short treatment of "The Hollow Men."

CHAPTER V

1 This final scene, which Eliot decided not to include in published texts of *Sweeney Agonistes,* may be found in Carol H. Smith's *T. S. Eliot's Dramatic Theory and Practice* (1963), pp. 62–63.

2 Helen Gardner, *The Art of T. S. Eliot* (1950), p. 132.

3 Nevill Coghill, "Sweeney Agonistes," in Richard March and Tambimuttu (eds.), *T. S. Eliot: a Symposium* (1948), pp. 82–87.

4 Eliot to Dobrée, in Bonamy Dobrée, "T. S. Eliot: a Personal Reminiscence," in Tate (ed.), *T. S. Eliot: The Man and His Work* (1967), p. 72.

5 Hoxie Neale Fairchild, *Religious Trends in English Poetry*: Vol. V, *Gods of a Changing Poetry* (1962), p. 564.

6 Dobrée, *op. cit.,* p. 70.

7 *Ibid.,* p. 75.

8 Eliot, "A Commentary," *The Monthly Criterion,* Vol. V, No. 2 (May, 1927), p. 190.

9 Eliot, review of recent books by Ludovici, Chesterton, Belloc, Hobson, and the authors of *Coal*, in *The Monthly Criterion*, Vol. VI, No. 1 (July, 1927), pp. 69–73.

10 Eliot, "A Commentary," *The Monthly Criterion*, Vol. VI, No. 5 (November, 1927), pp. 385–388.

11 Eliot, "A Commentary," *The Monthly Criterion*, Vol. VII, No. 2 (February, 1928), p. 98.

12 Eliot, "The *Action Française*, M. Maurras and Mr. Ward," *The Monthly Criterion*, Vol. VII, No. 3 (March, 1928), pp. 195–203.

13 Eliot, "A Reply to Mr. Ward," *The Criterion*, Vol. VII, No. 4 (June, 1928), pp. 372–376.

14 Eliot, "A Commentary," *The Criterion*, Vol. VIII, No. 30 (September, 1928), pp. 4–5.

15 Eliot, review of Freud's *The Future of an Illusion*, in *The Criterion*, Vol. VIII, No. 30 (December, 1928), pp. 350–352.

16 Eliot, "A Commentary," *The Criterion*, Vol. VIII, No. 32 (April, 1929), pp. 377–381.

17 Eliot, "A Commentary," *The Criterion*, Vol. VIII, No. 33 (July, 1929), pp. 575–579.

18 Eliot, "The Literature of Fascism," *The Criterion*, Vol. VIII, No. 31 (December, 1928), pp. 280–290.

19 Eliot, "Mr. Barnes and Mr. Rowse," *The Criterion*, Vol. VIII, No. 33 (July, 1929), pp. 682–691.

20 Eliot, "A Commentary," *The Criterion*, Vol. IX, No. 35 (January, 1930), pp. 182–184.

21 Eliot to Bonamy Dobrée, in Dobrée, *op. cit.*, pp. 81–82.

22 Stephen Spender, "Remembering Eliot," in Tate, *op. cit.*, p. 49.

23 Helen Gardner, *op. cit.*, p. 104.

24 Rose Macaulay, "The First Impact of *The Waste Land*," in Neville Braybrooke (ed.), *T. S. Eliot: a Symposium for His Seventieth Birthday* (1958), p. 33.

25 Grover Smith, *T. S. Eliot's Poetry and Plays: a Study in Sources and Meaning* (1956), pp. 146, 150.

26 Eliot to Bonamy Dobrée, in Dobrée, *op. cit.*, p. 81.

27 See Genesius Jones, *Approach to the Purpose: a Study of the Poetry of T. S. Eliot* (1964), pp. 112–113; Leonard Unger, *T. S. Eliot: Movements and Patterns* (1956), pp. 49–54; Grover Smith, *op. cit.*, pp. 144–145; B. C. Southam, *A Student's*

Guide to the Selected Poems of T. S. Eliot (1968), p. 112; Helen Gardner, *op. cit.*, pp. 115–116.

28 Allen Tate, "On Ash Wednesday," in his *Collected Essays* (1959); reprinted in Hugh Kenner (ed.), *T. S. Eliot: A Collection of Critical Essays* (1962), pp. 129–135.

29 See Genesius Jones, *op. cit.*, pp. 116–120.

30 Leonard Unger, *op. cit.*, pp. 62–64.

31 Eliot's understanding of love in its several forms will be made clearer by a reading of M. C. D'Arcy, *The Mind and Heart of Love* (1947), the work of a scholar closely associated with Eliot.

32 Eric Voegelin, "Immortality: Experience and Symbol," *Harvard Theological Review*, Vol. 60, No. 3 (July, 1967), pp. 235, 257.

CHAPTER VI

1 Wyndham Lewis, "Early London Environment," in Richard March and Tambimuttu (eds.), *T. S. Eliot: a Symposium* (1948), pp. 29–30.

2 See Frank Morley, "T. S. Eliot As a Publisher," in *ibid.*, pp. 69–70.

3 The preceding quotations from Eliot's Commentaries in *The Criterion* of 1931 all will be found in Volume X: pp. 307–314, 481–490, 709–716.

4 F. O. Matthiessen, *The Achievement of T. S. Eliot* (first published in 1935); Galaxy edition, 1959, with a chapter on Eliot's later work by C. L. Barber, pp. 137–143.

5 D. E. S. Maxwell, *The Poetry of T. S. Eliot* (1952), pp. 137–143.

6 Elizabeth Drew, *T. S. Eliot: The Design of His Poetry* (1952), p. 133.

7 Eliot, "A Commentary," *The Criterion*, Vol. XI, No. 42 (October, 1931), pp. 65–72.

8 Eliot, *The Use of Poetry and the Use of Criticism* (1933), pp. 68–69.

9 *Ibid.*, pp. 73–74.

10 *Ibid.*, pp. 155–156.

11 *Ibid.*, p. 26.

12 *Ibid.*, p. 139.

13 *Ibid.*, pp. 131–135.

14 *Ibid.*, pp. 136–137.

15 Frank Morley, "A Few Recollections of Eliot," in Allen Tate (ed.), *T. S. Eliot: The Man and His Work* (1966), pp. 104–107.

16 Wyndham Lewis, "Early London Environment" in March and Tambimuttu, *Eliot, op. cit.*, pp. 29–30.

17 Eliot, *After Strange Gods: a Primer of Modern Heresy* (1934), pp. 19–20.

18 See William Turner Levy and Victor Scherle, *Affectionately, T. S. Eliot: The Story of a Friendship: 1947–1965* (1968), p. 81.

19 Sir Herbert Read, "T. S. E.—a Memoir," in Tate, *Eliot, op. cit.*, p. 30.

20 *Ibid.*, p. 19.

21 *Ibid.*, p. 33.

22 *Ibid.*, pp. 35–40.

23 *Ibid.*, p. 43.

24 *Ibid.*, p. 53.

25 Eliseo Vivas, *D. H. Lawrence: the Failure and the Triumph of Art* (1960), p. 102.

26 *After Strange Gods*, pp. 57–63.

27 Eliot's Commentaries in *The Criterion*, from October, 1932, to July, 1933: Vol. XII, pp. 73–79, 224–249, 468–473, 642–647.

28 A full account of the production of *The Rock* will be found in two pieces by its director, E. Martin Browne: "T. S. Eliot in the Theatre: the Director's Memories," in Tate, *Eliot, op. cit.*, pp. 116–132; and "From *The Rock* to *The Confidential Clerk*," in Braybrooke (ed.), *T. S. Eliot: a Symposium for His Seventieth Birthday* (1958), pp. 57–69.

29 Herbert Hensley Henson to E. Lyttleton, January 3, 1934, in Evelyn Foley Braley (ed.), *More Letters of Herbert Hensley Henson* (1954), p. 91.

30 See Cyril Garbett (Archbishop of York), *In an Age of Revolution* (1952), p. 55.

31 See David E. Jones, *The Plays of T. S. Eliot* (1960), pp. 38–49; Carol H. Smith, *T. S. Eliot's Dramatic Theory and Practice* (1936), pp. 83–90; and the treatments by F. O. Matthiessen and Grover Smith, *op. cit.*

CHAPTER VII

1 Wyndham Lewis, letter to the editor of *The Spectator*, November 2, 1934; reprinted in W. K. Rose (ed.), *The Letters of Wyndham Lewis* (1965), pp. 222–225.

2 William Empson, "The Style of the Master," in Richard March and Tambimuttu (eds.), *T. S. Eliot: a Symposium* (1948), pp. 35–37.

3 Desmond Hawkins, "The Pope of Russell Square," in *ibid.*, pp. 44–47.

4 George Orwell, *Inside the Whale* (1940), reprinted in Sonia Orwell and Ian Angus (eds.), *The Collected Essays, Journalism and Letters of George Orwell* (1968), Vol. I, p. 512.

5 Hawkins, *op. cit.*, pp. 45–46.

6 Christopher Dawson, "Religion and the Totalitarian State," *The Criterion*, Vol. XIV, No. 54 (October, 1934), pp. 1–16.

7 Eliot, "A Commentary," *The Criterion*, Vol. XIV, No. 55, (January, 1935), pp. 260–264.

8 Eliot, "A Commentary," *The Criterion*, Vol. XIV, No. 56 (April, 1935), pp. 431–436.

9 Eliot, Commentaries in *The Criterion*, Vol. XV, Nos. 58 and 59 (October, 1935, and July, 1936), pp. 65–69, 265–269.

10 The planning and production of *Murder in the Cathedral* are described by the three men most nearly associated with Eliot in this undertaking. See E. Martin Browne, "The Dramatic Verse of T. S. Eliot," in March and Tambimuttu, *op. cit.*, pp. 196–207; Browne, "From *The Rock* to *The Confidential Clerk*," in Braybrooke (ed.), *T. S. Eliot: A Symposium for His Seventieth Birthday* (1958), pp. 57–69; Browne, "T. S. Eliot in the Theatre: the Director's Memoirs," in Tate (ed.), *T. S. Eliot: The Man and His Work* (1966), pp. 116–132; Robert Speaight, "Interpreting Becket and Other Parts," in Braybrooke, *op. cit.*, pp. 70–78; Speaight, "With Becket in *Murder in the Cathedral*," in Tate, *op. cit.*, pp. 182–193; Ashley Dukes, "T. S. Eliot in the Theatre," in March and Tambimuttu, *op. cit.*, pp. 111–118. See also T. S. Eliot and George Hoellering, *The Film of Murder in the Cathedral* (1952), pp. 7–14.

11 Hilaire Belloc, *The Old Road* (1911), pp. 89–90.

12 Henri Daniel-Rops, *Cathedral and Crusade* (translated by John Warrington, 1957), p. 216.

13 Grover Smith, *T. S. Eliot's Poetry and Plays* (Phoenix edition, 1960), pp. 183–184.

14 Ashley Dukes, "T. S. Eliot in the Theatre," *op. cit.*, p. 114.

15 Eliot, "A Commentary," *The Criterion,* Vol. XV, No. 61 (July, 1936), pp. 663–668.

16 Eliot, "A Commentary," *The Criterion,* Vol. XVI, No. 62 (October, 1936), pp. 63–69.

17 William G. Peck, "Divine Democracy," *The Criterion,* Vol. XVI, No. 63 (January, 1937), pp. 255–266; Eliot, "A Commentary," same number, pp. 289–293.

18 Eliot, "A Commentary," *The Criterion,* Vol. XVI, No. 64 (April, 1937), pp. 469–474.

19 Eliot, "A Commentary," *The Criterion,* Vol. XVI, No. 65 (July, 1937), pp. 669–670; Herbert Read and Eliot, "Correspondence," *The Criterion,* Vol. XVII, No. 66 (October, 1937), pp. 123–124.

20 See William Turner Levy and Victor Scherle, *Affectionately, T. S. Eliot* (1968), p. 79.

21 Eliot, "A Commentary," *The Criterion,* Vol. XVIII, No. 70 (October, 1938), pp. 58–62.

22 Eliot, "A Commentary," *The Criterion,* Vol. XVII, No. 68 (April, 1938), pp. 478–485.

23 Eliot, "A Commentary," *The Criterion,* Vol. XVII, No. 66 (October, 1937), pp. 81–86.

24 Eliot, "A Commentary," *The Criterion,* Vol. XVII, No. 69 (July, 1938), pp. 686–690.

25 Eliot, "Last Words," *The Criterion,* Vol. XVIII, No. 71 (January, 1939), pp. 269–275.

26 Eliot, "Poetry and Drama," in *On Poetry and Poets* (1957), pp. 75–95.

27 F. R. Leavis and Q. D. Leavis, *Lectures in America* (1969), pp. 51–52.

28 *Ibid.*, pp. 49–50.

29 Arthur M. Sampley, "The Woman Who Wasn't There: Lacuna in T. S. Eliot," *The South Atlantic Quarterly,* Vol. LXVII, No. 4 (Autumn, 1968), pp. 603–610.

30 Eliot, *After Strange Gods* (1934), p. 46.

31 Leavis, *op. cit.*, p. 53.

CHAPTER VIII

1 Philip Mairet, "Memories of T. S. E.," in Neville Braybrooke (ed.), *T. S. Eliot: a Symposium for His Seventieth Birthday* (1958), pp. 36–44.

2 Edwin Muir, "The Political View of Literature," reprinted in his *Essays on Literature and Society* (1949), pp. 138–139.

3 George Orwell, *Coming up for Air* (1939). See also Orwell's "Not Counting Niggers," in *The Adelphi*, July, 1939; reprinted in Orwell and Angus (eds.), *The Collected Essays, Journalism and Letters of George Orwell* (1968), Vol. I, pp. 394–398.

4 Eliot, *The Idea of a Christian Society* (1939), pp. 94–97.

5 *Ibid.*, pp. 15–16.

6 *Ibid.*, pp. 23, 63.

7 *Ibid.*, pp. 33–34.

8 Peter Kirk, "T. S. Eliot," in Melville Harcourt (ed.), *Thirteen for Christ* (1963), pp. 3–26.

9 *The Idea of a Christian Society*, p. 59.

10 *Ibid.*, p. 62.

11 *Ibid.*, pp. 63–64.

12 George Orwell, "The Rediscovery of Europe" (BBC Eastern Service talk, March 11, 1942), reprinted in Orwell and Angus, *op. cit.*, Vol. II, pp. 197–207.

13 Orwell, review in *Poetry London*, October-November, 1942; reprinted in Orwell and Angus, *op. cit.*, Vol. II, p. 236–242.

14 Vincent Buckley, *Poetry and the Sacred* (1968), p. 223.

15 Denis Donoghue, *The Ordinary Universe: Soundings in Modern Literature* (1968), pp. 260–261.

16 Eliot, *On Poetry*: an address by T. S. Eliot on the occasion of the twenty-fifth anniversary of Concord Academy (1947).

17 Martin D'Arcy, *Death and Life* (1942), p. 152.

18 For an argument that Eliot, in "Burnt Norton" and even in the later *Quartets,* has not fully accepted Christian revelation as Saint John of the Cross accepted it, see Sister Mary Gerard, "Eliot and John of the Cross," *Thought*, Vol. XXXIV, No. 132 (Spring, 1939), pp. 107–127.

19 The turning world and the still point are interestingly discussed

by Philip Wheelwright in *The Burning Fountain: a Study in the Language of Symbolism* (1954), Chapter XV.

20 See Helen Gardner, *The Art of T. S. Eliot* (1950), pp. 158–185.

21 That the "silent motto" was Eliot's, not Mary Stuart's, has been unearthed by Elizabeth Drew, whose chapter on *Four Quartets* is very good; see her *T. S. Eliot: the Design of His Poetry* (1949), p. 165, n.

22 Christopher Dawson, *Progress and Religion* (1929), pp. 75, 89–90. So far as I know, the only critic to have noticed Dawson's bearing on *Four Quartets* is James Johnson Sweeney, "*East Coker*: a Reading," in *The Southern Review*, Vol. VI, No. 4, (1941), pp. 771–791; reprinted in Unger (ed.), *T. S. Eliot: a Selected Critique* (1966), pp. 395–414.

23 Paul Elmer More, *Shelburne Essays*, Seventh Series (1910), pp. 201–202.

24 In Somerset, where Eliot's ashes are laid, churchyard yews are especially numerous. See Vaughan Cornish, *The Churchyard Yew and Immortality* (1946).

25 Miguel de Unamuno, *The Tragic Sense of Life* (translation by J. E. Crawford Flitch, 1923), pp. 248–249.

26 Martin D'Arcy, *op. cit.*, pp. 174–175.

27 T. O. Beachcroft, "Nicholas Ferrar and George Herbert," *The Criterion*, Vol. XII, No. 46 (October, 1932), pp. 24–42. For comments of members of the Criterion group on Ferrar, see Bernard Blackstone's review of *Nicholas Ferrar of Little Gidding*, by A. L. Maycock, *The Criterion*, Vol. XVIII, No. 70 (October, 1938), pp. 154–156; and Charles Smythe's review of *The Ferrar Papers*, edited by Bernard Blackstone, *The Criterion*, Vol. XVIII, No. 71 (January, 1939), pp. 366–371.

28 Anthony Thorlby, "The Poetry of 'Four Quartets,'" *The Cambridge Journal*, Vol. V, No. 5 (February, 1952), pp. 280–299.

CHAPTER IX

1 Emilio Cecchi, "A Meeting with Eliot," in Richard March and Tambimuttu (eds.), *T. S. Eliot: a Symposium* (1948), pp. 73–77.

2 Bertrand Russell to Lady Ottoline Morrell, May, 1914, in *Memoirs of Lady Ottoline Morrell: a Study in Friendship* (edited by Robert Gathorne-Hardy, 1963), p. 255.

3 John Cowper Powys, *The Meaning of Culture* (1928), p. 273.

4 Clive Bell, *Civilization: an Essay* (1928), Chapter VII.

5 R. H. Tawney, *Equality: Halley Stewart Lecture, 1929* (1931), pp. 98–118.

6 Eliot, *Notes towards the Definition of Culture* (1948), pp. 18–19.

7 *Ibid.*, p. 26.

8 *Ibid.*, pp. 36–37.

9 See Karl Mannheim, *Man and Society in an Age of Reconstruction: Studies in Modern Social Structure* (translated by Edward Shils, 1940), particularly the first chapter of Part II.

10 Raymond Williams, *Culture and Society, 1780–1950* (1958), pp. 241–243.

11 Eliot, *Notes, op. cit.*, pp. 43–44.

12 *Ibid.*, pp. 47–48.

13 For an interesting discussion of Burke on this point, see Harvey Mansfield, Jr., *Statesmanship and Party Government: a Study of Burke and Bolingbroke* (1965), Chapter 8.

14 Rowland Berthoff, *An Unsettled People: Social Order and Disorder in American History* (1971), p. xiii.

15 Eliot, *Notes, op. cit.*, p. 62.

16 *Ibid.*, pp. 81–82.

17 *Ibid.*, pp. 88–89.

18 Eliot, introduction to Josef Pieper's *Leisure, the Basis of Culture* (1952), pp. 11–14.

19 Eliot, *Notes, op. cit.*, pp. 91–92.

20 *Ibid.*, p. 109.

21 *Ibid.*, p. 122.

22 Eliot, "Yeats" (first annual Yeats Lecture, 1940), printed in Eliot, *On Poetry and Poets* (1957), pp. 301–302.

23 Eliot. "The Social Function of Poetry" (address delivered in 1943 and 1945), printed in *On Poetry and Poets, op. cit.*, pp. 15–16.

24 Eliot, *Notes, op. cit.*, p. 108.

25 Of all the analyses of *The Cocktail Party*, I find most illuminating Helen Gardner's "The Comedies of T. S. Eliot," in Allen Tate (ed.), *T. S. Eliot: The Man and His Work* (1966). There is much of value in D. E. Jones' *The Plays of T. S. Eliot* (1960).

26 Leslie Paul, "A Conversation with T. S. Eliot," *The Kenyon Review*, Vol. XXVII, No. 1 (Winter, 1965), pp. 19–20.

27 Helen Gardner, "The Comedies of T. S. Eliot," *op. cit.*, pp. 169–170.

28 Philip Rahv, "T. S. Eliot: the Poet as Playwright," in his *Literature and the Sixth Sense* (1969), p. 350.

29 There has appeared as yet no careful detailed study of Eliot's exploration of Time and Self; and the subject is too complex for extensive treatment in this book. An interesting discussion of Eliot on such matters, "Bergson, and the Problem of Time," may be found in Kristian Smidt's *Poetry and Belief in the Work of T. S. Eliot* (1949 and 1961), pp. 165–181. See also William T. Noon, "Modern Literature and Time," *Thought*, Vol. XXXIII, No. 31 (Winter, 1958–1959), pp. 571–603.

30 Michael Polanyi, *Personal Knowledge: Towards a Post-Critical Philosophy* (1958), p. 285.

31 See Kristian Smidt, *Poetry and Belief in the Work of T. S. Eliot*, *op. cit.*, p. 174.

32 Eliot, "Virgil and the Christian World," *On Poetry and Poets* (1957), p. 137.

CHAPTER X

1 Eliot, "A Commentary," *The Criterion*, Vol. XI, No. 42 (October, 1931), pp. 65–72.

2 Eliot, "A Commentary," *The Criterion*, Vol. XIII, No. 52 (April, 1934), pp. 624–628.

3 Eliot, "A Commentary," *The Criterion*, Vol. XIV, No. 55 (January, 1934), p. 264; Bernard Iddings Bell, "The Decay of Intelligence in America," *The Criterion*, same number, p. 200.

4 G. H. Bantock, *T. S. Eliot and Education* (1970).

5 Eliot, *Notes towards the Definition of Culture* (1948), pp. 95–103.

6 Eliot, *Notes*, *op. cit.*, pp. 99, 106–107.

7 Robert M. Hutchins, "T. S. Eliot on Education," *Measure*, Vol. I, No. 1 (Winter, 1950), p. 6.

8 Hutchins, "The Theory of Oligarchy: Edmund Burke," *The Thomist*, Vol. V (January, 1943), pp. 61–78.

9 Hutchins, "T. S. Eliot on Education," *op. cit.,* p. 8.

10 Eliot, "The Aims of Education," in four parts, *Measure,* Vol. II, Nos. 1, 2, 3, 4; reprinted in *To Criticize the Critic* (1965), pp. 61–124.

11 G. H. Bantock, *T. S. Eliot and Education, op. cit.,* p. 109.

12 For an English sociologist's ironical demolition of the new élite created by examinations, see Michael Young, *The Rise of the Meritocracy, 1870–2033: An Essay in Education and Equality* (1958). For accounts of what has been done to British schooling by the theories that Eliot opposed, see the essays in the two "Black Papers" edited by C. B. Cox and A. E. Dyson, *Fight for Education* and *The Crisis in Education* (1969).

13 Of many books touching on the decline of American culture, Thomas Griffith's *The Waist-High Culture* (1959) is particularly telling, because in part autobiographical. For England's precipitous descent to the level of Sweeney, see Christopher Booker, *The Neophiliacs: A Study of the Revolution in English Life in the Fifties and Sixties* (1969).

14 Seán Lucy, *T. S. Eliot and the Idea of Tradition* (1960), pp. 201–202.

15 Eliot, "The Lion and the Fox," *Twentieth Century Verse,* Nos. 6–7 (November-December, 1937), pp. 6–9.

16 R. H. S. Crossman, "Towards a Philosophy of Socialism," in Crossman (ed.), *New Fabian Essays* (1952), pp. 1–32.

17 W. L. Burn, "The Last of the Lynskey Report," *The Nineteenth Century and After,* Vol. 145, No. 4 (April, 1949), pp. 222–229.

18 See William Turner Levy and Victor Scherle, *Affectionately, T. S. Eliot* (1968), pp. 71, 79.

19 Eliot, "The Literature of Politics," in *To Criticize the Critic* (1965), pp. 136–144.

20 The only fairly detailed study of Eliot's political theories so far published is Rajendra Verma's *Royalist in Politics: T. S. Eliot and Political Philosophy* (1968); but that little book does not take up fully Eliot's political observations in *The Criterion,* or his other occasional excursions into the practical political controversies of his age.

21 Leslie Paul, "A Conversation with T. S. Eliot," *The Kenyon Review,* Vol. XXVII, No. 104 (Winter, 1965), pp. 11–21.

CHAPTER XI

1 Eliot, "The Function of Criticism," *Selected Essays, 1917–1932* (1932), pp. 12–22.

2 Eliot, "The Classics and the Man of Letters," *To Criticize the Critic and Other Writings* (1965), pp. 145–161.

3 Eliot, "What Is a Classic?", *On Poetry and Poets* (1957), pp. 71–73.

4 Eliot, "The Frontiers of Criticism," *On Poetry and Poets, op. cit.*, pp. 113–131.

5 John Wain, "A Walk in the Sacred Wood," *The London Magazine*, Vol. 5, No. 1 (January, 1958), pp. 45–53.

6 Eliot, "To Criticize the Critic," in *To Criticize the Critic, op. cit.*, pp. 11–26.

7 Eliot, "The Three Voices of Poetry," *On Poetry and Poets, op. cit.*, pp. 96, 98.

8 *Ibid.*, p. 111.

9 Grover Smith, *T. S. Eliot's Poetry and Plays: A Study in Sources and Meaning* (Phoenix edition, 1960), p. 248.

10 D. E. Jones, *The Plays of T. S. Eliot* (1960), p. 213.

11 Eliot to William Turner Levy, in Levy and Scherle, *Affectionately, T. S. Eliot* (1968), pp. 98–99.

12 Eliot, "A Dedication to My Wife," *Collected Poems, 1909–1962* (1963), p. 221.

13 W. B. Yeats, *A Vision* (edition of 1962), p. 219.

14 Aldous Huxley to Dr. Humphrey Osmond, December 16, 1958, in Grover Smith (ed.), *Letters of Aldous Huxley* (1969), pp. 857–858.

15 Eliot, Introduction to *The Sacred Wood* (seventh edition, 1950), pp. xv–xvi.

16 Eliot, *The Idea of a Christian Society* (1939), pp. 23–24.

17 Audrey Fawcett Cahill, *T. S. Eliot and the Human Predicament* (1967), pp. 1–4.

INDEX

For convenience, this index is divided into two parts. The first consists of names of persons and places, and titles of books, periodicals, poems, essays, and other publications. The second part includes general subjects and events.

NAMES AND TITLES

INDEX

INDEX

INDEX

TOPICS AND IDEAS

INDEX

About the Author

Both *Time* and *Newsweek* have described RUSSELL KIRK as one of America's leading thinkers.

He writes and speaks on political thought, educational theory, literary criticism, foreign affairs, and many other themes. His syndicated column, "To the Point," distributed by the Los Angeles Times Syndicate, appears in more than a hundred daily newspapers.

He has spoken on more than three hundred American campuses, and to many other audiences, including frequent television appearances. More than a million copies of his books have been sold to date.

Of his sixteen books, the best known is *The Conservative Mind*, probably the most widely read and reviewed work of political theory to be published in this century. It has been translated into several languages, and is available in paperback edition.

Born in Plymouth, Michigan, in 1918, Dr. Kirk now lives with his wife and three children at Mecosta, Michigan, in a haunted house built by his great-grandfather.